System Design on AWS

Mastering cloud design on AWS for secure, scalable production systems

Manish Kumar Atnere

www.bpbonline.com

First Edition 2027

ISBN: 978-93-09786-273

LIMITS OF LIABILITY AND DISCLAIMER OF WARRANTY

To View Complete
BPB Publications Catalogue
Scan the QR Code:

www.bpbonline.com

Dedicated to

My beloved mom:

Mrs. Bhagwati Atnere

and

My beloved father:

Late Mr. Shriram Atnere

About the Author

Manish Kumar Atnere is an innovative and results-driven cloud architect leader with over 20 years of experience architecting, automating, and managing scalable, secure, and high-performance infrastructure. He specializes in Kubernetes, AI/ML infrastructure, cloud platforms including AWS, Azure, and GCP, and infrastructure as code using Terraform. With a proven track record in designing and managing AI workloads, Manish Atnere excels in optimizing hybrid cloud environments and enabling DevSecOps and GitOps in enterprise settings.

Currently a lead cloud architect at leading software company, Manish architects containerized AI/ML workloads using AWS EKS and bare-metal clusters, integrating advanced AI data pipelines with Kubernetes. He has built end-to-end ML pipelines and RAG architectures using technologies like LangChain, FAISS, and vector databases, and developed automation tools for performance profiling and observability. His leadership in GitOps and DevSecOps pipelines has significantly enhanced release velocity and system reliability.

Manish holds multiple certifications including **AWS Certified Solutions Architect – Professional**, **AWS Certified Solutions Architect – Associate**, **Certified Kubernetes Administrator** (**CKA**), and has deep expertise in cloud-native architectures, AI/ML engineering, and secure infrastructure automation. His extensive hands-on experience and strategic insights make him uniquely qualified to guide readers in mastering system design on AWS with integrated AI capabilities.

About the Reviewers

- **Rahul Rao Juvvadi** is a Principal Software Engineer at Microsoft, where he architects large-scale, cloud-native enterprise finance platforms — distributed systems engineered for multi-region high availability, fault tolerance, horizontal scalability, and elastic compute, processing some of the highest transaction volumes of any financial systems in operation. With over two decades in enterprise system architecture, cloud platform engineering, and modern ERP design and implementation, he has delivered mission-critical, event-driven, and microservices-based systems across three continents, having worked and studied in India, Australia, and the United States.

  His work centers on resilient system design: asynchronous messaging and streaming architectures, high-throughput ledger platforms, close-orchestration systems, and integration patterns that balance scalability, availability, consistency, and compliance at global scale. An active independent researcher in AI, machine learning, blockchain, and enterprise systems, he has authored peer-reviewed publications on machine-learning anomaly detection, event-driven intercompany accounting, and smart contracts in supply-chain finance.

  Rahul is a Fellow of the Chartered Institute of Management Accountants (FCMA), a Fellow of CPA Australia (FCPA), and an IEEE Senior Member. He serves as an independent director at CognoWiz, is a technical reviewer for books on cloud architecture and enterprise systems, and mentors engineers at the intersection of technology and business.

- **Abhinav Srivastava** is an Engineering Manager leading the runtime for an enterprise-scale Agentic AI platform at Amazon, where he works on LLM orchestration, agentic system security, and production evaluation frameworks for autonomous AI workflows. With over 13 years of experience in distributed cloud infrastructure, MLOps, and large-scale data engineering on AWS, he is focused on the operational and security challenges that emerge when AI agents move from prototype to production. He is an active contributor to the AI engineering community, publishing practitioner articles on agentic AI governance and security, and serving as a technical reviewer and judge across IEEE conferences and global AI competitions.

- **Arun Sivakumar** is a mobile engineer with over a decade of software engineering experience. He is fascinated by AI and machine learning, and by how large language models are reshaping the way apps are built and used. He has worked across iOS and backend systems, in Objective-C, Swift, and Go, at startups in Singapore and the US. Driven by a passion for thoughtful UI/UX and scalable, resilient software, he contributes to open source and has served as a technical reviewer for books on AI.

Acknowledgement

I would like to express my sincere gratitude to my family and friends for their constant support and encouragement throughout the journey of writing this book especially my beloved parents and my beloved wife Megha Patil. Their patience and belief in me made it possible to stay committed to this effort.

I am also thankful to the BPB Publications team for their guidance, professionalism, and support in shaping this book into its final form. The contributions of reviewers, editors, and technical experts played a crucial role in refining the content and ensuring its quality.

I would like to acknowledge my colleagues and peers from the cloud and technology community, whose knowledge, discussions, and feedback over the years have greatly influenced my understanding and perspective.

Finally, my heartfelt thanks to the readers for their interest and support. I hope this book adds value to your learning journey and professional growth.

Preface

Cloud computing has transformed system design, development, and operations. AWS stands out as a leading platform, providing a broad range of services that support rapid innovation, scalability, security, and cost efficiency. However, selecting and implementing the right services requires a structured approach.

This book bridges the gap between understanding AWS services and applying them in real-world scenarios. It emphasizes architectural thinking, focusing on designing resilient, secure systems that align with business objectives. You will explore core AWS concepts, modern cloud patterns, and best practices based on the AWS Well-Architected Framework.

The content draws on practical experience and addresses common challenges for cloud engineers, solution architects, and DevOps professionals. Each chapter encourages critical thinking about trade-offs, service selection, and implementing production-ready solutions. Topics include networking, security, serverless, containers, observability, and AI/ML integration, all presented with clarity and practical relevance.

Whether you are preparing for an architect role, enhancing your skills, or building scalable systems on AWS, this book offers a clear and practical guide. It focuses not only on AWS itself, but also on designing systems that perform reliably, scale efficiently, and adapt to changing requirements.

This book provides a comprehensive guide for architects, engineers, and developers seeking to design, build, and operate production-grade systems on AWS. It progresses from foundational cloud concepts to advanced topics such as AI, Kubernetes, and security, concluding with system design interview preparation. Each chapter builds on the previous one, ensuring readers develop the necessary vocabulary and mental models for later material.

Chapter 1: Getting Started with AWS — The first chapter introduces AWS global infrastructure, including regions, availability zones, and VPCs as the core boundaries for all architectures. It emphasizes the AWS Well-Architected Framework and its six pillars: operational excellence, security, reliability, performance efficiency, cost optimization, and sustainability. These pillars serve as the foundation for evaluating design decisions throughout the book.

Chapter 2: Core AWS Services for Scalable Architecture — This chapter covers core AWS services common to most architectures: EC2 for compute, S3 for storage, VPCs for network isolation, and IAM for permissions and identity. It explains how these services integrate to form the foundation for more specialized solutions, helping readers understand the relationships among compute, storage, network, and identity.

Chapter 3 : Scaling with AWS Compute and Serverless — This chapter addresses managing variable demand. Application Load Balancers distribute traffic across instances, while scaling strategies adjust compute resources as needed. AWS Lambda introduces event-driven, serverless computing that scales automatically. The key lesson is understanding when to use managed infrastructure, serverless, or a combination of both.

Chapter 4 : Designing Distributed Systems in AWS — This chapter presents key architectural patterns for cloud-native applications: microservices for independent deployment, event-driven architecture with SNS, SQS, and EventBridge for loose coupling, and Step Functions for orchestrating serverless workflows. It emphasizes how these patterns enable systems to withstand partial failures without complete disruption.

Chapter 5 : Data Storage Strategies and Patterns on AWS — This chapter explains that storage solutions must be tailored to specific needs. It discusses SQL and NoSQL trade-offs, caching with ElastiCache and CDN, data consistency models, and replication strategies. The main takeaway is to align storage technology with access patterns and to use caching to reduce latency and cost while maintaining data integrity.

Chapter 6 : Load Balancing and Auto Scaling— Expanding on scaling concepts, this chapter details the three AWS load balancer types - Application, Network, and Gateway, and their appropriate use cases. It also covers Auto Scaling groups and both dynamic and scheduled scaling policies. The key point is how load balancing and Auto Scaling work together to maintain availability and cost efficiency automatically.

Chapter 7 : Monitoring and Observability Best Practices — This chapter emphasizes the importance of observability for safe operations. It covers CloudWatch for metrics, logs, and alarms, as well as observability strategies for distributed applications. The main lesson is to implement observability from the outset, ensuring timely incident detection through effective alarms and tracing.

Chapter 8 : Essential AWS AI/ML Services — This chapter presents managed AI services that enable architects to add intelligence to applications without managing machine learning infrastructure. Amazon Rekognition provides computer vision, Comprehend offers natural language processing, Polly converts text to speech, and Lex supports chatbots and voicebots. SageMaker is introduced as a comprehensive ML lifecycle platform. Each service is positioned as a modular component that integrates with event-driven architectures through API calls.

Chapter 9 : Advanced AWS AI Services — This chapter explores specialized and emerging AI services. Amazon Textract enables intelligent document processing, Amazon Bedrock facilitates generative AI integration, and Amazon Q serves as an AI assistant for cloud management. The key takeaway is how these services can be combined to create comprehensive intelligent document and data pipelines.

Chapter 10 : Designing and Deploying AI Applications on AWS — This chapter transitions from individual services to full AI application architectures. It covers SageMaker ML pipeline design, **retrieval-augmented generation** (**RAG**) architectures, and operational aspects of deploying and scaling SageMaker endpoints. The focus is on operationalizing models, including versioning, monitoring, drift detection, and retraining to maintain reliability.

Chapter 11 : Scaling and Automating AI Applications — Continuing from Chapter 10, this chapter addresses automating AI systems for production. It covers CI/CD pipelines for model deployment, serverless orchestration with Lambda and Step Functions, and cost optimization for inference workloads. The main lesson is that AI applications need automated deployment, continuous monitoring, and cost management from the outset.

Chapter 12 : Infrastructure as Code and DevOps Automation — This chapter advocates for **infrastructure as code** (**IaC**) as the standard for scalable environments. It compares CloudFormation, Terraform, and AWS CDK, and provides guidance on modular template design, testing, and validation. GitOps workflows, CI/CD pipelines, and drift detection are also discussed. The key point is that IaC serves as both a provisioning and governance tool, ensuring infrastructure is auditable, repeatable, and reviewable.

Chapter 13 : Securing and Governing AWS Architectures — This chapter provides an in-depth review of security, expanding on its introduction in *Chapter 1*. It covers IAM design, data encryption, GuardDuty for threat detection, and automated incident response. AWS Config and Security Hub support continuous compliance, while EventBridge routes high-severity findings for remediation. The main takeaway is to treat security as an ongoing, automated process.

Chapter 14 : AWS Fargate, ECS, and SAM — This chapter covers the container and serverless deployment layer above EC2. Fargate eliminates server management for containers, ECS offers orchestration for microservices, and the **Serverless Application Model** (**SAM**) simplifies infrastructure as code for Lambda applications. It explains how to select among these tools based on the desired balance of control and convenience.

Chapter 15 : Amazon Elastic Kubernetes Service Architecture — This chapter introduces EKS, AWS's managed Kubernetes service, and details its architecture, including the control plane, worker node management, networking, security, and observability. It highlights the division of responsibilities between AWS and the customer, which affects networking, upgrade strategies, and security controls.

Chapter 16 : Service Mesh and Autoscaling for EKS — This chapter examines advanced EKS networking and scaling features essential for production. It covers the Container Network Interface for Pod networking, Horizontal Pod Autoscaler for scaling workloads, service mesh for secure communication, and Karpenter for node autoscaling. Together, these components enable a self-scaling, self-healing cluster for diverse workloads.

Chapter 17 : Security and Best Practices in EKS — This chapter addresses the unique security considerations of Kubernetes compared to traditional AWS workloads. It reviews the AWS shared responsibility model in the Kubernetes context, discusses network security, data protection, and incident response for EKS. The main point is that Kubernetes security is layered, requiring controls at the cluster, namespace, Pod, and container levels.

Chapter 18 : System Design Interview Essentials — The final chapter applies previous concepts to the system design interview. It explains how to clarify requirements, define scope, communicate trade-offs, and address scaling, load balancing, security, reliability, and cost within time constraints. The key takeaway is that strong answers demonstrate structured thinking, problem decomposition, and justified design choices.

Code Bundle and Coloured Images

Please follow the link to download the
Code Bundle and the ***Coloured Images*** of the book:

https://rebrand.ly/ipovakt

The code bundle for the book is also hosted on GitHub at
https://github.com/bpbpublications/System-Design-on-AWS.
In case there's an update to the code, it will be updated on the existing GitHub repository.

We have code bundles from our rich catalogue of books and videos available at https://github.com/bpbpublications. Check them out!

Errata

We take immense pride in our work at BPB Publications and follow best practices to ensure the accuracy of our content to provide an indulging reading experience to our subscribers. Our readers are our mirrors, and we use their inputs to reflect and improve upon human errors, if any, that may have occurred during the publishing processes involved. To let us maintain the quality and help us reach out to any readers who might be having difficulties due to any unforeseen errors, please write to us at: errata@bpbonline.com

Your support, suggestions and feedback are highly appreciated by the BPB Publications' Family.

Piracy

If you come across any illegal copies of our works in any form on the internet, we would be grateful if you would provide us with the location address or website name. Please contact us at business@bpbonline.com with a link to the material.

If you are interested in becoming an author

If there is a topic that you have expertise in, and you are interested in either writing or contributing to a book, please visit www.bpbonline.com. We have worked with thousands of developers and tech professionals, just like you, to help them share their insights with the global tech community. You can make a general application, apply for a specific hot topic that we are recruiting an author for, or submit your own idea.

Reviews

Please leave a review. Once you have read and used this book, why not leave a review on the site that you purchased it from? Potential readers can then see and use your unbiased opinion to make purchase decisions. We at BPB can understand what you think about our products, and our authors can see your feedback on their book. Thank you!

For more information about BPB, please visit www.bpbonline.com.

Join our Discord space

Join our Discord workspace for latest updates, offers, tech happenings around the world, new releases, and sessions with the authors:

https://discord.bpbonline.com

Table of Contents

CHAPTER 1
Getting Started with AWS

Introduction

This book is designed to support readers at all skill levels, from beginners to intermediate learners and experts. Before moving forward, it is essential to ensure readers have a basic understanding of technical skills and the core concepts of software engineering and technology. Having a solid grasp of fundamental logic and principles will help you better comprehend the material and make the most out of this book.

Additionally, familiarity with general programming concepts, understanding of cloud computing basics, and some experience with software architecture will be highly beneficial. This foundation will enable you to follow along more easily as we explore complex **Amazon Web Services** (**AWS**) and system design patterns. However, even if you are new to some topics, the book aims to guide you step by step, helping you build confidence and deepen your knowledge progressively. We always encourage you to write down the essential points you learn from this book, which gives you clarity and lets you review them anytime with ease.

Structure

In this chapter, we will discuss the following topics:

- Computer tradition
- Concepts and history of AWS
- AWS infrastructure footprint
- AWS services overview
- AWS global services
- AWS regional-scoped services
- AWS service types

- AWS Console and CLI overview
- AWS technology terms

Objectives

In this chapter, you will learn about AWS and cloud concepts in general and the history behind them. You will also learn various use cases of AWS and the AWS infrastructure footprint geographically. In this chapter, we will also go through the AWS services and their types. After this, we will learn how to use the AWS Console and CLI.

Computer tradition

We are in the 21st century; every day, we come across various buzzwords such as *artificial intelligence, quantum computing, blockchain, content delivery network, social networking,* and so on. These areas have something in common. Just pause for a minute and think. The commonality among all of them is the infrastructure on which these platforms or technologies run. Now, let us take a step back and imagine you are in the 1980s, at the start of the *Computer Era*. There are a few things you can think of.

CPU for processing, hard drive for storage, operating system, peripherals like a monitor, keyboard, mouse, and network card to connect and interact with the world. All these components work together to perform tasks efficiently. Then, the evolution of the internet, where one local network can connect to another to form a larger network known as a **wide area network** (**WAN**). A WAN connects computers over large distances, such as between cities, countries, or continents. It enables communication beyond a single building or campus.

We can think of purchasing these components in large quantities, then partitioning them into smaller pieces and leasing them to various tenants. Tenants will pay for their use without the overhead of purchasing these components for the business, saving a substantial amount of money that can be used in the actual business rather than being burned on infrastructure.

This is where the evolution of *Cloud Computing (AWS)* took place in 2003. This was the time when Amazon realized this could be a great business model, allowing it to charge customers based on their usage. Instead of buying physical hardware, AWS lets you create and use virtual CPUs (EC2 instances, which are the virtual machine instances in AWS), memory, storage (EBS, which is a virtual hard drive in AWS, and **Simple Storage Service** (**S3**), which is an object storage service in AWS), and networking components in just a few clicks. This ability to instantly build a *virtual data center* has completely transformed how software is developed and deployed. Now companies do not need to invest in expensive hardware or wait weeks to set up infrastructure; with AWS, they can scale globally in minutes and only pay for what they use.

Table 1.1 shows how the traditional computer components resemble the AWS services. Moreover, AWS improved the way traditional computer components worked. This shows the real power of cloud computing in a nutshell.

Traditional computer component	Functionality	AWS service equivalent	AWS improvement
Central processing unit (CPU) (Processor)	Runs programs and handles processing	**Elastic Compute Cloud (EC2)**	Instantly create virtual servers, scalable
Random access memory (RAM) (Memory)	Stores data temporarily for faster access	EC2 Instance RAM / ElastiCache	Choose the amount per instance; add cache easily
Hard disk / SSD	Stores files and data	S3 (Storage), EBS (Block Storage)	Durable, scalable, pay-as-you-go
Motherboard	Connects all hardware	**Virtual Private Cloud (VPC)**, networking	Define connections between resources
Graphics card	Powerful visuals and graphics	EC2 GPU Instances	Rent high-end GPUs for ML, graphics
Network card	Connects to a network	VPC, Elastic Load Balancer	Build secure networks, balance traffic
Power supply	Keeps the system running reliably	**Availability Zones (AZs)**, Regions	Guaranteed uptime, redundancy
Keyboard/Mouse/Monitor	User interaction	AWS Console, CLI, SDKs	Manage resources via web/command/API

***Table 1.1**: Traditional computer components vs. AWS services*

System design, on the other hand, is about planning how these computing components, whether physical or virtual, work together to meet performance, scalability, and reliability goals. It is like drawing the blueprint before constructing a complex building. Good system design helps ensure that an application can handle many users, recover from failures, and deliver results quickly without wasting resources. It focuses on building efficient, fault-tolerant, and maintainable systems that can grow and adapt as demands change.

When AWS and system design come together, they form the backbone of modern cloud architecture. AWS provides the tools, virtual machines, databases, load balancers, and messaging systems, while system design defines how to assemble and use them effectively. By combining the flexibility of AWS with strong design principles, you can create systems that scale automatically under heavy load, stay available even when components fail, and remain cost-effective and easy to manage. Together, they enable developers to go beyond traditional infrastructure and build solutions that reliably and efficiently serve users around the globe.

Concept and history of AWS

When AWS began its journey, it started as an internal project within Amazon around 2002, created to help different engineering teams work more efficiently by standardizing infrastructure and tools. The idea soon evolved into something bigger, providing scalable IT infrastructure-as-a-service to other companies. In 2004, Amazon officially launched its first publicly available service, Amazon **Simple Queue Service** (**SQS**), which allowed developers to build distributed systems using reliable message queues. This marked the beginning of AWS as a commercial cloud provider. Over the following years, primary services like Amazon S3 in 2006 and **Amazon Elastic Compute Cloud** (**EC2**) later that same year shaped the foundation of modern cloud computing. The same year, these services were re-launched publicly. In 2007, services were launched in the European region. This way, we can now see that AWS is available in 26 Regions.

Numerical Fact: **AWS is now the pioneer and leader in the cloud market, accounting for around 31 to 32% of the market. It has around one million annual active users worldwide. In 2024, AWS had $107.6 billion of annual revenue.**

AWS helps you build highly scalable and sophisticated applications. You can use it in any industry, irrespective of the field. Various use cases involve social media, live streaming, gaming, website hosting, mobile applications, enterprise IT, backup and storage, artificial intelligence, deploying **large language models** (**LLMs**), machine learning, big data analytics, and so on.

AWS infrastructure footprint

From the preceding section, it is evident that AWS infrastructure is not present only in one place but spans across various regions globally. We can use regions as per our needs and service usage. You can imagine AWS as a distributed network infrastructure across the globe.

The AWS infrastructure footprint is among the most extensive and resilient cloud foundations in the world, enabling organizations to deploy applications globally with low latency and high fault tolerance. As of 2025, the AWS Cloud operates across *38 Regions*, encompassing *120* AZs.

Complementing these are more than 700 CloudFront Points of Presence, 43 Local Zones, and 31 Wavelength Zones, which help bring compute and storage closer to end users for ultra-low-latency performance. Each AWS Region is composed of multiple isolated AZs connected by high-speed, low-latency fiber networks spanning over 9 million kilometers worldwide, ensuring fault-tolerant and redundant connectivity. This global infrastructure allows customers to architect highly available, secure, and performant systems across continents, whether through edge delivery with CloudFront, which is a global **content delivery network** (**CDN**), hybrid deployments via Outposts, or regional redundancy with multi-AZ and multi-region fault tolerance.

We will learn more about the global footprint in the coming sections. In a nutshell, AWS's global infrastructure ensures that customer applications are fault-tolerant, robust, and highly available.

AWS Region

Think of an AWS Region as a large, specific area in the world where AWS has set up a cluster of data centers. Each region is a distinct geographic location, such as Northern Virginia in the US, Frankfurt in Germany, or Mumbai in India. These regions are entirely independent of one another, meaning they operate separately and do not share infrastructure. This separation helps AWS provide high fault tolerance and stability. Currently, AWS spans across 38 geographic regions. AWS services are region-scoped, meaning some are available only in a few regions and may not be available in others. For example, **Amazon Transcribe Call Analytics**, the streaming version of this service, is supported in US West (Oregon) but is not available in Asia Pacific (Mumbai). The following figure illustrates the examples for US regions us-east-1, us-east-2, eu-west-3, etc.:

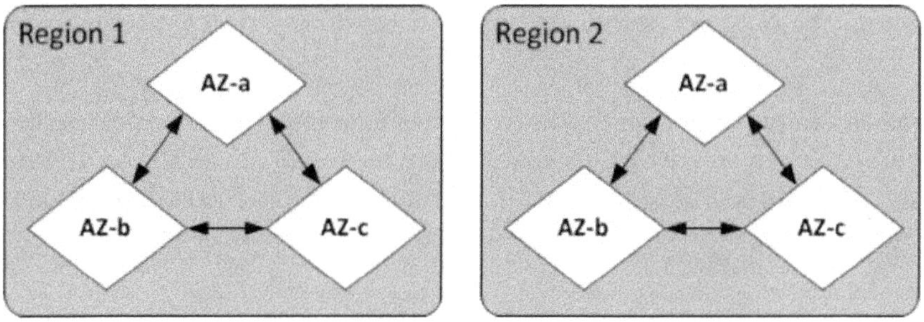

Source: Amazon docs

***Figure 1.1**: Availability regions*

Choosing an appropriate region is also essential. Consider the points below before choosing the right region for your application:

- **Available services**: Probably the service you are looking for is not present in your region, so you might need to switch to the region where that service is available.
- **Proximity**: To avoid latency (which is the time delay between when you send a request and when you get a response) issues, you need to select a region that is near your location or the location where the customer belongs. For instance, if an application has users in Japan, you will make sure that the application is deployed to a region where Japanese users will not face latency issues.
- **Pricing**: Sometimes the pricing in one region differs from the pricing in another region, so you might look for the cheaper pricing for your service.

- **Legal compliance**: Sometimes, local government requires that the data not leave the particular country where that data belongs. For example, US data governance and legal requirements ensure that data should not leave the US region without permission.

AWS Availability Zones

AZs within a region are separated by up to 60 miles (approximately 100 km) to reduce the risk of correlated failures while remaining close enough to support synchronous replication with single-digit millisecond latency. Each AZ consists of one or more data centers that are physically close enough to connect quickly but separated enough to avoid being affected by the same disaster, such as a power failure or flooding. These zones are connected by high-speed, redundant networks, allowing data and workloads to move between them smoothly.

The primary purpose of AZs is to make sure your applications stay up and running, even if something goes wrong in one zone. For example, if one AZ experiences an issue such as a power outage or technical failure, AWS can automatically reroute your operations to another AZ in the same region. This setup provides high availability, fault tolerance, and resilience for your systems, helping you avoid downtime caused by physical problems or outages in a single data center.

Every region has a minimum of 3 and a maximum of 6 Availability Zones. For example, us-east-2 has 3 Availability Zones, us-east-2a, us-east-2b, and us-east-2c. Kindly refer to **https://docs.aws.amazon.com/whitepapers/latest/aws-fault-isolation-boundaries/availability-zones.html**

Refer to the following figure:

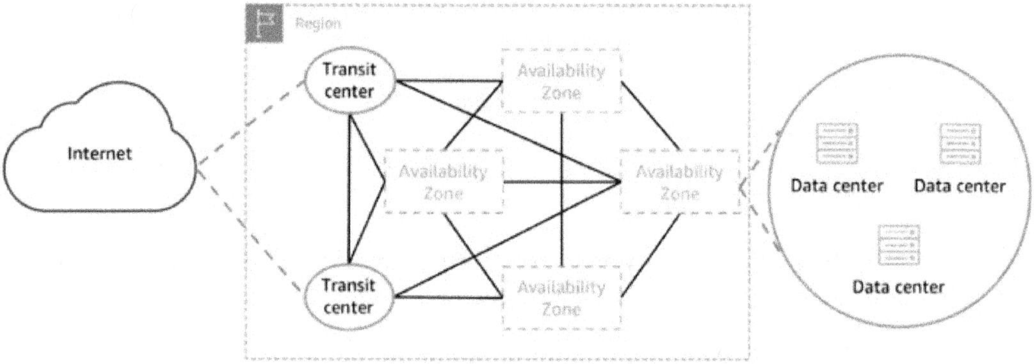

***Figure 1.2**: Availability Zones with physical data centers connected to each other and the internet*

AWS points of presence, also known as Edge Locations. As of late 2025, AWS operates a global network of over 410 **Points of Presence** (**PoPs**). These include more than 400 Edge Locations and 13 regional edge caches spread across over 90 cities in 48 countries worldwide. Points of Presence are data centers that cache and deliver content closer to end users, reducing latency and improving performance for services such as Amazon CloudFront (content delivery), Amazon Route 53 (DNS), and AWS Global Accelerator (network optimization).

To summarize:

- Over 410 PoPs globally
- More than 400 Edge Locations in more than 90 cities
- 13 Regional Edge caches

This extensive PoP network is a critical part of AWS's global infrastructure, enabling faster response times and higher availability for cloud applications everywhere. Refer to the following figure:

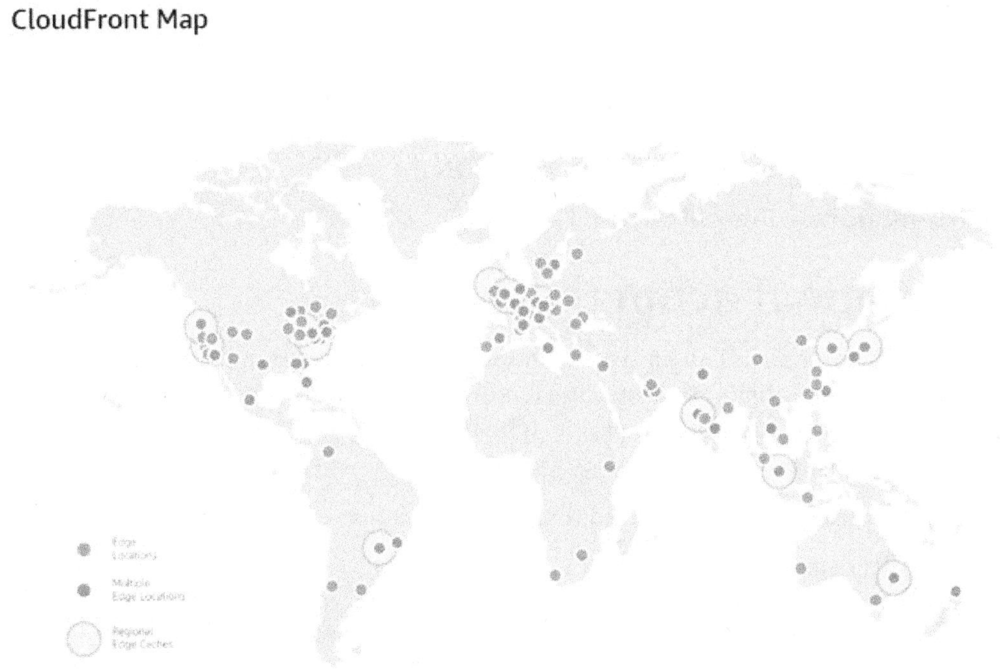

***Figure 1.3**: AWS Points of Presence; Edge Locations*
(Source: https://aws.amazon.com/cloudfront/features/)

AWS services overview

The AWS services capture the breadth and depth of Amazon Web Services' cloud ecosystem—an integrated suite of over 200 fully managed offerings spanning compute, storage, networking, databases, analytics, machine learning, security, and application integration. A few AWS services are Global Services, meaning they are not specific to any region; these are mostly core services like **Domain Name System** (**DNS**) and **Identity and Access Management** (**IAM**). At the same time, most others are region-scoped, such as EC2 and Lambda. We can also divide services by level of abstraction, which defines how much control and management responsibility users retain versus the cloud provider.

These services are building blocks that empower organizations to design resilient, elastic architectures that adapt to any workload—from startups deploying their first web app to enterprises running global-scale platforms.

AWS global services

The AWS services that are not specific to any region but are available at the global level mainly encompass services that are related to AWS admin or core network services. Due to the nature of these services, they are common across all regions, so the user does not need to worry about selecting a particular region. These services are as follows:

- IAM
- **Route 53** (DNS services)
- **CloudFront** (**content delivery network** (**CDN**))
- **Web application firewall** (**WAF**)

AWS regional-scoped services

The AWS services are specific to a particular region and mainly contain services that are related to AWS infrastructure or have some specific features. We need to select a particular region so that the latency factor would not be an issue, which provides a faster response to the end user. These services are as follows:

- Amazon **Elastic Compute Cloud** (**EC2**)
- Elastic Beanstalk
- Lambda
- Rekognition

AWS service types

Broadly, you can divide AWS services into three categories based on their level of abstraction, which defines how much control and management responsibility users retain compared to the cloud provider. For a few service types, users have to bear the overhead of provisioning and maintaining infrastructure, while for others, AWS takes care of it.

Infrastructure as a service

Infrastructure as a service (**IaaS**) is the most flexible cloud model, providing access to basic computing resources such as virtual machines, storage, and networks. As the name suggests, Infrastructure means this service mainly deals with the Basic infrastructure required to run any application. Just like for our Windows or Linux servers, we need storage, memory, network, and a processor. All these components or peripherals can be configured under the virtual machines service (EC2) in AWS. Similarly, for storage, the S3 service can handle storage hardware and other features, such as **input/output operations per second** (**IOPS**), Number of reads and writes, and versioning, which are configurable.

In User responsibility, the user has the responsibility to manage the operating system, applications, and data, while AWS helps to manage the physical hardware. The user does not need to worry about running infrastructure maintenance or patching. This avoids the overhead of server maintenance and patching for the User, allowing them to focus more on the actual business.

AWS examples are as follows:

- **Elastic Compute Cloud (EC2)**: This service allows you to launch virtual servers, known as instances, in the cloud. You have control over the operating system, storage, and networking, while AWS manages the underlying physical infrastructure.
- **Simple Storage Service (S3)**: This provides scalable object storage for any amount of data, and this data can have different data types like images, videos, and backups.
- **Elastic Block Storage (EBS)**: It offers persistent block storage volumes for use with EC2 instances, functioning like a traditional hard drive for your virtual server.
- **Virtual Private Cloud (VPC)**: VPC isolates resources in a virtual network from other resources for logical separation. This can include various resources such as EC2 instances, S3 Storage, Network devices, etc. This will ensure that communication within the VPC can occur without issue, but at the same time, there is no direct connectivity to another VPC without proper configuration in place. We will learn in the coming chapters how resources in one VPC can connect with resources in another VPC.

The IaaS model offers benefits to modern enterprises like the following:

- **Speed**: IaaS can help to provision any number of resources within minutes, perform testing, and launch new ideas to market much faster. You can focus on your core business activities because AWS fully manages the IT infrastructure and computing resources for you.
- **Performance**: Since distributed data centers are geographically distributed, they can be used to scale applications to locations physically closer to your customers. Just think whether this would be possible if you have a limited server capacity and no geographic reach. IaaS solutions offer many options to increase compute performance and reduce network latency.
- **Reliability**: IaaS provides a highly reliable environment where EC2 instances can be rapidly and predictably replaced.
- **Backup and recovery**: IaaS provides unlimited infrastructure for backup and disaster recovery. For instance, you can duplicate your applications across multiple servers so

that if one fails, another takes over. Similarly, you can automatically and frequently sync data backups to achieve redundancy and business continuity.

- **Pricing**: Compute, storage, and networking can be used as you go. Customers will pay only for the resources they use, encouraging more efficient IT resource management and promoting innovation by making cloud services affordable for small businesses. This is why we see many start-ups booming nowadays with very small initial expenditure.

Platform as a service

Platform as a service (**PaaS**) is a layer on top of IaaS that provides a way to develop, host, and manage applications without having to think much about the underlying infrastructure. It is your responsibility to manage your applications and data. AWS handles operating systems, runtime environments, middleware, and underlying infrastructure.

AWS examples are as follows:

- **AWS Elastic Beanstalk**: This service is for deploying and scaling hassle-free web applications and services.
- **AWS Lambda**: This is a compute service that runs your code in response to events, but where you do not need to worry about provisioning infrastructure; AWS will take care of it on the fly as and when it is needed.
- **Elastic Kubernetes Service (EKS)**: This is a service for container orchestration, which is a managed Kubernetes service by AWS. In this service, the user can quickly create a Kubernetes cluster, as most of the management will be handled by AWS. This means the user does not have to worry too much about managing and monitoring the worker nodes.

The benefits of PaaS are as follows:

- **Automated process management**: A PaaS platform enables organizations to automate information flows between systems, significantly reducing the need for repetitive manual work. This automation keeps data in sync across platforms in real time, making sure decision-makers always have the latest information. By connecting various applications, iPaaS helps break down information silos and provides businesses with a clear, unified view of their data to support smarter decisions.
- **Rapid integration at a large scale**: Connecting business applications the traditional way often takes months and holds back growth. With PaaS solutions, ready-to-use connectors and templates can drastically shorten the time needed to link complex systems, even as an organization grows or its data needs increase. It is possible to connect different technology stacks regardless of whether resources are on-premises, in private clouds, or spread across multiple cloud providers.
- **Seamless, secure, and less complex connectivity**: PaaS simplifies integration, enabling teams to connect systems without deep expertise or custom-coded solutions.

Security is built in, and managing integrations becomes straightforward; no dedicated specialists are needed. This helps companies quickly adapt their tech environments while maintaining strong data protection and reducing integration overhead.

Software as a service

It provides complete software solutions that are managed and delivered by a third party over the internet. You have to use the application. AWS handles all management, from the infrastructure to the application itself.

AWS examples are as follows:

- **AWS WorkMail**: A business email and calendar service.
- **Amazon SageMaker**: This service is used to build, train, and deploy machine learning models. This is a fully managed service in AWS.

The benefits of SaaS are as follows:

- **Cloud accessibility**: This service is independent of the device you use to access it; you need an internet connection. Usually, in a device-dependent software model, your business application can be accessed only from the device where it is installed. In contrast, a SaaS application can be accessed from any device. The SaaS model became more popular in the work-from-home and hybrid environment.
- **Lower upfront costs**: SaaS software is typically subscription-based, with no initial heavy investment in computing resources, since the vendor manages everything on its servers.
- **Reduced ongoing costs**: The ongoing costs are also significantly lower, since you only pay a subscription fee. You can confidently choose the plan that works for you. The vendor manages everything for you so you can focus on your core business.
- **Rapid deployment**: You do not need to install or configure software with SaaS. You can start using the application as soon as your subscription begins. This way, you can achieve rapid deployment.
- **On-demand scalability**: When you need more storage or services, you can add them without paying a high price to upgrade the infrastructure. This makes your application highly scalable.
- **Reliability**: SaaS vendors invest rigorously in cybersecurity and disaster recovery capabilities, ensuring your application has uptime of up to 99%. Even a few vendors claim 99.9% of uptime. This makes the application highly reliable.
- **Automatic updates**: Software vendors regularly release incremental updates and security patches for their applications, which automatically upgrade the applications without the need for IT support.

- **Integration**: Third-party SaaS applications can be integrated with other platforms and systems using APIs.
- **Real-time data and analytics**: SaaS applications often collect usage and performance data and can provide real-time insights.

The following table provides a quick reference for all AWS services that belong to different service types:

Infrastructure as a service (IaaS)	Platform as a service (PaaS)	Software as a service (SaaS)
Amazon Elastic Compute Cloud	AWS Elastic Beanstalk	Amazon WorkMail
Amazon Simple Storage Service	AWS Lambda	Amazon SageMaker
Amazon Elastic Block Store	Amazon Elastic Kubernetes Service (EKS)	Amazon DynamoDB
Amazon Virtual Private Cloud	Amazon Elastic Container Service (ECS)	Amazon WorkSpaces

***Table 1.2**: IaaS vs. PaaS vs. SaaS*

AWS Console and CLI overview

AWS Console or **Command Line Interface (CLI) version 2** is the tool with which you can create new services or configure them. This can be from creating a new instance of EC2, creating an S3 bucket, VPC, DynamoDB, or starting, stopping, and configuring any other services. Depending on the use case, we opt for either of them. If we want to create services just for our learning purposes or at a lower scale, we can use the AWS Console, while if we want to automate the provisioning of infrastructure or at a large scale, we can use the CLI.

AWS Console

To use the AWS Console, you first need to create an AWS account by signing up at **https://aws.amazon.com/** as shown in *Figure 1.4*. If you already have an account, you can sign in with your account details.

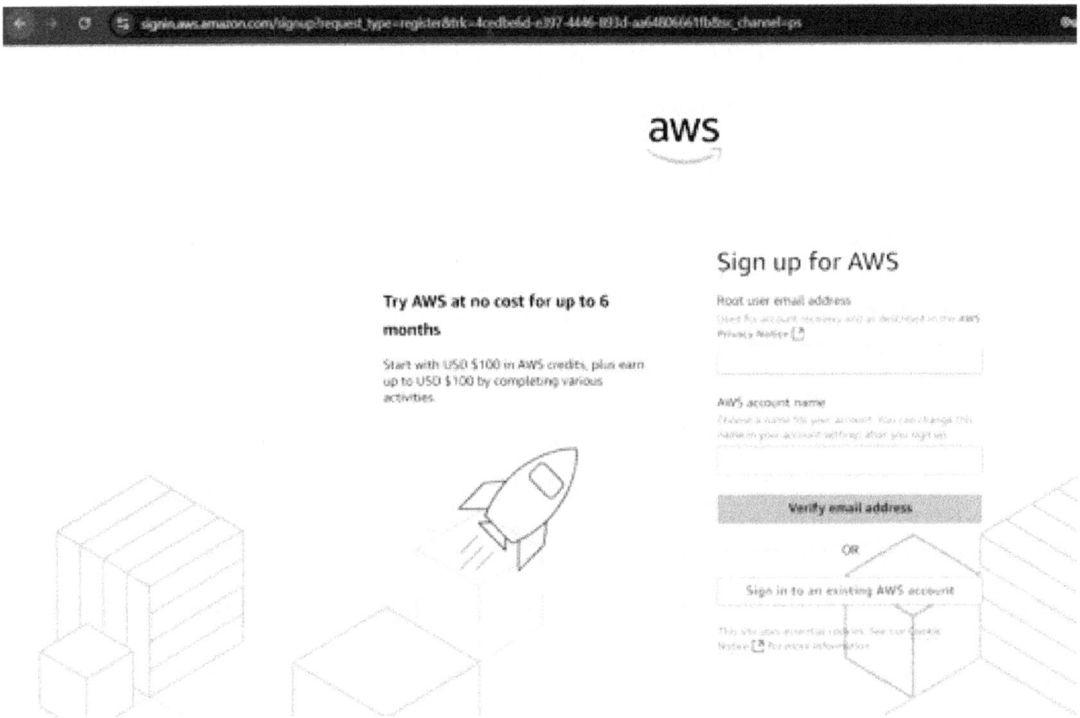

Figure 1.4*: AWS signup web page*

The AWS Console is shown in the following figure:

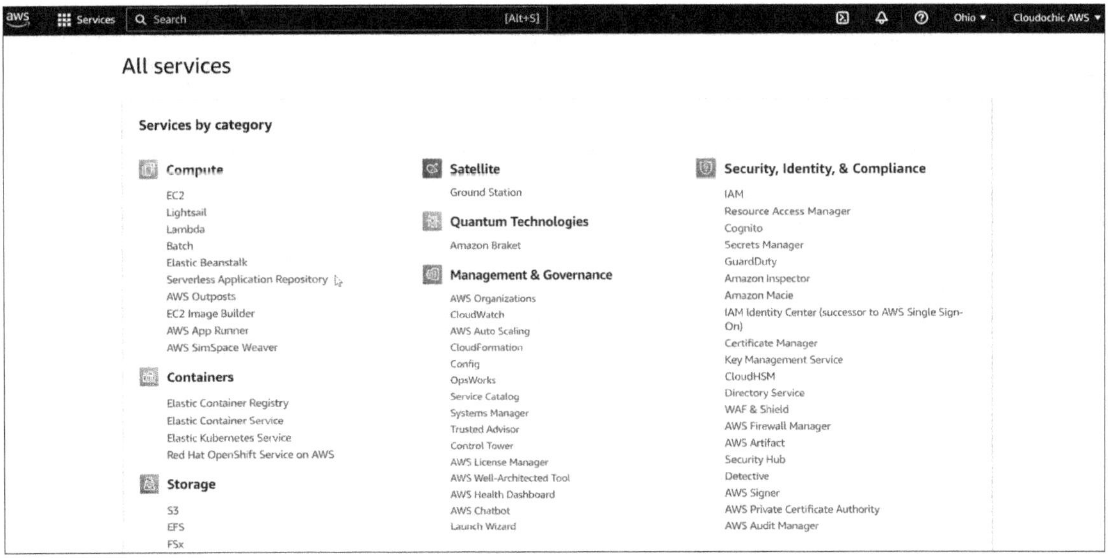

Figure 1.5*: AWS Console (sample image)*

The preceding figure shows the landing page you see as soon as you log in to your AWS Console. This page shows all the services available for consumption:

- The AWS Management Console is a web-based dashboard where you can see and manage all your AWS services.
- When you first log in, you are greeted by a home page with a search bar and shortcuts to your favorite services.
- You can click on any AWS service, like EC2 (virtual servers) or S3 (storage), to open its dashboard and set things up intuitively.
- The console lets you manage resources with simple point-and-click actions, no complicated commands necessary.
- You can search for any service by name, pin your most-used services, and customize the console to fit your workflow.
- Each AWS service has its own dedicated section in the console, with easy-to-understand menus and settings.
- The interface includes helpful tooltips and guided walkthroughs for new features, making it easy to learn as you go.
- You can view real-time resource activity, such as running server instances or storage usage, at a glance.
- The console provides integrated monitoring dashboards (like AWS CloudWatch) so you can track performance and spot potential issues early.
- AWS Console has features of security and access controls, which help you set up user accounts and permissions for your team.
- The console shows billing information, health notifications, and lets you chat with support if you have questions.
- You can choose in which region you would like to create services.
- For instance, you can start, stop, and terminate EC2 instances from the EC2 Dashboard. Similarly, you can create and configure any new service instance from here.

We will learn more about this in the upcoming chapters; this is just to familiarize you with the AWS Console.

AWS Command Line Interface

AWS CLI is a unified, open-source tool that enables developers and administrators to manage AWS services directly from their terminal or command prompt. By offering a consistent command structure across all AWS services, the CLI brings the full functionality of the AWS Management Console to the command line, allowing users to automate workflows, script repetitive operations, and perform real-time resource management. In this section, we will learn more about AWS CLI, as mentioned in the following list:

- Usually, in the software field, when we work at an Enterprise level, working on the AWS Console is not a feasible approach because you need to provide all the details manually. Then it will create services and objects for you. So, assume you need to make 100 EC2 instances with the same configuration; to do that, you need to manually create them in the AWS Console, which is time-consuming. Moreover, you cannot achieve automation by this approach. That is why we use the AWS CLI. For hands-on users or automation, AWS provides the CLI, which lets you control services by typing commands instead of clicking.
- The CLI is fast and powerful, perfect for advanced users or repetitive tasks, and works from your computer's terminal or command prompt.
- You first install the AWS CLI software on your Windows, Mac, or Linux computer. Setup is quick, and AWS provides clear instructions for every central operating system
- To connect the CLI to your AWS account, you use the AWS configure command, where you will be asked for your access key, secret key, default region, and output format (like JSON or text).
- With the CLI, you can start servers, create S3 buckets, set permissions, and do almost everything you can in the AWS Console, but often much faster and with more control.
- The CLI is great for automating repetitive tasks, running scripts, and managing many resources at once.
- Output from CLI commands can be easily formatted for readability or fed into other tools.
- Example of a simple CLI command: **`aws s3 ls`** (lists all your S3 buckets)
- CLI allows you to choose which AWS Region to work in, helping you manage resources closest to your users.

Whether you prefer an easy-to-use dashboard or command-line speed, AWS gives you both, letting you control your cloud in whatever way suits you best. Refer to the following image to see the AWS CLI:

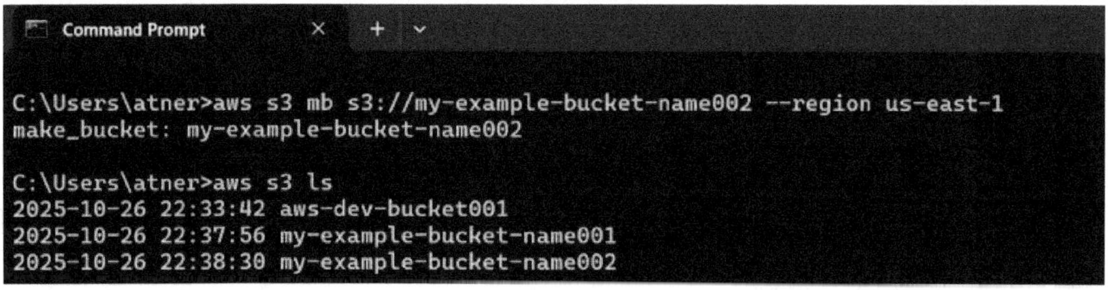

***Figure 1.6**: AWS Command Line Interface (sample image)*

The preceding figure shows the Command Line Interface window and how you can run any command from it. You can connect to EC2 and start and stop services. You can list all files in an S3 bucket and so on.

The AWS CLI has built-in help; just type `aws help or aws <service> help` to see available commands and options. This tool is popular with developers, system admins, and DevOps engineers because it saves time, reduces mistakes, and supports powerful automation. We will learn more about this in the upcoming chapters; this was just to familiarize you with the AWS CLI.

AWS technology terms

In this section, you will learn various technical terms that you will frequently use while working with AWS. These terms are also commonly used by other cloud computing providers. These terms are necessary to understand the context we will be talking about.

AWS technology terms are as follows:

- **Scalability**: It is the ability of a system to scale up or down its resources, like servers, storage, or processing power, as per the requirement. For example, during heavy shopping days like *Thanksgiving, Christmas*, or *Diwali*, an e-commerce site can automatically add new servers and can remove them when it's over.
- **Load balancing**: Load balancing is a networking concept in which the traffic can be divided and sent to multiple servers instead of overloading one server, which can prevent the server from crashing and make the system robust.
- **High availability**: High availability is another concept that means the system is Available every time without any downtime, regardless of the kind of traffic. There are various ways to make a system highly available, e.g., using Kubernetes for containerization (containerization packages software code and its dependencies into a lightweight executable, called a container, to ensure consistent operation across any infrastructure), deploying infrastructure across multiple **Availability Zones** (**AZs**), etc.
- **Database choices**: You have many flavors of database services available in AWS, depending on your requirements. This can be a relational or NoSQL database. Database services available in AWS are RDS, DynamoDB, etc.
- **Monitoring**: Monitoring refers to continuously observing and analyzing the performance, availability, and security of infrastructure, applications, and services to ensure everything runs efficiently. It helps detect issues early, optimize resource usage, and maintain reliability across dynamic environments. In AWS, we can do this with services like CloudWatch (covers metrics, logs, and alarms) and CloudTrail (tracks API-related activities).

- **Logging**: By means of logging and tracing, we can debug any issue and find out the sequence of steps involved and the exact cause of the issue. This is one of the important functionalities in enterprise-level applications.
- **Observability**: Observability in cloud computing means understanding the internal state and behavior of systems by analyzing their external outputs, specifically logs, metrics, and traces. It goes beyond traditional monitoring by not only identifying what went wrong but also helping explain why it happened. This helps teams to gain deeper insights into complex, distributed applications, improving performance, resilience, and user experience. In AWS, observability is achieved through services such as Amazon CloudWatch (for metrics, alarms, dashboards, and logs), AWS X-Ray (for request tracing and latency analysis), and AWS OpenTelemetry (for standardized telemetry collection), providing engineers with a unified view to detect, analyze, and optimize system health efficiently.
- **Automation with infrastructure as code**: Infrastructure provisioning is automated, with code templates used to generate new infrastructure. For example, CloudFormation templates help to automate the creation of AWS infrastructure. This helps you deploy or rebuild your infrastructure when needed.
- **DevOps**: In the earlier days, the development and operations teams used to work separately without being in sync. Once development is complete, the Operational team gets involved, significantly extending the end product timeline. DevOps is the opposite of this, integrating software development and IT operations to automate and streamline application delivery, improve reliability, and accelerate release cycles. AWS CodeCommit, CodePipeline, CodeBuild, CodeDeploy, and CloudFormation are a few examples.
- **CI/CD**: CI/CD is an automation process that stands for continuous integration and continuous deployment, which is a DevOps term, in which code deployment happens continuously, and the customer gets the newer version periodically, unlike the case with SDLC.
- **GitOps**: GitOps is a modern operational framework in which Git repositories are the single source of truth, containing both application code and infrastructure configuration, enabling teams to manage deployments, updates, and rollbacks entirely through version-controlled pull requests.
- **Security, compliance, and governance on AWS**: Security, compliance, and governance on AWS together form a comprehensive framework ensuring that cloud resources are protected, regulatory obligations are met, and organizational policies are enforced across dynamic environments. A few examples of AWS services include IAM for security, **Service Control Policies** (**SCP**) for governance, and AWS CloudTrail for compliance.
- **Cost optimization**: Cost optimization in AWS means using strategies and tools to ensure cloud resources are efficient and expenses are minimized, without sacrificing

performance or reliability. Cost management is one of the services in AWS for cost optimization.

- **Performance tuning**: Performance tuning in AWS is the practice of continuously optimizing cloud resources, configurations, and workloads to maximize speed, responsiveness, and efficiency. AWS offers specialized services such as AWS Compute Optimizer (for instance, right-sizing) and Amazon CloudWatch.

Conclusion

In conclusion, starting your journey with AWS system architecture opens the door to building reliable, scalable, and secure solutions in the cloud. By understanding the basics of AWS infrastructure, core services, and management tools, you gain the confidence to design systems that meet modern business needs while adapting to growth and change. This chapter lays a solid foundation for deeper learning, setting you up to explore more advanced architectural concepts and best practices as you move forward in your cloud journey.

In the next chapter, we will continue the discussion on services and will do a deep dive on the AWS Core services, which are the foundation building blocks, followed by storage and data durability services, which will help to achieve a scalable architecture.

References

1. **https://docs.aws.amazon.com/whitepapers/latest/aws-fault-isolation-boundaries/availability-zones.html**
2. **https://aws.amazon.com/cloudfront/features/**
3. **https://www.cloudflare.com/learning/network-layer/what-is-a-wan/**
4. **https://www.crn.com/news/cloud/2024/aws-google-microsoft-battle-over-76b-q1-cloud-market-share**
5. **https://aws.amazon.com/about-aws/global-infrastructure/regional-product-services/**

CHAPTER 2
Core AWS Services for Scalable Architecture

Introduction

A well-architected cloud solution begins with a deep understanding of the foundational **Amazon Web Services** (**AWS**) that enable scalable, reliable, and high-performing architectures. As cloud workloads evolve, scalability becomes a core requirement, ensuring applications and data can grow seamlessly to handle more users, traffic, and business demands while maintaining resilience and efficiency. In this chapter, readers are introduced to the essential building blocks of AWS compute, storage, networking, and database services and to modern scaling patterns such as Auto Scaling, load balancing, and serverless architectures that collectively empower organizations to meet fluctuating demands without complexity or downtime.

By exploring each core service in the context of scalability, this section provides practical insights and actionable design strategies for architects and developers. The goal is to equip you with the knowledge and real-world patterns necessary to build AWS solutions that can grow as needed, incorporate high availability across regions and zones, and optimize performance and cost, all while ensuring security and operational simplicity for modern cloud-native applications.

We will also learn about the **Identity and Access Management** (**IAM**) service, which enables you to perform administrative and access-related tasks. Also, you will learn what IAM users, groups, policies, and roles are, and how these services help us secure applications.

Structure

In this chapter, we will discuss the following topics:

- AWS Identity and Access Management
- Configure AWS CLI
- Amazon EC2 computer services

- Amazon S3 storage patterns
- Virtual Private Cloud

Objectives

This chapter examines four key pillars of AWS system architecture: **IAM, Amazon EC2 Compute Services, Amazon S3 Storage**, and networking with **Virtual Private Clouds** (**VPCs**).

IAM serves as the security backbone, providing robust mechanisms to control and audit resource access across your environment. By leveraging granular policies, roles, and federated identities, architects can enforce least-privilege and scalable security required for both single-account and multi-account AWS deployments. Amazon EC2 anchors the compute layer, empowering users to launch, customize, and scale virtual machines tailored to diverse workloads, with features such as Auto Scaling groups, managed OS images, and a broad selection of instance types. S3 storage patterns introduce highly durable, scalable object repositories with customizable access, lifecycle, and replication controls, enabling efficient backup, content delivery, and real-time analytics scenarios. The section on VPCs guides you in building secure, isolated network topologies with managed subnets, routing, endpoints, and network firewalls, blending connectivity, resilience, and policy enforcement for modern cloud-native ecosystems. By mastering these four building blocks, readers gain the toolkit to design, secure, and optimize cloud solutions for agility and scale.

High-level flowchart for building an AWS application

When building an application on AWS, we first establish IAM to define secure access boundaries with users, roles, and policies. After securing access, we provision compute resources using EC2 to support our workloads. We then add S3 as a scalable object storage tier for application data, logs, and artifacts. With compute and storage in place, we configure a VPC to provide networking through subnets, routing, and traffic controls, ensuring secure integration of these services. Finally, we create a custom VPC to serve as the foundation for the application architecture:

- **IAM Security Foundation**: Starts with IAM because every AWS resource, EC2, S3, VPC, requires secure access control. IAM is the gatekeeper.
- **IAM EC2**: Once security is understood, we move to EC2, where we launch our first compute resource. IAM roles and permissions are required to manage EC2 instances safely.
- **EC2 S3**: After compute, we explore S3, which is commonly used by EC2 instances for:
  - Storing logs
  - Hosting application assets

- Keeping backups
- Sharing data

This shows how compute and storage interact.

- **S3 VPC**: Next, we learn about VPC, the networking layer that controls:
  - How EC2 instances communicate.
  - How S3 is accessed.
  - How secure is our architecture.

  VPC ties together compute, storage, and security.
- **Create Our Own VPC**: Finally, you apply the concepts by building a VPC from scratch, which prepares you for designing real application architectures.

The following figure illustrates a high-level flowchart of the services' interaction:

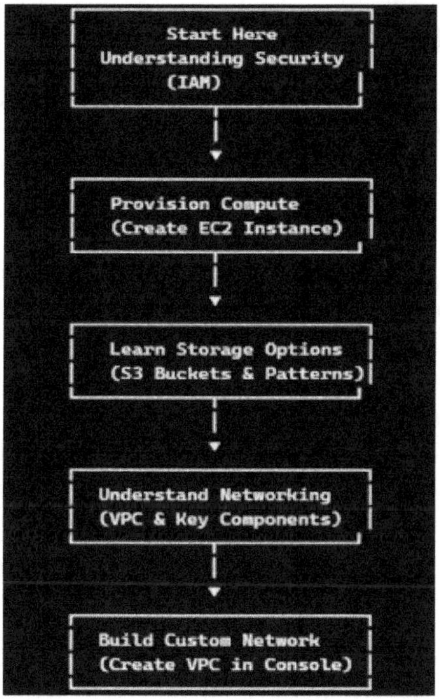

***Figure 2.1**: High-level flowchart of service interaction*

AWS Identity and Access Management

IAM is the primary security service that enables architects and administrators to define, manage, and enforce who can access AWS resources and what actions they can perform. When you set up your AWS environment, IAM lets you create users, groups, roles, and policies to structure access according to the organization's needs, ensuring strong separation of duties and granular control down to the service, resource, or even API level. IAM manages authentication (verifying who you are) and authorization (what you are allowed to do) for both human users and machine identities, handling every request with embedded policy evaluation to grant or deny access.

The service offers essential features, including **multi-factor authentication** (**MFA**), fine-grained permissions, policy conditions (such as IP address or MFA status), and federated access, which enables seamless integration with external identity systems (e.g., SAML, Active Directory) for centralized user management. IAM roles play a significant role in securing workloads by allowing services such as EC2, Lambda, and ECS to interact securely with other AWS services without hardcoding credentials. Integration with AWS CloudTrail, Config, and Security Hub ensures a rigorous audit trail and a strong compliance posture by capturing every authorization event and monitoring configuration changes. Fundamentally, IAM is not just about who can log in; it is the gatekeeper enforcing security, compliance, and policy, and is integral to well-architected AWS solutions that scale securely and efficiently.

IAM users, groups, policy, roles

IAM users, groups, and policies are central to the core AWS concepts of authentication and authorization. Authentication refers to who this user is, and authorization defines what actions or privileges that user is permitted to perform. An IAM user is an individual identity with unique credentials, used for people, applications, or systems requiring access to AWS. IAM groups are collections of users organized by similar responsibilities-such as developers, administrators, or auditors, making it easier to assign and manage permissions across multiple users by applying shared policies. Policies, expressed as structured **JavaScript Object Notation** (**JSON**) documents, precisely govern which AWS resources users (or groups of users) can access and what actions are allowed or denied. These three components work together to streamline access management, minimize risk, and enforce consistent security across your AWS environment. You can think of IAM's structure as analogous to familiar models in traditional operating systems, like Windows users, user groups, and permissions, offering a clear framework for newcomers. In this section, we will discuss these key concepts and their interrelationships within AWS.

IAM users

When you first sign up for AWS using your Username (which is your email address) and password, you create the Root user, a highly privileged and powerful account with full access to all AWS resources. This user has unrestricted access to all the AWS services and resources, and critical operations like modifying support and payment plans, closing accounts, etc., can be done by this account. This user's permissions cannot be limited by IAM policies, which makes it a highly privileged account. There are three critical points to remember about the Root user: first, securely store its credentials since losing them can make them difficult to recover; second, avoid using the Root user for daily operations; it should primarily be reserved for creating IAM users; and third, never share your Root user credentials with anyone to maintain security. You can configure MFA with this user for added protection.

IAM users, on the other hand, are individual identities that represent people, systems, and apps that need access to resources. IAM users have fewer privileges than the Root user, which is created and configured according to your specific access needs. IAM users can log in with a Username (which is not the email address) and a password, with the option to log in with access keys. There can be multiple IAM users, and IAM users can belong to groups that logically organize similar users. Each user has secret keys and access keys that can be downloaded from the AWS Console for programmatic access. This separation helps enforce security best practices by limiting the use of high-level accounts and managing permissions effectively. Refer to the following figure:

Figure 2.2: IAM Service Search

The preceding figure shows the AWS console after logging in (either as the root user or as an IAM user with **`IAMReadOnlyAccess`**). It is advisable not to use the root user for day-to-day work. Once logged in, search for IAM in the top search bar to find the IAM service:

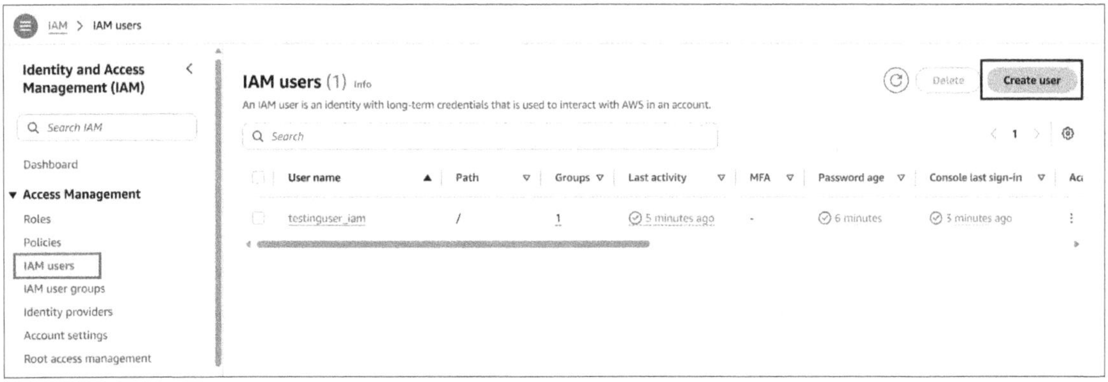

Figure 2.3: IAM users listing and creation

The preceding figure shows the AWS Console after following the steps in *Figure 2.2*. We can click **IAM users** in the left navigation pane to list all IAM users. Also, we can create new users by clicking on the **Create user** button.

A federated user is an AWS user who logs in to the AWS console using external credentials from an enterprise identity provider, rather than an AWS-specific IAM username and password. It is not created directly in AWS but is authenticated via an external identity provider (such as **Active Directory**, **Security Assertion Markup Language** (**SAML**), or OAuth). Through federation, the existing workforce or third-party identities assume IAM roles to access AWS resources without needing to maintain separate credentials in AWS. This enables organizations to centrally manage users, apply consistent policies and access controls, and streamline onboarding by leveraging enterprise identity systems. AWS IAM Identity Center (formerly AWS SSO) simplifies federated access and role management for seamless integration across accounts and applications. In big organizations, they usually use federated users.

IAM groups

IAM groups are a collection or set of users that have similar characteristics. For instance, in an organization, there are various Employees, and some employees are part of the Developer group, while others are part of the Tester or Auditor group. This way, the permission for each group differs from that of another. If a user is part of a group, they will inherit all the access permissions of that group.

One group can have multiple users, and the same users can be part of numerous groups. You cannot have one group inside another group in AWS groups. For best practices, it is always advisable not to create Users who are not part of any group, as shown in the following figure.

Figure 2.4 shows how to access the **User group** dashboard by clicking the **IAM user groups** link in the left navigation pane. It also shows the steps to create a user group in the AWS console by clicking the **Create group** orange button:

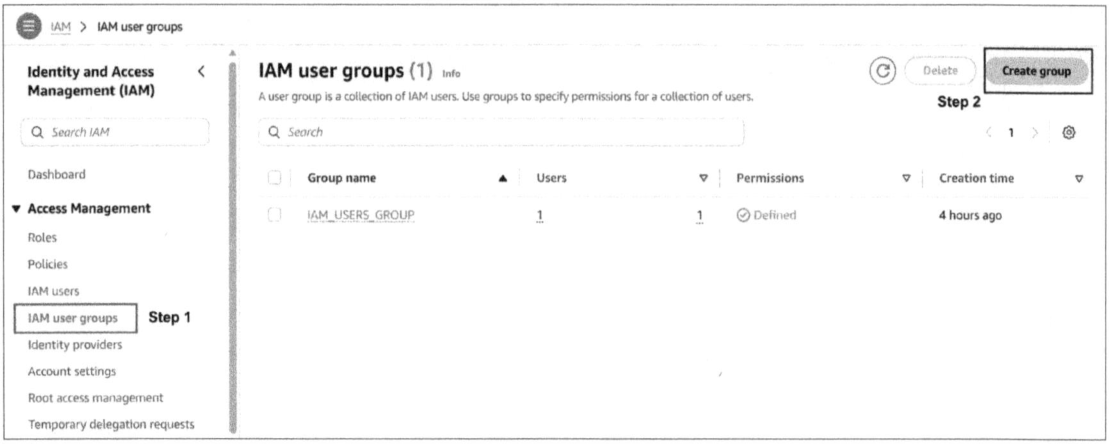

***Figure 2.4**: IAM groups-dashboard*

After clicking the **Create group** button, you will see the page in the following figure, which shows entering the **User group name**, followed by attaching permission policies to the user group:

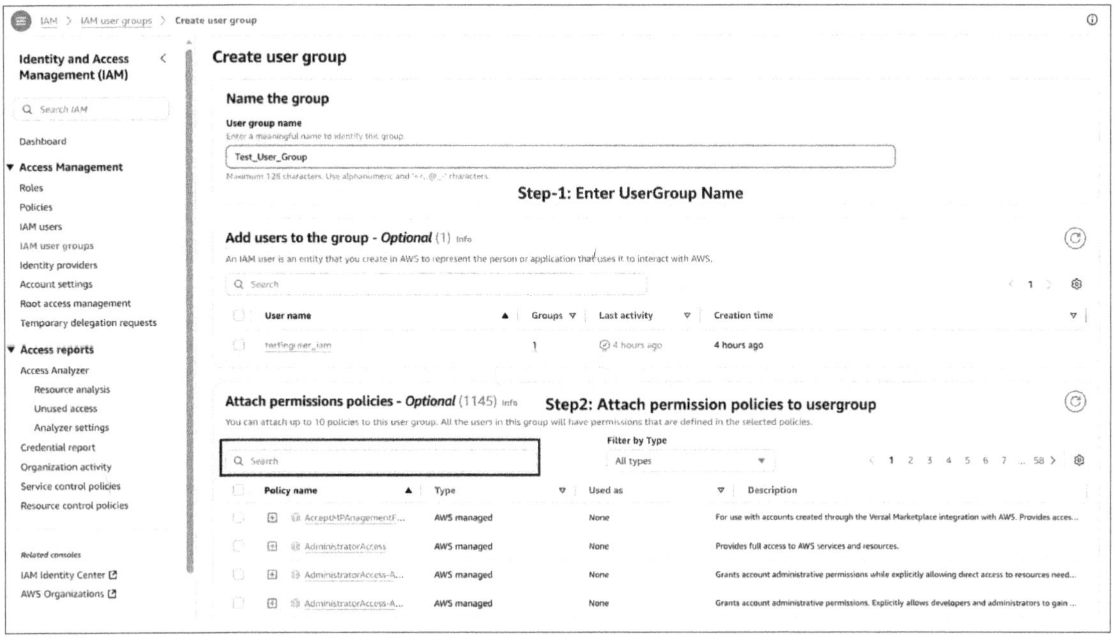

Figure 2.5: IAM group creation

After the above steps, the following figure shows the final creation of the user group by clicking on the **Create user group** button:

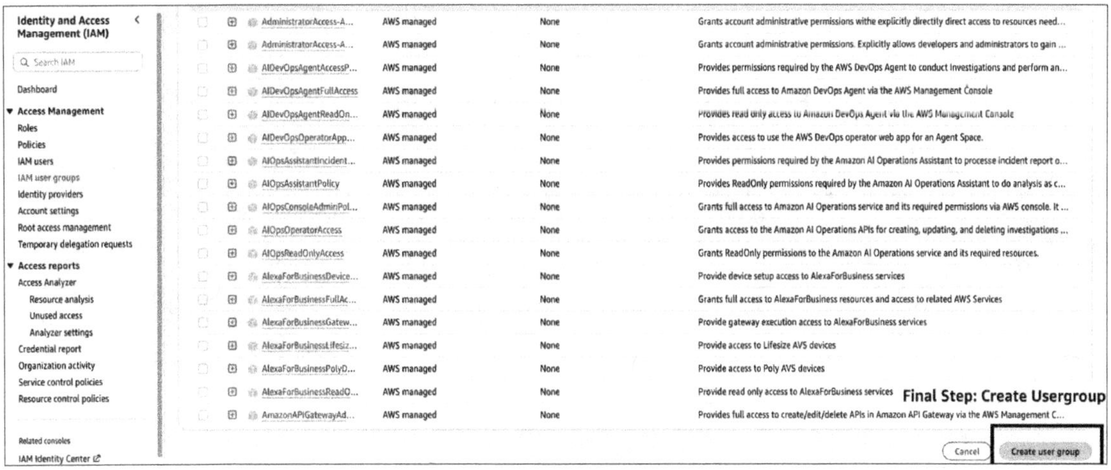

Figure 2.6: IAM groups-final step

IAM policies

In simpler words, IAM policies define what access or permissions a particular IAM group or user has on a particular service or resource. It forms the core mechanism for control in IAM. These are JSON-formatted documents that define permissions in a structured manner, specifying effect (allow/deny), actions (like **`ec2: StartInstances`**), resources (such as **`arn:aws:ec2:::instance/*`**), and optional conditions (e.g., requiring MFA or limiting access to specific IP ranges). Policies can be managed (AWS-defined or customer-managed) or inline (attached directly to a single user, group, or role) and are strictly evaluated to enforce least-privilege access. Deeply understanding how to create, attach, and audit both identity-based and resource-based policies ensures you maintain robust, compliant control over every AWS resource your organization uses. Refer to the following figure:

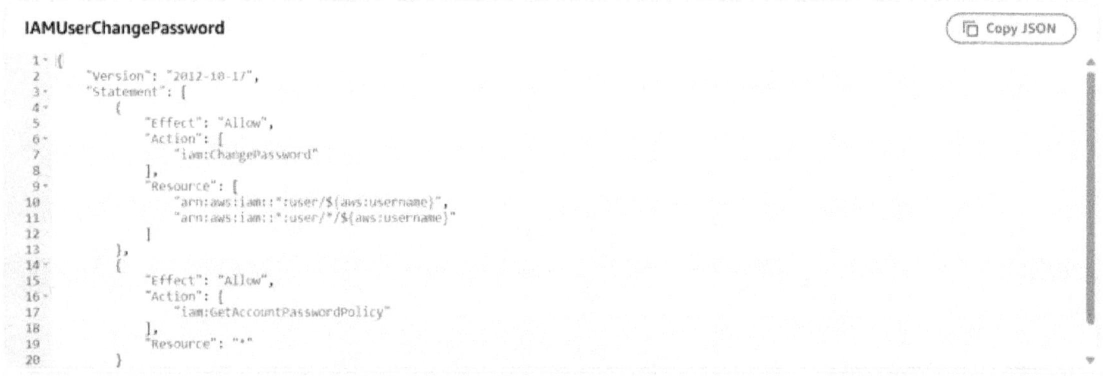


```
{
    "Version": "2012-10-17",
    "Statement": [
        {
            "Effect": "Allow",
            "Action": [
                "iam:ChangePassword"
            ],
            "Resource": [
                "arn:aws:iam::*:user/${aws:username}",
                "arn:aws:iam::*:user/*/${aws:username}"
            ]
        },
        {
            "Effect": "Allow",
            "Action": [
                "iam:GetAccountPasswordPolicy"
            ],
            "Resource": "*"
        }
```

***Figure 2.7**: IAM policies-allow*

The preceding figure shows the AWS Console, from which you can view the AWS policy in JSON format. The policy displays the actions allowed and the involved resources, as displayed in the following figure:

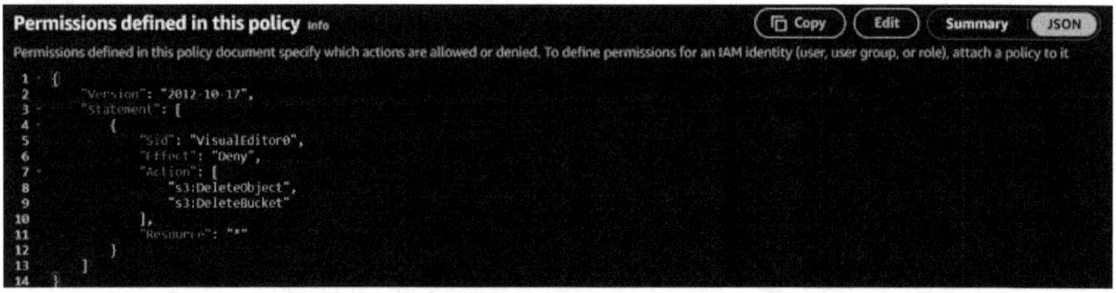


```
{
    "Version": "2012-10-17",
    "Statement": [
        {
            "Sid": "VisualEditor0",
            "Effect": "Deny",
            "Action": [
                "s3:DeleteObject",
                "s3:DeleteBucket"
            ],
            "Resource": "*"
        }
    ]
}
```

***Figure 2.8**: IAM policies-deny*

The preceding figure shows the AWS Console, from which you can view the AWS policy in JSON format. The policy displays the actions denied for all resources.

IAM roles

IAM roles in AWS are special identities that assign specific permissions to trusted users, applications, or services, allowing them to perform defined actions without requiring permanent credentials, such as passwords or access keys. Unlike IAM users, roles do not have long-term credentials. Instead, when someone assumes a role, AWS generates temporary security credentials for them that automatically expire, enhancing security.

We can take an example of an IAM role with permissions to access an S3 bucket and let an Amazon EC2 instance assume this role. The instance can then securely interact with the S3 bucket without embedding sensitive keys in the instance, reducing the risk of credential leaks. IAM roles are widely used to dynamically and securely delegate permissions across AWS accounts, services, and external identities. IAM roles provide EC2 with an option to fetch IAM details without requiring credentials. You can refer to the following figure:

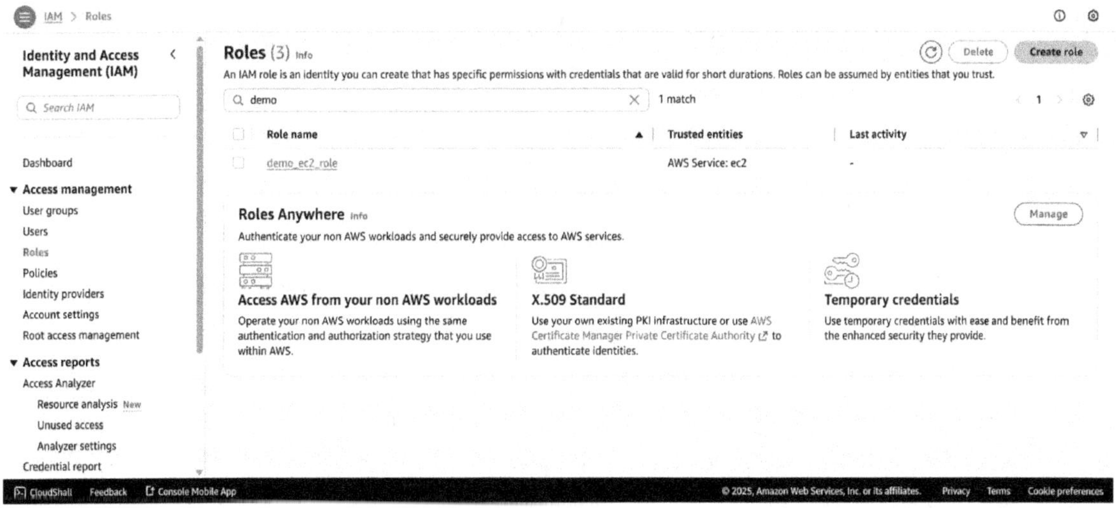

Figure 2.9: *IAM policies*

The preceding figure shows the AWS console. We have created an IAM role that provides an EC2 instance with the ability to fetch IAM details without requiring credentials.

Configure AWS CLI

To configure the AWS **Command Line Interface** (**CLI**) on your local machine, execute the following steps, depending on your operating system.

For Windows

Steps to configure CLI on the Windows platform are as follows:

1. Go to the official AWS CLI website and download the **Microsoft Installer File (MSI)** for the latest AWS CLI version.
2. Locate the downloaded `.msi` file and double-click to launch the setup wizard.
3. Open Command Prompt and enter the following command to verify the installation:
   ```
   aws --version
   ```
4. You should see output indicating the AWS CLI version installed.
5. Open Command Prompt and run:
   ```
   aws configure
   ```
6. Enter your AWS Access Key ID, Secret Access Key, default region, and output format when prompted. These credentials can be generated or downloaded from your AWS console under **My Security Credentials**.
7. Once configured, you can use AWS CLI commands to interact with AWS services directly from your Windows system.

For Linux

Steps to configure CLI on the Linux platform are as follows:

1. Use `curl` command to download the AWS CLI installation package:
   ```
   curl "https://awscli.amazonaws.com/awscli-exe-linux-x86_64.zip" -o "awscliv2.zip"
   ```
2. Ensure you have the `unzip` utility installed, then `unzip` the package:
   ```
   unzip awscliv2.zip
   ```
3. Run the install script with `sudo` privileges:
   ```
   sudo ./aws/install
   ```
4. Check that AWS CLI is installed correctly by checking the version:
   ```
   aws -version
   ```
5. Set up your credentials and default region by running:
   ```
   aws configure
   ```
6. You will be prompted to enter your Access Key ID, Secret Access Key, preferred region, and output format.
7. Once configured, you can use AWS CLI commands to interact with AWS services.

These steps should work on most Linux distributions, including Ubuntu, CentOS, and Amazon Linux.

For Mac

Steps to configure CLI on the Mac platform are as follows:

1. Use **curl** command to download the AWS CLI installation package:

   ```
   curl "https://awscli.amazonaws.com/AWSCLIV2.pkg" -o "AWSCLIV2.pkg"
   ```

2. Run the install script with **sudo** privileges:

   ```
   sudo installer -pkg AWSCLIV2.pkg -target /
   ```

3. Check that AWS CLI is installed correctly by checking the version:

   ```
   aws -version
   ```

4. Set up your credentials and default region by running:

   ```
   aws configure
   ```

5. You will be prompted to enter your Access Key ID, Secret Access Key, preferred region, and output format.
6. Once configured, you can use AWS CLI commands to interact with AWS services.

Amazon EC2 computer services

Elastic Compute Cloud (**Amazon EC2**) provides scalable, on-demand virtual server resources in the AWS cloud, enabling developers and organizations to deploy and manage compute capacity quickly and cost-effectively. EC2 allows you to launch configurable virtual machines, known as instances, tailored with various CPU, memory, storage, and networking configurations to fit diverse application needs. By leveraging features like Auto Scaling, Elastic Load Balancing, and **Amazon Machine Images** (**AMIs**), EC2 delivers elasticity and flexibility that support everything from simple web applications to complex, distributed systems.

With Amazon EC2, users reduce the need for upfront hardware investment while gaining the agility to scale computing resources dynamically based on demand. This service integrates tightly with storage options such as Amazon **Elastic Block Store** (**EBS**), networking capabilities like **Virtual Private Clouds** (**VPCs**), and security constructs including key pairs and security groups, forming a comprehensive platform for running virtually any workload securely and reliably.

Steps to create EC2 instance

Think of an AWS Region as a large, specific area in the world where AWS has set up a cluster of data centers. Each region is a distinct geographic location, such as Northern Virginia in the US, Frankfurt in Germany, or Mumbai in India. These regions are entirely independent of one another, meaning they operate separately and do not share infrastructure. This separation helps AWS provide high fault tolerance and stability. Currently, AWS spans across 38 geographic regions. AWS services are region-scoped, meaning some are available only in a few regions, while others are available in other regions.

Here are the steps to create an Amazon EC2 instance:

1. **Sign in to AWS Management Console**: Log in to the console.aws.amazon.com and navigate to the EC2 Dashboard by selecting EC2 service from the Top Search bar.
2. **Launch Instance Wizard**: Click on the orange **Launch Instance** button to start the process of creating a new virtual server. Provide your instance name, e.g., web-server-dev.
3. **Choose an Amazon Machine Image (AMI)**: Select a pre-configured operating system image suitable for your workload, such as Amazon Linux, Ubuntu, or Windows Server.
4. **Select an instance type**: Pick an instance type based on required CPU, memory, and networking performance (e.g., `t3.medium`, `m5.large`).
5. **Create a key pair (Your Login Credentials)**: A key pair is how you securely connect to your instance. Think of it as a digital key: AWS holds the lock, and you keep the key:
    a. Click **Create new key pair.**
    b. Give it a name like `my-ec2-key.`
    c. Choose RSA as the key type.
    d. Choose `.pem` format if you are on Mac or Linux, or `.ppk` if you are on Windows using PuTTY.
    e. Click **Create key pair**, and your browser will automatically download the key file.

    Important: **Save this file somewhere safe. You cannot download it again. Without it, you cannot connect to your instance.**
6. **Configure network settings**: This section controls who can connect to your server. The console will show a default VPC (your virtual private network on AWS) already selected; leave it as is for now.

    Under firewall (security groups), tick the following boxes based on what you need:

    - **Allow SSH traffic from**: Lets you connect to a Linux instance from your terminal. Change the dropdown from **Anywhere to My IP** for better security.
    - **Allow HTTPS traffic**: Check this if you plan to host a website
    - **Allow HTTP traffic**: Check this if you plan to host a website

    For a basic first instance, just enabling SSH from your IP is enough to get started.

7. **Configure storage**: Your instance needs a disk. The default is 8 GB of **General Purpose SSD (gp3)**, which is fine for learning. The Free Tier includes up to 30 GB of storage, so you can increase this if needed without extra cost during your free tier period.

8. **Add tags**: Optionally assign metadata tags (key-value pairs) to help organize and manage your instance.

9. **Review and launch**: On the right side of the wizard, you will see a Summary panel showing your choices, instance type, AMI, key pair, and storage. Take a moment to check that everything looks right. After review, click the orange Launch instance button.

   AWS will take about 30 to 60 seconds to start your server. You will see a success screen with a link to your instance ID.

10. **Access the Instance**: Click **View all instances** to go back to the EC2 dashboard. Once the instance state is *running*, use SSH or RDP with the key pair to connect and start working on your EC2 server.

    Select your instance by checking the checkbox next to it, then click the **Connect** button at the top. AWS gives you four connection options. For beginners, the easiest is **EC2 Instance Connect**, which opens a terminal directly in your browser with one click, no extra software needed. If you prefer your own terminal, click the **SSH client** tab and copy the example SSH command shown; it will look something like:

    ```
    ssh -i "my-ec2-key.pem" ec2-user@ec2-xx-xx-xx-xx.compute.amazonaws.com
    ```

    Run that in your terminal from the folder where your `.pem` key file is saved.

11. **Stop or terminate when done**: Click **View all instances** to go back to the EC2 dashboard. Once the instance state is *running*, use SSH or RDP with the key pair to connect and start working on your EC2 server. EC2 instances cost money when they are running, even on the Free Tier after the first 750 hours per month. When you are done experimenting:

    - Stop the instance if you want to keep it and come back later. A stopped instance does not incur compute charges, only storage charges.
    - Terminate the instance if you are done with it completely. This deletes the server permanently.

To do either, select your instance, click the Instance state dropdown at the top, and choose **Stop instance** or **Terminate instance**.

These steps enable users to provision flexible, scalable compute resources quickly within the AWS cloud, fitting the needs of diverse applications and architectures. Refer to the following figure:

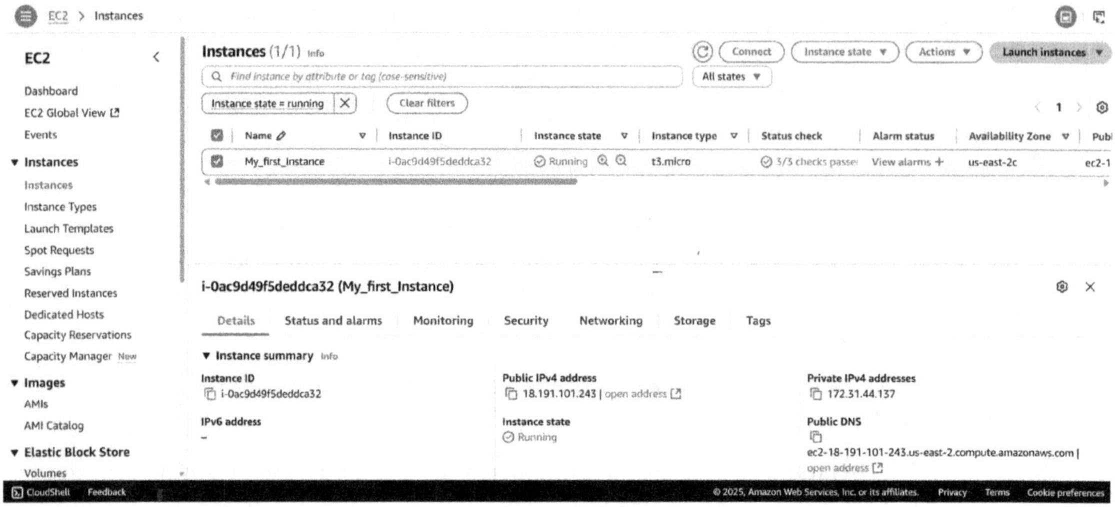

***Figure 2.10:** EC2 instance*

The preceding figure shows a created EC2 instance after following the above-mentioned steps.

EC2 instance types

Amazon EC2 offers a vast range of instance types optimized for different workload needs, grouped into categories based on compute, memory, storage, and acceleration requirements. The main instance families are:

- **General purpose**: Balanced CPU, memory, and networking, suitable for web servers, development environments, and small databases (e.g., T4g, M6i).
- **Compute optimized**: High CPU-to-memory ratio for compute-intensive tasks like batch processing and gaming (e.g., C7g, C6i).
- **Memory optimized**: Enhanced memory capacity for in-memory databases, in-memory caches, real-time analytics, and big data processing (e.g., R7g, R6i).
- **Storage optimized**: High, low-latency storage access for workloads requiring fast read/write to large local datasets (e.g., I4i, D3, H1).
- **Accelerated computing**: Specialized hardware like GPUs or FPGAs for machine learning, graphics rendering, and scientific simulations (e.g., P4, Inf2).
- **High-performance computing (HPC)**: Optimized for tightly coupled compute clusters requiring low latency and high throughput (e.g., Hpc6a).

Each family also offers various sizes, ranging from small virtual CPUs to massive instances with dozens of CPUs and terabytes of RAM, enabling precise scaling to meet workload demands.

Amazon EC2 offers various instance types to meet different requirements. Instance types are named by *instance family* and *size*. The first character of the family indicates the *series*. The second character shows the *generation*. The third character(s) represents options. After the period, the instance size is specified, such as small, 4xlarge, or metal for bare metal instances.

The *family* defines the primary purpose, such as compute, general, memory, or storage optimization. The *generation* indicates the hardware's recency and efficiency; higher numbers mean newer designs. The *capability* suffix specifies features like processor type, local storage, or enhanced network performance. The *size* determines the CPU, memory, and capacity available within the family.

When selecting an instance, identify your application's primary bottleneck. For CPU-bound workloads, use compute-optimized instances. For memory constraints, select memory-optimized options. If storage or network is the limitation, choose a family that addresses those needs. Base your decision on actual workload requirements, not just instance names. Match the instance type to your workload and confirm your choice through testing. The optimal EC2 instance eliminates your application's bottleneck without unnecessary resource costs.[5]

EC2 security groups

You can assume security groups as virtual firewalls in AWS for your Amazon EC2 instances, which enable you to control inbound and outbound network traffic at the instance level. You can define rules that specify which types of traffic are permitted to reach your instances by means of inbound rules and which outbound connections are allowed by outbound rules. In AWS, by default, all inbound traffic is denied, and all outbound traffic is permitted, but you can customize these rules to meet your security requirements.

We can associate one or more security groups with an EC2 instance during or after launch. Each security group contains a set of inbound and outbound rules that specify allowed protocols (such as TCP and UDP), ports, and source/destination IP address ranges, as well as other security groups. For instance, you can create an inbound rule to allow SSH access (port 22) from your office IP address only, enhancing security by limiting exposure. Security groups are stateful; if you allow inbound traffic on a port, the corresponding outbound traffic is automatically allowed. Properly configuring security groups is a fundamental practice for protecting your cloud network from unauthorized access and controlling communication between resources.

The rule of thumb is that if you are trying to connect to EC2 and experiencing a timeout issue, it means there is an issue with the security group. Otherwise, if you receive a *connection refused* error, it indicates an application-related issue. *Figure 2.11* shows the Inbound rules inside the security group attached to an EC2 instance. You can add, update, and delete ports and protocols as needed.

Figure 2.11: Security group-inbound rules

Figure 2.12 shows the outbound rules inside the security group attached to an EC2 instance. You can add, update, and delete ports and protocols as needed.

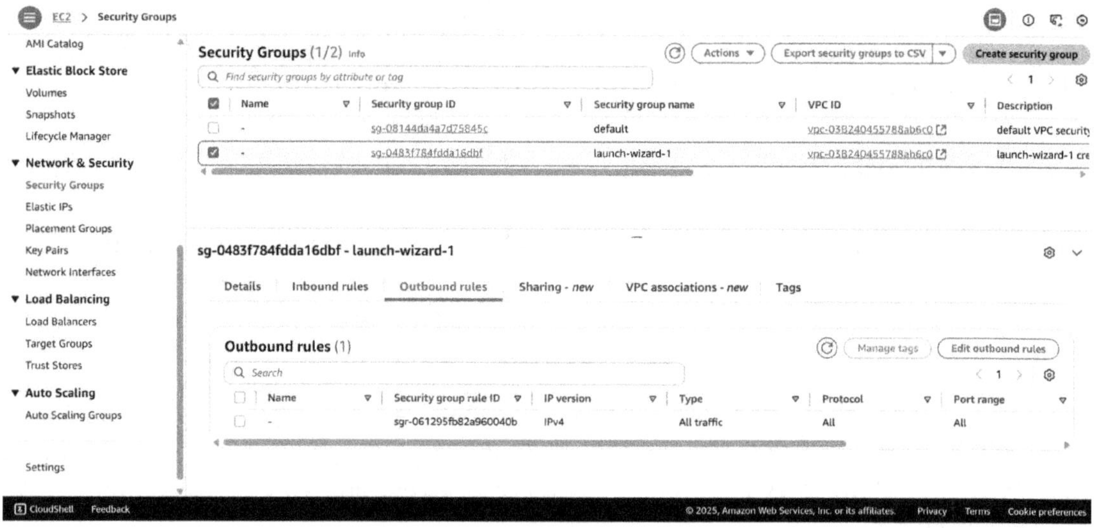

Figure 2.12: Security group-outbound rules

Amazon S3 storage patterns

Amazon Simple Storage Service (S3) is a highly scalable and durable object storage service provided by AWS, enabling users to store and retrieve large amounts of data. It organizes data into containers called buckets, within which files are stored as objects identified by unique keys. With Amazon S3, users benefit from automatic scaling, high availability, and robust security features, including encryption, access control policies, and versioning to protect against data loss or accidental deletion.

S3 is widely used for diverse use cases, including backup and restore, data archiving, content distribution, big data analytics, and hosting static websites. Its flexible storage classes enable cost optimization by matching storage cost to data access patterns, ranging from frequent access to long-term archival. The service integrates easily with other AWS offerings and provides a simple web service interface and APIs, making it a fundamental component in cloud-native architectures.[12]

Amazon S3 storage patterns are architectural strategies and best practices designed to ensure efficient, secure, and cost-effective use of S3 for modern cloud applications. One of the most important patterns is selecting the right storage class based on data access frequency: S3 Standard suits frequently accessed content, while S3 Standard-IA, S3 Glacier, and Glacier Deep Archive provide optimized, lower-cost options for infrequently or rarely accessed data. Utilizing S3 Lifecycle policies and S3 Intelligent-Tiering helps organizations automate the movement of data between storage classes based on usage patterns, thereby optimizing long-term costs without requiring manual intervention.

Tabular summary of the Amazon S3 storage classes is as follows:

Storage class	Description	Use cases	Availability	Cost characteristics
S3 Standard	General-purpose storage for frequently accessed data with low latency and high throughput	Websites, content distribution, mobile apps, analytics	99.99%	Higher cost, optimized for frequent access
S3 Intelligent-Tiering	Automatically moves data between access tiers based on changing patterns	Unknown or changing access patterns	99.9 to 99.99%	Monitoring and automation fees apply
S3 Standard-Infrequent Access (IA)	Storage for data accessed less frequently but requires rapid access when needed	Backups, disaster recovery	99.9%	Lower cost than Standard, retrieval fees apply
S3 One Zone-Infrequent Access (One Zone-IA)	Same as Standard-IA but data is stored in a single Availability Zone	Reproducible, non-critical data	99.5%	Lower than Standard-IA, no multi-AZ redundancy
S3 Glacier Instant Retrieval	Archive storage with milliseconds access time	Long-term archives requiring immediate access	99.99%	Low cost, retrieval fees apply

Storage class	Description	Use cases	Availability	Cost characteristics
S3 Glacier Flexible Retrieval	Archive for long-term storage(data retention time range is 90 days minimum), with retrieval times in minutes to hours	Compliance and archival data need occasional access	99.99%	Lowest storage cost, retrieval fees apply
S3 Glacier Deep Archive	Lowest cost storage for long-term (data retention time range is 180 days) data that can tolerate retrieval times of hours	Digital preservation, long-term archives	99.99%	Lowest storage cost, longer retrieval times

***Table 2.1**: AWS S3 storage classes*

This table helps in choosing the best storage class based on access frequency, cost sensitivity, latency requirements, and data durability needs.

Virtual Private Cloud

Amazon VPC is a foundational AWS service that enables you to launch AWS resources within a logically isolated virtual network that you design and control. It mimics a traditional network environment but operates within the AWS cloud, providing you with full control over your virtual networking stack, including IP address range selection, subnet creation, route tables, and Internet gateways. This isolation enables secure segmentation of resources, protecting them from unauthorized access and allowing for an architecture tailored to business needs.

Core components of a VPC include subnets (public and private segments within your IP space), route tables that define how traffic flows between your VPC's subnets and external destinations, and gateways for internet access or private connectivity. Additional features, such as security groups and **Network Access Control Lists** (**NACLs**) (which are subnet-level traffic filters in a VPC that allow or deny inbound and outbound traffic based on rules), act as firewalls, controlling traffic at the instance and subnet levels, thereby enhancing security. VPC also supports peering connections, VPNs, and dedicated Direct Connect lines, enabling hybrid cloud setups and integration with on-premises data centers. This flexibility and security make Amazon VPC essential for creating secure, scalable, and performant cloud architectures.

The key code components of an Amazon VPC include the following:

- **Classless Inter-Domain Routing (CIDR) block**: The IP address range (in CIDR notation) assigned to your VPC, defining the private IPv4 or IPv6 address space available for use.

- **Subnets**: Segments within the VPC's CIDR block, logically dividing the network into smaller address ranges. Subnets can be public (accessible from the internet) or private (isolated from internet access).
- **Route tables**: Define rules for routing network traffic between subnets, internet gateways, virtual private gateways, and peered VPCs.
- **Internet gateway (IGW)**: A gateway that enables communication between instances in your VPC and the internet.
- **Network Address Translation (NAT) gateway**: Allows instances in private subnets to initiate outbound internet traffic while preventing inbound connections from the internet.
- **Security groups**: Stateful firewalls associated with instances to control inbound/outbound traffic at the instance level.
- **Network access control lists (NACLs)**: Stateless firewalls that control traffic at the subnet boundary, offering an additional layer of security.
- **VPC peering**: Enables networking connectivity between two VPCs, allowing the private routing of traffic between them.
- **VPC endpoints**: Allow private connections between your VPC and supported AWS services without traversing the public internet.
- **Elastic IPs**: Static, public IPv4 addresses that can be associated with instances or network interfaces.

These components, together, form the building blocks for creating secure, isolated, and well-controlled networking environments in AWS, enabling you to customize connectivity, routing, and security according to your application requirements. This flexibility and security make Amazon VPC essential for creating secure, scalable, and performant cloud architectures.

When you create an EC2 instance, a Default VPC gets created by AWS; you can create your own VPC as per your requirement. In a production environment, it is always advisable to develop our own AWS VPC to keep the environment secure.

Steps to create a VPC from the AWS Console

To create a VPC from the AWS Console, please follow these steps as follows:

1. Sign in to the **AWS Console** | **VPC Dashboard** under the **Networking and Content Delivery** section.
2. Click on **Create VPC** or **Launch VPC** wizard to open the VPC creation interface.
3. Choose from predefined VPC templates (from *VPC and more*) or select the option to create a custom VPC.

4. Enter a name for your VPC, and specify the IPv4 CIDR block (e.g., 10.0.0.0/16, as per your requirement). Optionally, you can assign an IPv6 CIDR block.
5. Depending on the template, specify subnet ranges and Availability Zones for the public and private subnets.
6. For advanced setups, configure routing, enable DNS hostnames, assign a NAT gateway for private subnet internet access, and attach an IGW.
7. Review the configuration, then click **Create VPC**. The console will provision the VPC along with the configured subnets, gateways, and routing tables.
8. Once created, verify the VPC and related components (subnets, route tables, IGW) in the console's VPC Dashboard.

This process provisions an isolated virtual network environment in AWS where you can launch and manage resources securely according to your application needs. Refer to the following figure:

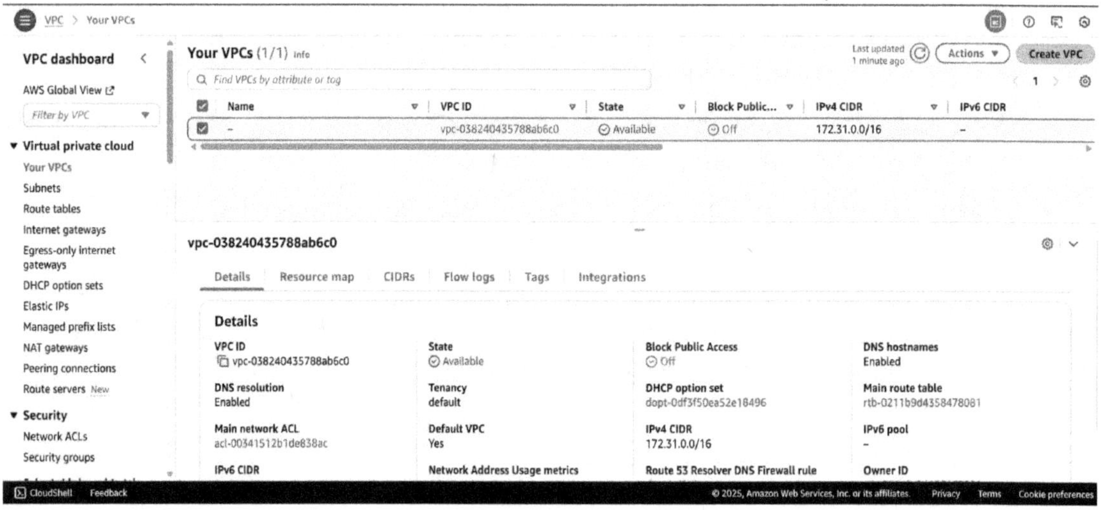

Figure 2.13: *Virtual Private Cloud*

Conclusion

In conclusion, we covered services in this section, which are the backbone of modern AWS architecture. We began with IAM services for security, and then we explored how to create an EC2 instance from the AWS Console. Then we learned about S3 storage patterns, where we discovered how S3 can be used to store a large number of objects that can be accessed from anywhere. We then learned about what a VPC is, its importance, and its key components. We also saw how we can create a VPC from the AWS Console. After completing this chapter, you are ready to proceed with advanced AWS services and features, which together will help you build an advanced architecture.

In the next chapter, we will continue the discussion on services, and you will deepen your understanding of load balancing with application and network load balancers, which ensure high availability and fault tolerance by efficiently distributing traffic. We will explore scaling strategies that dynamically adjust resources to meet fluctuating demands, and then we will introduce AWS Lambda and serverless architectures.

References

1. **https://docs.aws.amazon.com/AWSEC2/latest/UserGuide/concepts.html**
2. **https://docs.aws.amazon.com/s3/?icmpid=docs_homepage_featuredsvcs**
3. **https://docs.aws.amazon.com/AWSEC2/latest/UserGuide/using-vpc.html**
4. **https://docs.aws.amazon.com/AWSEC2/latest/UserGuide/security-iam.html**
5. **https://docs.aws.amazon.com/ec2/latest/instancetypes/instance-type-names.html**
6. **https://docs.aws.amazon.com/vpc/latest/userguide/vpc-network-acls.html**
7. **https://aws.amazon.com/blogs/aws/new-visualize-your-vpc-resources-from-amazon-vpc-creation-experience/**
8. **https://docs.aws.amazon.com/network-firewall/latest/developerguide/arch-igw-ngw.html**
9. **https://docs.aws.amazon.com/AmazonS3/latest/userguide/glacier-storage-classes.html**
10. **https://aws.amazon.com/s3/storage-classes/glacier/**
11. **https://docs.aws.amazon.com/AWSEC2/latest/UserGuide/ec2-security-groups.html**
12. **https://docs.aws.amazon.com/quickstarts/latest/s3backup/step-1-create-bucket.html**

Chapter 3
Scaling with AWS Compute and Serverless

Introduction

In today's digital world, applications must handle unpredictable workloads, sometimes serving a few users, other times supporting millions. Scaling is the process by which an application adjusts its computing resources automatically in response to demand. AWS provides powerful tools to make scaling simple, efficient, and cost-effective, primarily through its compute and serverless services.

This chapter explores how AWS compute options such as **Amazon EC2**, **Elastic Load Balancing** (**ELB**), **Auto Scaling**, and **AWS Lambda** help you build applications that stay reliable even when traffic changes suddenly. We will also look at container-based options like **AWS Fargate** and **Amazon ECS/EKS**, which make scaling containerized applications easier without managing servers directly.

You will learn the key principles of horizontal and vertical scaling, how AWS automatically handles scaling events behind the scenes, and how to design systems that grow smoothly with user demand. Finally, we will discuss how serverless computing changes the way we think about infrastructure, letting developers focus on writing code while AWS automatically manages scaling, uptime, and costs.

Structure

In this chapter, we will discuss the following topics:

- AWS concepts
- Load balancing
- AWS Lambda
- Integration patterns for core AWS services

Objectives

This chapter will cover how AWS enables scalable and reliable application performance through key compute and serverless services. You will examine how **Application Load Balancers** (**ALBs**) and **Network Load Balancers** (**NLBs**) distribute traffic efficiently across multiple servers, ensuring high availability and consistent performance for users. The chapter will also help you understand the principles of scaling, including horizontal and vertical scaling, and how autoscaling can automatically adjust resources to match application demand. You will examine **AWS Lambda**, learning how serverless functions execute code in response to events without requiring server management. In addition, you will explore the key benefits of serverless architecture, including reduced maintenance, improved scalability, and cost optimization. Finally, the chapter will introduce integration patterns for connecting key AWS services, such as **API Gateway**, **DynamoDB**, and **S3**, to design event-driven, cloud-native solutions that adapt seamlessly to real-world workloads.

AWS concepts

In this section, you will explore some fundamental AWS concepts that are essential for understanding how load balancing works and how it fits into a scalable cloud architecture. These foundations will help you follow the detailed explanations, design patterns, and best practices covered later in this chapter, including how different AWS services interact to deliver high availability and performance.

Vertical scaling

Vertical scaling in AWS refers to increasing the capacity of a single server or resource rather than adding more servers. It is often referred to as *scaling up* (or *scaling down* when capacity is reduced). In practice, this usually means changing an EC2 instance or database instance to a larger size with more CPU, RAM, or network performance so it can handle more users or heavier workloads. For example, upgrading from a small EC2 instance type to a larger one is a classic vertical scaling action that gives your application more capacity without changing the overall design or adding new instances.

A key benefit of vertical scaling is simplicity: the application code and architecture can often remain the same, and you simply provide more resources to the existing instance, which is helpful for stateful or legacy applications that are difficult to distribute across many servers. It also reduces infrastructure complexity by managing fewer instances. However, vertical scaling has clear limits: every instance family has a maximum size, and changing instance types can require a restart, which may cause brief downtime if not planned carefully. For sustained expansion and high availability, vertical scaling is usually combined with horizontal scaling so that applications can both scale up for quick performance boosts and scale out for fault tolerance and larger traffic spikes.

Figure 3.1 shows how the vertical scaling works. We can see that earlier we had a smaller instance with 2vCPUs of processing unit, 4 GB RAM of memory, and 50 GB of hard disk drive, which, after scaling up, becomes 8 vCPUs of processing unit, 32 GB RAM of memory, and 500 GB of hard disk drive.

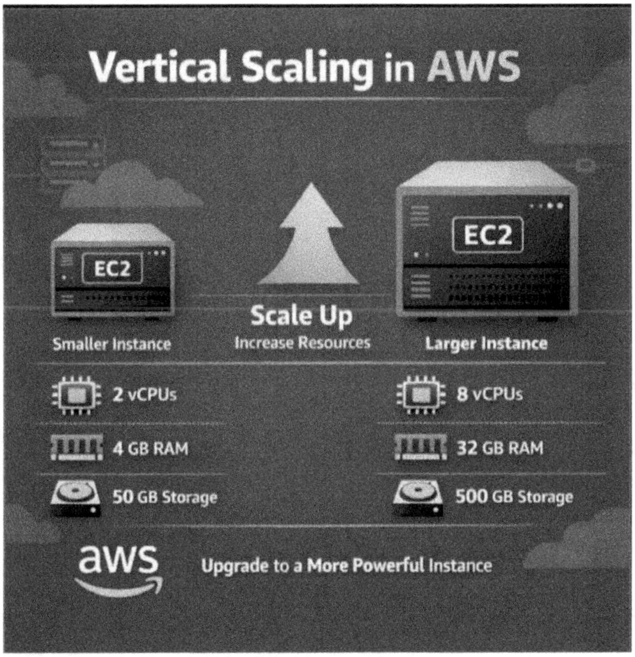

***Figure 3.1**: Vertical scaling*

Horizontal scaling

Horizontal scaling in AWS refers to adding more instances to handle increased load rather than scaling a single instance. In simple terms, you *scale out* by running the same application on multiple EC2 instances, containers, or serverless functions, and then use a load balancer to distribute user requests across them. This approach is common in stateless web applications and microservices, in which any instance can handle any request, and new instances can be added or removed automatically based on demand using services such as Auto Scaling and Elastic Load Balancing.

The main benefits of horizontal scaling are high availability, improved fault tolerance, and the ability to scale almost without limit by adding nodes across multiple Availability Zones. If one instance fails, traffic can be rerouted to the remaining healthy instances, keeping the application running with minimal disruption. Horizontal scaling can also reduce or avoid downtime, as new cases can be launched while the system remains live. However, it requires more careful architectural design: applications often need to be stateless or use shared data stores, and operating many instances introduces extra complexity in deployment, monitoring, and configuration management. This is why AWS provides managed services such as **Auto Scaling groups** (**ASGs**) (you will learn in the next chapter), load balancers, and managed databases to make horizontal scaling easier to implement in production systems.

Figure 3.2 shows how the horizontal scaling works. We can see that earlier we had only one instance involved, while after horizontal scaling, the number of instances extends to four, which will help to share the load on one server.

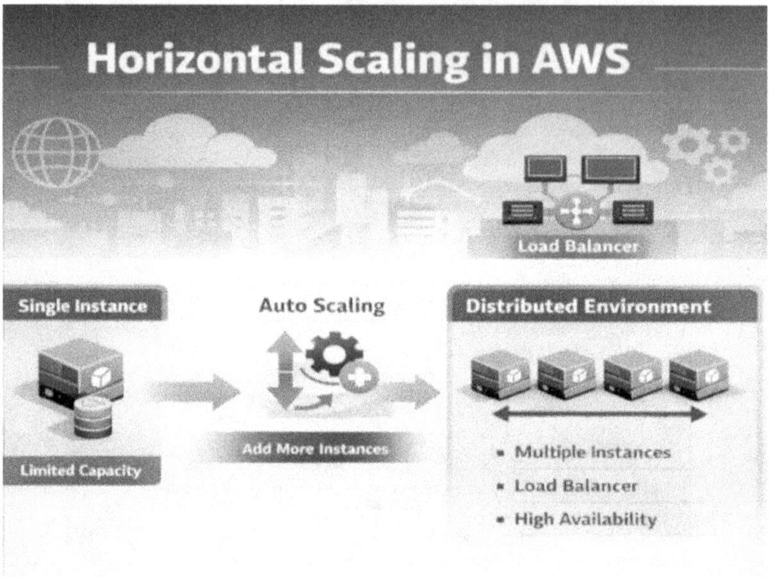

***Figure 3.2**: Horizontal scaling*

High availability

High availability in AWS entails designing systems to continue operating with minimal or no interruption, even when some components fail. It focuses on avoiding single points of failure by running your application across multiple **Availability Zones** (**AZs**) in a region and using redundancy at every critical layer. For example, instead of running a single EC2 instance in a single AZ, a highly available design runs multiple instances across at least two AZs. It places them behind a load balancer so traffic can be routed to healthy instances if one fails. Managed services such as Amazon RDS Multi-AZ, Amazon S3, and serverless services like AWS Lambda and API Gateway also provide built-in high availability by automatically replicating data or capacity across AZs.

To achieve high availability, AWS architectures commonly combine several building blocks: Multi-AZ deployments for compute and databases, ELB to distribute traffic and detect unhealthy targets, Auto Scaling groups to replace failed instances and handle traffic spikes, and Amazon Route 53 health checks and routing policies for DNS-level failover. This approach helps reduce downtime from hardware failures, AZ outages, or planned maintenance, and it supports stricter uptime goals such as 99.9% or higher. High availability is related to but different from disaster recovery: high availability is about staying online during component or AZ failures, while disaster recovery focuses on recovering from larger regional or catastrophic events, often using backups or multi-Region architectures.

Understanding load balancing

Load balancing is a technique that spreads incoming traffic across multiple servers so no single server is overloaded. In AWS, a load balancer sits in front of your application and receives all user requests, then forwards each request to one of the healthy backend targets, such as EC2 instances, containers, or Lambda functions. This improves availability because if one server fails, the load balancer automatically stops sending traffic to it and routes requests to other working servers instead. It also improves performance by preventing bottlenecks and ensuring less-busy resources serve users. *Figure 3.3* shows how load balancing works. When the client sends requests through the browser, the load balancer accepts the requests and distributes this traffic to various backend target groups.

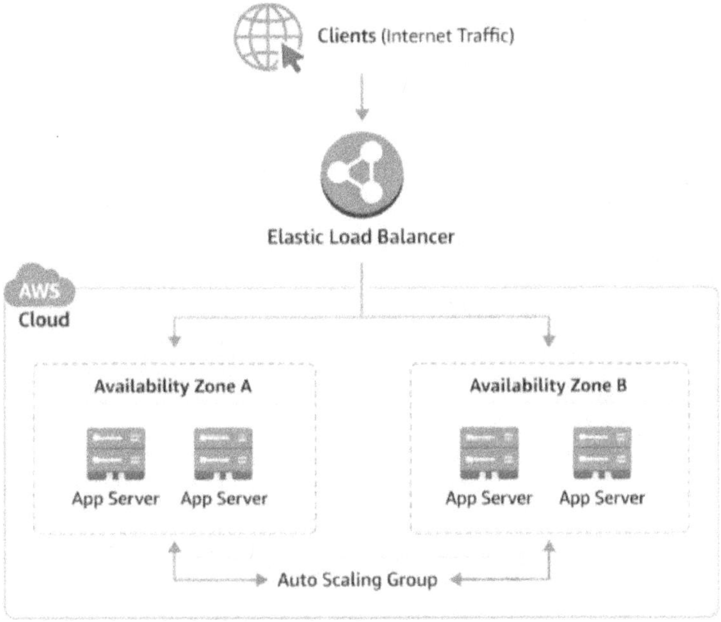

***Figure 3.3**: Load balancing in AWS*

Types of load balancers

AWS provides various types of load balancers for different use cases, primarily the **Application Load Balancer** (**ALB**), **Network Load Balancer** (**NLB**), and **Gateway Load Balancer** (**GWLB**). We will study these types of load balancers in detail in this section.

Application Load Balancer

An ALB is a Layer 7 load balancer that routes HTTP/HTTPS traffic based on the content of each request, including the URL path, host header, HTTP headers, query string, and HTTP methods. It uses listeners (e.g., HTTP:80 or HTTPS:443) and routing rules to route traffic to target groups that can include EC2 instances, **Elastic Container Service** (**ECS**)/**Elastic Kubernetes Service** (**EKS**) container instances, IP addresses, or Lambda functions. ALB continuously performs health checks and sends requests only to healthy targets, thereby improving application reliability and availability.

Key benefits of ALB include advanced routing features, such as path-based and host-based routing, which are ideal for microservices and monolithic apps that expose multiple endpoints behind a single entry point. It integrates tightly with ECS, enabling dynamic container registration and deregistration, and supports serverless patterns by invoking Lambda functions directly without additional middleware. ALB also offloads SSL/TLS termination, supports HTTP/2 and WebSocket, and offers features such as access logs, **web application firewall** (**WAF**) integration, and authentication (OIDC/Cognito) to secure and monitor traffic at the edge.

However, ALB also has limitations that architects must consider. It is optimized for HTTP/HTTPS and gRPC Remote Procedure Calls traffic only; therefore, it is not suitable for non-HTTP protocols such as raw TCP/UDP, for which a **Network Load Balancer** (**NLB**) is a better choice. Because it operates at Layer 7 and provides rich features, its performance and latency characteristics differ from those of NLB; in ultra–low–latency or extremely high-throughput scenarios, NLB may be preferable. Additionally, ALB is regional and zonal in scope and cannot be deployed directly on the public internet for global routing, such as Amazon CloudFront or Route 53. In many designs, it is used in conjunction with these services for international distribution, caching, and DNS-based traffic management.

Network Load Balancer

A **Network Load Balancer** (**NLB**) in AWS helps to handle very high traffic volumes at extremely low latency by operating at the network (OSI Layer 4) level rather than the application level. It forwards connections based on IP address and port and is ideal for TCP, UDP, and TLS traffic, such as database connections, gaming backends, IoT, or any workload that needs fast, stable network performance and does not require HTTP-aware features like path-based routing. An NLB can distribute traffic across targets such as EC2 instances, containers, and IP addresses within a VPC, and it can use static IP addresses or Elastic IP addresses per Availability Zone, which simplifies integration with existing network and firewall rules.

NLB is built for high availability and resilience; it can automatically scale with traffic, handle millions of requests per second, and perform health checks so that only healthy targets receive connections. Because it supports multi-AZ deployments, if one Availability Zone becomes unavailable, NLB can keep routing traffic to targets in other zones, helping you build fault-tolerant architectures. It also supports features like TLS offload, cross-zone load balancing (optional), and integration with services like Auto Scaling, ECS, and PrivateLink, making it a strong choice whenever you need ultra-low latency, protocol-level load balancing rather than advanced HTTP routing logic.

TLS offload: **The load balancer manages HTTPS encryption and decryption, reducing the processing burden on application servers.**

Cross-zone load balancing: **Traffic is distributed across all targets in every Availability Zone, rather than only within the originating zone.**

PrivateLink: **A private AWS connection that enables secure service access without exposing traffic to the public internet.**

Gateway Load Balancer

Gateway Load Balancer (**GWLB**) is a special type of load balancer in AWS that inserts and scales network security appliances, such as firewalls, intrusion detection/prevention systems (IDS/IPS), or deep packet inspection tools, into your traffic path transparently. It operates at the network (OSI Layer 3) and listens for IP packets, then forwards them to a target group of virtual appliances using the GENEVE protocol on port 6081, while preserving the original source and destination IP addresses. This allows traffic to flow *through* the security appliances without applications needing to be aware of them, and without complex routing changes in each VPC or subnet.

GWLB gives you a single logical gateway that distributes traffic across multiple appliance instances and automatically scales them up or down as demand changes, often using Auto Scaling groups in the background. It continuously checks the health of each appliance and forwards packets only to healthy instances, improving availability and making failover smoother during maintenance or outages. Traffic from other VPCs, on-premises networks, or the internet usually reaches GWLB via Gateway Load Balancer Endpoints, which are powered by AWS PrivateLink and keep all traffic within the AWS network rather than exposing it directly to the public internet. This design simplifies building centralized *inspection VPCs*, where all inbound, outbound, or east–west traffic can be inspected and filtered by your chosen thirdparty or custom virtual appliances in a scalable, consistent, and secure way.

Create load balancers from the AWS Console

Figure 3.4 shows the AWS console. We can select the load balancer of our choice from this screen, depending on our use case.

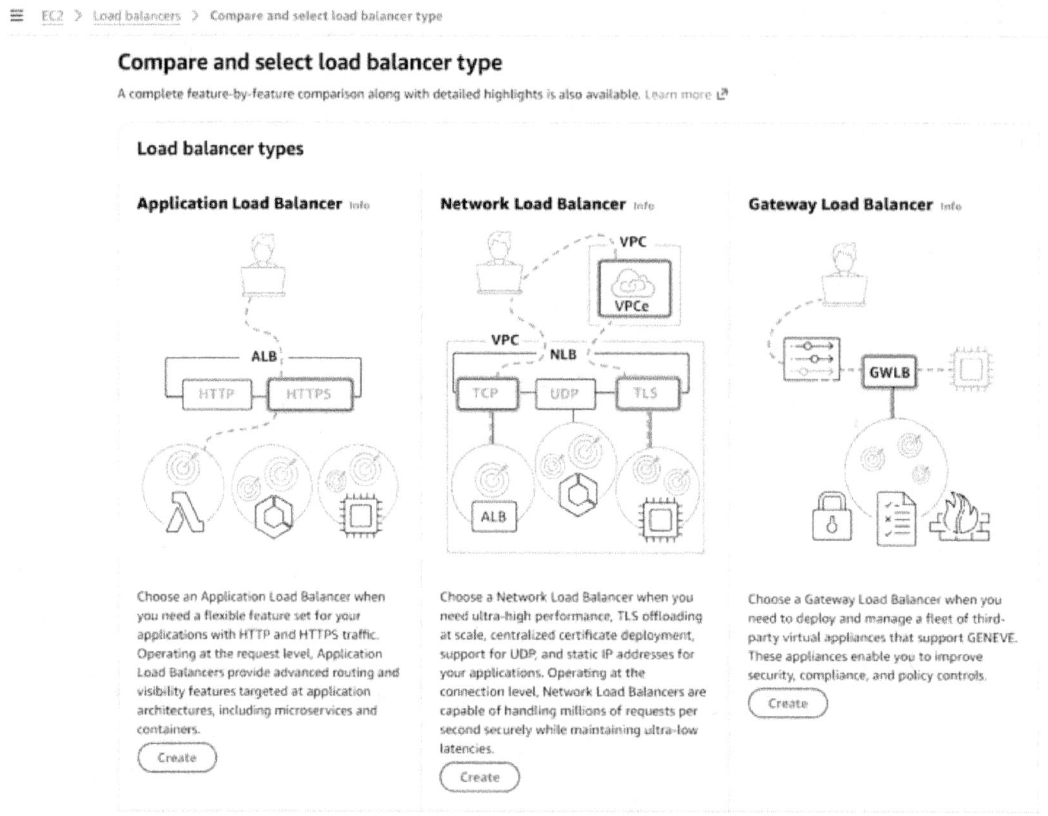

Figure 3.4*: Select the type of load balancer in AWS Console*

Steps to create load balancers are as follows:

1. **Open the EC2 console and start the wizard**:
   a. Sign in to the AWS Management Console and open the EC2 service.
   b. In the left menu, under load balancing, choose load balancers, then click **Create load balancer**.
   c. Select the type you need (for example, Application Load Balancer or Network Load Balancer).
2. **Set basic configuration**:
   a. Give your load balancer a name and choose the VPC and subnets where it will run.
   b. Choose whether it is internet-facing (public) or internal (private).
   c. Choose load balancer IP address type (Options IPv4, Dualstack, Dualstack without public IPv4)
   d. Configure at least one listener (for example, HTTP port 80 or HTTPS port 443).

3. **Configure security and health checks**:
   a. Create a security group by clicking on the **Create security group** link in blue, this will open a new browser window/tab.
   b. Configure the newly created security group to allow traffic on the listener ports.
4. **Create and Register targets and create**:
   a. Create or select a target group. While creating target group by clicking on **Create target group** link define its protocol/port, and set health check settings (path, interval, thresholds).
   b. Add your backend resources (EC2 instances, IPs, or Lambda functions) to the target group as registered targets.
   c. Review all settings and click **Create target group** button.
   d. Once the above step is completed, add the newly created target group in the **Create Load Balancer** window.
5. **Create load balancer after review**:
   a. Review all settings and click **Create Load Balancer** button.
   b. After the status becomes **Active**, test using the load balancer's DNS name in a browser or client.

Stickiness session in Elastic Load Balancer

Sticky sessions (also called session affinity) in ELB ensure that all requests from the same client are sent to the same backend target for a period of time, depending on our setup. This is useful for legacy or stateful applications that keep user session data in memory on each instance rather than in a shared store.

In a normal load balancing setup, each new request can be routed to any healthy instance according to the algorithm (for example, roundrobin or least outstanding requests). With stickiness enabled, the load balancer *remembers* which target handled a client's earlier request and continues to send subsequent requests from that client to the same target while the stickiness is active.

AWS Lambda

AWS Lambda comes under a serverless compute service that triggers a piece of code known as a function in response to events, without you provisioning or managing servers. It is a core building block in modern AWS architectures for building scalable, event-driven, and cost-efficient applications.

AWS Lambda lets you upload small units of code called functions, and AWS handles provisioning compute resources, scaling, and high availability. You pay only for the number of requests and the execution time of your functions, measured in milliseconds.

Lambda supports multiple runtimes such as Python, Node.js, Java, Go, .NET, and others. Functions can be triggered by many AWS services (for example, S3, DynamoDB, API Gateway, EventBridge) or called directly from your applications.

Lambda is ideal for applications that need to run code in response to specific events, rather than maintaining servers continuously. For instance, in a photo upload application, when a user uploads an image to storage like S3, Lambda can automatically trigger a function to resize the image, generate a thumbnail, and store the processed files in another bucket. The application does not need to manage servers or handle scaling during peak upload times, as Lambda executes code only when required and automatically scales to meet demand. This approach simplifies operations, reduces costs, and improves maintainability, particularly for event-driven workloads that require immediate responses to user actions or system events.

Lambda workflow

At a high level, Lambda follows an event-driven model. An event occurs in AWS or in your application, triggering a Lambda function to execute the following steps:

1. **An event happens (Either of the following events)**:
   a. An object is uploaded to S3.
   b. A record is added to a DynamoDB table.
   c. An HTTP request hits an API Gateway endpoint.
   d. A scheduled time is reached (cron-like schedule via EventBridge).
2. **Lambda is invoked**:
   a. AWS finds the proper function and runs your handler code with the event payload and a context object.
3. **Scaling and concurrency**:
   a. Lambda automatically creates more function instances when many events arrive in parallel and reuses warm instances to reduce cold-start latency.
4. **Completion and billing**:
   a. When the function finishes, AWS stops billing; there is no charge while the function is idle.

Key features

From an architectural perspective, Lambda provides several important capabilities as follows:

- **Automatic scaling**: Lambda scales from zero to thousands of concurrent executions based on incoming events, with no manual capacity planning.

- **Event-driven integration**: Lambda integrates natively with S3, DynamoDB, Kinesis, SNS, SQS, EventBridge, API Gateway, and many other AWS services, making it well-suited for decoupled, event-driven designs.
- **Fine-grained deployment controls**: Versions and aliases allow safe rollouts, blue/green deployments, and traffic shifting. Environment variables allow configuration without code changes.
- **Code reuse with layers**: Lambda layers let you share common libraries (for example, logging, SDK wrappers, validation) across many functions, reducing duplication.
- **Security and IAM integration**: Each function executes with an IAM role that controls what AWS resources it can access, enabling least-privilege designs.

Common architectural use cases

Lambda is often used as *glue* between AWS services. Lambda can be used for the following use cases:

- **Web and mobile backends**: Paired with API Gateway, Lambda can implement REST or GraphQL APIs without managing servers, handling tasks like authentication, business logic, and database access.
- **File and object processing**: S3 events trigger Lambda to process new files, such as image resizing, document conversion, metadata extraction, or data validation.
- **Stream and event processing**: Lambda consumes events from Kinesis or DynamoDB Streams to process logs, IoT data, clickstreams, or change data capture in near real time.
- **Automation and scheduled tasks**: Using EventBridge (or CloudWatch Events), Lambda runs scheduled jobs such as backups, cleanup, report generation, and cost optimization.
- **Lightweight data transformation**: Lambda functions transform, enrich, or route data as part of analytics or **extract, transform, and load** (**ETL**) pipelines, often in combination with S3, Kinesis, and data warehouses.

Serverless architecture benefits

Serverless architecture has the following benefits over EC2:

- **Cost efficiency**: Lambda pay-per-use with no idle cost is attractive for spiky or unpredictable workloads.
- **Faster delivery**: Teams focus on application logic, while AWS manages servers, OS patching, and scaling, thereby increasing developer agility.

- **Resilience and availability**: Lambda runs on AWS's managed infrastructure, with built-in multi-AZ fault tolerance for functions.
- **Supports multiple runtimes**: Lambda supports multiple runtimes like Python, Node. JS, etc.

Serverless architecture trade-off

We need to consider the following Serverless architectural trade-offs while deciding whether to go serverless or not:

- **Execution limits**: Functions have maximum runtime (*approx. 15 mins*), memory, and package size limits that shape which workloads are suitable.
- **Cold starts**: Infrequently used functions or functions with heavy runtimes can experience higher startup latency, which matters for latency-sensitive APIs.
- **State management**: Lambda itself is stateless; state must live in external services such as DynamoDB, S3, or ElastiCache, which need to be reflected in the architecture design.

Integration patterns for core AWS services

Integration patterns describe common ways that AWS services communicate with each other so your systems remain simple, reliable, and easy to grow. In simple terms, they answer *who calls whom, when, and how.*

Importance of integration patterns

In a modern AWS system, no service exists in isolation. Your applications need to send requests, publish events, process messages, and execute workflows across multiple managed services and, at times, SaaS systems.

Integration patterns give reusable *shapes* for these interactions:

- Reduce tight coupling between services.
- Handle failures and retries consistently.
- Make systems easier to evolve as requirements change.

At a high level, AWS integration patterns fall into four simple groups: APIdriven, message-driven, event-driven, and workflow-driven.

API-driven integration or request-response pattern

API-driven integration occurs when one service calls another and waits for an immediate response, as when a user clicks a button and expects a result on the same screen. The main AWS services here are Amazon API Gateway and AWS AppSync, often calling Lambda, containers, or backend services:

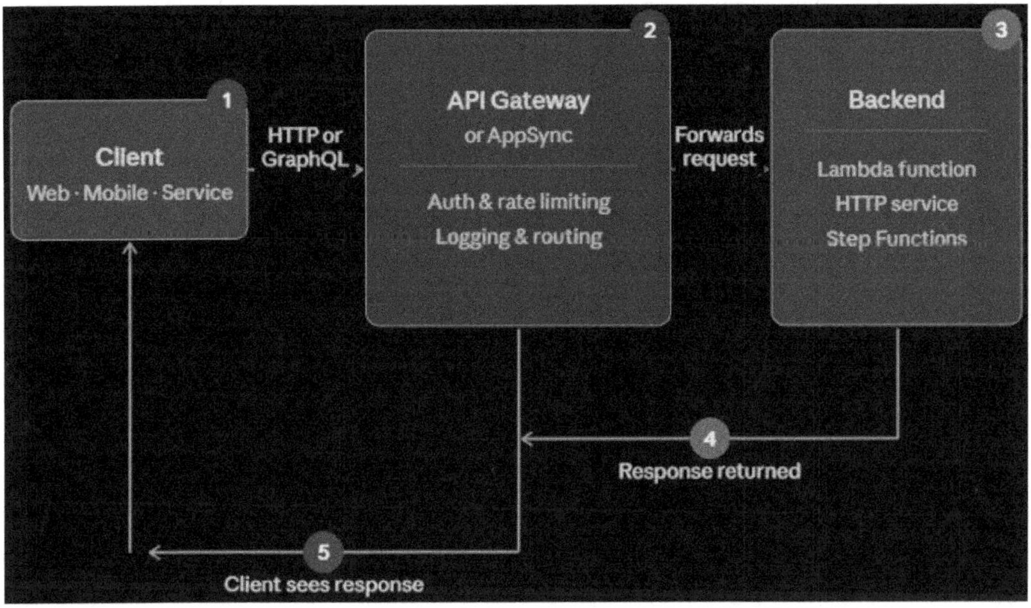

***Figure 3.5**: API driven integration*

The preceding figure demonstrates the steps as follows:

1. In step 1, a client (a web app, a mobile app, or another service) sends an HTTP or GraphQL request.
2. In step 2, API Gateway or AppSync receives it and applies security, rate limits, and logging.
3. In step 3, the request is forwarded to a backend (for example, a Lambda function, an HTTP service, or a Step Functions workflow).
4. The backend processes the request and returns a response that the client sees right away, in steps 4 and 5.

Message-driven integration using Queues or Publish-Subscribe pattern

Message-driven integration uses messages to connect services without them needing to talk directly. AWS uses two core services for this: Amazon SQS (Queues) and Amazon SNS (Pub/

Sub topics). The **Publish-Subscribe** (**Pub-Sub**) model is an asynchronous messaging pattern in which publishers send messages to a message broker, which then distributes them to subscribers.

In simple terms:

- **Queues (SQS)**: One producer sends messages to a queue, and one or more consumers pull and process them later:
  - Good for spreading work across workers, smoothing traffic spikes, and retrying failed work.
  - The producer does not care who processes the message or when, as long as it is processed at least once.
- **Pub/sub topics (SNS)**: One publisher sends a message to a topic, and many subscribers receive copies of that message:
  - Good for broadcasting events or notifications to multiple systems simultaneously.
  - Subscribers can be **Simple Queue Service** (**SQS**) queues, Lambda functions, HTTP endpoints, or even emails and SMS.

Event-driven integration

In event-driven integration, an event triggers some specified actions. The primary AWS service here is Amazon EventBridge, which integrates closely with Lambda, Step Functions, SQS, and many AWS and SaaS services.

A simple view of how it works is as follows:

- A service publishes an event, such as *OrderCreated* or *UserSignedUp*, to an event bus.
- EventBridge uses rules to match events and route them to targets like *Lambda, Step Functions, SNS, SQS*, or other services.
- Producers do not know who is listening; new consumers can be added later by creating new rules.

Workflow and orchestration patterns

Some business processes need multiple steps, decisions, retries, and human-like flow control. Workflow patterns coordinate these steps in a visible, controlled way. AWS Step Functions is the leading orchestration service for this.

In simple terms:

- You define a state machine that describes each step, the order, and what to do on success or failure.

- Step Functions calls other services (Lambda, API Gateway, DynamoDB, ECS, and over 200 AWS service APIs) and tracks progress.
- Built-in patterns handle *call and move on, call and wait until the long-running job finishes,* or *wait for a callback,* which are common in real workflows.

Conclusion

This chapter explored the foundational elements of resilient AWS architectures, starting with core concepts of scaling and high availability that ensure systems handle varying loads and failures gracefully. Load balancing with ALBs for HTTP-aware routing and NLBs for high-performance TCP/UDP traffic provides even distribution and fault tolerance across targets. AWS Lambda introduces serverless compute, automatically scaling event-driven functions without server management, enabling benefits such as pay-per-use pricing, reduced operational overhead, and seamless integration with other services. Finally, integration patterns using API Gateway, SNS, SQS, EventBridge, and Step Functions enable decoupled, flexible connections between core AWS services, promoting event-driven designs that are easier to maintain and evolve. Together, these building blocks would allow architects to develop robust, cost-effective systems that adapt to growth and change while minimizing downtime and complexity.

In the next chapter, we will examine building the architecture and design patterns essential for distributed systems on AWS. It introduces microservices, event-driven, and serverless architectures that enable scalable, loosely coupled components.

References

1. **https://docs.aws.amazon.com/elasticloadbalancing/latest/application/introduction.html**
2. **https://aws.amazon.com/elasticloadbalancing/application-load-balancer/**
3. **https://aws.amazon.com/elasticloadbalancing/gateway-load-balancer/**
4. **https://aws.amazon.com/elasticloadbalancing/getting-started/**
5. **https://docs.aws.amazon.com/elasticloadbalancing/latest/userguide/load-balancer-getting-started.html**
6. **https://docs.aws.amazon.com/lambda/latest/dg/welcome.html**
7. **https://aws.amazon.com/lambda/**
8. **https://aws.amazon.com/integration-on-aws/**
9. **https://aws.amazon.com/integration-on-aws/**
10. **https://docs.aws.amazon.com/step-functions/latest/dg/connect-to-resource.html**

CHAPTER 4
Designing Distributed Systems in AWS

Introduction

In this chapter, we will learn to design distributed systems in **Amazon Web Services** (**AWS**) that are scalable, resilient, and flexible enough to meet the demands of modern applications. Distributed systems break down bigger applications into smaller, independent components that work together across multiple environments and services. AWS provides a variety of managed services and architectural patterns to simplify and improve the reliability of this design.

We will start with a microservices architecture, which splits a monolithic system into smaller services with specific functionality that can be developed, deployed, and scaled independently to improve agility, fault tolerance, and other features. We will also explore a service mesh for automating communication, traffic routing, and observability across microservices. Then we will cover event-driven architectures using **Simple Notification Services** (**SNS**), **Simple Queue Services** (**SQS**), and EventBridge. Finally, we will look at AWS serverless offerings (e.g., Lambda and Step Functions) for building distributed workflows without managing servers or infrastructure.

By the end of this chapter, we will learn how these AWS components and design principles combine to create efficient, decoupled, and highly available distributed systems that can scale seamlessly as business needs evolve.

Structure

In this chapter, we will discuss the following topics:

- AWS concepts
- Microservices architecture
- Event-driven architecture
- Serverless patterns

Objectives

Designing distributed systems in AWS focuses on creating loosely coupled applications using modern architectural patterns. At its core, microservices architecture breaks large applications into independent services that communicate through **application programming interfaces** (**APIs**) or events, enabling faster innovation and resilience. Service Mesh further enhances this model by managing inter-service communication, security, and observability without modifying application code.

Distributed systems on AWS often follow an event-driven architecture using SNS, SQS, and EventBridge to enable asynchronous communication and automated responses to system events. Combined with serverless patterns powered by AWS Lambda and Step Functions, these designs remove infrastructure overhead while delivering agility, fault tolerance, and cost efficiency. Together, these components form the foundation for building responsive, scalable distributed applications in the AWS Cloud.

AWS concepts

In this section, you will explore some fundamental AWS concepts that are essential for understanding how to design distributed systems in AWS that are scalable, resilient, and flexible enough to meet the demands of modern applications. These foundations will help you follow the detailed explanations, design patterns, and best practices covered later in this chapter, including how different AWS services interact to deliver scalable, reliable, and loosely coupled applications using modern architectural patterns.

Monolithic applications

A monolithic application is a software system in which all features are packaged, deployed, and scaled as a single unit, typically sharing a single codebase and database. It usually combines the presentation layer **user interface** (**UI**), business logic, and data access layer into a tightly coupled structure, often running as one process or server.

In this design, modules within the application are tightly coupled, so a change in one area (for example, billing) may require rebuilding and retesting the entire application. A monolithic application has simple deployment steps, which can be advantageous for small teams or early-stage products. However, over time, it becomes harder to maintain, slows down release cycles, and prevents independent scaling of specific functionalities.

Monolithic applications run into several problems as they grow in size and complexity:

- **Scalability issues**: You must scale the entire application even if only one part needs more resources, which wastes resources and limits fine-grained scaling.

- **Slow and risky deployments**: Any slight change requires rebuilding, retesting, and redeploying the entire application, increasing deployment time and the risk that a single bug can bring down the whole system.
- **Tight coupling and low flexibility**: Components share the same codebase and often the same database, so changes in one module can have unintended consequences in others, making it difficult to adopt new technologies or frameworks.
- **Reliability concerns**: A failure in a single part can bring down the entire application because everything runs as a single process or deployment unit.
- **Growing complexity and technical debt concerns**: As features accumulate, the codebase becomes harder to understand, test, and maintain, slowing down development and making it harder for new developers to be productive.

Microservices

In contrast to monolithic application which is a single, unified piece of software where all features, **user interface** (**UI**), business logic, and data access live in one codebase and are deployed together as one unit microservices architecture takes the opposite approach. In microservices, instead of one big application, you build many small, independent services, each responsible for a specific business capability such as orders, payments, or catalog. Each microservice has its own codebase and often its own database, and exposes a clear API (for example, **Hypertext Transfer Protocol** (**HTTP**)/**Representational State Transfer** (**REST**) or messaging) so other services interact with it only through these well-defined interfaces. As services are independent, you can deploy, scale, and update them separately. If one service needs more capacity, you scale only that service instead of the whole application.

In AWS, microservices usually run on managed compute services such as **Elastic Container Service** (**ECS**), **Elastic Kubernetes Service** (**EKS**), or Lambda, with API Gateway or load balancers in front, and asynchronous communication handled by services such as SNS, SQS, and EventBridge. This setup improves fault isolation, enables teams to use different languages or data stores per service, and supports faster, more frequent releases by making changes smaller and safer. Microservices are not limited to containerized environments; they can also run perfectly well on **Elastic Compute Cloud** (**EC2**) instances. In AWS, you can package each microservice as a separate process or service on its own Auto Scaling group of EC2 instances, put them behind load balancers, and let them communicate via HTTP, **gRPC Remote Procedure Call** (**gRPC**), or messaging services like SNS and SQS, just as you would if they were running in containers.

The following figure illustrates the difference between monolith and microservice architectures: in a monolith, the modules for users, threads, and posts are deployed as a single API service, whereas in microservices, they are deployed as three individual services:

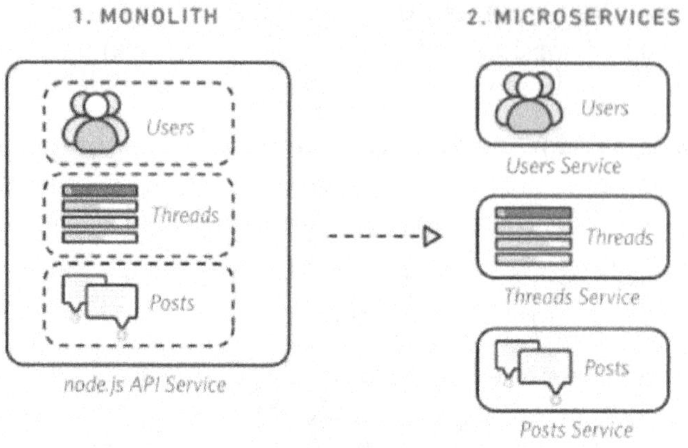

***Figure 4.1**: Monolith vs. microservices*

Microservices architecture

As discussed in the previous section on microservices architecture and its requirements, this section examines in greater detail the various components of microservices. We will examine service mesh and its implementation using *Istio*.

AWS service mesh

A service mesh in AWS is a dedicated software layer that manages how microservices communicate, without modifying the application code. Instead of each service implementing its own logic for retries, timeouts, security, and traffic routing, a service mesh centralizes these concerns, thereby making communication more reliable, observable, and secure.

Explaining service mesh

A service mesh is a special software layer that sits between your microservices and manages all the network traffic between them. Instead of each service handling its own retries, timeouts, security, and metrics, the mesh handles these concerns consistently across all services.

In practice, each service runs a small network proxy (called a sidecar) alongside it, and all incoming and outgoing calls flow through this proxy. A central control component configures these proxies, telling them how to route traffic, enforce policies, and collect telemetry, so you get features like traffic shifting, **Mutual Transport Layer Security** (**mTLS**) encryption, and detailed observability without changing application code. In the following figure, we can see how external traffic flows from the proxy container to the main microservice container:

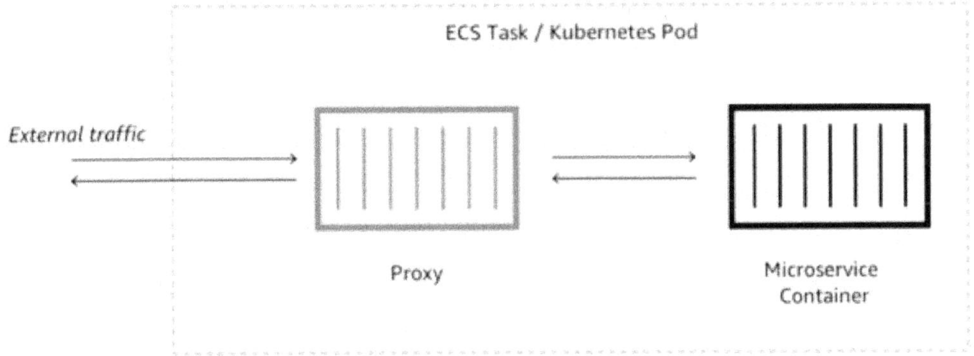

Figure 4.2: *Proxy and main service container*

All communication with external requests, as well as with other microservices, flows through this proxy container; this way, the main microservice is not exposed to other services. For instance, in an e-commerce website with multiple microservices (e.g., Order, Return, Payment, Shipping), each microservice will have its own proxy(sidecar) that communicates with other microservices.

All these sidecars together form the **data plane**, which handles requests, applies load balancing, enforces policies, and collects telemetry, such as metrics and traces. Above this sits the **control plane**, which stores configuration, knows which services exist (service discovery), and pushes routing (service routing), security, and observability rules down to the proxies in near-real time.

Need for service mesh

In modern application architectures, applications are often built as collections of small, independently deployable microservices. Different teams can develop these services using their preferred languages and tools. However, for the overall application to function properly, these microservices must communicate effectively. Application performance hinges on the speed and reliability of inter-service communication. Developers need to monitor and optimize across all services, but achieving full visibility is challenging given the system's distributed architecture. As applications grow and scale, managing this communication becomes increasingly complex.

In the e-commerce example, one team might build the payment microservice in Python, while another develops the order service in `Node.js`. With different technology stacks, developers must manually handle communication between services and implement logging and monitoring in custom ways. This adds significant overhead, distracting teams from their core goal of delivering successful microservices. A service mesh solves this by using network proxies to automatically manage these concerns, freeing developers to focus on business logic.

So, the two main drivers for service mesh adoption are:

- **Service observability**: As the number of services and workloads grows, developers struggle to see how everything connects and performs together. Teams need clear views of upstream and downstream dependencies, plus detailed insights into application-layer communication between services and workloads.
- **Service control**: Administrators require precise control over which services can communicate and what they do. This includes fine-grained governance of service behavior, policies, and interactions in a microservices environment, with strong security enforcement to meet compliance requirements.

Benefits of service mesh

A service mesh provides a centralized infrastructure layer for managing the complexities of communication among services in a distributed application. Various benefits of service mesh are as follows:

- **Smart traffic control**: Handles routing, load balancing, retries, timeouts, and circuit breaking to prevent one slow service from affecting the whole system.
- **Easier deployments**: Support canary releases, blue/green deployments, and traffic splitting to roll out new versions safely.
- **Improved visibility**: Service mesh collects metrics, logs, and traces from all service-to-service communication in a single place, making it easy to spot performance issues or failures across microservices.
- **Automatic security**: Enables mTLS encryption and authentication between services without changing application code, keeping internal traffic secure.
- **Developer focus**: Proxies handle networking concerns, so teams can focus on business logic rather than custom retry or monitoring code.

Istio

Istio is an open-source service mesh platform for managing communication between microservices in complex, distributed applications. Initially designed for Kubernetes environments like Amazon EKS, Istio adds a transparent layer of proxies (based on Envoy) next to each service to handle traffic routing, security, and observability without requiring changes to your application code. Istio operates through two main components: the data plane (Envoy sidecar proxies that intercept all service traffic) and the control plane (components such as Pilot for traffic management, Citadel for security, and Mixer/Galley for telemetry and policy). Key features include intelligent traffic routing (for canary deployments or A/B testing), automatic mTLS encryption between services, retries and circuit breakers for resilience, and rich metrics/logs/traces for debugging.

In an AWS architecture, Istio runs well on EKS clusters and offers advanced customization for multi-cluster or hybrid setups. Architects use Istio when they need fine-grained control over service interactions, Zero Trust security, or detailed observability across Kubernetes-based microservices, making it a popular choice for production-grade service meshes beyond AWS's managed offerings.

In *Figure 4.3*, we can refer to the various components, like the Data Plane and the Control Plane of Istio, and their interactions. Data Plane consists of services and proxy, while Control Plane consists of Istiod, Pilot, Citadel, and Galley. The figure also shows ingress (incoming) traffic and egress (outgoing) traffic from services. This is how all microservices communicate via Sidecar Proxies.

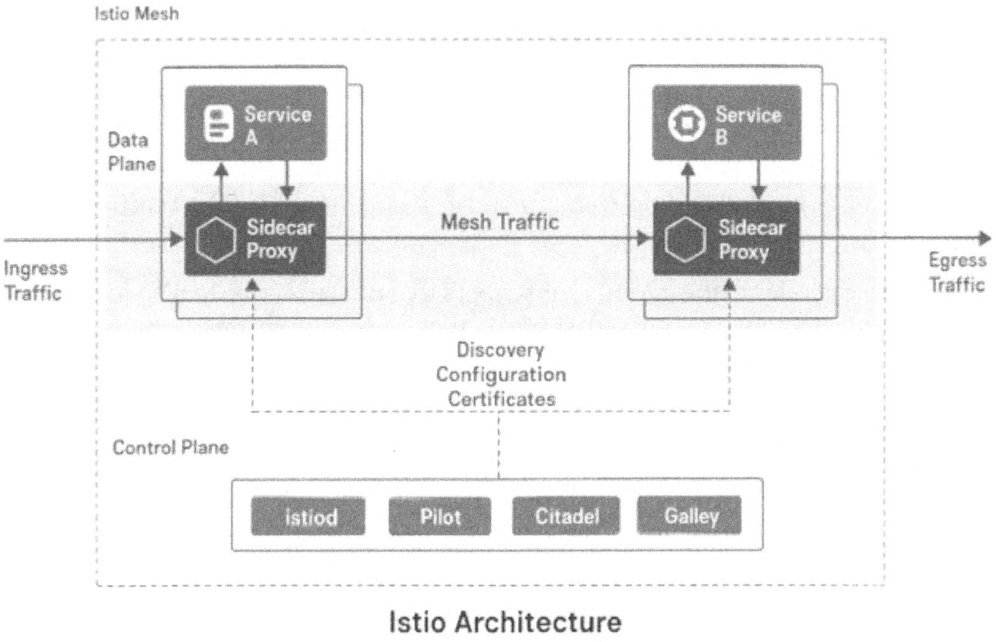

***Figure 4.3**: Istio architecture*

Event-driven architecture

In event-driven integration, an event triggers some specified actions. Key AWS services for event-driven architectures include SNS, SQL, and Amazon EventBridge. Amazon EventBridge integrates closely with Lambda, Step Functions, SQS, and many AWS and SaaS services.

Simple Notification Service

SNS is a managed service by AWS. It is a publisher-subscriber (pub / sub) messaging service that enables event-driven architectures by allowing publishers to send messages to topics, which are then asynchronously distributed to multiple subscribers. Publishers (such as an order service) send events, such as *OrderPlaced*, to an SNS topic without knowing or waiting for who will receive them, thereby decoupling systems and improving scalability.

SNS handles asynchronous communication by pushing messages immediately to subscribers like Lambda functions, SQS queues, HTTP endpoints, email, or SMS, without the publisher blocking or polling. This *fire-and-forget* model supports parallel processing (fan-out), where a single event triggers multiple independent actions, for example, notifying inventory via SQS, billing via Lambda, and users via email, all in near real-time. Subscribers process at their own pace, with SNS providing retries, dead-letter queues for failures, and message filtering for targeted delivery.

In event-driven AWS architectures, SNS serves as a central event hub: an e-commerce order event can be distributed to fulfillment (SQS), analytics (Kinesis), and notifications (email / SMS) simultaneously, enabling loose coupling, resilience, and automatic scaling to handle millions of messages per second. As a serverless service, SNS eliminates infrastructure management, charging only for published and delivered messages, making it ideal for reactive, distributed systems.

In *Figure 4.4*, we can refer to the various subscribers that can subscribe to SNS for notifications. SNS and EventBridge are push-based services that push notifications, in contrast to SQS, which is a pull-based service:

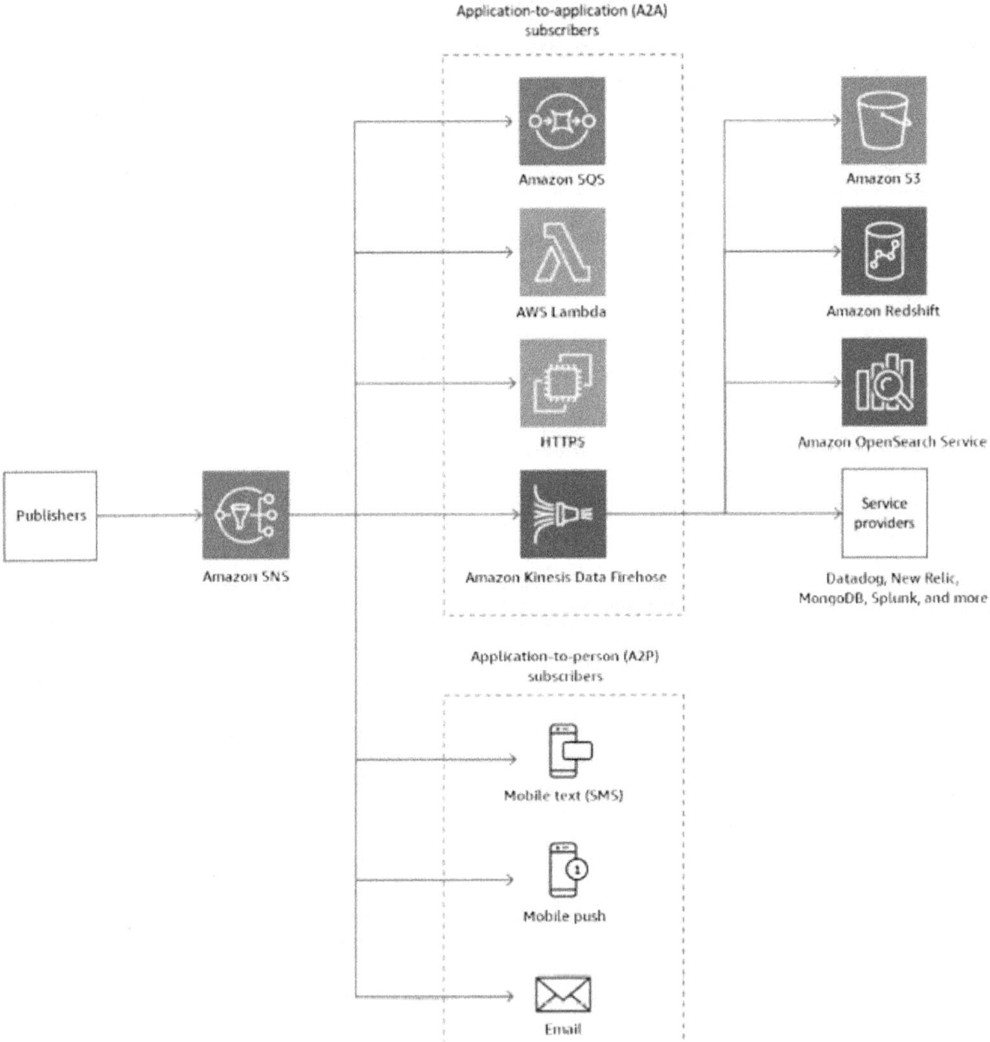

***Figure 4.4**: Simple notification service*

Simple Queue Service

SQS is a queuing service by AWS. It is a fully managed message that decouples components of distributed applications by storing messages until they are processed. Producers send messages to an SQS queue, and consumers poll the queue to retrieve and process them at their own pace, enabling reliable, scalable communication without direct service-to-service dependencies.

SQS supports two queue types: Standard queues for high-throughput workloads with at-least-once delivery and best-effort ordering, and **first-in-first-out** (**FIFO**) queues for strict message ordering and exactly-once processing. Its key features include automatic scaling to handle any volume, message durability across multiple Availability Zones, visibility timeouts to reduce the chances of duplicate processing (by hiding a message from other consumers while one consumer is processing it. Duplicates can still occur in Standard queues), dead-letter queues for failed messages, and server-side encryption for security.

In event-driven architecture, SQS excels at asynchronous processing and load leveling. For example, an e-commerce order service publishes order events to an SQS queue; multiple worker instances (EC2, Lambda, or ECS tasks) consume these messages in parallel to handle fulfillment, inventory updates, or notifications without blocking the frontend. This pattern provides back-pressure handling during spikes (via a message buffer in the queue), fault tolerance (if a consumer fails, messages remain available), and decoupling (producers do not wait for consumers, enabling independent scaling). Often used in combination with SNS for fan-out scenarios, SQS is a core building block for resilient, serverless event-driven systems on AWS. In the following figure, we can see that the producer sends a message, which gets queued in SQS and will eventually get processed and consumed by the consumer:

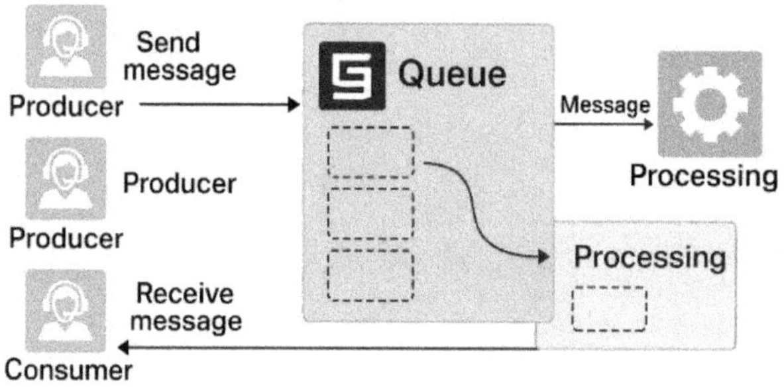

***Figure 4.5**: Simple Queue Service*

EventBridge

EventBridge is a serverless service that connects applications using events, making it easier to build event-driven architectures across AWS services, custom apps, and **software as a service** (**SaaS**) partners. Events, simple notifications like *OrderCreated* or *FileUploaded*, flow through EventBridge's event buses (default, custom, or partner), where rules filter and route them to targets such as Lambda, SQS, SNS, Step Functions, or other services based on content patterns.

In event-driven architecture, EventBridge acts as a smart router: producers publish events without knowing their consumers, and rules match patterns (e.g., events from S3 with specific bucket names) to trigger actions automatically. This enables loose coupling; services react independently to changes, plus features like schema discovery, event archiving for replays, Pipes for transformations, and real-time integration with a growing catalog of AWS services and SaaS partners, including *Zendesk*, *Shopify*, and other third-party applications.

For example, an e-commerce *PaymentProcessed* event can route simultaneously to inventory updates (via SQS), notifications (SNS), workflows (Step Functions), and analytics, all scaling automatically without direct wiring between systems. EventBridge simplifies reactive systems by handling routing, filtering, and reliability, reducing complexity in distributed AWS architectures. EventBridge provides simple, consistent methods for ingesting, filtering, transforming, and routing events, enabling faster application development.

It provides two primary mechanisms for event handling: event buses and pipes:

- **Event buses**: They act as intelligent routers that receive events from diverse sources, like custom applications, AWS services, or third-party SaaS, and deliver them to one or more targets across your organization. They are ideal for scenarios with many-to-many routing, including optional event transformations before reaching targets.
- **EventBridge pipes**: They focus on point-to-point integrations, pulling events from a single source, processing them, and delivering them to a single target. Pipes also support advanced transformations and data enrichment along the way.

Pipes and event buses complement each other effectively. A typical pattern uses a pipe to direct events to an event bus as the target, for instance, capturing events from a DynamoDB stream via a pipe, then routing them through the event bus to multiple downstream targets according to predefined rules. In the following figure, we can see the EventBridge architecture where Event Bus, Pipes, and a schedule are involved:

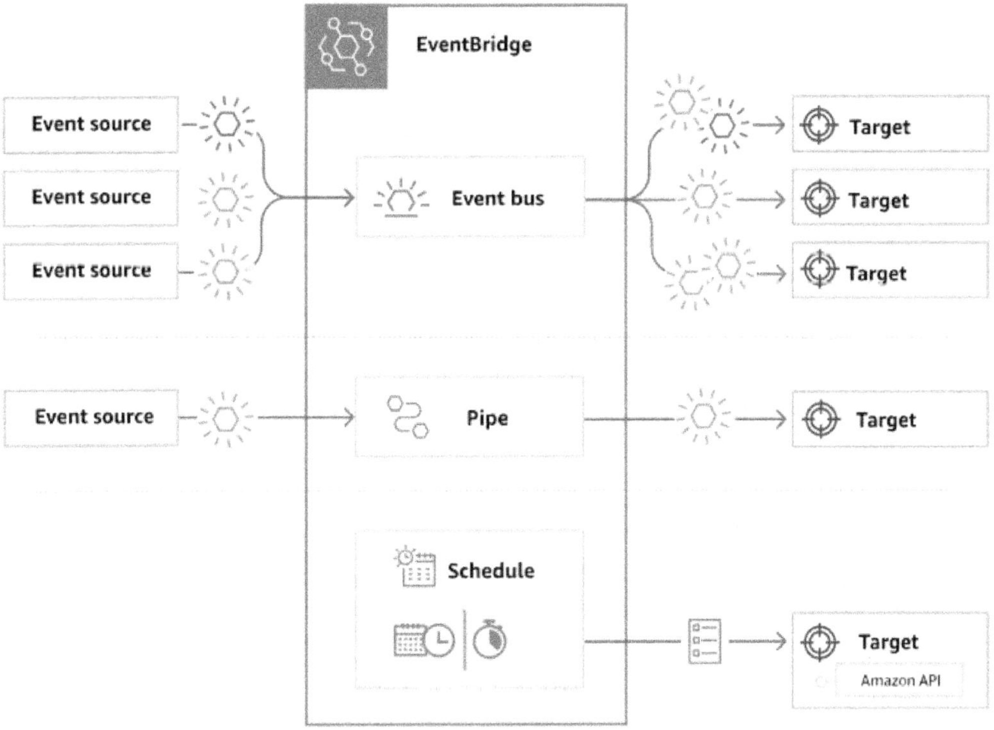

***Figure 4.6**: EventBridge architecture*

Serverless patterns

Serverless patterns in AWS leverage managed services like Lambda, API Gateway, Step Functions, and DynamoDB to build applications without provisioning or managing servers. These patterns emphasize event-driven, stateless designs in which compute scales automatically with demand and you pay only for actual usage.

This will help to avoid the overhead of provisioning, managing, and configuring the actual server for the application. These are created on demand and can be scaled out or scaled in response to request traffic. Serverless patterns promote loose coupling, automatic scaling, and resilience by design. Combine them with Cognito for auth, X-Ray for tracing, and CloudWatch for observability to create production-ready architectures that adapt to variable loads efficiently.

Lambda

AWS Lambda serverless patterns form the foundation of event-driven, scalable architectures where code runs in response to triggers without managing servers. Lambda functions execute small, focused units of business logic, triggered by events from API Gateway, S3, DynamoDB, SNS, SQS, EventBridge, or schedules, automatically scaling from zero to thousands of concurrent invocations based on demand.

Lambda patterns emphasize stateless design (store state externally in DynamoDB/S3), provisioned concurrency (which maintains a specified number of AWS Lambda instances ready to respond immediately, reducing cold start delays) for low latency, and Lambda layers (which enable you to share common code, libraries, or dependencies across multiple Lambda functions) for code reuse. They deliver zero idle costs, sub-second scaling, and seamless integration with hundreds of AWS services, enabling resilient architectures that adapt to variable workloads efficiently.

Step Function

Step Function is an orchestration service that coordinates multiple AWS services into reliable workflows using state machines, making it ideal for complex, multi-step processes without requiring custom error-handling or retry code. It is also a serverless service by AWS.

Step Function models applications as state machines defined in **Amazon States Language** (**ASL**), which can be expressed in **JavaScript Object Notation** (**JSON**), or **YAML Ain't Markup Language** (**YAML**), describing states like Task (invoke Lambda/service), Choice (branching), Parallel (concurrent execution), Map (iterate arrays), Wait, and Fail/Succeed. Two workflow types serve different needs: standard for long-running (up to one year), auditable workflows with durable execution history; express for high-volume, short-duration workloads (up to five minutes) with lower costs.

Direct integrations with more than 200 AWS services (Lambda, DynamoDB, ECS, SageMaker, etc.) via **Software Development Kit** (**SDK**) calls or optimized APIs eliminate glue code, while visual workflow diagrams in the console provide execution history, debugging, and monitoring. Step Functions simplifies serverless by centralizing workflow logic, providing built-in resilience (retries, dead-letter queues), visibility (100% execution traces), and compliance (audit trails). Combine Lambda for compute, EventBridge for triggers, and DynamoDB for state to build fault-tolerant, scalable applications such as e-commerce pipelines or **machine learning** (**ML**) inference workflows, dramatically reducing operational complexity. In the figure here, we can see a sample Step Function with a default path and a conditional path:

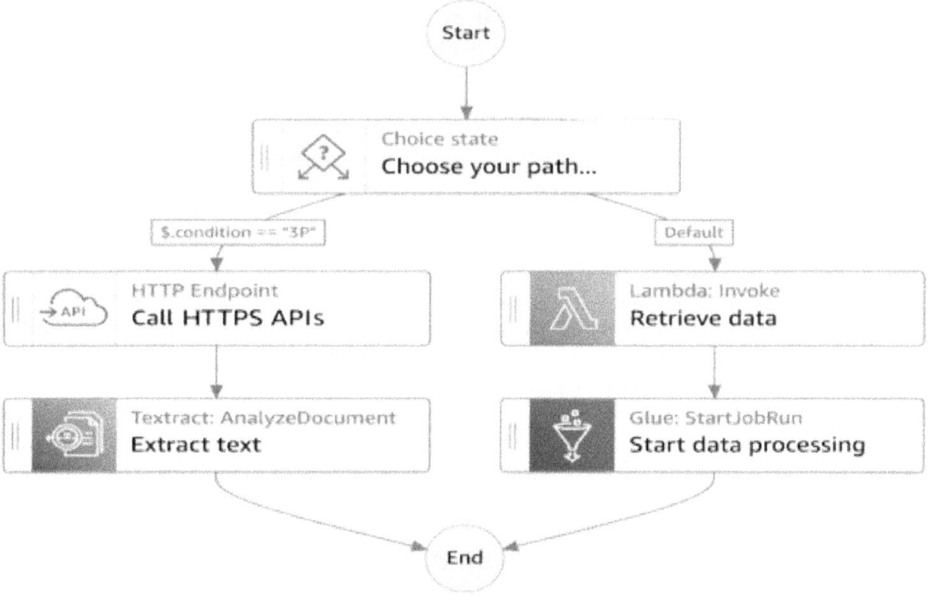

Figure 4.7: *Sample Step Function flow*

Conclusion

This chapter explored the foundational elements of designing distributed systems in AWS, from breaking monoliths into independent microservices to orchestrating them with advanced patterns. Microservices architecture enables teams to build, deploy, and scale services separately, while AWS service mesh provides the secure, observable communication layer needed for reliable inter-service interactions.

Event-driven architecture, powered by SNS for pub/sub fan-out, SQS for decoupled queuing, and EventBridge for intelligent event routing, decouples components, enabling reactive systems that scale independently and handle failures gracefully. Serverless patterns using Lambda for event-triggered compute and Step Functions for workflow orchestration eliminate infrastructure management, adding resilience through built-in retries, branching, and visibility. Together, these concepts form a cohesive toolkit for creating flexible, fault-tolerant AWS architectures that adapt to growth, reduce operational overhead, and accelerate delivery in modern distributed environments.

In the next chapter, we will examine building the architecture and design patterns essential for distributed systems on AWS. It introduces microservices, event-driven, and serverless architectures that enable scalable, loosely coupled components. We will also be exploring how to choose and architect persistent storage solutions like Amazon S3 for object data, DynamoDB for NoSQL scalability, RDS and Aurora for relational workloads, and ElastiCache for high-performance caching. You will discover patterns for data partitioning, multi-region replication, eventual consistency trade-offs, and integrating storage with serverless and event-driven systems to build durable, performant architectures that match your application's needs.

References

1. **https://aws.amazon.com/compare/the-difference-between-monolithic-and-microservices-architecture/**
2. **https://aws.amazon.com/what-is/service-mesh/**
3. **https://aws.amazon.com/documentation-overview/sns/**
4. **https://docs.aws.amazon.com/sns/latest/dg/welcome.html**
5. **https://tutorialsdojo.com/amazon-sqs/**
6. **https://aws.amazon.com/blogs/mt/event-driven-architecture-using-amazon-eventbridge/**
7. **https://docs.aws.amazon.com/eventbridge/latest/userguide/eb-what-is.html**
8. **https://aws.amazon.com/awstv/watch/494f68011a4/**
9. **https://docs.aws.amazon.com/step-functions/latest/dg/welcome.html?nc2=type_a**

Join our Discord space

Join our Discord workspace for latest updates, offers, tech happenings around the world, new releases, and sessions with the authors:

https://discord.bpbonline.com

CHAPTER 5

Data Storage Strategies and Patterns on AWS

Introduction

Data is central to every cloud application, and your approach to storage, replication, and delivery affects both user experience and infrastructure costs. **Amazon Web Services** (**AWS**) provides a comprehensive suite of purpose-built storage services: **Amazon S3** for object storage, **Amazon Elastic Block Store** (**EBS**) for block storage, **Amazon EFS** and **Amazon FSx** for shared file systems, and **Amazon DynamoDB** and **Amazon Aurora** for distributed databases. Each service is optimized for specific access patterns and workloads. Instead of applying a single storage solution universally, modern AWS architectures treat storage selection as a strategic decision. This chapter begins by examining how distributed storage operates in AWS, including data partitioning, replication, and load balancing across **Availability Zones** (**AZs**) to ensure durability and scalability. It also explains how to select the appropriate storage model based on access patterns, latency, and cost. The chapter then discusses data consistency models, from strong consistency for financial transactions to eventual consistency for social feeds, and introduces the **consistency, availability, and partition tolerance** (**CAP**) trade-off that every distributed system architect must consider.

Building on this foundation, the chapter explores how to optimize storage performance and efficiency at scale. **Amazon ElastiCache** provides in-memory caching near your application, using strategies such as lazy loading, write-through, and **time to live** (**TTL**) to reduce repeated database reads. **Amazon CloudFront** distributes cached content to global edge locations, ensuring low latency for users worldwide. These caching layers address different parts of the request path and are most effective when combined. The chapter concludes with distributed system design patterns, including microservices decomposition, event-driven architecture, event sourcing, CQRS, the saga pattern, circuit breakers, and self-healing observability, that equip teams to build AWS architectures that are resilient, loosely coupled, and adaptable.

Structure

In this chapter, we will discuss the following topics:

- Distributed storage
- Data consistency models
- Caching strategies with ElastiCache
- Content delivery network
- Distributed system design patterns

Objectives

The objective of this chapter is to teach how to align storage design with application and business requirements, rather than treating storage as a single generic layer. It aims to help readers understand when to use object, block, file, and database services on AWS, and how to combine them into robust, scalable, and cost-effective architectures for both operational and analytical workloads.

This chapter also focuses on recognizing and applying common cloud data patterns, such as data lakes on Amazon S3, tiered storage and lifecycle policies, databaseperservice in microservices, and patterns for ingesting, curating, and serving data, to build systems that can evolve. By the end, readers should be able to evaluate trade-offs between durability, performance, latency, governance, and cost, and design storage layers that are secure, well-governed, and optimized for their applications on AWS.

Distributed storage

Distributed storage is a method of storing data by splitting and distributing it across multiple servers, often in multiple data centers, while presenting a single logical system to the user. Applications read and write data through **application programming interfaces** (**APIs**) or file interfaces without needing to know where the data physically lives.

In AWS, distributed storage underpins almost every major storage and database service, enabling horizontal scaling, high durability, and global reach. By combining many commodity servers into clusters, AWS can store petabytes to exabytes of data and still meet strict performance and reliability goals.

Core storage models in AWS

AWS offers several storage models, each built on distributed storage but optimized for different access patterns:

- **Object storage (Amazon S3)**: This storage model stores data as objects in buckets, accessed via HTTP APIs, and is ideal for unstructured data like backups, media, and logs. Amazon S3 is AWS's flagship distributed object storage service, designed for virtually unlimited scale, high durability, and flexible access patterns. It has the following characteristics:
  - **Logical model**: Data is stored as objects in buckets within a region; each object has a key and an optional version ID.
  - **Physical layout**: Behind each bucket is a large, multi-tenant cluster that stores objects across many nodes and multiple **Availability Zones** (**AZs**) for durability and availability.
  - **Storage classes**: S3 offers multiple storage classes (S3 Standard, S3 Intelligent-Tiering, S3 Express One Zone, S3 Standard-IA, S3 Glacier, etc.) to balance cost, latency, and retrieval patterns. S3's design makes it suitable as a central data lake, backup target, logging sink, and origin for content delivery networks.
- **Block storage (Amazon EBS)**: This storage model presents virtual disks to compute or database systems, optimized for low-latency transactional workloads. Block storage in AWS appears to applications as local disks but uses distributed techniques for durability and scalability. Amazon EBS volumes are network-attached block devices that store data redundantly within an AZ to protect against hardware failure and provide consistent performance. These systems enable databases and transactional workloads to benefit from distributed durability while maintaining familiar block semantics.
- **File storage (Amazon Elastic File System, Amazon FSx)**: This storage model exposes shared file systems via standard protocols, useful for applications that expect **Portable Operating System Interface** (**POSIX**) or **Server Message Block** (**SMB**) semantics. AWS file services provide shared file systems backed by distributed storage clusters:
  - **Amazon Elastic File System (EFS)**: Amazon EFS stores file data across multiple AZs in a region and supports concurrent access from hundreds or thousands of **Elastic Compute Cloud** (**EC2**) instances, with strong file consistency and standard file semantics.
  - **Amazon FSx File System**: FSx provides managed file systems (e.g., Windows File Server, Lustre, NetApp ONTAP, and OpenZFS) built on highly available, distributed storage and integrates with Windows and **high-performance computing** (**HPC**) ecosystems.

  These services are well-suited to legacy applications, home directories, content management systems, and HPC workloads that require shared file access.
- **Database storage (DynamoDB, Aurora)**: This storage model uses custom distributed storage layers to support high-throughput, low-latency queries and strong durability guarantees. Many AWS databases implement their own distributed storage engines to meet database-specific requirements.

- **Amazon DynamoDB**: Uses a distributed, **solid-state drive** (**SSD**)-backed storage layer to partition and replicate data, supporting high request rates and predictable low-latency access.
- **Amazon Aurora**: Combines a relational query engine with a distributed and Auto Scaling storage subsystem that offloads many traditional database storage concerns (like manual provisioning and replication).

These designs allow databases to scale horizontally while maintaining data integrity and durability guarantees expected from enterprise-grade systems.

Key properties of distributed storage

Distributed storage in AWS focuses on several fundamental properties that shape both architecture and behavior:

- **Scalability**: Capacity and throughput grow horizontally by adding more nodes, without changing application code.
- **Durability and availability**: Data is replicated across multiple AZs, so it survives hardware failures and even full data center loss.
- **Performance**: Workloads can be parallelized across many disks and servers, and data can be placed closer to consumers to reduce latency.
- **Cost efficiency**: Commodity hardware, tiered storage classes, and pay-as-you-go pricing help keep storage costs manageable at large scale.

Data distribution, partitioning, and replication

To scale and remain resilient, AWS services distribute and replicate data across many nodes and locations:

- **Partitioning (sharding)**: Data is split into partitions (or shards) based on keys or internal hashing and placed on different storage nodes, allowing parallel reads and writes.
- **Replication**: Each partition is stored in multiple copies across distinct servers and AZs, so the system can continue operating when nodes or entire facilities fail.
- **Elastic membership**: New nodes can be added to the cluster, and data is rebalanced automatically, so capacity and throughput increase without downtime.

These mechanisms are largely hidden from application developers, who interact with logical buckets, volumes, tables, or file systems.

Design considerations for architects

When integrating distributed storage services into an AWS architecture, several practical considerations guide service selection and design:

- **Access patterns and interface**: Choose object, file, block, or database storage depending on how applications read and write data and which protocols they expect.
- **Performance and latency**: Consider throughput, **input/output operations per second (IOPS)**, and typical request sizes, as well as region and AZ placement, and the effect of network hops between compute and storage.
- **Cost and lifecycle**: Use appropriate storage classes, lifecycle policies, and backup strategies to align storage costs with business value and data retention requirements.

Documenting these choices clearly in the architecture helps teams operate and evolve systems safely over time.

Data consistency models

Data consistency models in AWS describe when and how data changes become visible to applications that read the same data, often from different servers or regions. We need to choose the right model, which is essential for balancing correctness, performance, and availability in a distributed cloud architecture.

Different consistency models

A consistency model is a set of rules that defines what a read operation is allowed to return after one or more writes have happened to the same piece of data. In a distributed system, data is replicated or partitioned across multiple nodes, so updates cannot reach every copy at the same time. Consistency models provide a *contract* between applications and the storage system about how quickly changes will be visible and in what order. This contract influences how developers design application logic, error handling, and user experience.

Importance of consistency in AWS

In AWS, most storage and database services are distributed and replicated to improve durability and fault tolerance. This replication introduces timing gaps where some nodes have newer data while others still hold older versions.

The chosen consistency model determines whether a read can return stale data and under what circumstances. For example, a banking system usually requires strict guarantees, while a social feed can tolerate brief inconsistencies in exchange for higher availability and lower latency.

Strong consistency

Strong consistency means that once a write is confirmed, any subsequent read of that data returns the latest value, regardless of which node or replica serves the request. From the application's perspective, the system behaves like a single up-to-date copy of the data, even though it is distributed underneath.

Strong consistency often requires coordination between replicas before acknowledging writes, which can increase latency or reduce availability during network partitions. It is typically used for workloads where incorrect or stale data would cause serious issues, such as financial balances or inventory that must never go negative.

Eventual consistency

Eventual consistency allows replicas to be temporarily out of sync, but guarantees that if no new updates occur, all replicas will eventually converge to the same latest value. During this convergence window, different reads may return different versions of the same data depending on which replica responds.

This model favors high availability and low latency, because writes can be accepted locally and propagated asynchronously to other replicas. Eventual consistency is suitable for systems where small windows of stale data are acceptable, such as social media timelines, activity feeds, and analytics dashboards.

Read-your-writes and related models

Between pure strong and pure eventual consistency, there are intermediate client-centric models that shape what individual users see:

- Read-your-writes consistency guarantees that once a client updates an item, subsequent reads by the same client will always return at least that updated value.
- Other models (such as monotonic reads or session consistency) ensure that a client never goes *back in time* to older versions once it has seen a newer one.

These models aim to give predictable behavior to each user session while still allowing the system to relax global strictness for better performance.

Consistency and the CAP trade-off

Consistency models are closely linked to the CAP theorem. As per the CAP theorem, in the presence of network partitions, a distributed system must choose between strict consistency and full availability. Partition tolerance is non-negotiable in large-scale cloud systems, so architects decide where to sit on the spectrum between stronger consistency and higher availability.

Stronger consistency usually means more coordination, which can increase latency or cause operations to fail during partitions. Weaker or eventual consistency allows operations to proceed even when parts of the system are unreachable, at the cost of temporarily inconsistent views of data.

AWS services exposing consistency

AWS services exhibit different default consistency behaviors, and some allow per-request tuning:

- Many NoSQL and distributed database services support eventually consistent reads by default, with options to request stronger reads when needed, often at higher cost or latency.
- Object storage and log-oriented services may use a mix of strong and eventual consistency depending on the type of operation (for example, new writes versus overwrites or deletes).
- **AWS DynamoDB** service defaults to eventually consistent reads but supports strongly consistent reads.
- **AWS S3** returns strongly consistent reads for new object writes.
- **EC2** APIs are eventually consistent in many operations due to the distributed control plane.

This flexibility allows architects to match consistent behavior to specific access patterns rather than enforcing a single global model.

Design guidelines for architects

When choosing consistency models in AWS architectures, the key is to align guarantees with business requirements, not just technical preferences:

- Classify data and operations by risk. Identify which reads must be absolutely correct and which can tolerate short-term staleness.
- Use stronger consistency for critical invariants (such as money transfers, security rules, and entitlement checks) and more relaxed models for non-critical views (such as counters, recommendations, or feeds).
- Document the consistent behavior of each service and operation in your architecture so that application teams understand what guarantees they get and where they may see stale data.

A clear understanding and intentional use of AWS consistency models help avoid subtle bugs and create systems that behave predictably under load and failure.

Caching strategies with ElastiCache

Caching in AWS is about moving data closer to where it is needed so applications feel fast and responsive, even under heavy load. Two of the most important tools for this are Amazon

ElastiCache, which caches data in memory near your application, and a CDN such as Amazon CloudFront, which caches content near your users.

Caching matters

In a typical cloud application, every request that accesses a database or a remote origin server incurs latency and cost. As traffic increases, repeatedly fetching the same data can overload back-end systems and slow operations. Caching reduces this pressure by storing frequently accessed data in faster, closer layers so that most requests can be served without touching the original data source. When implemented well, caching can enhance user experience, reduce infrastructure costs, and improve resilience during traffic spikes.

Caching close to the app with ElastiCache

Amazon ElastiCache service is a fully managed in-memory data store that applications typically access from within the same **Virtual Private Cloud** (**VPC**), often just a few network hops away. Because data lives in memory rather than on disk, reads and writes can complete in microseconds, making it ideal for hot, frequently accessed data.

ElastiCache supports Redis **Open Source Software** (**OSS**), Valkey, and Memcached, so teams can use familiar commands and data structures for caching. AWS manages the heavy lifting, provisioning, patching, scaling, and replacing failed nodes so architects can focus on how the cache fits into the overall design rather than on cluster maintenance.

Application of ElastiCache

ElastiCache Serverless enables you to create a cache without worrying about capacity planning, hardware management, or cluster design. You simply provide a name for your cache, and you receive a single endpoint that you can configure in your Valkey, Memcached, or Redis OSS client to begin accessing your cache. Key benefits are:

- **No capacity planning**: ElastiCache Serverless removes the need for you to plan for capacity. ElastiCache Serverless continuously monitors the memory, compute, and network bandwidth utilization of your cache and scales both vertically and horizontally. It allows a cache node to grow in size while, in parallel, initiating a scale-out operation to ensure that the cache can scale to meet your application requirements at all times.
- **Pay-per-use**: With ElastiCache Serverless, you pay for the data stored and compute utilized by your workload on the cache.
- **High availability**: ElastiCache Serverless automatically replicates your data across multiple AZs for high availability. It automatically monitors the underlying cache nodes and replaces them upon failure. It offers a 99.99% availability **service level agreement** (**SLA**) for every cache.

- **Automatic software upgrades**: ElastiCache Serverless automatically upgrades your cache to the latest minor and patch software versions without any availability impact to your application. When a new major version is available, ElastiCache will send you a notification.
- **Security**: Serverless always encrypts data in transit and at rest. You can use a service-managed key or use your own customer-managed key to encrypt data at rest.

The following figure illustrates how ElastiCache Serverless works:

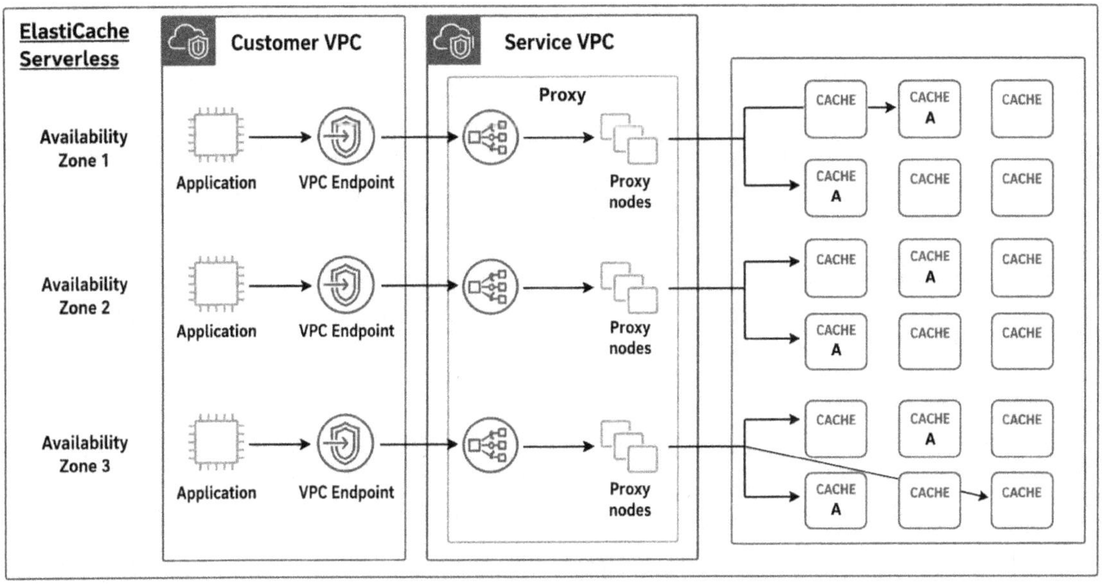

Figure 5.1: ElastiCache Serverless

Common ElastiCache patterns

When ElastiCache sits between your application and your database or API, several practical patterns emerge:

- **Database query caching**: The application checks the cache first for query results; if there is a miss, it queries the database, stores the result in the cache, and returns it to the caller.
- **Session and token caching**: User sessions, authentication tokens, or permissions are stored in ElastiCache so that every request does not have to hit a central database or identity service.
- **Computation and aggregation caching**: Expensive calculations, aggregations, or recommendation results are computed once and then reused from the cache for many subsequent requests.

In all of these cases, ElastiCache acts like a high-speed notebook that remembers recent answers so that the system does not have to *rethink* them every time.

Core caching strategies

Behind these patterns are a few key strategies that shape how data flows into and out of the cache:

- **Lazy loading (cacheaside)**: The application reads from the cache first; if the key is absent, it loads data from the backend, stores it in the cache, and returns it. This keeps the cache focused on data that is actually used but allows occasional stale values until entries expire or are refreshed.
- **Writethrough caching**: When the application writes to the database, it also writes to the cache in the same flow, so reads always see fresh values in the cache. This reduces cache misses at the cost of extra work on write paths and the risk of populating the cache with data that might be rarely read.
- **Timetolive (TTL)**: Each cache entry gets an expiration time, after which it is automatically evicted and can be loaded again from the backend. TTL helps prevent forgotten keys from living forever and provides a simple way to balance freshness and performance.

In practice, systems often mix these approaches, for example, using lazy loading everywhere and write-through plus longer TTLs only for a handful of critical keys.

Content delivery network

A CDN in AWS is a globally distributed layer of cache servers that brings your application's content physically closer to users so it loads faster and more reliably. In AWS, this role is provided by Amazon CloudFront, which uses hundreds of edge locations (points of presence) around the world to cache static assets like images, JavaScript, CSS, video, and even API responses, reducing latency and offloading traffic from your origin servers, such as S3 buckets, **Application Load Balancer(ALB)/Network Load Balancer** (**NLB**), or custom HTTP origins. When a user requests content, CloudFront routes the request to the nearest edge location; if the object is already cached, it is served directly from there; and if not, CloudFront fetches it once from the origin, returns it to the user, and keeps a cached copy for subsequent requests controlled by cache behaviors and TTL settings.

CloudFront and caching at the edge with a CDN

Amazon CloudFront is a global CDN service that accelerates the delivery of static and dynamic web content (e.g., HTML, CSS, JavaScript, images, videos, and APIs) by caching it at edge locations near users worldwide. When a viewer makes a request, CloudFront routes it to the nearest edge location, serves the content from cache if available, and only returns to the origin (e.g., an S3 bucket or HTTP server) on a cache miss, thereby reducing latency and offloading work from the backend. Integrated security features like **Transport Layer Security** (**TLS**) encryption, **distributed denial of service** (**DDoS**) protection through **AWS Shield**, and integration with AWS **Web Application Firewall** (**WAF**) help protect applications at the edge, while edge compute options such as CloudFront Functions and Lambda@Edge allow custom logic, like URL rewrites, header manipulation, or simple personalization, to run close to users without changing origin code.

While ElastiCache accelerates traffic inside your AWS environment, a CDN such as Amazon CloudFront pushes cached content out to edge locations around the world, closer to your users. Instead of every user request traveling all the way to your origin (e.g., an S3 bucket, an Application Load Balancer, or a custom HTTP server), nearby edge locations can serve cached copies directly.

This edge caching greatly reduces latency for static and semi-static content such as images, CSS, JavaScript, video segments, and API responses that do not change frequently. It also reduces the load on your origins, which can significantly cut costs and improve resilience during traffic spikes or regional incidents.

CloudFront decides what to cache

CloudFront applies caching rules called cache behaviors to decide how responses are stored and reused at the edge:

- **Cache keys**: CloudFront can use parts of the request, such as the URL path, query string, headers, and cookies, to form a cache key, so different variations (for example, language or device type) can be cached separately.
- **TTL and origin headers**: You can control how long CloudFront keeps an object in cache by configuring minimum, default, and maximum TTLs, and by respecting or overriding Cache-Control headers from your origin.
- **Path-based behaviors**: Different URL patterns can have different caching rules, for instance, long TTLs for static assets under/static/and shorter or no caching for dynamic endpoints under/api/.

By tuning these behaviors, architects can strike a careful balance between freshness and performance for each part of an application.

Combining ElastiCache and CDN

Most real systems benefit from using both ElastiCache and a CDN together, each handling a different segment of the request path:

- At the edge, CloudFront caches responses and static assets so users around the world experience low latency and fewer round-trips to your origin.

- Behind the scenes, near your compute and databases, ElastiCache absorbs repeated reads and computational work, keeping back-end systems responsive and stable.

For example, an e-commerce site might serve product images and static pages through CloudFront while using ElastiCache to store shopping cart data, recommendations, and precomputed price calculations. In this layered approach, each request passes through multiple cache tiers, and very few requests need to reach the slowest or most expensive components.

Practical design considerations

When weaving caching into an AWS architecture, several practical questions help avoid subtle issues:

- **Consistency and invalidation**: Architects must decide how quickly changes need to appear to users and design invalidation strategies (such as explicit DELETE/PURGE, versioned URLs, or short TTLs) that match those expectations.
- **Failure behavior**: Applications should be prepared for cache misses or cache failures by falling back gracefully to the primary data store, possibly degrading non-critical features while keeping core flows working.
- **Observability and tuning**: Metrics such as cache hit ratio, latency, and eviction rates should be monitored so TTLs, cache sizes, and key patterns can be iteratively tuned over time.

When handled thoughtfully, caching with ElastiCache and CDN becomes a quiet but essential layer in AWS architectures, making systems feel fast, efficient, and robust long before raw infrastructure limits are reached.

Distributed system design patterns

Distributed system design patterns in AWS provide reusable approaches to address network realities, failures, and growth while keeping systems understandable to teams. Instead of solving every problem from scratch, architects reach for well-known patterns that have been proven to work at scale in the cloud.

Decomposition and microservices patterns

A natural starting point in AWS is deciding how to break a large system into smaller, independent pieces. Microservices patterns help define boundaries so that each service can evolve and scale at its own pace while still contributing to a coherent whole.

APIdriven microservices expose clear, versioned contracts, often through Amazon API Gateway, Application Load Balancers, or service meshes, so teams can change internals without breaking callers. Event-driven microservices build on this by publishing and consuming events instead of calling each other directly, which reduces coupling and makes the system more flexible in the face of changing requirements.

Event-driven and event sourcing

In an event-driven architecture, services communicate by sending events that describe what happened, rather than by issuing direct commands that demand immediate action. An order service might emit *OrderPlaced*, while a payment service reacts to that event independently, creating a natural flow of loosely coupled actions across the system.

Event sourcing takes this further by treating the sequence of events as the source of truth. Instead of only storing the current state of an entity, the system stores every state-changing event in order, allowing it to reconstruct the state at any time and to analyze the full history of how that state evolved. This pattern fits well with AWS streaming and messaging services, and it supports powerful audit and analytics capabilities at the cost of extra complexity in modeling and replaying events.

Event-driven design on AWS typically uses EventBridge, SNS, SQS, and Lambda to connect services through events rather than direct calls. Event sourcing can be implemented with DynamoDB, Kinesis, or EventBridge to store and replay state-changing events over time.

Practical CQRS and read/write separation

Command Query Responsibility Segregation (**CQRS**) emerges naturally as systems grow and reads and writes start to place very different demands on storage. CQRS separates the write model, which handles commands and enforces business rules, from one or more read models optimized for querying and display.

In an AWS context, this may mean using one data store and schema for validated writes and another for fast, denormalized reads, with events or streams connecting the two. Reads become much faster and more scalable, while writes can remain strict and carefully validated, though architects must accept that read models are often eventually consistent with the authoritative write model.

As an example, **DynamoDB** manages write operations, while **Lambda** uses **DynamoDB Streams** to propagate updates to **Aurora** or **RDS**. This approach enables more advanced read queries. Also, this approach enables the application to process writes quickly while maintaining fast and flexible reads.

Saga pattern for distributed transactions

In a distributed system, a single business action often involves multiple services and data stores, but traditional two-phase commit is often too rigid and fragile. The saga pattern addresses this by breaking a long-running transaction into a series of local transactions in different services.

Each local transaction performs its part and then publishes an event that triggers the next step; if something fails, compensating actions roll back or adjust previous steps, rather than relying on a global lock. In AWS, sagas often run on top of messaging or event services, enabling business-level consistency while remaining available and loosely coupled.

As an example of the Saga pattern, **AWS Step Functions** orchestrate the transaction flow, **Lambda** executes each local step, and **DynamoDB** stores the state for each service.

Resilience patterns

Network calls fail, time out, and sometimes slow down in ways that can cascade through a system if not controlled. Resilience patterns help keep these problems local instead of letting them spread and take down the entire application.

A circuit breaker watches calls to a dependency and *opens* the circuit when failures pass a threshold, short-circuiting new calls for a while and often returning a fallback response instead. Bulkhead patterns isolate resources, such as connection pools or thread pools, between components, so one misbehaving part cannot starve others of capacity. Complementing these, retry with exponential backoff and fail-fast patterns reduces the risk of storms of retries overwhelming already-strained services.

Observability and self-healing patterns

As distributed systems grow, understanding what is happening at runtime becomes a design concern, not an afterthought. Observability patterns emphasize consistent logging, metrics, and tracing across services so that teams can see end-to-end flows and identify where problems begin.

On top of this visibility, self-healing patterns use automation to detect and recover from failures quickly. Auto Scaling, health checks, and blue/green or canary deployments are all examples where design patterns blend with AWS capabilities to keep systems running reliably even as components fail or are replaced.

Putting patterns together in AWS

In practice, no single pattern stands alone; real AWS architectures combine several of them to fit specific domains and constraints. A system might use microservices and API gateways at the edges, event-driven communication and sagas in the middle, and CQRS and event sourcing for critical business records.

By treating these patterns as a vocabulary, architects can reason more clearly about trade-offs in consistency, coupling, resilience, and evolution, and then map those choices onto AWS services that support them well.

Conclusion

Modern AWS architectures stand on a foundation of distributed ideas: storage that spans AZs, data that is replicated with clear consistency guarantees, and traffic that is shaped and steered intelligently across fleets of services. Together, distributed storage, well-chosen consistency and replication strategies, and layered caching with ElastiCache and global CDNs turn inherently unreliable networks and commodity hardware into platforms that feel durable, responsive, and predictable to end users. These capabilities only reach their full potential when paired with thoughtful load balancing and traffic management, so that requests flow smoothly, failures are isolated, and capacity grows elastically rather than explosively.

At the same time, technology alone is not enough; the chapter's patterns, microservices, event-driven flows, CQRS, sagas, circuit breakers, and bulkheads give teams a language for shaping systems that can evolve safely over time. By combining these design patterns with AWS primitives for storage, caching, and traffic control, architects can create systems that degrade gracefully instead of collapsing, that expose clear contracts instead of hidden coupling, and that remain observable and operable as they scale. The result is an architecture that does more than *run in the cloud*: it embraces distribution as a deliberate design choice, turning complexity into a set of managed, well-understood trade-offs.

In the next chapter, the focus will shift to load balancing and Auto Scaling, two closely related capabilities that keep AWS-based systems responsive and cost-efficient as demand changes. You will explore how load balancing distributes incoming requests across multiple instances or containers to prevent any single resource from becoming a bottleneck, and how Auto Scaling automatically adjusts capacity up or down in response to real-time metrics such as traffic or **central processing unit** (**CPU**) utilization. Building on the distributed principles covered so far, this chapter will show how these mechanisms work together to absorb sudden spikes, handle failures gracefully, and align infrastructure usage with actual workload patterns, setting the stage for highly available and economically optimized architectures.

References

1. **https://docs.aws.amazon.com/pdfs/whitepapers/latest/build-e2e-data-driven-applications/build-e2e-data-driven-applications.pdf**
2. **https://aws.amazon.com/what-is/database-storage/**
3. **https://aws.amazon.com/s3/**
4. **https://docs.aws.amazon.com/whitepapers/latest/aws-overview/storage-services.html**
5. **https://aws.amazon.com/caching/best-practices/**
6. **https://docs.aws.amazon.com/AmazonElastiCache/latest/dg/WhatIs.html**
7. **https://aws.amazon.com/elasticache/**

8. https://docs.aws.amazon.com/AmazonElastiCache/latest/dg/WhatIs.corecomponents.html
9. https://docs.aws.amazon.com/AmazonElastiCache/latest/dg/Strategies.html
10. https://docs.aws.amazon.com/AmazonElastiCache/latest/dg/Strategies.html
11. https://docs.aws.amazon.com/AmazonCloudFront/latest/DeveloperGuide/header-caching.html
12. https://docs.aws.amazon.com/AmazonCloudFront/latest/DeveloperGuide/DownloadDistValuesCacheBehavior.html
13. https://docs.aws.amazon.com/AmazonCloudFront/latest/DeveloperGuide/header-caching.html
14. https://docs.amazonaws.cn/en_us/AmazonElastiCache/latest/dg/WhatIs.corecomponents.html
15. https://aws.amazon.com/blogs/storage/modify-images-cached-in-amazon-cloudfront-using-amazon-s3-object-lambda/

Chapter 6
Load Balancing and Auto Scaling

Introduction

Amazon Web Services (**AWS**) provides a family of managed load balancers, application, network, gateway, and classic, that distribute traffic across **Elastic Compute Cloud** (**EC2**) instances, containers, IPs, and even Lambda functions to improve availability and fault tolerance. **Application Load Balancers** (**ALBs**) focus on HTTP/HTTPS and advanced routing for modern microservices; **Network Load Balancers** (**NLBs**) handle ultra-low-latency **Transmission Control Protocol** (**TCP**)/**User Datagram Protocol** (**UDP**) flows at scale; **Gateway Load Balancers** (**GWLBs**) sit in front of virtual appliances like firewalls; and **Classic Load Balancers** (**CLBs**) remain primarily for legacy architectures. Well-designed entry points align the load balancer type, listener configuration, health checks, and target group strategy with the application's protocol, performance profile, and security requirements.

Behind these front doors, **Auto Scaling groups** (**ASGs**) provide the elasticity that defines cloudnative design, combining launch templates, capacity bounds (minimum, maximum, desired), and scaling policies to continuously match compute capacity to real-world demand. Dynamic scaling policies, such as target-tracking based on metrics like CPU utilization or request count per target, respond to live load, while scheduled (and predictive) strategies pre-provision capacity for known peaks, such as business hours or product launches, balancing resilience, performance, and cost efficiency. Thoughtful integration of load balancers with multi-**Availability Zones** (**AZs**) ASGs, health checks, and scaling policies creates self-healing, right-sized architectures that form the backbone of production-grade systems on AWS.

Structure

In this chapter, we will discuss the following topics:

- AWS load balancer types
- Auto Scaling groups

- Designing auto scaling groups and policies
- Dynamic and scheduled scaling strategies

Objectives

This section aims to equip readers with a clear understanding of the primary AWS load balancer offerings, Application, Network, Gateway, and Classic, and how to select the right type for different workloads and architectures. It focuses on building the ability to design and configure these load balancers for high availability, fault tolerance, and secure, efficient traffic distribution across targets such as EC2 instances, containers, and serverless endpoints. Readers should be able to reason about protocol requirements, routing patterns, and observability needs to choose and configure load balancers that align with real-world application demands.

In parallel, the objective is to enable readers to design robust ASGs and policies that maintain optimal capacity through both dynamic and scheduled scaling. By the end of this section, readers should be able to define ASG boundaries, attach them to load balancers, and implement metrics-driven scaling (e.g., based on **central processing unit** (**CPU**) utilization or request rate) alongside time-based scaling for predictable traffic patterns, such as business hours or marketing campaigns. The goal is to give practitioners the skills to construct self-healing, cost-efficient, and performance-aware architectures where load balancing and scaling work together as an integrated control plane for elasticity.

AWS load balancer types

AWS offers several types of load balancers, each designed for a slightly different role in your architecture. Thinking about them clearly will help you choose the right one for each workload and avoid accidental complexity.

Understanding AWS load balancers

At a basic level, a load balancer sits in front of your application and decides which backend target should handle each incoming request. Instead of sending all traffic to a single EC2 instance or container, it distributes requests across multiple targets so that none of them gets overwhelmed. In AWS, this capability is provided by **Elastic Load Balancing** (**ELB**), which automatically scales capacity as traffic increases or decreases. ELB works with targets in multiple AZs, giving you both distribution and built-in high availability out of the box.

In cloud environments, traffic patterns are unpredictable, and applications frequently scale up and down. A load balancer absorbs these fluctuations, smoothing traffic and allowing ASGs to add or remove instances without changing how clients connect.

Load balancers also act as a control point for security and observability. They integrate with services such as **Transport Layer Security** (**TLS**) termination, security groups, and health checks, ensuring that only healthy, authorized targets receive traffic.

Four faces of AWS load balancing

When people talk about *AWS load balancers*, they usually mean one of four flavors under the ELB family:

- **CLB**: The original, now mainly for legacy migrations, supports both basic Layer 4 and Layer 7 behaviors. *It is not recommended for new architectures*, but it still appears in older deployments and exam questions.
- **ALB**: Focused on HTTP/HTTPS and WebSocket traffic, operating at the application layer (Layer 7). It understands URLs, headers, and hostnames, making it ideal for modern web and API traffic.
- **NLB**: Focused on ultra-high performance at the connection level (Layer 4). NLB can handle a large number of requests per second with very low latency, primarily for TCP, TLS, and UDP.
- **GWLB**: Focused on steering network traffic through virtual appliances such as firewalls or intrusion detection systems. It operates at the network layer and gives you a single gateway to distribute traffic across a fleet of security appliances.

Application Load Balancer in practice

ALB is the default choice for most HTTP and HTTPS workloads. It operates at Layer 7, which means it looks inside the HTTP request and can route traffic based on paths, hostnames, headers, and query strings. In practice, this lets you simplify architectures that would otherwise require multiple load balancers or custom routing logic. For example:

- You can run multiple microservices behind a single ALB using path-based routing, such as: **`/api/orders`** and **`/api/payments`**, mapped to different target groups.
- You can use host-based routing to support multiple domains, such as orders.abc.com and billing.abc.com, all terminating on the same ALB listener.
- You can integrate ALB with container platforms like Amazon **Elastic Container Service** (**ECS**) and **Elastic Kubernetes Service** (**EKS**) so that each service or task is registered as a target automatically.

ALB also supports features that are important in real applications, such as WebSockets, HTTP/2, TLS offload, and detailed access logs. Health checks run at the HTTP level, letting you verify that specific URLs are healthy before sending production traffic to a target.

Network Load Balancer for high performance

NLB is built for raw performance and low latency rather than a deep understanding of HTTP. It operates at Layer 4, working with connections defined by IP addresses and ports, and can handle millions of connections per second with very small overhead.

A key feature of NLB is support for static IP addresses, including elastic IPs, which is useful when clients or partners need to allowlist fixed IPs. NLB is also well-suited for protocols beyond HTTP, such as custom TCP or UDP services, gaming backends, and financial trading systems that are extremely sensitive to latency. As it works at the connection layer, NLB does not perform advanced HTTP routing like ALB, but it integrates tightly with features such as TLS termination and PrivateLink. Its health checks operate at the TCP or HTTP level, depending on configuration, ensuring that unhealthy targets are removed quickly from rotation.

Gateway Load Balancer for security appliances

GWLB exists to solve a specific but important problem: how to scale and manage virtual network appliances in the cloud. Many organizations rely on third-party firewalls, intrusion detection systems, or deep packet inspection tools, and GWLB helps deploy these as a scalable service inside AWS. GWLB combines a transparent network gateway with a load balancer that distributes traffic across a fleet of virtual appliances. From the client's point of view, traffic flows as if through a single gateway, but behind the scenes, GWLB balances connections across multiple appliance instances and runs health checks to keep flows on healthy devices.

Architecturally, GWLB is often placed in a dedicated security **Virtual Private Cloud (VPC)** and integrated with AWS Transit Gateway. This lets you centralize security inspection for traffic between VPCs and between on-premises networks and AWS, enforcing consistent policies while reducing operational overhead.

Common patterns with ALB, NLB, and GWLB

Modern AWS architectures often combine multiple load balancer types in a single design. Each type handles a different concern, and together they create a layered, resilient system. Some common patterns include:

- **ALB in front of microservices**: A single internet-facing ALB terminates TLS and routes to multiple target groups, each backing a separate microservice running on ECS, EKS, or EC2.
- **NLB for edge protocols**: An NLB exposes non-HTTP protocols such as **gRPC Remote Procedure Call (gRPC)** over TCP, game servers, or **Internet of Things (IoT)** brokers, often with static IP addresses that clients can connect to directly.
- **GWLB security hub**: Traffic from many VPCs is routed through a central security VPC via Transit Gateway and GWLB, where it passes through third-party firewalls before reaching its destination.
- **ALB + NLB combination**: In some architectures, NLB provides a fixed IP front door, and traffic is then passed to ALB for richer HTTP-level routing behind the scenes.

These patterns let you balance user experience, security, and operational complexity while using each load balancer where it is strongest.

Auto Scaling groups

ASGs are one of the quiet, behind-the-scenes heroes of AWS architectures, constantly adjusting capacity so your application stays responsive without wasting money on idle servers. Instead of guessing how many instances you need, you describe the rules, and the group does the scaling work for you.

Core concepts

Auto Scaling in AWS automatically matches supply (EC2 capacity) to demand (your workload). Amazon EC2 ASGs monitor metrics such as CPU utilization or request rate and add or remove instances to keep performance stable as traffic changes. This turns your infrastructure into a living system that can grow during busy periods and shrink during quiet hours. When combined with load balancers, Auto Scaling helps you build applications that stay available even when individual instances fail.

The ASG is the central concept, a logical group that manages a fleet of EC2 instances as a single unit. Within this group, you define how many instances you want, what type they should be, and how they should scale in and out. Scaling policies tell the ASG when to change capacity based on metrics or schedules. Together, the group definition (what to run) and policies (when to change) form the control loop that keeps your application aligned with demand.

Launch templates and instance configuration

Every ASG revolves around three numbers: minimum, maximum, and desired capacity. The minimum is the floor: the fewest instances you are willing to run, even at quiet times.

The maximum is the ceiling: the maximum number of instances the group will ever launch, protecting you from runaway scaling and unexpected costs. The desired capacity is the group's target under normal conditions, and scaling policies adjust this value within the minimum-maximum range.

Defining minimum, maximum, and desired capacity

Let us have a look at the definitions of these three types of capacity:

- **Desired capacity**: It represents the initial capacity of the ASG at the time of creation. An ASG attempts to maintain the desired capacity. It starts by launching the specified number of instances for the desired capacity and maintains that number as long as there are no scaling policies or scheduled actions attached to the ASG.
- **Minimum capacity**: It represents the minimum group size. When scaling policies are set, they cannot decrease the group's desired capacity below the minimum capacity.

- **Maximum capacity**: It represents the maximum group size. When scaling policies are set, they cannot increase the group's desired capacity higher than the maximum capacity.

The minimum and maximum size limits also apply in the following scenarios:

- When you manually scale your ASG by updating its desired capacity.
- When scheduled actions run that update the desired capacity. If a scheduled action runs without specifying new minimum and maximum size limits for the group, then the group's current minimum and maximum size limits apply.

An ASG always tries to maintain its desired capacity. When an instance terminates unexpectedly (for example, due to a spot instance interruption, a health check failure, or human action), the group automatically launches a new instance to maintain its desired capacity. The following figure shows the desired and minimum capacity settings for ASGs:

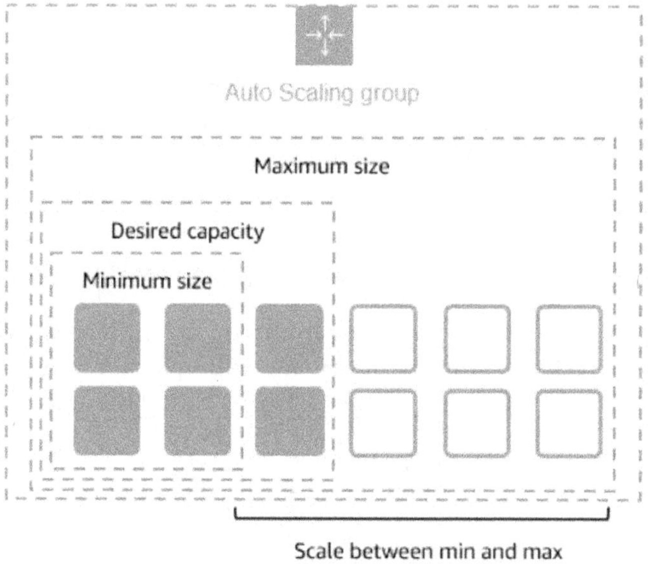

Figure 6.1: Auto Scaling groups minimum, desired, and maximum capacity

The following figure shows the ASG setting:

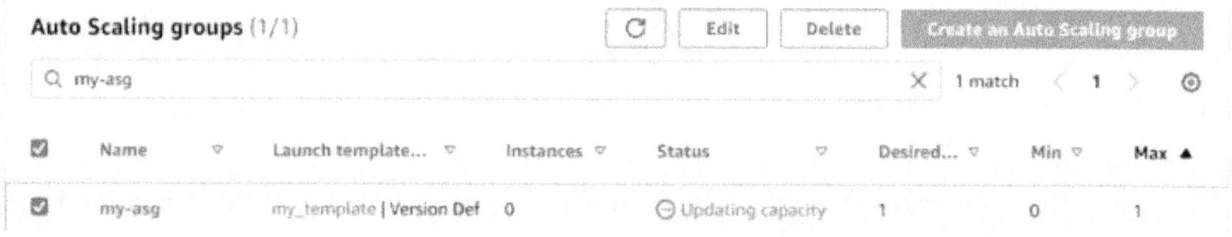

Figure 6.2: Auto Scaling groups setting

Health checks and self-healing behavior

An ASG continuously monitors the health of its instances. If an instance fails health checks, either EC2 checks or load balancer checks when integrated, it is marked unhealthy and terminated. The group then automatically launches a replacement instance to maintain the desired capacity, creating a self-healing environment. This means you do not have to manually react to hardware failures, kernel panics, or application crashes on individual nodes.

Dynamic scaling policies

Dynamic scaling policies react to live metrics to adjust capacity. Target tracking policies are the most intuitive: you pick a metric (like average CPU) and a target value, and the ASG automatically scales to keep the metric near that target. Step scaling policies add or remove capacity in increments based on how far the metric deviates from the threshold. Simple scaling policies are older and react to a single alarm by performing a fixed scale-out or scale-in action, usually with cooldown periods.

Scale-in protection in an AWS Auto Scaling group prevents designated instances from being terminated when the group reduces capacity. This feature is valuable for instances performing critical tasks, running special processes, or those that should not be interrupted temporarily.

For example, if an instance is processing a large file upload or running a long background job, you can enable scale-in protection to ensure it remains active while less critical instances are terminated. After the task is complete, you can remove the protection and allow the instance to be terminated if necessary. This approach provides greater control during scaling and helps prevent service disruptions.

Multi-AZ distribution and high availability

ASGs are designed to work across multiple AZs, not just one. When configured with multiple subnets in different AZs, the group spreads instances across them, improving fault tolerance if one AZ has issues. When combined with a multi-AZ load balancer, this distribution means the application can continue serving traffic even if an entire AZ becomes impaired. Running across two or more AZs is a core AWS best practice for reliability and is often a baseline for production designs.

Integrating Auto Scaling groups with load balancers

In most production architectures, an ASG sits behind an ALB or NLB. New instances that join the group are automatically registered with the load balancer's target group, and terminated instances are deregistered.

This integration ensures traffic is always routed only to healthy, in-service instances. It also allows the load balancer's health checks to drive replacement decisions in the ASG, further improving resilience. In the following figure, we can see how ELB integrates with ASG. An

ASG consists of a number of EC2 instances that, together, form a target group for the load balancer:

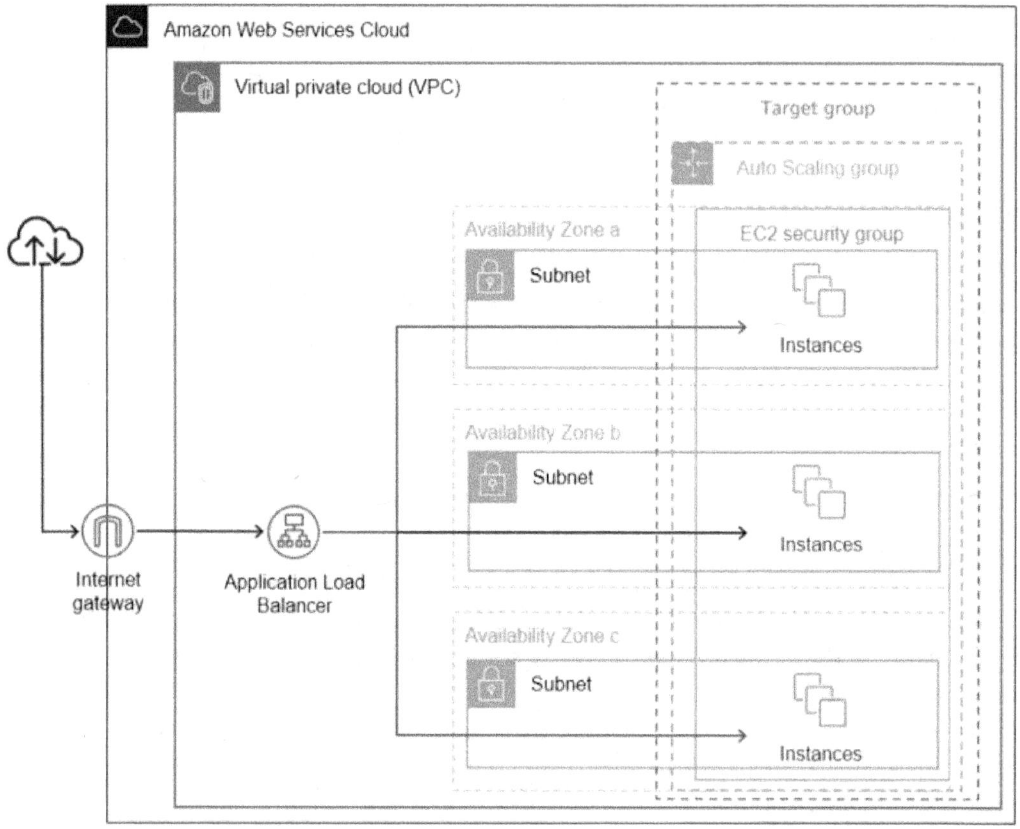

Figure 6.3: Load balancer integration with Auto Scaling group

Scheduled and predictive scaling strategies

Sometimes demand follows a predictable pattern: daily peaks, weekday spikes, or monthly reporting jobs. Scheduled scaling lets you tell the ASG to adjust min, max, and desired capacities at specific times, such as scaling up before business hours and scaling down at night. Predictive scaling goes a step further by analyzing historical traffic patterns and automatically forecasting future demand. The ASG then launches instances ahead of the expected surge so they are warm and ready when traffic arrives, reducing the lag between demand and capacity.

Lifecycle hooks, warm pools, and instance refresh

Lifecycle hooks let you pause the instance lifecycle at key moments to run custom logic. For example, when an instance is launching, a hook can pause it so configuration management tools or initialization scripts can finish before the instance enters service.

Warm pools keep a set of pre-initialized instances in a *warm* state, ready to be brought into service quickly when the group scales out. Instance refresh uses the ASG to roll out changes gradually, replacing instances in batches using the latest launch template, while preserving capacity and availability.

Scaling best practices for cost and reliability

Effective auto scaling requires a balance between cost and reliability. Choosing target tracking policies with realistic utilization targets keeps instances busy enough to be cost-efficient while maintaining a buffer for sudden spikes.

Designing groups to span multiple AZs and integrating them with load balancers improves resilience without significant operational overhead. Features like warm pools, lifecycle hooks, and instance refresh should be used thoughtfully to reduce scale-out latency, automate configuration, and roll out changes safely, all while respecting min and max capacity limits to control spend.

Designing Auto Scaling groups and policies

Designing Auto Scaling groups and policies starts with a simple idea: your application should have the right amount of capacity at the right time, not too little that users see errors, and not too much that you waste money. An ASG is a logical collection of EC2 instances that share a common configuration (launch template), subnets, and scaling rules. You define the minimum, maximum, and desired number of instances, and the service automatically launches or terminates instances to stay within those limits. Typically, you spread the group across at least two AZs and, for web or application tiers, place it behind a load balancer so traffic is evenly distributed and the system can survive the loss of a single instance or even an entire AZ.

Once the group shape is clear, the real design work is in the scaling policies. At the basic level, you can scale manually (changing the desired capacity yourself), on a schedule (for predictable patterns like business hours), or dynamically based on metrics. Dynamic scaling usually relies on CloudWatch metrics such as average CPU, request count per target, or custom application latency. Target tracking policies keep a metric near a fixed value (for example, *keep the average CPU at 60%*), while step scaling policies add or remove instances based on how far a metric exceeds a threshold, which is useful for sudden spikes. Cooldown periods prevent excessive flapping by giving the system time to settle between scaling actions, and health checks (from EC2 and the load balancer) ensure unhealthy instances are replaced automatically. A well-designed ASG combines all of this: a robust launch template (AMI, security groups, IAM role), multiAZ placement, sensible min/max/desired capacity, and carefully chosen policies tied to application metrics rather than just infrastructure metrics, so the group tracks real user demand instead of just CPU noise.

Understanding auto scaling design goals

Understanding Auto Scaling design goals starts with a simple idea: you want your architecture to stay fast, reliable, and affordable, even when traffic is unpredictable. Everything else in Auto Scaling exists to serve those core aims in a repeatable, automated way:

- **Keep performance steady under changing load**: A primary goal of Auto Scaling is to keep your application responsive, regardless of traffic levels. Instead of users feeling every spike, the system quietly adds or removes capacity to keep response times within an acceptable range.

- **Avoid overprovisioning and reduce cost**: Another central design goal is cost efficiency: running *enough* capacity rather than *as much as possible*. In a static environment, teams often overprovision for peak traffic, leaving expensive instances idle for most of the day. Auto scaling counters this by scaling down when demand is low, reclaiming capacity that is no longer needed, and lowering the bill without human intervention. Good designs often include techniques such as instance diversification and spot instances for non-critical workloads to further optimize spend.

- **Improve availability and fault tolerance**: Auto Scaling is also about resilience, designing systems that keep working when individual resources fail. Instances will eventually crash, hosts will fail, and sometimes, the entire AZ may experience issues. The design goal here is that users never notice these failures. Auto Scaling contributes by replacing unhealthy instances, maintaining a baseline capacity, and spreading workloads across multiple AZs to avoid a single infrastructure bottleneck.

- **Automate operations and reduce human toil**: Manual capacity management does not scale with modern cloud workloads. One of the quieter but powerful goals of Auto Scaling is to encode operational decisions, when to grow, when to shrink, into policies and schedules. This automation reduces the need for middle-of-the-night scaling changes or manual interventions before every marketing campaign. It also standardizes behavior across environments, so your staging, pre-production, and production stacks follow the same rules, reducing the risk of human error.

- **Handle predictable patterns proactively**: Many workloads have traffic patterns that are easy to anticipate: weekday peaks, end-of-month reporting, and holiday sales. A key design goal is to be proactive about these patterns rather than react to them at the last minute.

- **Scheduled and predictive scaling**: They aim to have the right capacity in place before the surge begins, so customers never experience slow warm-up periods. This reduces the *lag* between increased demand and additional instances coming online, which is especially helpful for applications with long startup times.

Designing Auto Scaling groups

Effective Auto Scaling requires a balance between cost and reliability. Choosing target tracking policies with realistic utilization targets keeps instances busy enough to be cost-efficient while maintaining a buffer for sudden spikes.

Designing groups to span multiple AZs and integrating them with load balancers improves resilience without significant operational overhead. Features like warm pools, lifecycle hooks, and instance refresh should be used thoughtfully to reduce scale-out latency, automate configuration, and roll out changes safely, all while respecting min and max capacity limits to control spend.

Designing Auto Scaling policies

Auto Scaling policies control when and how the group adds or removes instances. Simple designs start with target-tracking policies that keep a key metric, such as average CPU or requests per target, near a chosen value, letting AWS automatically adjust capacity as demand changes. For more control, you can add step policies that react more aggressively to big spikes or scheduled policies that increase capacity before known peaks (such as business hours) and reduce it afterward to save cost, ensuring the system stays responsive without overprovisioning.

Dynamic and scheduled scaling strategies

Dynamic and scheduled scaling are two complementary ways to keep your AWS applications responsive while controlling cost. Both use Auto Scaling groups as the engine, but they answer different questions: dynamic scaling asks: *How should I react to load right now?* While scheduled scaling asks: *What capacity do I need at a known time in the future?*

Different types of scaling strategies

There are three different types of scaling strategies as discussed in the upcoming subsections.

Manual scaling

You can manually adjust the number of EC2 instances in your Auto Scaling group at any time. This process of manually changing the instance count is called manual scaling. Manual scaling is an alternative to auto scaling, especially if you want to make one-time capacity changes.

Dynamic scaling

Dynamic scaling continuously adjusts capacity based on live metrics from CloudWatch, such as CPU utilization, request rate per target, queue depth, or custom application metrics. You define a minimum and maximum number of instances, and scaling policies decide when to add or remove instances inside that range. Target tracking policies are the most common; you specify a desired value (for example, keep average CPU at 70% or keep SQS messages per instance near 100), and the system automatically scales out when the metric rises and scales in when it falls. Step scaling can layer on top of this, adding more instances when the metric crosses higher thresholds, which helps handle sudden spikes. This approach works best for workloads where traffic is variable or partially unpredictable, because capacity follows demand in near real time without manual intervention.

Predictive scaling

Predictive scaling analyzes historical load data to detect daily or weekly patterns in traffic flows. It uses this information to forecast future capacity needs, enabling Amazon EC2 Auto Scaling to proactively increase the capacity of your Auto Scaling group to match anticipated load.

Predictive scaling is well-suited for situations where you have:

- Cyclical traffic, such as high use of resources during regular business hours and low use of resources during evenings and weekends.
- Recurring on-and-off workload patterns, such as batch processing, testing, or periodic data analysis.
- Applications that take a long time to initialize cause a noticeable latency impact on application performance during scale-out events.

Scheduled scaling

Scheduled scaling is designed for predictable patterns, such as business-hour peaks, batch windows, or weekly traffic cycles. You create scheduled actions that set new desired, minimum, and maximum capacities at specific times or on recurring cron-like schedules (e.g., scale out every weekday at 7:00 am and scale in at 6:00 pm in a given time zone). This allows you to pre-warm capacity before known peaks, so users never see slow start-ups, and then automatically reduce capacity during off-hours to save money. In more advanced setups, predictive scaling uses historical metrics to forecast future load and automatically creates scheduled actions to match that forecast, while dynamic policies still handle unexpected extra demand. Well-designed architecture usually blends these strategies: scheduled or predictive scaling sets a smart baseline for known patterns, and dynamic scaling fine-tunes capacity minute by minute as real traffic fluctuates.

Limitations:

- The names of scheduled actions must be unique per Auto Scaling group.
- A scheduled action must have a unique time value. If you attempt to schedule an activity at a time when another scaling activity is already scheduled, the call is rejected and returns

an error indicating that a scheduled action with this scheduled start time already exists.

As of this writing, we can create up to 125 scheduled actions per Auto Scaling group.

Conclusion

In this chapter, we explored how AWS helps applications stay both highly available and responsive to changing traffic by combining load balancing with automatic scaling. We looked at an overview of AWS load balancer types, seeing how Application, Network, and GWLBs each serve different kinds of traffic and protocols, and how choosing the right one shapes your architecture's performance and resilience. We then covered load balancer configuration best practices, such as using multi-AZ target groups, health checks, secure listener configurations, and consistent tagging, so that traffic is routed only to healthy targets and can survive instance or Availability Zone failures.

In this chapter, we also learned how to design Auto Scaling groups and policies to keep *the right amount of capacity at the right time* by defining sensible minimum, maximum, and desired capacities and tying them to application-aware metrics. Building on that, we examined dynamic and scheduled scaling strategies: dynamic scaling reacts in real time to CPU, request rate, or custom metrics, while scheduled scaling anticipates known peaks and quiet periods to balance performance with cost. Together, these concepts give you a toolkit for building AWS architectures that automatically balance user experience, reliability, and efficiency without constant manual intervention.

In the next chapter, the focus shifts from scaling and load balancing to monitoring and observability, so you can actually see how your architecture behaves in real time. You will learn to collect and visualize key metrics, logs, and traces so issues can be detected at an early stage, rather than later.

The chapter will walk through best practices for setting clear SLIs and SLOs, designing meaningful dashboards, and creating actionable alerts rather than noisy ones. It will also introduce observability patterns such as structured logging, distributed tracing, and using correlation IDs, so you can follow a single request as it moves through multiple services. Together, these ideas will help you build AWS systems that are not only scalable and resilient but also transparent and easier to operate over time.

References

1. **https://aws.amazon.com/elasticloadbalancing/gateway-load-balancer/**
2. **https://aws.amazon.com/blogs/networking-and-content-delivery/scaling-strategies-for-elastic-load balancing/**
3. **https://docs.aws.amazon.com/whitepapers/latest/building-scalable-secure-multi-vpc-network-infrastructure/using-gwlb-with-tg-for-cns.html**

4. https://docs.aws.amazon.com/autoscaling/ec2/userguide/as-scaling-target-tracking.html
5. https://docs.aws.amazon.com/autoscaling/ec2/userguide/predictive-scaling-policy-overview.html
6. https://docs.aws.amazon.com/autoscaling/ec2/userguide/warm-pool-instance-lifecycle.html
7. https://aws.amazon.com/blogs/compute/scaling-your-applications-faster-with-ec2-Auto Scaling-warm-pools/
8. https://docs.aws.amazon.com/AWSEC2/latest/UserGuide/create-launch-template.html
9. https://docs.aws.amazon.com/AWSEC2/latest/UserGuide/ec2-launch-templates.html
10. https://docs.aws.amazon.com/autoscaling/ec2/userguide/what-is-amazon-ec2-Auto Scaling.html
11. https://docs.aws.amazon.com/autoscaling/ec2/userguide/scale-your-group.html
12. https://docs.amazonaws.cn/en_us/autoscaling/ec2/userguide/asg-capacity-limits.html
13. https://docs.amazonaws.cn/en_us/autoscaling/ec2/userguide/ec2-Auto Scaling-scaling-manually.html
14. https://docs.amazonaws.cn/en_us/autoscaling/ec2/userguide/ec2-Auto Scaling-predictive-scaling.html
15. https://docs.amazonaws.cn/en_us/autoscaling/application/userguide/application-Auto Scaling-predictive-scaling.html
16. https://docs.amazonaws.cn/en_us/autoscaling/ec2/userguide/ec2-Auto Scaling-scheduled-scaling.html

Join our Discord space

Chapter 7
Monitoring and Observability Best Practices

Introduction

In a modern **Amazon Web Service** (**AWS**) architecture, load balancers, **Auto Scaling groups** (**ASGs**), and observability work together as a single control system that keeps applications fast, resilient, and cost-efficient. Load balancers control how traffic enters and flows through your system: **Application Load Balancers** (**ALBs**) handle HTTP-aware features like path-based and host-based routing; **Network Load Balancers** (**NLBs**) provide ultra-low-latency front doors for **Transmission Control Protocol** (**TCP**)/**User Datagram Protocol** (**UDP**) traffic and static IPs; and **Gateway Load Balancers** (**GWLBs**) steer traffic through fleets of security appliances, such as firewalls, intrusion detection systems, and traffic inspection appliances. Behind these entry points, ASGs continually adjust **Elastic Compute Cloud** (**EC2**) capacity based on demand, automatically replace unhealthy instances, and spread workloads across multiple **Availability Zones** (**AZs**) so your application can survive individual instance or AZ failures without manual intervention.

Observability ties all of this together by giving you the visibility needed to operate and evolve your architecture safely. CloudWatch metrics, logs, and alarms provide the basic signals for understanding system health, driving scaling policies, and catching problems early, while distributed tracing and structured logging help you follow a single request as it crosses multiple services. With these foundations in place, you can tune performance and cost as an ongoing loop, using the data you collect to refine instance sizes, scaling thresholds, and service choices, and you can troubleshoot common load balancing and scaling issues in a structured way, moving quickly from symptoms (errors, timeouts, odd scaling) to root causes and durable fixes.

Structure

In this chapter, we will discuss the following topics:

- Monitoring with AWS CloudWatch, logs, and alarms
- Observability patterns for distributed applications

- Performance optimization and cost management
- Troubleshooting common load balancing and scaling issues

Objectives

Monitoring, observability, performance, and troubleshooting are the practical muscles of your AWS architecture. This section aims to give you enough clarity to design and operate them with confidence. You will learn how to use CloudWatch metrics, logs, and alarms to keep a constant pulse on your systems and how to apply observability patterns such as structured logging, correlation IDs, and distributed tracing so that even complex, microservice-based applications become understandable. The goal is not just to collect data, but to design your workloads so that questions like: *Is it healthy? Where is it slow? What just broke?* These can be answered quickly and repeatedly.

At the same time, this section will help you connect performance optimization with cost management, treating them as an ongoing feedback loop rather than one-time tuning. You will see how load balancing and Auto Scaling choices affect both user experience and your AWS bill, and how to troubleshoot common issues such as failing health checks, uneven traffic distribution, or unstable scaling behavior using the signals you have instrumented. By the end, you should be able to design architectures that monitor themselves, scale intelligently, surface the right information when something goes wrong, and continuously balance reliability with efficient spend.

Monitoring with CloudWatch, Logs, and Alarms

Monitoring with CloudWatch is about having a single place to watch how your AWS environment behaves in near-real time. It collects metrics (time-series data, such as **central processing unit** (**CPU**) usage or request counts), application and service logs, and events so you can see trends, spot issues early, and understand the impact of changes using dashboards and graphs. You can use it out of the box with many AWS services and send your own custom metrics and logs, providing a unified observability layer for your applications and infrastructure.

Logs and alarms are the pieces that turn raw data into actionable signals. CloudWatch Logs lets you centralize logs from EC2, containers, Lambda, and other services so you can search, filter, and analyze them when debugging, auditing access patterns, or investigating security incidents. On top of metrics and logs, you define alarms that monitor specific thresholds or anomaly patterns. When a condition is met, they change state and can notify you (email or Slack via **Simple Notification Service** (**SNS**)) or even trigger automated actions like scaling or remediation. Together, metrics, logs, and alarms form a feedback loop that helps you detect problems quickly, respond automatically where it makes sense, and continuously improve the reliability of your AWS workloads.

AWS CloudWatch

Monitoring with Amazon CloudWatch is about giving your AWS architecture a live *control room* view, where you can see how every major component is behaving and react before users feel pain. CloudWatch continuously collects data from AWS services and your own applications, including metrics, logs, and events, and brings it together into dashboards, charts, and alerts that show health and performance in near-real time. Instead of logging in to individual servers or consoles, you design your systems so that all important signals flow into CloudWatch, then use that central layer to watch trends, investigate anomalies, and drive automation.

From an architect's perspective, monitoring with CloudWatch starts with metrics. Services like EC2, **Relational Database Service** (**RDS**), Lambda, and ELB automatically publish key metrics (for example, CPU utilization, latency, and request count), and you can add custom metrics for business-level or application-level indicators such as queue depth or orders per minute. You then build alarms on top of these metrics, defining thresholds and evaluation periods so that when a metric crosses a threshold, say, an error rate or latency, the alarm changes state and can notify operators or trigger actions like Auto Scaling. CloudWatch Logs complements the numbers by aggregating application and system logs into log groups, where you can search, query with Logs Insights, and even turn log patterns into new metrics via metric filters, closing the loop between symptoms and root cause. Finally, CloudWatch dashboards pull all of this together into visual, role-specific views (for example, per-service or per-environment), and cross-account observability lets you monitor multi-account architectures from a single place, turning CloudWatch into the backbone of operational visibility in AWS.

CloudWatch Metrics

Monitoring with CloudWatch Metrics is about turning the behavior of your systems into numbers you can watch, reason about, and automate against. CloudWatch treats a metric as a stream of time-stamped data points, such as *CPU utilization was 56% at some time, 52% after a second*, and stores and visualizes it in graphs so you can see patterns over minutes, days, or months. AWS services (for example, EC2, S3, Lambda, RDS, **Elastic Block Store** (**EBS**)) publish many of these metrics automatically, covering things like CPU usage, network traffic, **input/output** (**I/O**) operations, latency, and error counts, and you can also publish your own custom metrics for application or business signals such as queue depth, checkout failures, or number of active users. For EC2 service, you can choose between basic monitoring (typically 5-minute intervals) and detailed monitoring (1-minute data points), which provides a finer-grained view and supports faster detection of performance anomalies when you care about short spikes. A few other services, like Lambda, API Gateway, and many other services, publish at 1-minute resolution by default.

In day-to-day architecture, these metrics become the backbone of your feedback loops. You group related metrics on dashboards to get a live view of a service (for example, request count, latency, and error rate for an **application programming interface** (**API**)), and you use alarms that monitor specific metrics or combinations of metrics via metric math to decide when something needs attention or an automated response. An alarm might fire when average CPU utilization stays above a threshold, when the error rate exceeds a percentage, or when a composite metric that blends CPU, memory, and network metrics indicates overall stress. In response, it can send notifications or adjust the capacity of an Auto Scaling group. Over time, you refine which metrics matter, add custom ones where the built-in set is not enough, and use anomaly detection and trend analysis to move from reactive firefighting to proactive capacity planning and reliability engineering based on CloudWatch Metrics.

CloudWatch Logs

Monitoring with CloudWatch Logs is about giving your AWS systems a single, reliable place to tell their story in plain text. Instead of doing SSH into individual servers and tailing log files, you stream logs from EC2 instances, containers, Lambda functions, and many managed services into centralized log groups, each containing one or more log streams per source. These logs can include application messages, HTTP access logs, OS logs, and audit trails, and they are stored durably with flexible retention so you can keep short-lived debug data for days or critical security / audit records for months or years. Once the data lands in CloudWatch Logs, you can search and filter it in near real time, use Logs Insights to run queries for troubleshooting and trend analysis, and even build dashboards that combine log-derived metrics with traditional CloudWatch metrics.

Logs should not be considered *set-and-forget* data. In AWS, CloudWatch log groups retain logs indefinitely unless a retention period is specified. Without one, logs accumulate continuously, which can lead to significant costs, particularly in large environments with high log volumes.

In architectural design, logging serves not only for troubleshooting but also for cost control and long-term system management. Effective designs determine the required log retention period for security, debugging, audits, or compliance and set retention accordingly. For example, detailed logs may be kept for 30 days, audit logs for 90 days, and older data archived as needed. This strategy maintains a clean, predictable, and cost-effective environment while ensuring necessary visibility.

The real power of monitoring with CloudWatch Logs comes from turning raw text into structured signals and automated workflows. You define metric filters to watch for patterns such as *ERROR* lines, 5xx responses, throttling errors, or specific exception types and convert each match into a CloudWatch metric data point, which can then drive alarms and automated responses in the same way as native service metrics. You can also stream logs in real time to downstream systems (for example, Kinesis, OpenSearch Service, or Lambda) using subscription filters, where they can feed security analytics, centralized SIEM platforms, or custom processing pipelines. For larger organizations, cross-account and cross-Region log centralization lets you aggregate logs from many environments into a single *observability* account, adding metadata such as source account and Region so you can quickly slice and dice during investigations. In an AWS architecture, this approach turns CloudWatch Logs from a simple storage service into a core monitoring fabric that connects application behavior, operational visibility, and automated remediation.

CloudWatch Agent

Monitoring with the CloudWatch Agent is about extending AWS's visibility into what is happening inside your servers and containers, not just around them. While many AWS services publish basic metrics to CloudWatch automatically, the agent runs on your Amazon EC2 instances, onpremises servers, and containers to collect richer system-level data such as memory usage, detailed CPU breakdown, disk I/O, filesystem space, and perprocess statistics. It can also tail local log files and send them to CloudWatch Logs, and in recent versions, it can forward OTLP trace data as a collector layer, while X-Ray or another OTLP-compatible backend still processes and stores the traces, giving you a single, unified way to push metrics, logs, and trace data into the CloudWatch observability platform.

In a typical architecture, you install and configure the CloudWatch Agent once, often using automation like Systems Manager, user data, or configuration management, and then treat it as a standard part of every compute node. The configuration file defines what to collect (for example, which filesystems, which log files, which processes to watch) and where to send it, including the option to send metrics to CloudWatch, Amazon Managed Service for Prometheus, or both. Once the agent is running, all the data it sends appears alongside native CloudWatch metrics and logs, so you can build dashboards, alarms, and metric-math expressions that blend infrastructure signals from inside the OS with service-level metrics from AWS. For architects, this turns the CloudWatch Agent into a key building block for consistent, deep monitoring across hybrid environments, enabling capacity planning, performance tuning, and faster incident diagnosis using a single, standard telemetry pipeline.

CloudWatch Logs agent

Monitoring with the CloudWatch Logs agent is about ensuring that every important log line your systems produce is securely collected, centralized, and searchable without requiring you to SSH into servers or manually copy files. You install the agent on your EC2 instances (and, in older patterns, on on-premises servers) and point it at the log files you care about, such as application logs, web server access logs, or system logs. Then the agent tails those files and streams new entries to CloudWatch Logs in near-real time. Each instance typically sends its data into a log group, with one or more log streams per instance or application, so you can keep a clean structure while still being able to filter or aggregate across the whole fleet. Once the logs are in CloudWatch, you can search, filter, and run interactive queries with Log Insights, making it much easier to troubleshoot issues, correlate events across instances, and keep an audit trail of what happened and when.

From an architectural perspective, the CloudWatch Logs agent turns local, fragile log files into durable, centralized telemetry that can drive automation. Since logs now flow into CloudWatch, you can define metric filters that look for patterns such as *ERROR* lines, 5xx status codes, or specific exception names and convert them into metrics that power alarms and dashboards, closing the loop between logs and monitoring. You can also attach subscription filters to stream the same log data to other services such as Kinesis or Lambda for further processing, security analytics, or long-term storage, without changing your applications. In practice, you treat the Logs agent (or its unified successor) as a standard part of your instance baseline: every server has it, every important log file is configured, and your operations, security, and compliance processes all assume that anything written to a log will end up in CloudWatch Logs, where it can be searched, analyzed, and acted upon.

Note: **CloudWatch Logs agent has been deprecated and the CloudWatch agent is now the current unified agent for collecting both host metrics and logs.**

Observability patterns for distributed applications

For distributed applications on AWS, *observability patterns* are about having a consistent way to see what is happening inside many small, loosely coupled services just by looking at their external signals: metrics, logs, and traces. Instead of treating monitoring as an afterthought, you design each service to emit structured telemetry (for example, consistent log fields, dimensions, shared trace IDs) and send it to a centralized observability platform built from services such as CloudWatch, X-Ray, and the **AWS Distro for OpenTelemetry** (**ADOT**). It is a supported distribution that enables you to collect, process, and send metrics, logs, and traces from your applications and infrastructure to observability backends. With these patterns in place, a single user request that hops across APIs, queues, and functions can be followed end-to-end, and you can quickly move from a symptom such as *checkout is slow*, to the specific service, dependency, or network segment causing the degradation.

In practice, these patterns show up as repeatable building blocks you apply across teams and workloads. You standardize cross-cutting concerns such as correlation IDs in logs, golden-signal metrics (latency, traffic, errors, saturation), and default tracing middleware so every new microservice or serverless function is *born observable* with minimal extra work. You then layer on centralized dashboards, **service level objective** (**SLO**)-based alerts, and multi-account visibility so operators see the health of an entire distributed system rather than isolated components and can respond quickly when failures or performance issues emerge. Over time, these observability patterns help teams move from reactive debugging to proactive reliability engineering, using rich telemetry to guide design decisions, capacity planning, and continuous improvement of complex AWS architectures.

Core concepts

Auto Scaling in AWS automatically matches supply (EC2 capacity) to demand (your workload). Amazon EC2 ASGs monitor metrics such as CPU utilization and request rate, and add or remove instances to maintain performance as traffic changes. This turns your infrastructure into a living system that can grow during busy periods and shrink during quiet hours. When combined with load balancers, Auto Scaling helps you build applications that stay available even when individual instances fail.

The ASG is the central concept: a logical group that manages a fleet of EC2 instances as a single unit. Within this group, you define how many instances you want, what type they should be, and how they should scale in and out. Scaling policies tell the ASG when to change capacity based on metrics or schedules. Together, the group definition (what to run) and policies (when to change) form the control loop that keeps your application aligned with demand.

SLOs, error budgets, and alerting patterns

Let us learn about SLOs, error budgets, and alerting patterns, which give distributed systems on AWS a shared language for how *reliable is reliable enough?* Instead of relying on adhoc uptime claims, the following:

- **SLO**: SLOs are clear, numeric targets for how well a service should perform from the user's point of view, such as *99.9% of checkout requests succeed within 300 ms over 30 days*. They are built on top of **service level indicators** (**SLIs**) such as availability, latency, and error rate, and provide teams with a common definition of *good enough* reliability that can be measured and reported over time. In AWS, SLOs are typically mapped to CloudWatch metrics or metric expressions and can be modeled as period-based or request-based objectives, for example, *99.5% of 1-minute periods meet the latency goal* or *99.9% of all requests in a month succeed.*
- **Error budgets**: An error budget is the small amount of failure you are willing to tolerate while still meeting your SLO, turning reliability into something you can spend deliberately instead of chasing perfection. If your SLO is 99.9% successful requests, your error budget for that period is 0.1% of requests being slow or failing; you can think of it as the *allowance* that can be consumed by incidents, risky releases, or experiments. For time-based SLOs, the budget is typically expressed in minutes of allowed downtime per period (e.g., monthly, yearly). When the error budget is being burned too quickly, it is a signal to slow down changes, prioritize hardening work, or temporarily freeze deployments until reliability is back under control.
- **Alerting patterns**: Alerting patterns describe how you turn SLOs and error budgets into practical, meaningful alerts that focus on user impact rather than raw infrastructure noise. Instead of paging on every metric crossing a fixed threshold, modern patterns use burn-rate-based alerting: you alert when the service is consuming its error budget faster than acceptable over short and long windows (for example, *using 2% of the monthly budget in 1 hour*). This helps distinguish between brief, harmless blips and serious, sustained issues in distributed workloads spanning many services and regions.

For distributed applications on AWS, SLOs, error budgets, and alerting patterns work together as a control system for reliability across many microservices, queues, and serverless components. Teams define SLOs for critical user journeys or services (such as *search latency* or *checkout success rate*), track how quickly each service burns its error budget, and wire alerts to fire when budget consumption indicates real user pain rather than just internal metric noise. This shared framework lets product and **site reliability engineering** (**SRE**) teams make informed trade-offs, deciding when it is safe to ship faster and when to focus on stabilizing the system, while keeping distributed workloads aligned to clear, user-centric reliability goals.

End-to-end request tracing in microservices

Tracing is a way to follow a single user request as it flows through many different services, like tracking a parcel as it moves through multiple warehouses and trucks until it reaches the customer. In a microservices architecture, an application is split into many small, independent services, each owning its own logic and often its own data, and those services communicate with each other over APIs, queues, or streams to fulfill a single user action, such as *place order* or *watch video*. When something becomes slow or fails, it can be hard to identify the problem by looking at isolated logs or CPU graphs, because the request might have passed through ten different services on its journey.

End-to-end request tracing solves this by assigning each request a unique trace ID at the entry point (for example, an API Gateway or edge service) and passing that ID with every call between services. Each service record's *spans*, including timing and metadata on what it did, which downstream service it called, whether it succeeded, and how long it took, are tagged with the same trace ID. Later, a tracing system can reconstruct the full call graph as a timeline: you see the original user request at the top, then a tree of spans showing which microservices were involved, how much time each one consumed, and where errors or retries occurred. In AWS, you typically implement this using standard trace context headers, libraries, or middleware in each service, and a backend such as AWS X-Ray (which now supports OpenTelemetry natively via the OTLP endpoint). For architects, this pattern turns a distributed system from a *black box* into something you can reason about: you can answer questions like: *Which service is responsible for most of the latency? Which downstream dependency is flaking out? How does a single customer action flow across our microservice landscape?* Using concrete, visual traces instead of guesswork.

Real user and synthetic monitoring patterns

Real user and synthetic monitoring are two complementary ways to answer the question, *What experience are users actually having with our system?* in a distributed AWS application.

Real User Monitoring (**RUM**) watches genuine users as they interact with your application in production. A small snippet on the frontend (web or mobile) records metrics such as page or screen load times, client-side errors, and user journeys and sends them back to your monitoring system. This shows how fast the app feels on real networks, devices, and browsers and highlights issues that only appear in real-world conditions, for example, a specific region with a slow **Domain Name System** (**DNS**) or a particular browser version that consistently throws JavaScript errors. It is the closest you can get to standing over a user's shoulder and watching their experience at scale. AWS RUM service offers this functionality.

Synthetic monitoring takes the opposite approach: instead of waiting for real people, you run scripted *robots* that simulate typical user flows on a schedule. CloudWatch Synthetics (Canaries) is one such offering provided by AWS. These synthetic checks can log in, search, add items to a cart, or hit critical APIs every minute from multiple regions, and then report whether each step succeeded and how long it took. Since, they do not depend on real traffic, they are ideal for catching problems in the middle of the night or right after a deployment, and for validating external dependencies like DNS, **Transport Layer Security** (**TLS**), and **content delivery network** (**CDN**) availability. In practice, robust architectures combine both real-user monitoring to understand the actual experience and long-term trends and synthetic monitoring as an earlywarning system that continuously probes your most important paths, even when real traffic is low.

Network-level observability for distributed systems

Network-level observability is about seeing how traffic actually moves through your distributed system, not just whether individual services think they are healthy. In an AWS architecture, requests often cross **Virtual Private Clouds** (**VPCs**), regions, load balancers, service meshes, and hybrid links like Direct Connect, so a user-visible slowdown might be caused by a congested link, a misconfigured route, or an overloaded firewall rather than a broken application. Network observability patterns aim to make these invisible paths visible: you collect flow data, latency, and connectivity metrics from the network fabric itself, then correlate that with application metrics and logs to understand where time is spent and where packets are dropped or delayed.

Practically, this means treating network telemetry as a first-class signal alongside application metrics. You enable features such as VPC Flow Logs, CloudWatch Network Monitor, and Internet Monitor, along with container network observability for **Elastic Kubernetes Service** (**EKS**) to capture who is talking to whom, how much data is flowing, and what latency and error profiles exist between components. That data feeds into dashboards that show, for example, how healthy connectivity is between key services, which paths are approaching bandwidth limits, or which microservice is generating the most cross-AZ or cross-Region traffic (and therefore cost). When something goes wrong- say, increased latency in a user journey- you can drill from high-level SLO or API metrics down to specific network segments, links, or security controls (like network firewall or web application firewall) that are causing the issue, reducing guesswork in complex distributed systems. Over time, these patterns help you design networks that are not only functional but also explainable and debuggable, which is essential when many independent services and teams share the same underlying AWS connectivity fabric.

Observability for serverless and event-driven architectures

Observability for serverless and event-driven architectures is about making sense of systems where there are no always-on servers to log into, and requests often hop through many managed services. Instead of watching a few big application servers, you are dealing with short-lived Lambda functions, managed queues and streams, API Gateway endpoints, Step Functions workflows, and third-party APIs, all wired together with events. In this world, you design your system so that each function invocation, message, and state transition emits useful telemetry logs, metrics, and traces into a central place, because you cannot rely on SSH access or local log files when something goes wrong. The goal is to be able to answer these questions just by looking at the signals the system produces: *What happened to this specific request?* Or, *why is this workflow slow today?*

In practice, observability patterns for serverless and event-driven designs focus on a few key habits. Each Lambda or serverless container emits structured logs (often JSON) that always include correlation IDs or trace IDs, so you can follow an event as it moves from API Gateway to Lambda, through SNS or SQS, into downstream functions and databases. Lambda Powertools (now AWS Lambda Powertools) is the recommended library for structured logging, tracing, and metrics in Lambda. You rely heavily on managed metrics such as invocation counts, durations, errors, and throttles for each function and event source, and you also add custom metrics for business outcomes such as *orders placed* or *payments failed*. Tracing, via AWS X-Ray or OpenTelemetry-based tooling, ties this together by showing a service map and timelines of how a single request touches multiple services, including retries and fan-out/fan-in patterns. Since serverless systems are highly distributed, you also invest in good dashboards and alerts built on these signals, so that when latency spikes or error rates rise, you can quickly see which function, event source, or external dependency is responsible, even though there is no traditional server to log into.

Performance optimization and cost management

Designing ASGs and policies starts with a simple idea: your application should have *the right amount of capacity at the right time*, not too little that users see errors, and not too much that you waste money. An ASG is a logical collection of EC2 instances that share a common configuration (launch template), subnets, and scaling rules. You define the minimum, maximum, and desired number of instances, and the service automatically launches or terminates instances to stay within those limits. Typically, you spread the group across at least two AZs and, for web or app tiers, place it behind a load balancer so traffic is evenly distributed and the system can survive the loss of a single instance or even an entire AZ.

Once the group shape is clear, the real design work is in the *scaling policies*. At a basic level, you can scale manually (adjusting the desired capacity yourself), on a schedule (for predictable patterns like business hours), or dynamically based on metrics. Dynamic scaling usually relies on CloudWatch metrics such as average CPU, request count per target, or custom application latency. Target tracking policies keep a metric near a fixed value (for example, *keep an average CPU at 65%*), while step scaling policies add or remove instances based on how far a metric crosses a threshold, which is useful for sudden spikes. Cooldown periods prevent excessive flapping by giving the system time to settle between scaling actions, and health checks (from

EC2 and the load balancer) ensure unhealthy instances are replaced automatically. A well-designed ASG combines all of this: a robust launch template (**Amazon Machine Image** (**AMI**), security groups, **Identity and Access Management** (**IAM**) role), multi-AZ placement, sensible min/max/desired capacity, and carefully chosen policies tied to *application* metrics rather than just infrastructure metrics, so the group tracks real user demand instead of just CPU noise.

Performance optimization

In this section, we will learn about various optimization techniques to improve performance. We can categorize into three categories: compute optimization, storage efficiency, and database performance tuning.

Compute optimization

Optimizing compute with AWS CloudWatch is about turning raw metrics into smart decisions about how much compute you really need and where performance is being left on the table. Instead of guessing instance sizes or relying on one-time benchmarks, you use CloudWatch to watch how your EC2 instances, containers, and serverless functions behave over time, CPU, memory (via the CloudWatch Agent), network, disk, and application-level metrics. By looking at real usage trends, you can spot underutilized instances that are safe to downsize, overworked ones that need more capacity, and burstable instances whose CPU credits are running low, which may require a different family or scaling approach.

In a well-designed architecture, CloudWatch sits at the center of a feedback loop for compute optimization. Metrics feed CloudWatch alarms, which in turn drive Auto Scaling policies so that capacity automatically scales out when key indicators (such as CPU, latency, or queue depth) rise, and scales in when they fall, reducing waste. Historical data is then used for rightsizing and recommendations, often in combination with services like AWS Compute Optimizer and Cost Explorer, helping you choose better instance types and sizes for each workload. Over time, this metric-driven approach lets you refine your compute layer continuously: you keep enough headroom for performance, avoid paying for idle capacity, and adjust scaling rules as traffic patterns evolve, all anchored by observability in CloudWatch rather than assumptions.

AWS Compute Optimizer analyzes your resource usage and provides actionable recommendations to right-size compute resources. It suggests optimal EC2 instance types, Auto Scaling group settings, EBS volumes, and Lambda memory configurations to enhance performance and minimize waste with projected savings. This service enables informed capacity decisions based on actual usage rather than estimates.

Storage efficiency

Storage efficiency with AWS CloudWatch is about seeing how your disks and databases are actually being used, so you can stop wasting space and avoid running out at the worst possible moment. Instead of treating storage as a black box, you use CloudWatch metrics and alarms to monitor metrics such as how busy your **Elastic Block Store** (**EBS**) volumes are, how often they are idle, how much burst capacity they have left, and how much free space your RDS databases still have. For example, EBS metrics such as volume throughput, queue length, and BurstBalance indicate whether a volume is oversized and mostly idle, or undersized and constantly burning through burst credits, which can cause sudden slowdowns. Similarly, RDS metrics such as AllocatedStorage and free storage space help you see when a database is approaching capacity, and CloudWatch alarms can trigger notifications or automated Lambda functions to increase storage before it affects applications.

In an AWS architecture, these storage signals become part of your wider optimization and automation story. By looking at trends over weeks or months, you can identify volumes and databases that are consistently underutilized and candidates for downsizing, moving to cheaper storage tiers, or cleaning up old data. You can also detect heavily used volumes or DBs that need more IOPS, throughput, or capacity, and plan upgrades instead of waiting for incidents. Combined with cost-focused tooling like AWS Cost Explorer and Compute Optimizer, CloudWatch gives you the raw, time-series evidence to back your storage decisions: what to shrink, what to grow, and where to add automation so that storage scales smoothly with demand while keeping costs in check.

Database performance tuning

Database performance tuning with AWS CloudWatch is about turning your databases from *black boxes* into clearly observable systems that you can adjust with confidence. For Amazon RDS and Aurora, CloudWatch exposes a rich set of metrics that describe CPU usage, memory pressure, I/O behavior, connections, cache hit ratios, and storage health, all in near-real time. By watching these signals over time, you can tell whether a slowdown is caused by insufficient compute (high CPU utilization), storage bottlenecks (high read / write latency or queue depth), connection saturation, or inefficient queries that generate excessive I/O. You can then tune accordingly by right-sizing instance classes, adjusting storage type or throughput, adding read replicas, or optimizing indexes and queries rather than guessing at the cause of poor performance.

CloudWatch also integrates closely with higher-level database observability tools such as Performance Insights and CloudWatch Database Insights, which surface query-level and wait-state information to help you pinpoint exactly which **Structured Query Language** (**SQL**) statements are consuming resources. These metrics can be graphed, combined with metric math, and wrapped in alarms so that you get alerted when key thresholds are breached, for example, sustained high CPU utilization, growing replication lag, or low freeable memory before they turn into visible outages. In an AWS architecture, the practical goal is to design databases with tuning in mind: enable and review the right CloudWatch and Performance Insights metrics, define alarms on the signals that matter, and use what you see to drive a continuous tuning loop of schema changes, query optimization, and capacity adjustments.

Cost management

In this section, we will learn about various ways to manage costs, which will help reduce the company's overall budget. We can categorize them into three categories: serverless rightsizing, network cost control, and database transfer and egress saving.

Serverless rightsizing

Serverless rightsizing with AWS CloudWatch is about making sure your *payperuse* services are actually sized to how they are used, not just left at default settings. In the serverless world, with Lambda functions, Aurora Serverless, **Elastic MapReduce** (**EMR**) Serverless, serverless endpoints, and other managed services, you do not choose instance types; you still choose capacity ranges, memory sizes, and concurrency limits. CloudWatch becomes your main lens into how well those choices match reality: it records metrics such as invocations, duration, memory usage, concurrent executions, throttles, error rates, and cold starts for Lambda, as well as capacity usage and latency for serverless databases and analytics jobs. By looking at these metrics over time, you can see patterns like *this function always uses only a fraction of its memory,* or *this endpoint constantly runs near its concurrency limit,* which are strong signals that you can dial capacity down to save money or up to protect performance.

In an AWS architecture, the practical rightsizing loop for serverless looks like this: start with conservative defaults, observe real behavior in CloudWatch, then adjust. If CloudWatch shows your Lambda functions consistently using far less memory than allocated and finishing quickly, you can reduce memory (and cost) while watching latency and error rates to ensure user experience stays healthy. If you see frequent throttles or long durations for a given function, you might increase memory (which also increases CPU usage) or tune the code to run more efficiently. For serverless databases and analytics services, you monitor capacity usage, queue times, and latency to refine configured capacity ranges or quotas so they scale smoothly without being overprovisioned for long periods. Over time, CloudWatch metrics, dashboards, and alarms turn serverless rightsizing into a continuous, low-friction process: you review trends, tweak resource settings, and let the platform automatically scale within well-chosen boundaries that balance performance and cost.

Network cost control

Auto Scaling policies control *when* and *how* the group adds or removes instances. Simple designs start with target tracking policies that keep a key metric, like average CPU or requests per target, near a chosen value, letting AWS adjust capacity automatically as demand changes. For more control, you can add step policies that react more aggressively to big spikes, or scheduled policies that increase capacity before known peaks (such as business hours) and reduce it afterward to save cost, ensuring the system stays responsive without overprovisioning.

Data transfer and egress savings

Data transfer and egress savings with AWS CloudWatch start with one simple idea: you cannot reduce what you cannot see. In an AWS architecture, data charges often hide in the background traffic between Regions, across the public internet, or from AWS to external partners and users. CloudWatch helps you turn this invisible flow into something you can measure and act on by exposing metrics from services that move data (like load balancers, **Network Address Translation** (**NAT**) gateways, DataSync, and others) and by centralizing logs that describe who is moving what, where, and how often. You can track throughput, bytes in and out, and request counts over time, then correlate those trends with specific paths, for example, a file transfer service sending large objects to partners, or a data migration workload running more frequently than expected. Once you see clear patterns, it becomes easier to make design changes: move chatty services into the same AZ or VPC, switch cross-region calls to asynchronous replication or bulk transfer, or use edge services and caching to keep content closer to users instead of repeatedly serving it from a single Region.

From an architectural point of view, CloudWatch becomes part of your cost-optimization feedback loop for network traffic and egress. You can build dashboards that highlight the top producers of outbound traffic and configure alarms when certain thresholds are exceeded, for instance, unusually high bytes out from a specific transfer server or data pipeline. Logs from datatransfer services can be streamed to CloudWatch Logs and searched to answer detailed questions like: *Which jobs moved the most data this week?* Or, *which partner or endpoint is responsible for this spike?* That visibility lets you refine retention policies, batch transfers more efficiently, compress data, or redesign flows to use cheaper paths (such as private connectivity or regional endpoints) instead of expensive public egress. Over time, data transfer stops being a vague line item on the bill and becomes a set of intentional, observable design choices, guided by CloudWatch metrics and logs rather than surprises at the end of the month.

Monitoring and FinOps practices

Monitoring and FinOps with AWS CloudWatch go hand in hand: one gives you the visibility, the other gives you the discipline to act on what you see. At a basic level, CloudWatch collects metrics, logs, and traces from your AWS services and applications, so you can understand how resources are behaving, how often errors occur, and how performance changes over time. FinOps (cloud financial operations) takes this telemetry and turns it into better decisions about where to spend, where to save, and how to align costs with business value. In an AWS architecture, this means using CloudWatch dashboards and alarms not just to detect outages, but also to flag underutilized instances, chatty services that drive data transfer costs, or functions that are overallocated in memory.

In practice, a Monitoring and FinOps mindset with CloudWatch looks like designing **key performance indicators** (**KPIs**) and alarms that balance reliability and cost. You track classic health metrics, CPU, latency, error rates, and queue depth, but you also watch utilization trends and correlate them with your cost reports from tools like Cost Explorer or Cost and

Usage Reports. When you see a service running hot, you improve performance or scale it out; when you see a service consistently idle, you rightsize, change purchasing models, or even retire it. Over time, CloudWatch becomes the shared language between engineering and finance: engineers instrument services with meaningful metrics and logs, while FinOps practitioners use that same data to build budgets, forecasts, and optimization plans. The result is an architecture that is observable by design and financially accountable by default. Issues are detected early, resources are sized intentionally, and every scaling and resiliency choice is made with both reliability and cost in mind.

Troubleshooting common load balancing and scaling issues

Monitoring and troubleshooting load balancing and scaling issues with AWS CloudWatch is about turning vague symptoms like *the site is slow* into concrete signals you can see and act on.

On the scaling side, CloudWatch sits between your Auto Scaling policies and real workloads. Metrics such as average CPU utilization, request count per target, queue depth, and scale-in/scale-out activity help you determine whether your scaling rules are too aggressive, too slow, or tied to the wrong signals. In this section, we will examine the details of load balancing and scaling problems.

Recognizing load balancing and scaling problems

Recognizing load balancing and scaling problems usually starts with a feeling: *the system is up, but something does not feel right*. In AWS architectures, these issues often show up as slow responses, uneven traffic across instances, or Auto Scaling behavior that seems out of sync with what users are experiencing.

Before you can see that something is wrong, you need a clear picture of what normal looks like for your application. In a well-designed AWS setup, traffic comes in through a load balancer, is spread fairly across healthy targets, and your ASGs quietly add or remove instances as demand changes.

At steady state, you generally see: CPU and memory in a comfortable band, response times stable, and error rates low and flat during normal hours. Scaling events are predictable: maybe a few new instances in the morning as users log in, and a scale-in late at night when activity drops.

Early warning signs at the load balancer

Many problems first appear at the load balancer edge, often before the application outright fails. Some common symptoms are:

- Rising 4xx/5xx error codes at the load balancer, while your application logs show timeouts or connection errors.
- Target health flapping, instances repeatedly moving between healthy and unhealthy status.
- Uneven request distribution, where one or two targets get a much higher load than others in the same target group.

When you see these patterns, it often means health checks are misconfigured, target registration is incomplete, or some instances are slower and causing the load balancer to *stick* to the ones that respond more quickly. It can also point to issues like missing subnets in one AZ, which leaves fewer healthy targets to share the work.

Symptoms of poor scaling behavior

Scaling problems show up in a different way: instead of traffic being unfair, capacity is simply not keeping up with demand, or it is constantly overreacting. Typical signals include:

- CPU, memory, or request-per-target metrics stay high for long periods during peak, with little or no scaling out.
- Very spiky instance counts, where the ASG rapidly adds and removes instances, causing instability and cold starts.
- Users report slowness at predictable times (e.g., every weekday at 8 a.m.), even though scaling is supposedly automatic.

These patterns usually mean thresholds are too high, scaling metrics are poorly chosen, or cooldown periods are preventing the group from reacting quickly enough. Sometimes it is a capacity-planning issue: the minimum and maximum sizes are set too low, or the instance type is too small for the actual workload.

Key metrics and logs to check

When you suspect load balancing or scaling problems, the fastest way to confirm your intuition is to look at a small, consistent set of key metrics and logs. These signals tell you whether traffic is arriving, how it is being spread, and whether your capacity is keeping up with demand.

Metrics on the load balancer

For your load balancers, a handful of CloudWatch metrics quickly indicate whether they are performing well. Focus on:

- **Request count and new connections (for example, RequestCount, NewFlowCount)**: Shows how much traffic is actually reaching the load balancer and how it changes over time. Rising traffic with flat capacity is a warning sign.

- **Target health (HealthyHostCount, UnHealthyHostCount, or similar)**: Tells you if the load balancer has enough healthy backends to send traffic to; a growing unhealthy count usually explains spikes in errors or latency.
- **Error rates (HTTPCode_ELB_5XX, HTTPCode_Target_5XX)**: A rise in 5xx codes at the load balancer or target level points to failures either at the edge or inside your application.
- **Latency metrics (TargetResponseTime, processing times in logs)**: Steadily increasing latency without a traffic drop suggests capacity or routing issues.

By putting these metrics on a single dashboard, you can quickly see whether the problem is a lack of capacity, unhealthy targets, or something else at the edge.

Metrics on Auto Scaling groups and instances

On the scaling side, you care about whether the group is the right size and whether individual instances are overloaded. Useful metrics include:

- **GroupDesiredCapacity, GroupInServiceInstances)**: It shows how the Auto Scaling Group is responding. If the desired capacity stays low while CPU utilization is high, your policies are probably too conservative.
- **Instance-level CPU, network, and disk metrics (CPUUtilization, NetworkIn/Out, DiskReadBytes/WriteBytes)**: Consistently high utilization across many instances usually points to under-scaling or under-sized instances.
- **Scaling event counts and alarm states**: Frequent scale-out and scale-in events in a short period indicate flapping policies, while long periods with no events during heavy load suggest thresholds or cooldowns are mistuned.

Watching these metrics together helps you see whether the load balancer is starved of healthy targets because the group is too small, or whether instances are simply misconfigured.

Load balancer access logs

Metrics tell you *how much* and *how often*; access logs tell you *what* and *who*. For ALBs, NLBs, and **Classic Load Balancers** (**CLBs**), access logs contain details such as:

- Timestamps, client IP, and target IP are useful for seeing where traffic is coming from and which backends handle which requests.
- Status codes from the load balancer and backend (`elb_status_code`, `target_status_code`, or `backend_status_code`) help you distinguish between problems at the edge (for example, SSL or routing) and failures inside the application.
- Processing times (request, backend, response) highlight whether latency comes from the client, the load balancer, or the backend service.

- Request paths, methods, and user agents let you see if a specific API, URL path, or client type is responsible for the spike in errors or slow responses.

In practice, you might filter logs for 5xx responses from the last 15 minutes and then look for common paths or patterns that often point directly to a misbehaving service or a bad deployment.

Application and system logs

Finally, scaling and balancing symptoms often show up first in your application and system logs, even before metrics cross alarm thresholds. You can look for:

- Timeouts, connection reset errors, and retry storms in application logs, especially around known peak times.
- Messages from your Auto Scaling service (for example, instance launch and termination events) around the same timestamps as user complaints.
- Operating system logs showing resource exhaustion, such as too many open files, out-of-memory kills, or disk-full events, which can make an otherwise healthy instance appear unhealthy to the load balancer.

Combining these logs with your metrics lets you trace a story: traffic rises, latency climbs, errors appear in the access logs, and then the application logs show timeouts or resource limits being hit. Over time, building this habit helps you recognize load balancing and scaling problems quickly and confidently, often before they turn into full outages.

Timeouts, high latency, and connection errors

Timeouts, high latency, and connection errors are often the first user-facing signs that something is wrong with your load balancing or scaling design, even when all instances are technically *up*. In an AWS architecture, these symptoms usually mean that requests are taking too long to reach a healthy target, the target is taking too long to respond, or the connection is being dropped somewhere along the path.

Understanding timeouts

From the user's point of view, timeouts show up as pages that never finish loading or error messages like *504 Gateway Timeout*. In AWS, a 504 from an **Application Load Balancer** (**ALB**) typically means one of two things: it could not establish a connection to the target in time, or it connected, but the target did not send a full response before the idle timeout expired. **Network Load Balancers** (**NLB**) operate at the connection level, not the HTTP level, so they do not return HTTP error codes such as 504. If a connection times out or is reset, the client receives a TCP-level failure, such as a connection reset or timeout, rather than an application-layer response.

When this happens, you often see a rise in 5xx error metrics on the load balancer, increased average latency, and sometimes a drop in the number of healthy targets if overloaded instances start failing health checks. Taken together, these symptoms are a strong hint that your backends are struggling or that network rules are preventing traffic from flowing cleanly between the load balancer and your instances.

Understanding high latency

High latency is the slow drift that often comes before full-blown timeouts. Instead of immediate failures, users notice that every request feels sluggish: API calls take seconds instead of milliseconds, and pages seem to *hang* before rendering.

In CloudWatch, you typically see average and response times climbing, even if total traffic has not changed very much. This can be caused by overloaded instances (CPU, memory, or I/O saturation), inefficient application code, or insufficient capacity added by your ASG during busy periods.

Connection errors and resets

Connection errors are the more abrupt result of timeouts and latency. They appear as *connection reset by peer*, *broken pipe*, or similar messages in client or server logs, indicating that one side closed the TCP connection unexpectedly.

In the context of AWS load balancers, you may see metrics like reset counts increase when the load balancer or target closes idle or long-running connections after a timeout, or when an application shuts down sockets without a graceful close. Network issues, such as security groups or network **access control lists** (**ACLs**) that do not allow return traffic on ephemeral ports, can also cause connection establishment failures and intermittent resets.

Network and security group misconfigurations

Network and security group misconfigurations are among the most frustrating causes of load balancing and scaling issues because, on the surface, all your AWS resources appear healthy, yet traffic still does not flow as you expect. We will focus on how these mistakes manifest from an application perspective and how to recognize them quickly when debugging load balancing and scaling problems.

Understanding misconfigurations

From a user's perspective, network and security group problems often look exactly like application issues: timeouts, connection errors, and intermittent failures. Requests may hang until they time out, or clients might see *connection refused* or *connection reset* errors even when your instances are running.

On dashboards, you might notice that the load balancer's request count is lower than expected, or that a whole AZ appears to be idle while others are busy. Health checks may start to fail for a subset of instances, causing them to be marked unhealthy even though the application is working fine when accessed locally from inside the instance.

Common security group issues around load balancers

The most common problems happen at the boundary between the load balancer and your targets. Typical security group mistakes include:

- The load balancer's security group can reach the instances, but the instance security group does not allow inbound traffic from the load balancer on the correct ports (for example, port 80 or 443 for HTTP/HTTPS, or a custom port for your service).
- Health check ports are different from the main application port, but the security group only allows one of them. The result is that the application might be reachable directly, while health checks fail and the load balancer *drains* those targets.
- Instances in an ASG are launched with a different security group than the one you expect, so the new instances never become healthy behind the load balancer, even though they look fine in the EC2 console. As a rule of thumb, always define the security group in the launch template rather than in the ASG configuration, and use **infrastructure as code** (**IaC**) to prevent drift.

When these mistakes happen, you often see increasing counts of 5xx errors from the load balancer, a growing number of unhealthy targets, and sometimes a pattern where only a subset of instances ever receive traffic.

VPC, subnet, and routing pitfalls

Beyond security groups, VPC-level configuration can quietly break load balancing and scaling behavior. For example:

- Instances are launched into private subnets that do not have a route to the load balancer's subnets, or vice versa, so connections cannot be established even though both sides are *up*.
- You enable cross-zone load balancing but only attach subnets in a single AZ for the ASG, leaving the other zones with no targets to send traffic to. This can look like uneven load distribution or zone-specific failures.
- Network ACLs are configured too strictly and block ephemeral ports that are needed for return traffic, causing intermittent connection drops and the strange *works sometimes* behavior.

These issues can be especially confusing because metrics such as CPU and memory usage on individual instances may appear normal; the real problem is that the traffic never reaches them in the first place.

Misconfigurations confuse scaling behavior

Network and security group problems also interfere with Auto Scaling in subtle ways. Imagine an Auto Scaling group that correctly launches new instances under load, but:

- The security group on the new instances does not allow traffic from the load balancer, so they never pass health checks and are eventually terminated. From the outside, it looks like the group is constantly scaling up and down without actually adding usable capacity.
- Only some subnets are correctly configured with routes and permissions. Instances in misconfigured subnets are technically *InService* from the ASG perspective but never receive traffic, so a small subset of instances ends up carrying all the load and becoming hotspots.

When you see scaling events happening with no improvement in latency or error rates, network and security group misconfigurations should be high on your list of suspects.

Building good habits to avoid problems

To reduce the chances of these misconfigurations, it helps to adopt a few consistent habits:

- Treat security group rules as part of your application's contract: for each service, clearly define which ports must be open from which sources (load balancer, other services, bastion hosts) and keep that definition in code.
- Always test new Auto Scaling or load balancing setups in a staging environment by simulating real traffic and verifying that instances in every AZ receive requests and pass health checks.
- When debugging, trace a single failing request *hop by hop*: from client to load balancer, from load balancer to instance, and from instance back out, checking at each step that the corresponding security groups, routes, and ACLs allow the traffic you expect.

By viewing network and security group settings as active participants in your load balancing and scaling design, rather than just background configuration, you make it much easier to recognize when they are the hidden cause of timeouts, uneven traffic, and ineffective scaling.

Conclusion

In this chapter, you saw how monitoring and observability turn an AWS architecture from a black box into a system you can understand, trust, and steadily improve. By combining metrics, logs, and alarms in AWS CloudWatch with clear observability patterns, you learned how to build feedback loops that keep your distributed applications healthy, performant, and cost-efficient.

You explored how to capture the right signals, service-level metrics, structured logs, and actionable alarms so that production issues reveal themselves quickly rather than hiding behind vague symptoms. Observability patterns such as centralized logging, trace propagation, and correlation IDs help you follow a single user request as it crosses load balancers, microservices, queues, and databases, making it far easier to debug complex failures and regressions.

Finally, you learned to recognize and troubleshoot common load balancing and scaling issues, timeouts, uneven traffic, misconfigured health checks, and network or security group problems, using a small, consistent set of metrics and logs. When monitoring and observability are built in from the start, these incidents become opportunities to tighten your architecture rather than emergencies that threaten reliability. With these practices in place, you leave this chapter equipped to watch your systems in production with confidence and to evolve them safely as your workloads and business grow.

In the next chapter, you will move from observing and operating systems to teaching them, exploring how AWS AI and machine learning services like Amazon SageMaker, Rekognition, Comprehend, Polly, and Lex can be woven into real applications to add intelligence, automation, and richer user experiences.

References

1. **https://www.amazonaws.cn/en/cloudwatch/features/**
2. **https://docs.aws.amazon.com/prescriptive-guidance/latest/patterns/centralize-monitoring-by-using-amazon-cloudwatch-observability-access-manager.html**
3. **https://aws.amazon.com/blogs/mt/using-amazon-cloudwatch-metrics-math-to-monitor-and-scale-resources/**
4. **https://aws.amazon.com/blogs/mt/monitoring-data-ingestion-tasks-with-amazon-cloudwatch-metrics-and-alarms/**
5. **https://aws.amazon.com/blogs/mt/simplifying-log-management-using-amazon-cloudwatch-logs-centralization/**
6. **https://docs.aws.amazon.com/prescriptive-guidance/latest/implementing-logging-monitoring-cloudwatch/welcome.html**
7. **https://aws.amazon.com/blogs/mt/observing-agentic-ai-workloads-using-amazon-cloudwatch/**
8. **https://docs.aws.amazon.com/AmazonCloudWatch/latest/monitoring/**
9. **https://docs.aws.amazon.com/AmazonCloudWatch/latest/logs/**
10. **https://docs.aws.amazon.com/pdfs/whitepapers/latest/availability-and-beyond-improving-resilience/availability-and-beyond-improving-resilience.pdf**
11. **https://aws.amazon.com/blogs/mt/alarming-on-slos-in-amazon-search-with-cloudwatch-application-signals-part-1/**

12. **https://aws.amazon.com/blogs/mt/slos-made-easier-with-nobl9-and-cloudwatch-metrics-insights/**
13. **https://docs.aws.amazon.com/wellarchitected/latest/devops-guidance/o.si.5-set-and-monitor-service-level-objectives-against-performance-standards.html**
14. **https://docs.aws.amazon.com/AmazonCloudWatch/latest/monitoring/CloudWatch-RUM.html**
15. **https://aws.amazon.com/blogs/networking-and-content-delivery/network-observability-for-modern-applications/**
16. **https://aws.amazon.com/blogs/aws/monitor-network-performance-and-traffic-across-your-eks-clusters-with-container-network-observability/**
17. **https://aws.amazon.com/blogs/containers/monitoring-network-performance-on-amazon-eks-using-aws-managed-open-source-services/**
18. **https://aws.amazon.com/cloudops/monitoring-and-observability/**
19. **https://docs.aws.amazon.com/whitepapers/latest/aws-caf-operations-perspective/observability.html**
20. **https://aws.amazon.com/marketplace/build-learn/application-performance-monitoring-observability/observability-for-aws-serverless-applications**
21. **https://aws.amazon.com/blogs/mt/observability-using-native-amazon-cloudwatch-and-aws-x-ray-for-serverless-modern-applications/**
22. **https://docs.aws.amazon.com/prescriptive-guidance/latest/patterns/serverless-more-patterns-pattern-list.html**
23. **https://docs.aws.amazon.com/AmazonRDS/latest/**
24. **https://docs.aws.amazon.com/prescriptive-guidance/latest/amazon-rds-monitoring-alerting/publishing-performance-insights-to-cloudwatch.html**
25. **https://docs.aws.amazon.com/emr/latest/EMR-Serverless-UserGuide/monitoring-usage.html**
26. **https://docs.aws.amazon.com/sagemaker/latest/dg/serverless-endpoints-monitoring.html**
27. **https://docs.aws.amazon.com/elasticloadbalancing/latest/**
28. **https://docs.aws.amazon.com/AmazonCloudFront/latest/DeveloperGuide/http-504-gateway-timeout.html**
29. **https://aws.amazon.com/blogs/apn/how-to-proactively-detect-and-repair-common-misconfigurations-on-aws-using-availabilityguard-nxg/**

Chapter 8
Essential AWS AI/ML Services

Introduction

Modern **Amazon Web Services** (**AWS**) architectures increasingly blend traditional services with managed **artificial intelligence** (**AI**) capabilities, and this section introduces some of the most important building blocks. Amazon SageMaker gives you an end-to-end environment for the machine learning lifecycle: you can prepare data, build and train models, tune them, and then deploy them into production without managing your own **machine learning** (**ML**) infrastructure. On top of general purpose ML, AWS also offers specialized AI services that solve common problems out of the box, so you can add intelligence to applications with simple **application programming interface** (**API**) calls instead of building complex models from scratch.

Amazon Rekognition lets you work with computer vision to detect objects, faces, text, and even inappropriate content in images and videos. Amazon Comprehend focuses on natural language processing, helping you extract entities, sentiment, and key phrases from unstructured text. Amazon Polly turns text into natural-sounding speech in many voices and languages, making it easy to build spoken interfaces or narrated content. Amazon Lex provides conversational AI, handling speech recognition and language understanding, so you can build chatbots and voice bots that integrate with channels such as web, mobile, and contact centers. Together, these services form a practical toolkit for architects who want to integrate AI into real systems without becoming machine-learning experts.

Structure

In this chapter, we will discuss the following topics:

- Artificial intelligence concept
- AWS Artificial Intelligence services
- Amazon Rekognition

- Amazon Comprehend
- Amazon Polly
- Amazon Lex
- Machine learning concept
- Amazon SageMaker

Objectives

This chapter provides practical guidance for AWS Solutions Architects to integrate managed AI services into real-world architectures without requiring deep machine learning expertise. You will learn how to use Amazon Rekognition and Amazon Comprehend as specialized microservices for computer vision and natural language understanding, integrating them into event-driven pipelines with S3, Lambda, Step Functions, and event buses. The chapter demonstrates how to embed these AI capabilities directly into user flows and data pipelines, such as moderating content uploads, extracting insights from customer feedback, processing compliance documents, and enriching media libraries with searchable metadata. Additionally, you will see how Amazon Polly and Amazon Lex enhance the interaction layer: Polly delivers lifelike speech across web, mobile, and contact center solutions, while Lex provides intent recognition and multi-turn dialog for chatbots and voicebots that integrate with Lambda and Amazon Connect.

The second half of the chapter focuses on Amazon SageMaker as the foundation of a production ML platform, emphasizing the architect's role in operational excellence. You will learn how SageMaker supports the entire ML lifecycle, including data preparation, experimentation, training, hyperparameter tuning, and model registration. The chapter also covers responsible model operationalization, such as designing MLOps pipelines with SageMaker Pipelines and Model Registry, implementing approval workflows for environment promotion, and configuring Model Monitor to detect data drift and prediction degradation in live traffic. The objective is to ensure you can build, deploy, and manage models as governed, versioned, and continuously monitored services that evolve safely within your AWS architecture.

Artificial intelligence concept

AI in an AWS architecture is best understood as a set of capabilities you add to systems, rather than as a single, monolithic *AI engine*. Instead of forcing every feature to be hand-coded, you selectively introduce services that can see, listen, read, and converse on your behalf. In practice, this might mean using computer vision to understand what is in an uploaded image, natural language processing to extract meaning from customer emails, or conversational interfaces that let users talk to your application instead of clicking through menus. As an architect, your focus is not on inventing new algorithms but on determining where these intelligent behaviors fit within user journeys, workflows, and data flows.

On AWS, AI shows up as managed, task-focused services that you compose just like any other building block, similar to how you choose a database or a queue. You can call an API to analyze a document, generate speech from text, or understand a chat message, without managing models, **graphics processing units** (**GPUs**), or complex training pipelines. These services usually sit behind clear, versioned endpoints, integrate with existing security and networking patterns, and scale automatically with demand. In a well-designed solution, AI is woven in where it creates obvious value: reducing manual effort, improving user experience, or unlocking insights from data that would be too slow or expensive for humans to process alone. The goal is to make intelligence a first-class, reliable component of the architecture, rather than a fragile experiment running on the side.

AWS Artificial Intelligence services

AWS Artificial Intelligence services give architects a set of readymade *intelligence APIs* they can drop into solutions without building or training models themselves. Instead of managing GPUs, data pipelines, and training jobs, you call specialized services that already know how to see, read, listen, and converse. For example, you can use computer vision services to detect objects and text in images, natural language services to extract entities and sentiment from documents, or texttospeech services to generate lifelike audio. Each capability runs on a managed endpoint, integrates with standard AWS security and networking patterns, and scales automatically with demand, so you can treat it much like any other managed service in your architecture.

From a solution architecture perspective, these AI services are building blocks you place at key points in user flows and data pipelines. An upload workflow might call vision APIs as soon as a file lands in S3, a support system might send tickets to a language service to classify and route them, and a customerfacing portal might rely on conversational AI to handle routine questions before handing off to a human. Because the services are accessed via simple **Hypertext Transfer Protocol Secure** (**HTTPS**) calls and **Software Development Kits** (**SDKs**), they fit naturally alongside existing components such as Lambda, API Gateway, S3, and event buses. The result is that you can incrementally add intelligent behavior, better search, smarter routing, and richer user experiences without turning your entire system into a machine learning project.

Amazon Rekognition

Amazon Rekognition service lets you add image and video analysis to your applications without building, tuning, or training machine learning models yourself. At a high level, you send images or videos to Amazon Rekognition via an API, and it returns structured **JavaScript Object Notation** (**JSON**) describing what it detects: objects, people, text, or even inappropriate content. This makes it a natural building block in an AWS solution architect's toolbox for problems like content moderation, identity verification, media search, and security analytics. As a fully managed service, it requires no model training or infrastructure management on your part.

Rekognition offers a set of prebuilt capabilities that cover the most common image and video analysis needs. These include:

- **Object and scene detection**: Detects thousands of common objects, scenes, and activities (for example, person, bicycle, traffic, classroom, running) in images and videos.
- **Face detection and analysis**: Finds faces in an image or video frame and returns attributes such as whether the person is smiling, whether the eyes are open, the presence of glasses or facial hair, and an estimated age range.
- **Face recognition and comparison**: Let us you compare a face in an image to a face in another image or to a stored collection of faces to find matches, which is useful for building signin flows or access-control systems.
- **Face liveness**: Helps detect whether a real person is present in front of a camera instead of a spoof (such as a printed photo or replayed video), which strengthens remote identity verification workflows.
- **Content moderation**: Classifies images and videos for potentially unsafe or inappropriate content, such as explicit adult content or graphic violence, so you can automatically flag or block user uploads.
- **Text detection (Optical Character Recognition (OCR))**: Extracts printed text from images and video frames, even when it is skewed or on noisy backgrounds, useful for reading signs, packaging, or screenshots.
- **Celebrity recognition**: Identifies known public figures, which helps media and entertainment companies autotag and search their photo and video libraries.
- **Custom labels**: Train domain specific detectors (for example, your own products, industrial parts, or brand logos) using your labeled images, without needing ML expertise.

Since these are exposed as simple APIs, you can plug them into web apps, mobile apps, or backend workflows with only a few lines of code using the AWS SDKs.

Rekognition presence in an AWS architecture

In a typical architecture, images and videos are stored in Amazon S3, and your application or a serverless workflow calls Rekognition to analyze that media and store the results. Rekognition itself is fully managed and scales automatically, so you do not provision any servers or GPUs for the vision models. You pay based on the number of images processed and the duration of the video analyzed (per minute), while Rekognition Custom Labels follows a different pricing model where you are charged per hour for both training and inference (i.e., the hours your model is actively running to process images), making it suitable for both small experiments and large-scale production workloads.

A common pattern for images looks like this:

1. A client (web or mobile) uploads an image to an S3 bucket.
2. S3 events trigger (S3 event type triggers is *s3:ObjectCreated:Put*) an AWS Lambda function. It is worth noting that the Lambda needs appropriate IAM permissions as a prerequisite to both reading from S3 and calling Rekognition APIs.
3. The Lambda function calls Rekognition APIs (for example, DetectLabels, DetectModerationLabels, DetectText, or CompareFaces) with the S3 object reference.
4. Rekognition returns JSON with labels, bounding boxes, confidence scores, or moderation flags.

The Lambda function writes metadata to a datastore (DynamoDB - for fast key-value lookups by image ID; OpenSearch—for full-text or label-based search across large media libraries; or **Relational Database Service** (**RDS**)—when the metadata needs to join with relational business data). So, the application can search or filter on it later, and optionally send notifications via Amazon **Simple Notification Service** (**SNS**) or EventBridge.

For video, the pattern usually becomes asynchronous because analysis of longer clips takes more time. A reference workflow is:

1. Video files are uploaded to S3 or ingested from a stream.
2. A jobscheduler Lambda function submits video analysis jobs to Rekognition (for example, StartLabelDetection, StartFaceDetection, StartContentModeration), respecting account concurrency limits.
3. Rekognition processes the video and, when finished, publishes a completion event to Amazon SNS.
4. An SNS subscription (often another Lambda) receives the event, calls the corresponding *Get* API (such as GetLabelDetection) to retrieve results, and stores them in S3, DynamoDB, or a search index.
5. Downstream services or dashboards use this metadata for search, analytics, or workflow automation (for example, sending flagged clips to a human review queue).
6. This design lets you scale processing across thousands of videos while keeping your own compute layer simple and eventdriven.

Example of content moderation workflow

As an example, imagine a social platform where users upload photos and short videos. You want to prevent unsafe content from appearing publicly while minimizing manual review effort. A typical Rekognition based moderation workflow would be:

1. **Upload**: A user uploads media to a dedicated S3 bucket. The object key might embed tenant or user IDs for easier tracking. (It is worth noting that, for large video files,

multipart uploads should be used to improve reliability and throughput; however, it is important to note that multipart uploads do not generate a standard S3 PUT event. Instead, they emit a CompleteMultipartUpload event only after all parts are assembled. Your Lambda trigger configuration must therefore listen for both *s3:ObjectCreated:Put* and *s3:ObjectCreated:CompleteMultipartUpload* event types, or use the broader *s3:ObjectCreated:** wildcard, to ensure the function fires consistently regardless of how the upload was performed.)

2. **Event trigger**: The S3 object creation event triggers a Lambda function.
3. **Moderation call**: The function calls Rekognition's content moderation API (DetectModerationLabels for images or StartContentModeration for videos) with the S3 object reference.
4. **Classification**: Rekognition returns a list of moderation labels (for example, *explicit nudity, violence, visually disturbing*) along with confidence scores.

The following are some pointers regarding policy decisions:

- If all labels are below your threshold, the object is marked as *approved* in a metadata store (like DynamoDB) and is immediately visible.
- If any label crosses the threshold, the object is either blocked or routed to a human review queue (for example, an internal moderation console backed by **Amazon SQS** or **Amazon Augmented AI** (**A2I**)).

Notification and audit

SNS can notify admins or workflows when content is flagged, and CloudWatch Logs captures the decision details for audits or modelthreshold tuning.

This architecture is attractive for solution architects because it is loosely coupled: S3 events, Lambda, Rekognition, and downstream systems interact via events and APIs, and the system scales automatically as upload volume grows.

Example of identity verification and liveness

Another common pattern is remote identity verification, say, a digital bank onboarding new customers. A Rekognition based flow might look like:

1. The user captures two things from a mobile app:
    - A photo or scan of a government ID.
    - A live selfie video or images.
2. The app uploads both assets to S3 over HTTPS. From a security, privacy, and Compliance point of view, the S3 bucket should be private with no public access, using pre-signed URLs for uploads rather than direct credentials on the client. The bucket should be

in a specific region that complies with the user's data residency requirements, which is especially important in banking. Server-side encryption (SSE-KMS) should be explicitly recommended for this bucket given the sensitivity of the data being stored.

3. A backend (Lambda or container on ECS/EKS) starts a workflow that uses:
   - Face liveness detection to confirm there is a real human in front of the camera, not a photo or replay.
   - ID document analysis (often combined with other AWS AI services) to extract and validate the text on the document.
   - Face comparison to check whether the selfie matches the face on the ID.
4. If everything passes, the system updates the user profile to *verified* and issues credentials; if not, it may ask for another capture or route the case to manual review.

From an architectural perspective, Rekognition handles the complex vision tasks, while your solution focuses on orchestration, data storage, security controls, and user experience.

Designing with security, privacy, and governance in mind

Since Rekognition often works with sensitive images and biometric data, security and governance are central design concerns. **Identity and Access Management** (**IAM**) policies should tightly control which roles can call Rekognition APIs and which S3 buckets hold source media and derived metadata. You can use VPC endpoints so traffic between your **Virtual Private Cloud** (**VPC**) and Rekognition stays on the AWS network instead of traversing the public internet.

Datahandling policies should specify how long to retain images and analysis results, and in which Regions, to meet regulatory or customer requirements. Encryption at rest (S3, DynamoDB, RDS) and in transit (**Transport Layer Security** (**TLS**)) is standard, and you may implement pseudonymization or tokenization for identifiers linked to people. CloudTrail can be enabled to log all API calls to Rekognition for auditing and investigation.

Use cases of Amazon Rekognition

In this section, we will learn various use cases where Amazon Rekognition can be applied.

For an AWS Solutions Architect, Rekognition is most compelling when:

- You need computer vision capabilities but do not want to build or train custom models.
- You are already on AWS and want tight integration with S3, Lambda, Step Functions, SNS/SQS, or other services.

The problem fits the built-in feature set (general labels, faces, text, moderation), or you can train a domain-specific model using Custom Labels rather than creating a full ML pipeline.

Rekognition often appears as a specialized *AI microservice* that plugs into broader solutions, moderating content flows, enriching media libraries with searchable metadata, or hardening identity verification, all while benefiting from AWS's managed scaling, payperuse pricing, and operational model.

Amazon Comprehend

Amazon Comprehend is a fully managed and **natural language processing** (**NLP**) service that helps you extract insights from unstructured text without building your own machine learning models. At its core, you send text or documents to the service, and it returns structured JSON describing what it *understands*: entities (people, places, organizations), key phrases, sentiment, language, topics, and more. For a solutions architect, Comprehend plays the same role for text that services like Rekognition play for images; it becomes a generalpurpose *text understanding* microservice you can plug into many architectures, such as customerfeedback analytics, document processing, or compliance workflows.

Amazon Comprehend offers a rich set of prebuilt NLP functions that cover most common text analysis needs. Key capabilities include:

- **Language detection**: Identifies the dominant language of a document, which is useful when you ingest content from multiple regions and want to route it for translation or region specific handling.
- **Entity recognition**: Detects named entities such as people, locations, organizations, dates, quantities, and more, and labels each occurrence with a type and confidence score.
- **Key phrase extraction**: Pulls out the main *talking points* or concepts from a piece of text, helping you quickly summarize what a document is about at a high level.
- **Sentiment analysis**: Classifies text as Positive, Negative, Neutral, or Mixed, often used for product reviews, support tickets, or social media monitoring.
- **Syntax analysis**: Breaks text into tokens and tags each word with its part of speech, which can support more advanced linguistic processing.
- **Personally identifiable information (PII) detection:** Automatically detects and can help you redact Personally Identifiable Information such as names, addresses, or IDs in emails, tickets, and documents.
- **Events detection**: Extracts *whodidwhatwhenwhere* structures from documents, turning narrative text into a set of event objects you can feed into analytics or graph systems. It is worth noting that it is currently available only in English and for a limited set of event types (primarily financial/news events).
- **Topic modeling**: Discovers topics across a collection of documents stored in S3 and groups documents by those topics, which is useful for organizing large text corpora.

In addition to these managed models, Comprehend also supports custom classification and custom entity recognition, where you provide labeled examples and it trains a model specific to your domain (such as your own ticket categories or internal codes).

Comprehend presence in an AWS architecture

Architecturally, Amazon Comprehend is usually not the system of record; it sits in the middle of a dataprocessing flow that ingests text, analyzes it, and stores structured insights for downstream services. Text can come from many sources: API payloads, S3 documents, Kinesis streams, logs, or databases. You then invoke Comprehend synchronously via APIs (for short texts) or asynchronously via batch jobs (for large document sets in S3).

A common pattern looks like this:

1. Text is collected from applications (for example, reviews, support tickets, or chat logs) and stored in S3 or pushed into a stream (Kinesis Data Streams or Kinesis Data Firehose).
2. An AWS Lambda function or AWS Step Functions state machine orchestrates calls to Comprehend, choosing the right APIs (DetectSentiment, DetectEntities, DetectKeyPhrases, DetectPiiEntities, or custom classification).
3. Comprehend returns structured JSON results, which are persisted into DynamoDB, Amazon OpenSearch Service, or a data warehouse such as Amazon Redshift for querying and dashboards.
4. Amazon QuickSight, custom analytics dashboards, or downstream microservices use this enriched data to power search, reporting, alerting, or personalization.

Since Comprehend is fully managed and scales with demand, you focus on designing the ingestion, orchestration, storage, and access patterns rather than managing NLP infrastructure.

Example of customer feedback analytics workflow

Consider an architecture where a **software as a service** (**SaaS**) product collects customer feedback from multiple channels: inapp surveys, email, and public reviews. You want to understand customer sentiment, trending issues, and top-requested features. A Comprehendbased workflow could be:

1. **Ingestion**:
   - Web and mobile apps send feedback to an API endpoint running on Amazon API Gateway and AWS Lambda.
   - Email feedback is ingested via Amazon **Simple Email Service** (**SES**) and stored in S3, while third-party review data is periodically imported and also written to S3.

2. **Normalization**: A Lambda function standardizes each message into a common JSON format (user ID, channel, timestamp, raw text) and writes it to a central S3 bucket or Kinesis stream.

3. **Text analysis with Comprehend**:

   - For each piece of text, a Lambda function calls DetectSentiment, DetectEntities, and DetectKeyPhrases to get sentiment, entities (for example, product names or locations), and main topics.

   - A custom classification model, trained beforehand, tags each message into your own categories such as *Billing*, *Performance*, or *UX issue*.

4. **Storage and search**: The enriched records are stored in DynamoDB or streamed into Amazon OpenSearch Service so product teams can search by sentiment, category, or entity (for example, all negative feedback mentioning *checkout*).

5. **Analytics and alerting**:

   - Amazon QuickSight dashboards show sentiment over time, top key phrases, and distribution of categories by region.

   - EventBridge or Lambda can trigger alerts when negative sentiment about a specific feature crosses a threshold, so teams act before issues escalate.

This architecture lets you continuously convert raw text into actionable insights, with Comprehend acting as the reusable NLP layer across all feedback channels.

Example of document processing and compliance

Another strong use case is intelligent document processing and compliance, especially when handling sensitive information and long documents such as contracts or insurance forms. A typical workflow includes the following:

1. **Document intake**: Documents arrive as **Portable Document Formats** (**PDFs**) or Word files and are stored in an S3 bucket.

2. **Text extraction**: An upstream OCR process (often Amazon Textract) extracts raw text and structured fields, writing the text output back to S3.

3. **NLP enrichment with Comprehend**:

   - Batch jobs (Comprehend asynchronous APIs) process the text files in S3 to detect entities, PII, key phrases, and events.

   - Custom entity recognition models detect domain specific concepts like policy numbers, claim IDs, or regulatory terms unique to your organization. Training a custom entity recognizer requires a minimum of 200 annotated documents per entity type.

- PII detection identifies sensitive elements that must be redacted or access controlled, helping you comply with data protection regulations.

4. **Knowledge organization and indexing**:
   - Results are stored in a metadata store and indexed in OpenSearch, enabling search by entities like a specific company name, product, or actions.
   - Topic modeling groups documents into logical categories, which simplifies building knowledge bases and recommendation systems.

5. **Compliance and workflows**:
   - Workflows built with Step Functions or thirdparty systems can route documents with specific entities or PII patterns to legal or compliance teams for review.
   - Audit logs (CloudTrail, CloudWatch Logs) capture when documents were analyzed and what PII was detected or redacted.

Here, Comprehend reduces manual review, accelerates data extraction, and ensures consistent handling of sensitive information across large volumes of text.

Designing with security, privacy, and governance in mind

Since **Amazon Comprehend** processes potentially sensitive text, customer messages, contracts, and support logs, security and governance are design priorities. IAM policies should tightly scope which roles or services can call Comprehend APIs and which S3 buckets hold input and output. Encryption at rest (S3, DynamoDB, OpenSearch indices) and in transit (TLS) should be enabled by default, and you can use VPC endpoints for private connectivity from your VPC to Comprehend. It is worth noting that not all Comprehend features are available via VPC endpoints, and the availability of a specific region and feature should be verified before designing.

When using PII detection, it is important to define clear retention and masking policies: for example, automatically redacting PII before indexing documents or limiting which internal users can view unredacted text. CloudTrail can log all calls to Comprehend, allowing you to audit who analyzed which documents and when. Combined with tagging and separate environments (dev/test/prod), this provides a controlled, auditable NLP layer that integrates well with enterprise governance frameworks.

Use cases of Amazon Comprehend

For an AWS Solutions Architect, Comprehend is a strong choice when you need to understand or organize large volumes of text without building and operating custom NLP models. It integrates naturally with core AWS services such as S3, Lambda, Step Functions, Kinesis, and OpenSearch, making it easy to drop into existing data pipelines and event-driven architectures.

When the built-in capabilities (entities, sentiment, key phrases, PII, topics) are not enough, custom classification and custom entity recognition give you a path to adapt the service to your own domain with minimal ML expertise.

In the broader context, Amazon Comprehend is the text analytics counterpart to other AI building blocks: it turns unstructured language into structured signals that your systems can search, aggregate, and act on, enabling smarter feedback loops, automated document workflows, and more personalized user experiences across your AWS solutions.

Amazon Polly

It is a service that turns written text into audio in many languages and voices. It is a fully managed TTS service by Amazon. Instead of you building speech models or running audio infrastructure, Polly exposes simple APIs: you send text, choose a voice and format, and receive an audio stream or file you can play, store, or distribute. For a solutions architect, Polly acts as a *voice layer* you can plug into web, mobile, contact center, and IoT architectures to add narration, guidance, or conversational output without operating any media servers.

The core capabilities of Amazon Polly include the following:

- At its core, Amazon Polly provides highquality standard and neural voices across dozens of languages and dialects, covering both realtime and batch use cases. Neural TTS voices use deep learning to sound more fluid and human, while standard voices offer a more cost-efficient option for large-volume workloads such as bulk audio generation. You can select from many male and female voices, often with regional accents, so the voice matches your brand and audience.
- Polly gives you finegrained control over how text is spoken. Using **Speech Synthesis Markup Language** (**SSML**), you can adjust pronunciation, pauses, emphasis, speech rate, pitch, and even specialized *styles*, such as a newscaster voice, for certain voices. Custom lexicons let you define how specific words, acronyms, or brand names should be pronounced, which is crucial for technical domains or internal terminology. Polly also supports speech marks, timing metadata describing when particular words or phonemes are spoken, so you can synchronize audio with onscreen text, captions, or character animations.
- Polly supports both *singleshot* synthesis (convert text to an audio file) and lowlatency streaming, where audio starts playing as it is generated, from an integration perspective. Streaming is particularly important for conversational agents, **Interactive Voice Response** (**IVR**) systems, or live applications that must respond quickly to user input.

Polly presence in an AWS architecture

In AWS architectures, Polly usually sits behind an API or eventdriven workflow that takes text from your systems and returns audio to users or downstream components. Applications commonly invoke Polly through the AWS SDK from Lambda functions, containerized services (**Elastic Container Service (ECS) / Elastic Kubernetes Service (EKS)**, or serverside frameworks, then store the resulting audio in Amazon S3 for reuse and distribution. Because Polly is fully managed and globally available, you do not manage codecs, media servers, or scaling; you focus on when and how to generate speech and how to deliver it. Polly has a character limit per API request. The *SynthesizeSpeech* API (real-time synthesis) supports up to 3,000 billed characters or 6,000 total characters because **Speech Synthesis Markup Language (SSML)** tags are not counted as billed characters. The *StartSpeechSynthesisTask* API (asynchronous jobs) supports up to 100,000 billed characters or 200,000 total characters, including SSML tags.

A typical pattern is: userfacing apps call an API Gateway endpoint; the back end (Lambda or a container) generates or retrieves text, calls Polly to synthesize speech, and returns a streaming URL or presigned S3 URL to the client. Another pattern is pregeneration: periodic jobs convert articles, help content, or training material into audio files and publish them as part of your content delivery stack via S3 and Amazon CloudFront.

Polly also fits naturally into multiservice AI solutions: text may be produced by other services (for example, contactcenter transcripts analyzed by Amazon Comprehend, or responses generated by chatbots), and Polly becomes the final step that turns that text into an audible experience.

Example of voice-enabled web or mobile app

Consider a learning platform that wants to offer *listen-to-this-lesson and read-aloud* features for accessibility and convenience. A Polly based workflow might look like this:

1. **Content storage**: Lessons are stored as structured text.
2. **Audio generation service**:
    - When a lesson is published or updated, an event (for example, via Amazon EventBridge) triggers a Lambda function.
    - The function fetches the lesson's text, wraps it in SSML to control pacing, emphasis, and pronunciation of domainspecific terms, and calls Polly with an appropriate neural voice and output format (commonly **Moving Picture Experts Group Audio Layer III (MP3)**).
3. **Storage and delivery**: The resulting audio file is stored in an S3 bucket, optionally fronted by CloudFront for global, lowlatency delivery.
4. **Client integration**:
    - Web and mobile clients display a **Play audio** button that streams the S3 / CloudFront URL with a native media player.
    - Since audio is pregenerated, playback starts quickly and scales cheaply as more learners access the content.

If you also want dynamic playback (for example, reading parts of the UI, search results, or chat replies), clients call an API that triggers on-demand synthesis with Polly's realtime streaming, returning an audio stream that starts playing immediately. This architecture combines batch and realtime usage: static content is pre-rendered, while adhoc responses are generated on the fly.

Example of contact center and IVR workflow

Another common pattern is building or enhancing contact-center and IVR systems with natural sounding prompts and responses. A typical workflow could be:

1. **Call handling**: A customer call lands in a telephony or contact center solution such as Amazon Connect or a thirdparty **Private Branch Exchange** (**PBX**).
2. **Dynamic prompt generation**:
   - The IVR or agent-assist application constructs text responses from customer data, business rules, or analytics (for example, *Hello Sam, your balance is 55 dollars*).
   - The backend sends this text to Polly, choosing a voice aligned with your brand and the caller's language.
3. **Speech delivery**: Polly returns an audio stream that is played back in near real time to the caller, using streaming for low latency where needed.
4. **Reuse and caching**:
   - Frequently used prompts (*press 1 for Office hours, 2 for Billing-related queries*) can be pregenerated as audio files stored in S3 and reused by the IVR, minimizing repeated synthesis calls.
   - Less predictable or highly personalized prompts (balances, status messages, onetime codes) are generated on demand. It is worth noting that latency considerations for on-demand synthesis in IVR contexts are of utmost importance. Callers are sensitive to delays, so streaming synthesis (SynthesizeSpeech with audio streaming) should be used here rather than waiting for a full audio file to generate before playback begins.

In more advanced scenarios, upstream services such as Comprehend or other analytics can shape what text gets spoken (for example, summarizing previous call interactions or adapting tone based on customer profile), while Polly remains the consistent, scalable voice engine.

Designing with security, privacy, and governance in mind

Architecting with Polly involves not only voice quality but also the secure and efficient handling of generated audio and input text. IAM policies should restrict which services or roles can call Polly APIs and access related S3 buckets, especially when the spoken text contains sensitive information such as account details or health data. Audio files stored in S3 should use encryption at rest, appropriate access controls, and presigned URLs, or CloudFront signed URLs can limit who can stream the audio and for how long.

Cost optimization often means balancing realtime versus pregenerated usage, choosing between neural and standard voices, and caching frequently used outputs instead of synthesizing the same sentences repeatedly. For governance and auditing, logging API calls and synthesis jobs (for example, with CloudTrail and CloudWatch Logs) helps track when and how sensitive content is converted to speech. With these patterns in place, Polly becomes a reliable, governed component in larger voice enabled solutions rather than an adhoc utility.

Use cases of Amazon Polly

Use Amazon Polly whenever you want your AWS solution to *speak* to users in a natural, scalable way rather than just displaying text. It is a good fit for any scenario where content is primarily text today, articles, alerts, messages, instructions, and you want to add audio without building your own texttospeech engine. Typical examples include: reading news or blog posts aloud in a mobile app, narrating elearning content, generating audio versions of documentation, or making dashboards and notifications accessible to users who prefer or require audio.

Polly is also a strong choice for voicedriven and telephony use cases. You use it to power prompts and responses in IVR/contact center flows (often with Amazon Connect), to give your chatbots a voice, or to read out realtime information like account balances, order status, and alerts. Because you pay per character and can cache the audio, it works well for both highvolume, repeated messages (standard prompts, menus) and longform content (articles, training modules). In short, reach for Polly whenever you need reliable, lifelike speech from text as a reusable capability in your architecture. It is worth noting that neural voices cost significantly more per character than standard voices, roughly 4 times more.

Amazon Lex

It is a fully managed and conversational AI service that lets you build chatbots and voicebots for applications, websites, and contact centers without building your own speech recognition or language understanding stack. It combines **automatic speech recognition** (**ASR**) to convert speech to text with **natural language understanding** (**NLU**) to determine what the user wants (their *intent*) and what information they provide (their *slots*). As a solutions architect, you treat Lex as the conversational front end of your system: it handles user messages or voice input, then routes requests into your backend services using AWS integrations like Lambda, Amazon Connect, and other APIs.

The core capabilities of Amazon Lex include the following:

- Amazon Lex organizes conversations around a few core concepts: bots, intents, slots, and utterances. A bot contains one or more intents, each representing a user goal such as *book a hotel*, *check product prices*, or *reset password*. For each intent you define, sample utterances (example phrases users might say) and slots, which are pieces of information the bot must collect, such as dates, locations, or product names. Intent names must be unique within a bot and follow specific naming conventions (alphanumeric and underscores only).

- Under the hood, Lex uses ASR and NLU (the same underlying technology inspired by Alexa) to map incoming text or speech to one of your defined intents and to extract slot values. It supports multiturn conversations, meaning the bot can ask follow-up questions to fill missing slots, confirm information, and handle corrections (corrections in previous intent). Lex V2 adds features such as better context management, improved fallback strategies when the bot is unsure, and assisted BERT-based NLU that uses large language models to improve intent and slot resolution across varied user phrasing. It is worth noting that Lex V2 improves intent resolution through BERT-based NLU enhancements and, more recently, generative AI-powered conversation features, which are distinct from a full LLM integration. Architects requiring true large language model-based conversational AI should consider Amazon Bedrock, combined with Lex or as a standalone solution.
- Lifecycle and deployment features are built in. You can version bots, intents, and slot types, run regression tests on real interaction logs via a test workbench, and deploy to multiple channels (web chat, mobile, Facebook Messenger, Slack, SMS, Amazon Connect) from a single configuration.

Lex presence in an AWS architecture

In a typical AWS architecture, Lex sits at the edge as the conversational interface, while business logic and data live in downstream services. Users interact with the bot through channels such as:

- A web or mobile chat widget embedded in your application. Embedding Lex in a web or mobile app requires the AWS Amplify SDK or direct API calls with Cognito-based authentication
- A voice call handled by Amazon Connect.
- Thirdparty messaging platforms like Slack or Twilio SMS.

The highlevel flow is:

1. The user sends a message or speaks; the channel sends text or audio to Lex.
2. Lex runs ASR (if audio) and NLU to determine the intent and extract slots.
3. Lex optionally invokes an AWS Lambda function (or, indirectly, other services) for fulfillment, retrieving data, triggering workflows, or updating systems.
4. The Lambda function returns a response message and, if needed, new prompts or session attributes to Lex.

5. Lex responds to the user with text or synthesized speech, and the conversation continues until the intent is fulfilled.

Lambda integration is central. It lets your bot call internal APIs, query DynamoDB, integrate with CRM or ticketing systems, and persist conversation context. You can also use DynamoDB or other datastores directly from Lambda to store user preferences, conversation state, or transaction details, and use Amazon CloudWatch to monitor bot metrics such as intent recognition accuracy and conversation completion rates.

Example of customer support chatbot workflow

Imagine a SaaS company that wants a support chatbot to handle common queries and reduce load on human agents. A Lex based workflow might look like this:

1. **Frontend integration**:
    - The web app includes a chat widget that communicates with an API tier or directly with Lex via a channel integration.
    - When the user types any instructions, the chat widget sends the text to Lex.
2. **Intent recognition and slot filling**:
    - Lex maps the utterance to an intent (like *PasswordReset* or *LoginIssue*), if the utterance does not match any defined intent with sufficient confidence, Lex triggers the *FallbackIntent*.
    - If required slots are missing (for example, username or account email), Lex prompts the user: *Please provide username?*
    - As the user responds, Lex fills slots and maintains the conversation context across turns.
3. **Lambda fulfillment**:
    a. Once Lex has enough information, it triggers a Lambda function associated with the intent.
    b. The Lambda function calls internal APIs or a user directory to verify identity, initiate a password-reset flow, or open a support ticket if the issue is more complex.
    c. Lambda returns a response message (*I have emailed you a password reset link. Anything else I can help with?*).
4. **Escalation and logging**:
    - If Lex hits a *FallbackIntent* (the user's need does not match any intent or confidence is low), the bot can offer suggested phrases or escalate to a live agent through a chat or telephony system.

- All interactions and outcomes are logged to CloudWatch and optionally stored for analytics, training improvements, and testset generation using the Lex test workbench.

This architecture scales automatically with user traffic and offloads repetitive queries while still offering a path to human support when needed.

Example of voicebot with Amazon Connect

Lex also integrates tightly with Amazon Connect to power IVR and voice selfservice experiences. A typical call center workflow includes the following:

1. **Inbound call**: A customer calls a support number hosted in Amazon Connect. Connect routes the call to a contact flow that includes a Lex bot.
2. **Natural language entry point**: Instead of *press 1 for billing, 2 for support*, the IVR says:

   Please briefly describe how I can help you today.

   The caller responds in natural language (**`I want to check the status of my order`**).
3. **Intent and slot handling**: Connect passes the caller's audio to Lex, which performs ASR and NLU to identify an intent such as *CheckOrderStatus* and extract or prompt for an order ID and other details. Lex manages multiturn dialog to clarify and confirm information (*Did you mean order XXX placed on March 3rd?*).
4. Backend integration:
   - Lex invokes a Lambda function to look up the order in a backend system (for example, via API Gateway to microservices or directly to a database). It is worth knowing that Lambda functions invoked by Lex through Amazon Connect have a maximum execution timeout of 8 seconds
   - The Lambda function returns a summary (**`Your order has shipped and you will receive between 9.00 am to 11.00 am tomorrow`**), which Connect plays back to the caller using text-to-speech.
5. **Routing and handoff**: If the user asks for something beyond selfservice capability, the flow can transfer the call to a live agent, passing along the gathered context (intent, slots, prior steps) so the agent does not need to ask for the same information again.

This design leverages Lex for understanding and orchestration, while Connect handles telephony, agent routing, and call recording.

Designing with security, privacy, and governance in mind

Since Lex often sits directly in front of customers, security, reliability, and governance are key architectural concerns. IAM policies should tightly control which roles and applications can invoke Lex and which Lambda functions or data sources those bots can reach. Sensitive information in user messages, such as account numbers, email addresses, or health details, should be handled carefully in fulfillment code, with encryption at rest in DynamoDB or other storage and TLS in transit.

Monitoring and improvement are continuous activities. Lex provides built-in metrics and dashboards for intent-recognition success, fallback rates, conversation length, and other **key performance indicators** (**KPIs**), which you can surface through CloudWatch and external observability tools. Using the test workbench and historical transcripts, you can build regression test sets to validate new intents or dialog changes before deploying them broadly, reducing the risk of breaking existing flows. Versioning of bots, intents, and slot types allows you to promote configurations safely between development, staging, and production environments and roll back if necessary.

With these patterns, Amazon Lex becomes a robust conversational layer in your AWS architectures, enabling natural language interfaces for support, sales, internal tools, and more, while relying on familiar AWS building blocks, Lambda, Connect, API Gateway, DynamoDB, and CloudWatch, for the underlying logic, data, and operations.

Use cases of Amazon Lex

Use Amazon Lex when you want users to interact with your system through natural conversation, text, or voice, instead of clicks and forms. It is a good fit for chatbots that answer FAQs, help users navigate your product, reset passwords, check order status, or perform simple transactions across channels such as web chat, mobile apps, or messaging platforms. Lex handles speech recognition and language understanding for you, so you focus on defining intents (what the user wants), slots (the key pieces of information you need), and the business logic behind each flow.

Lex is also a strong choice for voice and contact-center scenarios, especially when combined with services like Amazon Connect. You can use it to build selfservice IVR flows that collect information, route calls, and hand off to agents when needed, all while keeping context from the conversation. More broadly, choose Lex whenever you need: multiturn dialogues (backandforth questions to gather details), integration with AWS backends (Lambda, APIs, databases), and a managed, scalable conversational engine instead of rolling your own NLP stack.

Machine learning concept

In the context of AWS solution architecture, machine learning is less about abstract math and more about building systems that learn from data and improve over time. Instead of hardcoding every rule (*if X then Y*), you feed historical examples into a model so it can recognize patterns and make predictions on its own. In practical terms, that might mean forecasting demand from past sales, ranking search results based on user behavior, classifying support tickets by topic, or detecting fraudulent transactions in a stream of payments. The architect's job is to decide where these learned decisions fit into the overall flow of an application: at the edge for realtime personalization, in the data platform for batch scoring, or behind APIs that other services can call.

On AWS, machine learning becomes another set of services you compose into your design, much like databases or queues. For custom models and end-to-end workflows, you lean on platforms like Amazon SageMaker to handle data preparation, training, tuning, and deployment, so you do not have to manage GPU fleets or handroll deployment pipelines. For many common use cases, you can skip model building entirely and use prebuilt AI APIs, for vision, language, speech, and conversational interfaces, that plug into existing architectures through simple HTTPS calls. In a well-architected system, ML is treated as an operationalized capability: models are versioned and monitored, inferences are logged and measured, and scaling, security, and cost are designed just as carefully as for any other microservice. The end goal is not *to have machine learning,* but to weave datadriven decisionmaking into the architecture wherever it creates clear value.

Amazon SageMaker

Amazon SageMaker is a fully managed machine learning platform that helps you build, train, and deploy models at scale without stitching together separate tools and infrastructure. It provides an integrated environment, SageMaker Studio, where data scientists and engineers can explore data, experiment with algorithms, track versions, and push models into production using the same set of managed services. For a solutions architect, SageMaker is the central *ML workbench* in an AWS design: it connects to data in S3 and other sources, runs training on elastic compute, hosts models for realtime or batch inference, and includes governance and monitoring features to operate ML safely in production.

Amazon SageMaker spans the entire ML lifecycle, from data preparation to model monitoring. Key capabilities include:

- **Data preparation**: Tools like SageMaker Data Wrangler and SageMaker Lakehouse let you connect to S3, Redshift, and other data sources, explore and clean data, engineer features, and publish transformed datasets into S3 or feature stores. (*Note*: *As of late 2024, AWS rebranded and restructured several SageMaker components under Amazon SageMaker Unified Studio, with SageMaker Lakehouse being introduced as part of that broader unification effort)*
- **Model building and training**: You can use builtin algorithms, preconfigured frameworks (TensorFlow, PyTorch, XGBoost, etc.), or bring your own Docker containers. Training jobs spin up managed clusters of EC2 instances on demand, read data from S3, write model artifacts back to S3, and then automatically tear down the infrastructure so you only pay while training is running. It is to be noted that training jobs support Spot Instances for up to 90% of cost reduction.

- **AutoML and JumpStart**: SageMaker Autopilot can automatically build and tune models for tabular problems. While SageMaker Autopilot excels at tabular problems, it has expanded to support text classification, image classification, and time series forecasting, making it a broader AutoML solution than tabular-only workflows suggest. SageMaker JumpStart provides pre-trained and foundation models that you can fine-tune or deploy with minimal code.
- **Experiment management and debugging**: Features like SageMaker Experiments, Debugger, and Clarify track training runs, surface metrics, detect training issues, and analyze model bias and explainability.
- **Deployment and inference**: You can deploy models to realtime HTTPS endpoints, serverless inference, asynchronous inference, or run batch transform jobs for offline scoring. SageMaker Inference Recommender helps choose optimal instance types and configurations, while autoscaling and multiAZ options provide resilience and elasticity.
- **Pipelines and ModelOps**: SageMaker Pipelines, Model Registry, Model Monitor, model cards, and dashboards support **continuous integration/continuous deployment** (**CI/CD**), approval workflows, lineage tracking, and ongoing drift detection for models in production.

These capabilities mean you can standardize on SageMaker for ML development while still integrating with the rest of your AWS ecosystem.

SageMaker presence in AWS architecture

In a reference AWS architecture, SageMaker sits between your data platform and your application layer as the *ML factory* and model serving layer. Typical data flows start with raw data in Amazon S3, data warehouses like Redshift, or lakehouse patterns that unify multiple stores via SageMaker Lakehouse. AWS Glue is commonly used alongside SageMaker for data cataloging and **extraction, transform, and load** (**ETL**). Data engineers and data scientists use SageMaker Studio to access these datasets, perform exploratory data analysis and feature engineering, and then configure training jobs that run at scale on managed compute.

Once trained, models and their metadata are registered in the SageMaker Model Registry and associated with lineage information that tracks which data, code, and parameters produced each version. Deployment then follows one of several patterns:

- Realtime inference endpoints behind Amazon API Gateway or an internal API, used by microservices and frontend applications.
- Asynchronous inference for large payloads, where requests are queued and processed in the background.
- Batch Transform jobs that read from S3, score large datasets, and write predictions back to S3 for offline analytics.

Applications, such as web apps, backend services, or analytics jobs, consume predictions via these endpoints or from the scored datasets, often combining them with business rules or other service calls. Model monitoring runs alongside, using SageMaker Model Monitor to compare live traffic data and prediction quality against training baselines, sending CloudWatch metrics and EventBridge events when drift or anomalies occur.

Example of endtoend tabular ML workflow

Consider a fraud detection model for an ecommerce platform that processes transaction data. A SageMaker centric workflow might look like this:

1. **Data preparation**:
   - Transaction logs, customer profiles, and historical fraud labels are stored in S3 and possibly Redshift.
   - A data scientist uses SageMaker Studio with Data Wrangler to pull this data, join tables, handle missing values, and engineer features (for example, transaction velocity, geolocation anomalies), then exports a curated training dataset back to S3.
2. **Model building and training**:
   - The scientist starts a training job using XGBoost or a custom PyTorch model, pointing it at the training data in S3 and selecting an instance type optimized for CPU or GPU.
   - SageMaker spins up the cluster, trains the model, writes artifacts to S3, and tears down the compute resources after completion.
   - SageMaker Experiments tracks hyperparameters and metrics across runs, while Autopilot or hyperparameter tuning jobs explore multiple configurations automatically.
3. **Model registration and approval**:
   - The best model version is registered in the SageMaker Model Registry with performance metrics and documentation in a model card.
   - An approval workflow, often orchestrated by EventBridge, Lambda, and possibly a human approval step, promotes the model from *Candidate* to *Approved for staging/ production.*
4. **Deployment and serving**:
   - The approved model is deployed to a managed realtime endpoint with autoscaling policies.
   - The ecommerce transaction service calls this endpoint synchronously for each transaction, passing features and receiving a fraudrisk score and explanation attributes.

5. **Monitoring and retraining**:
   - SageMaker Model Monitor tracks input feature distributions, prediction outputs, and, where available, ground truth labels to detect drift.
   - When drift or performance degradation is detected, an automated SageMaker Pipeline kicks off a new training cycle with the latest data, evaluates the new model, and, if it passes thresholds and approvals, rolls it into production.

This pattern illustrates how SageMaker supports a full ModelOps loop, from data to deployment to ongoing improvement, within a governed AWS environment.

Example of using SageMaker with foundation models

Modern architectures often need to incorporate **foundation models** (**FMs**) and generative AI into existing systems. SageMaker provides JumpStart and other FM integrations so you can deploy or fine-tune large language models and vision models for tasks like classification, summarization, or recommendations. A typical workflow includes the following:

1. **Model selection**: A data scientist opens SageMaker Studio JumpStart, browses a catalog of FMs and solution templates, and chooses a model that fits the use case (for example, a text generation LLM or a vision model for image classification).
2. **Finetuning and evaluation**:
   - The team finetunes the chosen model on domain specific data stored in S3 using managed training jobs and, optionally, LoRA or parameter efficient techniques to reduce compute cost.
   - Results are tracked with experiments, and performance is evaluated on holdout datasets and through human review.
3. **Deployment and integration**:
   - The model is deployed with a SageMaker realtime endpoint that supports autoscaling and secure network access.
   - Applications (for example, an internal knowledge assistant or a customer support summarization service) call the endpoint via API Gateway or directly from backend services, passing prompts or content and receiving generated text or embeddings.
4. **Governance and monitoring**:
   - Model cards, lineage tracking, and dashboards capture how the FM is used, data sources, and risk assessments.
   - Model Monitor and external observability tools watch for quality, drift, and anomalous patterns in requests and responses, and pipelines support safe iterations as prompts, guardrails, or fine-tuning data evolve.

For a solutions architect, this demonstrates how SageMaker becomes the controlled interface for generative AI inside an enterprise, rather than adhoc model hosting.

Designing with security, privacy, and governance in mind

Production SageMaker architectures must address isolation, security, and cost efficiency from the outset. Multiaccount patterns, separating dev, test, and prod environments, are used to isolate workloads and apply leastprivilege IAM policies around Studio workspaces, training jobs, and endpoints. **AWS Control Tower** and **Service Catalog** are the recommended mechanisms for managing multi-account SageMaker environments at scale. Data access is typically mediated via IAM roles, S3 bucket policies, and lakehouse or catalog tooling so that notebooks and jobs see only the datasets they are authorized to use.

Encryption at rest (S3, EBS, EFS, model artifacts) and in transit, private VPC connectivity for endpoints, and controlled egress are standard. Costaware design includes choosing appropriate instance types, using spot training where possible, shutting down Idle Studio resources, and preferring batch or serverless inference for spiky or offline workloads. Governance capabilities, such as ML lineage tracking, model registry approvals, model cards, and CloudTrail logs for all SageMaker APIs, provide the traceability needed for audits and regulatory requirements.

With these patterns, Amazon SageMaker becomes the backbone of your ML platform on AWS, giving your architectures a consistent, managed way to turn data into models and models into reliable, monitored services that integrate cleanly with the rest of your cloud environment.

Use cases of Amazon SageMaker

Use Amazon SageMaker when you need to build, train, and deploy your own machine learning models as part of an application or platform, not just call a prebuilt AI API. It is the right choice when you have specific data, domain logic, or accuracy requirements that generic services (like Rekognition, Comprehend, or Lex) cannot meet, or when you want tight control over the full ML lifecycle, data prep, experimentation, training, tuning, deployment, monitoring, and retraining. Typical examples include fraud detection tuned to your transaction patterns, demand forecasting for your specific business, recommendation systems, predictive maintenance from sensor data, or custom NLP and computer vision models tailored to your domain.

SageMaker is also a good fit when you want to industrialize ML: multiple models, teams, and environments, all managed with consistent tooling and MLOps practices. You use it when you need features like managed training infrastructure (including GPUs), built-in algorithms and popular frameworks, hyperparameter tuning, experiment tracking, realtime and batch endpoints, CI/CD for models, and monitoring and drift detection in production. In solutionarchitecture terms, reach for SageMaker when *ML is a product feature you own and evolve,* not just a oneoff experiment or a simple call to a managed AI API.

Conclusion

In this chapter, we explored how AWS's AI services let you add intelligence to solutions without building your own machine learning stack, and how each service fills a distinct role in a larger architecture. Amazon Comprehend turns unstructured text into structured insights, such as entities, key phrases, sentiment, topic modeling results, and PII, so logs, tickets, documents, and feedback streams can feed analytics, search, and automated workflows. Amazon Rekognition applies advanced analysis to images and video, detecting objects, faces, text, and unsafe content. This enables you to moderate user uploads, enhance media libraries with searchable metadata, and improve security and identity verification. However, its processing model is significantly different from that of Comprehend.

We then saw how Amazon Polly and Amazon Lex enable natural human interaction layers on top of these intelligent backends. Polly converts text into natural sounding speech in many languages and voices, making it easy to add narration, accessible *readout* features, and spoken responses into web, mobile, and contact-center applications. Amazon Lex provides the conversational interface itself: it understands user intent and orchestrates multiturn dialogs for chatbots and voicebots, integrating with backend services through AWS Lambda and Amazon Connect. Together, these services form a powerful toolkit for solution architects: Comprehend and Rekognition extract meaning from text and media, while Polly and Lex turn that understanding into voice and chat-driven user experiences, allowing you to design end-to-end intelligent applications on AWS.

In the next chapter, we will move from using prebuilt AI APIs to designing richer, endtoend intelligent workflows that combine several specialized services. You will see how Amazon Textract enables intelligent document processing, extracting structured data and text from forms, invoices, and contracts as the first step in automated backoffice pipelines. We will then introduce Amazon Bedrock as the foundation for generative AI, showing how to integrate foundation models into your solutions for tasks like summarization, content generation, and advanced questionanswering without managing model infrastructure. Finally, we will look at Amazon Q, which encompasses the AI cloud assistant for helping developers and operators work more efficiently, Amazon Q Business for enterprise knowledge assistants and Amazon Q Developer for coding assistance and tying together many of the patterns you have learned so far.

References

1. **https://aws.amazon.com/rekognition/**
2. **https://aws.amazon.com/es/video/watch/39d72e62618/**
3. **https://docs.aws.amazon.com/prescriptive-guidance/latest/image-classification/rekognition.html**
4. **https://aws.amazon.com/comprehend/features/**

5. https://docs.aws.amazon.com/comprehend/latest/dg/what-is.html
6. https://aws.amazon.com/comprehend/
7. https://docs.aws.amazon.com/comprehend/latest/dg/doc-history.html
8. https://docs.aws.amazon.com/sagemaker/latest/dg/a2i-task-types-general.html
9. https://docs.aws.amazon.com/sagemaker/latest/dg/how-it-works-mlconcepts.html
10. https://aws.amazon.com/video/watch/24ffd20457c/
11. https://aws.amazon.com/sagemaker/ai/mlops/
12. https://docs.aws.amazon.com/sagemaker/latest/dg/whatis.html
13. https://docs.aws.amazon.com/next-generation-sagemaker/latest/userguide/what-is-sagemaker.html
14. https://docs.aws.amazon.com/next-generation-sagemaker/latest/userguide/what-is-sagemaker.html
15. https://docs.aws.amazon.com/sagemaker/latest/dg/whatis-features.html
16. https://docs.aws.amazon.com/sagemaker/latest/dg/how-it-works-mlconcepts.html
17. https://aws.amazon.com/blogs/machine-learning/best-practices-and-design-patterns-for-building-machine-learning-workflows-with-amazon-sagemaker-pipelines/
18. https://aws.amazon.com/blogs/machine-learning/automate-modelops-with-amazon-sagemaker-unified-studio-part-1-solution-architecture/
19. https://aws.amazon.com/blogs/machine-learning/build-an-amazon-sagemaker-model-registry-approval-and-promotion-workflow-with-human-intervention/
20. https://aws.amazon.com/lex/features/
21. https://docs.aws.amazon.com/lexv2/latest/dg/how-it-works.html
22. https://docs.aws.amazon.com/lexv2/latest/dg/latest-features.html
23. https://docs.aws.amazon.com/lex/latest/dg/how-it-works.html
24. https://aws.amazon.com/video/watch/749d538f351/
25. https://aws.amazon.com/documentation-overview/lex/
26. https://aws.amazon.com/polly/
27. https://aws.amazon.com/polly/features/
28. https://docs.aws.amazon.com/polly/latest/dg/neural-voices.html
29. https://aws.amazon.com/rekognition/pricing/
30. https://github.com/awsdocs/amazon-polly-developer-guide/blob/master/doc_source/limits.md

Chapter 9
Advanced AWS AI Services

Introduction

As **Amazon Web Service** (**AWS**) evolves, intelligence moves closer to where data resides. This section introduces services that reflect this shift. Amazon Textract converts documents into data by automatically reading forms, tables, and handwritten notes, enabling invoices, contracts, and reports to flow into your systems without manual entry. These services integrate *understanding* and *prediction* into your architecture via **application programming interface** (**API**) calls, not custom models.

Amazon Bedrock and Amazon Q extend AI deeper into how teams build and operate on AWS. Bedrock provides managed access to foundation models for text, images, and code, enabling generative AI features such as summarization, content creation, and intelligent search without managing infrastructure. **Amazon Q** serves as an **artificial intelligence** (**AI**) assistant for your cloud, helping you explore architectures, query accounts, and analyze configurations and code using natural language. This section also covers practical integration patterns, including how these AI services fit into workflows, interact with event buses, APIs, and data lakes, and which use cases benefit most from this intelligence layer.

Structure

In this chapter, we will discuss the following topics:

- Artificial intelligence concept
- Amazon Textract
- Amazon Bedrock
- Amazon Q
- AWS service integration use cases

Objectives

This chapter explains how to treat AI-powered capabilities as standard building blocks in AWS architectures rather than as separate experimental projects. You will learn how Amazon Textract converts scanned documents into structured data. The goal is to help you identify where these services fit into workflows such as ingestion pipelines, analytics platforms, and back-office automation, enabling you to design smarter, easier-to-maintain solutions.

You will also see how newer services like Amazon Bedrock and Amazon Q fit into the bigger architectural picture. Bedrock gives you managed access to foundation models for generative AI so you can add features like summarization, content generation, or intelligent search with clear integration patterns and guardrails, while Amazon Q acts as an AI assistant over your AWS environment and code, helping teams understand and operate complex systems. Throughout, we will focus on concrete integration use cases: which events trigger these services, how results flow to other AWS services (like S3, Lambda, Step Functions, or data lakes), and how to design these interactions so they are secure, observable, and cost-aware.

Artificial intelligence concept

Artificial Intelligence in an AWS architecture is best understood as a set of capabilities you add to systems, rather than as a single, monolithic *AI engine*. Instead of forcing every feature to be hand-coded, you selectively introduce services that can see, listen, read, and converse on your behalf. In practice, this might mean using computer vision to understand what is in an uploaded image, natural language processing to extract meaning from customer emails, or conversational interfaces that let users talk to your application rather than click through menus. As an architect, your focus is not on inventing new algorithms but on determining where these intelligent behaviors fit within user journeys, workflows, and data flows.

On AWS, AI appears as managed, task-focused services you compose alongside other building blocks, such as a database or queue. You can call APIs to analyze documents, generate speech, or interpret chat messages without managing models, **graphics processing units** (**GPUs**), or training pipelines. These services use clear, versioned endpoints, integrate with existing security and networking, and scale automatically. In well-designed solutions, AI reduces manual effort, improves the user experience, and unlocks insights from data that are too complex or costly for humans. The goal is to make intelligence a reliable, first-class component of your architecture, not a fragile side experiment.

Amazon Textract

Amazon Textract is an intelligent document processing service that goes beyond traditional **Optical Character Recognition** (**OCR**) by understanding document structure and meaning, not just characters. Unlike basic OCR, Textract recognizes printed and handwritten text, detects form fields and values, extracts tables, and answers targeted questions, all delivered as structured

JavaScript Object Notation (JSON). This enables solutions architects to convert **Portable Document Format (PDFs)**, scans, and images, such as invoices, forms, contracts, and receipts, into machine-readable data for automated workflows, analytics, and generative AI applications.

Textract excels at understanding both content and layout. It detects text blocks, lines, and words with confidence scores and preserves geometric details, such as bounding boxes and orientation, enabling downstream systems to locate each element precisely. Using the AnalyzeDocument APIs with appropriate feature flags, Textract returns several categories of structured results:

- **Text**: Printed and handwritten text extracted from the page, suitable for indexing and fulltext search.
- **Forms (key–value pairs)**: Identification of fields like *Invoice Number* or *Date* and the values associated with them, preserving the logical relationships rather than just raw text.
- **Tables**: Structured representation of rows, columns, and cells, including merged cells, headers, and footers, so you can reconstruct tables as **comma-separated values** (**CSV**) or database rows.
- **Queries**: Ability to ask targeted questions and get back specific answers, even if the layout varies across document templates.
- **Signatures and layout**: Detection of signatures and higher-level layout elements like titles, sections, and checkboxes, which support compliance and review scenarios.

> Note: **It is important to note that LAYOUT and SIGNATURES are separate AnalyzeDocument feature flags and must be specified independently in API calls, passing one does not automatically enable the other, and combining them may affect processing time and cost.**

These capabilities are available via synchronous APIs for small documents and asynchronous jobs for large or multi-page sets, allowing you to balance low latency and high throughput.

Textract presence in an AWS architecture

In most AWS solutions, Textract is central to an intelligent document processing pipeline: documents arrive through capture channels, Textract extracts structured data, and downstream services process it. Documents usually land in Amazon S3 from web or mobile uploads, enterprise content systems, email ingestion, or batch backfills. S3 events or orchestration services like AWS Step Functions coordinate Textract calls.

A common architectural pattern looks like this:

- **Ingestion and storage**:
  - Scanned PDFs, images, or office documents are uploaded to an S3 bucket dedicated to raw documents.

- S3 event notifications trigger an AWS Lambda function or a Step Functions state machine to start processing. In case of high-volume document processing, placing an SQS queue between S3 events and Lambda is recommended to buffer bursts and avoid Lambda throttling.

- **Document analysis with Textract**:
  - For smaller documents, a Lambda function calls synchronous APIs like AnalyzeDocument or AnalyzeExpense with the appropriate FeatureTypes (FORMS, TABLES, QUERIES, LAYOUT).
  - For larger or bulk workloads, asynchronous operations (StartDocumentAnalysis/ GetDocumentAnalysis) are used, with progress tracked through Amazon SNS or Amazon SQS.
- **Postprocessing and enrichment**:
  - The JSON response, containing text, key–value pairs, and table structures, is parsed by Lambda or containerized services and converted into normalized records for storage in **DynamoDB**, **Relational Database Service** (**RDS**), or data lakes.
  - Business rules or additional AI services (for example, Amazon Comprehend for entity extraction or sentiment) further enrich the data.
- **Downstream workflows**:
  - Cleaned and structured data drives approvals, payments, case creation, or analytics dashboards.
  - Human-in-the-loop review **user interfaces** (**UIs**) (often built with Step Functions, API Gateway, and frontend apps) allow operators to validate or correct fields flagged by confidence thresholds.

With Textract handling complex document understanding, your architecture can focus on orchestration, validation, storage, and integration with line-of-business systems.

Example of invoice and receipt processing pipeline

A common use case is automating accounts payable by extracting data from invoices and receipts. A Textract-driven pipeline typically works as follows:

- **Capture**:
  - Vendors email invoices that are automatically saved into S3, or employees upload receipt photos via a web or mobile expense app.
  - Each new object in a bucket triggers an S3 event that invokes a Lambda function.
- **Classification and extraction**:
  - The Lambda function determines the document type (invoice, receipt, generic form) based on metadata or machine-learning classification.

  - For invoices and receipts, it calls specialized Textract APIs (for example, AnalyzeExpense) that return vendor names, invoice numbers, line items, subtotals, taxes, and totals as structured fields.
  - For generic forms, it uses AnalyzeDocument with FORMS and TABLES to retrieve key–value pairs and tables.
- **Validation and enrichment**:
  - A processing service compares extracted vendor and invoice **identifiers (IDs)** against master data in an **enterprise resource planning** (**ERP**) or **customer relationship management** (**CRM**) system, checking for duplicates or mismatches.
  - If confidence scores are low for critical fields, such as the total amount, the document is routed to a review queue for human verification through a simple web UI.
- **Posting and analytics**:
  - Once validated, the pipeline posts the invoice to the ERP or accounting system through APIs and stores structured records in a data warehouse for reporting.
  - Dashboards display spend by vendor, category, or region, all based on data originally locked in unstructured PDFs.

AWS reference architectures and opensource examples extend this pattern to support large backfills, using **DynamoDB**, **Simple Queue Service** (**SQS**), and batch operations to scale processing to millions of documents.

Example of intelligent document processing with gen AI

Textract is a key component in modern intelligent document processing solutions that combine extraction with generative AI. A typical pattern includes:

- Use Textract to extract text, layout, forms, and tables from complex documents.
- Store the normalized text and structured fields in a vector store (or data lake).
- Feed that content into generativeAI services (for example, via Amazon Bedrock) to power use cases such as question-answering over document collections, summarization, or automated drafting of responses.
- Maintain a feedback loop where corrections by reviewers inform future rules or model updates. This feedback loop typically stores human corrections in a datastore, uses them to retrain or fine-tune models with SageMaker, or updates Textract Queries configurations.

This approach preserves Textract's strengths in high-fidelity extraction and structure while adding advanced reasoning and summarization from generative models.

Designing with security, privacy, and governance in mind

Since Textract often processes sensitive documents, such as financial records, identity documents, and healthcare forms, security and governance must be central to the architecture. **Identity and Access Management** (**IAM**) roles should strictly control which services can access Textract and which S3 buckets store raw and processed documents, with encryption enabled at rest and in transit. **Virtual Private Cloud** (**VPC**) endpoints can keep traffic between your VPC and Textract off the public internet. Data-retention policies should specify how long to retain raw images versus extracted fields.

At scale, you will rely on asynchronous APIs, SQS queues, and Step Functions to coordinate thousands or millions of documents, implementing retry and dead-letter strategies for robustness. CloudWatch metrics and logs, combined with business-level KPIs such as straight-through-processing rates, help you monitor accuracy and throughput and decide where to add human review. **Amazon Augmented AI** (**A2I**) integrates directly with Textract for human review workflows. With these patterns in place, Amazon Textract becomes a foundational component of advanced AWS AI solutions that turn static documents into live, governed data assets that flow through your cloud architectures.

Use cases for Amazon Textract

Use Amazon Textract when you need to convert documents into structured data automatically, not just extract text from images. It is a good fit when:

- You process forms and PDFs at scale, such as invoices, receipts, tax forms, loan applications, insurance claims, and onboarding forms, and want to extract key fields and tables into systems like DynamoDB, RDS, or data lakes without manual entry.
- You need more than basic OCR: identifying key–value pairs, tables, checkboxes, handwriting, and layout so your application recognizes that *Invoice Number* is a label and *INV00123* its value, or can extract full rows from financial tables.
- You are building intelligent document workflows, such as S3 upload | event/Lambda | Textract | validation/rules | storage | human review for low-confidence fields.
- You handle regulated or sensitive content that should not pass through ad hoc desktop tools. Textract provides an API with IAM, logging, and regional controls that align with enterprise security standards.

In short, use Textract when the document serves as the *API boundary* to your system, and you want to automate understanding of the document, its field names, values, and tables, enabling other services to act on it programmatically.

Amazon Bedrock

Amazon Bedrock is a fully managed platform on AWS for building generative AI applications using **foundation models** (**FMs**) from Amazon and third-party providers via a single, consistent API. Instead of provisioning GPUs, hosting models, and managing safety and orchestration, Bedrock provides a managed layer where you select a model, configure security and guardrails, optionally integrate your enterprise data, and call it like any other AWS service. For solutions architects, Bedrock serves as the central generative AI runtime, with other services managing retrieval, business logic, and workflow orchestration.

Amazon Bedrock provides access to a catalog of foundation models for text, code, images, and embeddings via a unified API, along with tools to evaluate and select the best model for each use case. You can switch or upgrade models without rewriting your application, which is crucial in a rapidly evolving model landscape. Bedrock also supports customization, fine-tuning, instruction tuning, and **retrieval-augmented generation** (**RAG**), enabling you to tailor general-purpose models to your domain while keeping proprietary data private within your AWS account. Fine-tuning in Bedrock is available only for selected models. Not all models in the Bedrock catalog support this feature, so before designing a fine-tuning workflow, availability for the chosen model needs to be verified. On top of raw models, Bedrock adds higher-level building blocks:

- **Knowledge bases** implement managed RAG, automatically embedding and indexing your documents, then retrieving relevant chunks and augmenting prompts at runtime.
- **Agents** enable you to define task-oriented *AI workers* that call APIs, query knowledge bases, and orchestrate multi-step workflows using tools like Lambda and external services.
- **Guardrails and safety** offer configurable controls over allowed topics, PII handling, toxicity filters, and output shaping, enforcing organizational policies on model usage.
- Bedrock Flows and AWS Step Functions integrations let you design complex workflows by chaining prompts, parallelizing calls, and combining multiple Bedrock components with other AWS services. Bedrock Flows has the responsibility of prompt chaining within the generative AI layer, while Step Functions orchestrates broader workflows including non-AI steps.

These capabilities turn Bedrock from *just an API to a model* into a platform for building production-grade generative AI systems.

Bedrock presence in an AWS architecture

In a reference architecture, Amazon Bedrock resides in a dedicated generative-AI account or VPC-isolated environment, exposing model and agent endpoints to other workloads via VPC interface endpoints or API Gateway. Applications, including web and mobile apps, internal tools, or backend microservices, send prompts or structured tasks to Bedrock, often through an API tier that handles authentication, authorization, and request shaping.

Data flows typically look like this:

1. **Data preparation and indexing**:
   - Enterprise documents, knowledge bases, and logs are stored in S3, databases, or search systems.
   - A knowledge base in Bedrock connects to this data (often via a vector index) and runs an embedding pipeline to chunk and index content.
2. **Application request**:
   - A user interacts with a UI (chat, search, workflow tool) that sends a request to your backend.
   - The backend calls Bedrock's InvokeModel, knowledge-base query, or Agent APIs, passing user input and any application-level context.
3. **RAG and reasoning**:
   - For knowledge bases, Bedrock converts queries into vectors using an embedding model, retrieves similar content, and augments the prompt with this context before calling the **foundational model** (**FM**).
   - For agents, Bedrock interprets input, selects the appropriate action group or API, invokes operations (via Lambda or OpenAPI endpoints), and iterates until it can respond or requires more user input.
4. **Response and orchestration**:
   - The FM returns a response that may include structured tool outputs, natural-language text, or JSON for your backend to continue the workflow.
   - Step Functions or Bedrock Flows can orchestrate multistep sequences, such as parallel document summarization or chained question answering across multiple data sources.

Security is enforced via IAM, VPC endpoints, logging (CloudTrail and CloudWatch), and centralized governance in a generative AI account, following landing-zone patterns for separation of duties and cost tracking.

Example of enterprise knowledge assistant

A common Bedrock use case is an internal knowledge assistant (RAG) that answers questions about company policies, architecture documents, or product manuals. A typical workflow includes:

1. **Content ingestion**:
    - PDFs, wikis, and design docs are stored in S3 or existing repositories.
    - A data-prep job cleans and chunks content, then a Bedrock knowledge base indexes it using an embedding model.
2. **User interaction**:
    - Employees use a web UI to ask questions.
    - The UI sends the question and user context (role, team, allowed domains) to the backend API.
3. **RAG call to Bedrock**:
    - The backend calls the knowledge-base query API, which:
    - Embeds the query into a vector.
    - Retrieves the most relevant document chunks from the vector index.
    - Constructs an augmented prompt combining the question and retrieved context.
    - Bedrock invokes the chosen FM with this augmented prompt, optionally applying guardrails to enforce tone, redaction, or policy boundaries.
4. **Response and citation**:
    - The model produces an answer and may reference specific documents or sections used as context.
    - The backend returns the answer with links to source documents, enabling users to verify and explore further.

This pattern keeps data within your AWS environment while leveraging powerful FMs. You can swap models or adjust retrieval strategies without changing the UI or core application logic.

Example of agentic workflow for API orchestration

Another effective pattern uses **Bedrock Agents** to orchestrate calls to enterprise APIs, converting natural-language requests into multi-step workflows. For example, consider an internal *cloud operations assistant* that provisions resources and monitors system health:

- **Agent configuration**:
    - **Define an agent in Bedrock with**:
        - Instructions describing its role
        - Action groups connected to OpenAPI schemas covering internal APIs and possibly direct AWS operations via Lambda
        - A knowledge base containing runbooks and architecture standards.

- **User request**:
  - An engineer types, *Create an EC2 instance with configuration t2 micro for team ABC* via chat or **command line interface** (**CLI**).
  - The request is sent to the agent endpoint.
- **Agent orchestration**:
  - The agent uses the FM to interpret the request, generates a rationale, and selects the appropriate action group to call.
  - It extracts required parameters from the conversation (team name, environment, region) and invokes a provisioning API or Lambda function to create the EC2 instance.
  - If information is missing, the agent asks follow-up questions. If an operation fails, it can roll back or escalate based on your logic.
- **Response and audit**:
  - The agent reports its actions, including resource names and links to monitoring dashboards.
  - All actions are logged through your APIs and CloudTrail, giving you full auditability of automated changes.
  - This approach shifts your architecture from simple *chat completion* to structured, verifiable workflows while allowing engineers to interact in natural language.

Note: **While Bedrock Agents can orchestrate infrastructure provisioning via Lambda action groups, real-world implementations require approval workflows, IAM boundaries, blast radius controls, and guardrails before allowing agents to make direct AWS resource changes.**

Designing with security, privacy, and governance in mind

Since Bedrock often handles sensitive data and can trigger side-effect actions (via agents and tools), design with strong security and governance boundaries. Typical patterns include:

- A dedicated generative-AI account hosting Bedrock access, model evaluation tools, and shared knowledge bases, integrated into your landing zone with centralized logging and cost allocation.
- VPC interface endpoints to keep Bedrock traffic private, and IAM policies that constrain which models, agents, and knowledge bases each workload can use.
- Guardrails configured per use case to enforce safety, block disallowed topics, and standardize tone and output structure, especially for customer-facing applications.

- Step Functions or Bedrock Flows to ensure that long-running or multi-step AI workflows are observable, retryable, and decoupled from frontend latency constraints.

Cost is managed by selecting appropriate models for each workload (e.g., smaller, cheaper models for high-volume or low-risk tasks, and larger models only when needed) and by using techniques such as retrieval-augmented generation and caching to avoid unnecessary recomputation. These patterns make Amazon Bedrock a secure, governed foundation for generative AI capabilities across your AWS solutions, rather than a one-off experiment attached to individual applications.

Use cases for Amazon Bedrock

Use Amazon Bedrock to build or integrate **generative AI** deeply into your applications without managing models or infrastructure yourself.

It is a strong fit when:

- You need access to multiple foundation models (text, code, images, multimodal) and want to select or change models as requirements evolve, avoiding vendor lock-in.
- You are building enterprise-grade generative AI features, chatbots, assistants, content summarizers, code helpers, RAG/search over your documents, document analyzers, or workflow agents, and prioritizing security, VPC integration, governance, guardrails, and compliance.
- You want to customize models with your data (fine-tuning or RAG/knowledge bases) without exposing it to public models, maintaining clear control over privacy and access.
- You need AI agents that call tools/APIs, chain steps, and integrate with existing systems, but you prefer not to build orchestration, observability, and scaling layers yourself.

In solution architecture, choose Bedrock when generative AI is a core **part of your platform** serving multiple teams and use cases, and you need a managed, multi-model, secure foundation rather than isolated calls to a single external LLM.

Amazon Q

Amazon Q is a generative AI assistant from AWS designed to operate within your cloud and business environments, enabling work through natural language rather than isolated queries. It acts as an intelligent layer over your AWS infrastructure and enterprise data: developers use it to analyze code or troubleshoot architecture, business users to summarize documents or build dashboards, and operators to investigate incidents or generate reports. This conversational interface integrates with the AWS Console, **integrated development environments (IDEs)**, and collaboration tools. For AWS Solutions Architects, **Amazon Q** offers a cross-cutting capability to accelerate development, operations, analytics, and workflows without requiring each team to build a custom assistant.

The following pointers discuss the core capabilities of Amazon Q:

- Amazon Q is offered in two main personas today: Amazon Q Developer for builders and operators, and Amazon Q Business for knowledge workers and line-of-business scenarios.
- Amazon Q Developer focuses on software and cloud engineering tasks. It can generate and refactor code, propose tests, explain errors, and help modernize applications, and it does so with deep awareness of AWS services, best practices, and your own codebases when connected. In the AWS Console, it can answer architecture questions, recommend instance types, troubleshoot configuration and network issues, and even help analyze costs across services.
- Amazon Q Business is an enterprise knowledge and workflow assistant that connects to a wide range of systems, wikis, intranets, file shares, ticketing systems, CRMs, email, and more, to provide unified search, summarization, and task automation from a single chat interface. Amazon Q Business primarily operates on **indexed unstructured content** via built-in connectors, while structured data access, such as Amazon Redshift, requires **specific connector configuration** and has inherent limitations compared to direct SQL querying.

It is worth noting that **Amazon Q Developer relies on Amazon's proprietary coding models** rather than directly exposing Bedrock foundation models, whereas Q Business more directly leverages the Bedrock generative AI platform for knowledge retrieval and summarization.

Q presence in an AWS architecture

Amazon Q is a managed assistant, not a standalone app. It connects to your AWS accounts and enterprise systems via secure connectors, IAM, and AWS Console configuration. Q serves the following from a solution architecture perspective:

- A developer-side companion that reduces friction when building and operating workloads on AWS by embedding guidance directly into the Console, CLI, and IDE and automating routine cloud management tasks.
- A business-side assistant that sits in front of your internal data stores and SaaS systems, using connectors to index content and then answer questions, summarize, or take actions across those systems.

Data from connected systems like Confluence, SharePoint, S3, Jira, ServiceNow, and Salesforce is indexed so Q can retrieve relevant information when prompted, following a retrieval-augmented generation pattern. It is to be noted that Q Business connectors sync on a scheduled basis and not in real time. Q interprets user intent using generative models, searches indexed sources (including AWS documentation and account context for developers), and synthesizes answers that may include links, code snippets, or suggested actions.

For automation, Q can be granted permissions to perform actions in integrated applications, such as creating or updating tickets, posting comments, triggering pipelines, or making AWS changes within defined IAM policies. This enables Q to orchestrate many routine tasks that would otherwise require switching between consoles and tools.

Example of Q Developer in cloud workflow

Imagine a team building and operating a microservices application on AWS. Amazon Q Developer can streamline both development and operations:

- **Design and implementation assistance:**
  - In the AWS Console, an engineer can ask, *What is the simplest and highly available architecture for this API behind API Gateway and Lambda?* Q then suggests patterns, explains trade-offs, and links to relevant AWS reference architectures.
  - In the IDE, developers can ask Q to generate boilerplate code for Lambda functions, infrastructure templates, or tests, or to explain unfamiliar inherited code.
- **Troubleshooting and optimization:**
  - When an application experiences latency spikes, engineers can ask Q in the Console, *Why is XXX service down?* Q inspects CloudWatch metrics, configurations, and common bottlenecks to suggest causes and remediation steps.
  - For cost reviews, a DevOps engineer can ask, *Where are my EC2 costs this month, and how can I reduce it?* Q analyzes cost and usage data and suggests right-sizing or architectural optimizations.
- **Actionable automation:**
  - With proper permissions, Q can recommend and execute actions such as creating EC2 test environments, updating autoscaling configurations, or generating cost report dashboards, all controlled by assigned IAM roles.
  - In this scenario, Q does not replace observability tools or IaC; it rides alongside them, making it easier for engineers to query, understand, and safely modify their AWS environments using natural language.

Example of Amazon Q for RAG

Consider a large organization with knowledge spread across tools like Confluence, SharePoint, S3, Salesforce, and internal databases. Amazon Q Business provides a unified assistant layer:

- **Data and connector setup**:
  - The architecture team configures Q Business to connect to core systems (wikis, ticketing, CRM, file shares, S3 buckets) using built-in connectors and defines which repositories and fields it can access.

- Q indexes content and builds a semantic understanding of documents, multimedia, and structured records for seamless search and summarization.

- **Unified question-answering with citations:**
  - A developer can ask, *What are the latest requirements for an XXX API?* Q combines specification documents, Jira tickets, and design notes to provide a unified answer with citations for verification and deeper review.
  - A sales rep might ask, *Summarize my last three opportunities with customer ABC and compose a follow-up email.* Q uses CRM records and emails to generate a tailored summary and draft message.

- **Task and workflow automation**:
  - Q can create or update tickets in tools like Jira or ServiceNow (*Open a P4 bug for this issue and link the logs*), update CRM entries, or trigger workflows, reducing context switching for users.
  - Over time, enterprises can define advanced agentic behaviors, so Q not only answers questions but also coordinates multi-step workflows, such as onboarding new employees or executing standard incident-response playbooks across systems.
  - From a solution architecture standpoint, Q Business is an opinionated implementation of the *enterprise RAG and agent* pattern, where AWS handles the heavy lifting of connectors, indexing, model orchestration, and security.

Designing with security, privacy, and governance in mind

Since Amazon Q accesses many systems and can perform actions on your behalf in some configurations, security and governance are key design priorities. Q uses AWS IAM and per-connector settings to ensure it only accesses data and performs actions permitted to users. For Q Business, access control mirrors existing user permissions, preventing unauthorized data access. Architects should also consider:

- **Account and environment scoping**: Use separate accounts or organizational units to manage Q's connections and capabilities, aligned with your landing-zone strategy and data-classification policies.

- **Data residency and logging**: Ensure Q's deployment regions comply with regulatory requirements and that all interactions are logged (e.g., CloudTrail, CloudWatch) for audit and incident investigation.

- **Guardrails and review**: Define which connectors and actions are initially enabled, review outputs for critical workflows (e.g., security or financial operations), and gradually expand Q's authority as confidence grows.

With these design patterns, Amazon Q becomes a powerful, governed assistant layer across both AWS and enterprise systems, helping your teams build, operate, and use cloud-native solutions more efficiently while keeping control, security, and architectural standards firmly in your hands.

Use cases of Amazon Q

Use Amazon Q when you want an AI assistant that understands your *own* organization's data and tools, not just general web knowledge. It is a good fit for companies where people spend a lot of time searching across wikis, SharePoint, tickets, code, CRM, and internal docs, or asking the same questions of subjectmatter experts. In that scenario, Amazon Q can sit on top of those systems, respect existing permissions, and answer *What does our policy say about X?*, *How do we deploy service Y?*, or *Summarize these documents for my project* directly in chat form. It is particularly useful for **information technology** (IT), **human resources** (HR), finance, and operations teams that live in different lines-of-business apps but need one place to ask questions and get consistent, cited answers.

Use Amazon Q when you want AI to **take actions**, not just answer questions. Its integrations and plugins enable updating tickets, generating fresh reports from SaaS apps, and drafting emails, **requests for proposals** (RFP), and internal documents based on your systems and data. For engineering teams, the developer-focused version helps them understand legacy code, suggest refactors, and assist with cloud changes. In short, use Amazon Q to boost employee productivity and decision-making across internal systems with an AI that is enterprise-aware, permission-aware, and deeply integrated into your AWS and SaaS environments.

AWS service integration use cases

AWS service integration is most effective when higher-level AI services combine into complete workflows instead of isolated APIs. This section explores how Amazon Textract, Amazon Bedrock, and Amazon Q collaborate to integrate documents, historical metrics, generative AI, and AI assistants across your architecture.

Amazon Textract intelligent document processing as foundation

Amazon Textract serves as the intake layer for processing documents, forms, invoices, contracts, medical records, or applications. Typically, scanned PDFs or images are stored in an S3 bucket, triggering a serverless pipeline (often using Lambda and Step Functions). Textract extracts text, key-value pairs, and tables, producing structured JSON that is normalized into domain entities such as *invoices, claims,* or *applications*.

These entities feed downstream systems such as loan origination platforms, ERPs, claims engines, or data lakes. Integration becomes critical here. Clean, structured fields from Textract, amounts, dates, product lines, and customer IDs serve as inputs for time-series models, search indices, and generative AI layers. Architecturally, Textract acts as the *document edge* of your AI landscape, converting files into data that other services can process and automate.

Amazon Bedrock generative AI as reasoning and interaction layer

Amazon Bedrock offers the generative AI foundation that complements Textract and SageMaker Canvas. After their processing, Bedrock models can explain results, summarize data, or auto-draft responses for users. A typical integrated workflow might look like this:

1. Textract ingests a batch of loan applications, extracting fields and scoring completeness.
2. SageMaker Canvas uses historical approvals, repayments, and macro features to project portfolio-level risk or funding needs.
3. Bedrock powers a generativeAI layer that:
    - Summarizes the key risk factors per application.
    - Draft personalized approval or *need-more-information* messages to applicants.
    - Generates portfolio summaries and scenario analyses for risk officers.

In invoice processing, Textract extracts line items, SageMaker Canvas predicts future spend, and Bedrock generates narrative explanations, variance analyses, and vendor-specific insights for finance teams. This is typically implemented as a backend service that pulls data from document and forecast stores, constructs context-rich prompts, and uses Bedrock to produce human-readable text, recommendations, or reasoning.

Amazon Q bringing AI to builders and business users

Amazon Q operates at a higher level as an assistant, enabling builders and business users to interact with AI-enhanced systems via natural language. While Bedrock provides the generative AI platform, Q is the packaged assistant integrated into IDEs, the AWS Console, and collaboration tools.

For developers and cloud engineers, Q can help design, implement, and operate the Textract/SageMaker Canvas/Bedrock pipelines:

- Proposing reference architectures for intelligent document processing.
- Explaining how to set up eventdriven workflows and error handling around Textract.
- Suggesting datamodeling approaches for SageMaker Canvas and code snippets for integrating Bedrock into microservices.

For business users, Q serves as the *front door* to insights generated by these services:

- A finance analyst can ask, *how our forecasted payables changed this week, and which vendors contribute most to the variance,* and Q can combine SageMaker Canvas outputs with ledger data to respond.
- An operations manager can ask, *show me invoices Textract flagged as low confidence this month and summarize the most common issues,* and Q can query document-processing logs, then use generative capabilities to summarize themes.

In well-designed architectures, Q connects to your data sources (data lake, document repositories, forecast outputs) and operational tools, serving as a conversational interface atop pipelines built with Textract, SageMaker Canvas, and Bedrock.

End-to-end service integration example

In this section, we will see Intelligent Order-to-Cash as an example of end-to-end service integration. To illustrate, consider an *Intelligent Order-to-Cash* system:

- Order capture and contracts:
    - Customer purchase orders and contracts arrive as PDFs and emails.
    - Amazon Textract extracts customer details, order lines, prices, and terms, normalizing them into structured orders in your ERP and data lake.
- Planning and forecasting:
    - Historical orders, lead times, and fulfillment data are aggregated into timeseries datasets.
    - Amazon SageMaker Canvas predicts future order volume and revenue by product and region, which feeds supplychain and staffing plans.
- Insights and automation:

  An internal analytics or *operations copilot* service uses Amazon Bedrock to:
    - Summarize large contract portfolios.
    - Explain demand changes by product.
    - Generate risk and opportunity narratives for leadership reports.
- Human interaction via Amazon Q:
    - Cloud and ops teams use Amazon Q inside the AWS Console to troubleshoot pipeline failures or request architecture changes.
    - Finance and sales users query Q in chat tools for operational questions, getting synthesized answers with links back to underlying systems.

In this integrated design, each service has a distinct role: Textract converts documents into data; SageMaker Canvas transforms data into forward-looking signals; Bedrock converts signals and context into reasoning and narratives; and Amazon Q delivers a conversational, action-oriented experience for users. This exemplifies advanced AWS AI service integration, treating each managed service as a composable building block within a comprehensive, end-to-end intelligent system.

Conclusion

Together, these services demonstrate how AWS makes AI a practical component of everyday architecture. Amazon Textract enables systems to *read* documents, converting PDFs and forms into clean, structured data for automation and analytics. Amazon SageMaker Canvas analyzes historical time-series data to provide forward-looking predictions that improve capacity, inventory, and staffing planning. Amazon Bedrock offers a generative AI foundation with secure access to powerful models for summarization, content generation, and intelligent search. Amazon Q acts as an AI assistant atop your business data and tools. Combined, they form a toolkit that integrates documents, predictions, generative experiences, and enterprise search into smarter, more adaptive, and user-friendly architectures.

The next chapter shifts from using ready-made AI services to building custom machine learning capabilities tailored to your business needs. You will learn how Amazon SageMaker Pipelines Design transforms data preparation, training, tuning, and validation into repeatable, automated workflows that teams can trust and evolve. We will explore RAG architecture and Vector Search Integration, demonstrating how to combine large language models with your data via vector databases and retrieval systems to ensure accurate, context-grounded answers. Finally, deploying and scaling models with SageMaker endpoints will guide you through moving trained models from notebooks to production, including autoscaling inference endpoints, A/B testing, canary rollouts, and monitoring, making ML a reliable service in your architecture rather than a fragile experiment.

References

1. **https://aws.amazon.com/blogs/machine-learning/improve-data-extraction-and-document-processing-with-amazon-textract/**
2. **https://aws.amazon.com/ai/generative-ai/use-cases/document-processing/**
3. **https://aws.amazon.com/blogs/machine-learning/create-a-document-lake-using-large-scale-text-extraction-from-documents-with-amazon-textract/**
4. **https://aws.amazon.com/blogs/architecture/amazon-bedrock-baseline-architecture-in-an-aws-landing-zone/**
5. **https://aws.amazon.com/video/watch/5e4470d1b90/**

6. **https://docs.aws.amazon.com/amazonq/latest/qdeveloper-ug/what-is.html**
7. **https://aws.amazon.com/video/watch/19ae78412a5/**
8. **https://aws.amazon.com/q/**
9. **https://aws.amazon.com/blogs/machine-learning/build-generative-ai-solutions-with-amazon-bedrock/**
10. **https://aws.amazon.com/blogs/machine-learning/orchestrate-generative-ai-workflows-with-amazon-bedrock-and-aws-step-functions/**
11. **https://aws.amazon.com/bedrock/**
12. **https://aws.amazon.com/blogs/machine-learning/streamline-workflow-orchestration-of-a-system-of-enterprise-apis-using-chaining-with-amazon-bedrock-agents/**
13. **https://docs.aws.amazon.com/prescriptive-guidance/latest/forecast-demand-new-product/architecture.html**
14. **https://docs.aws.amazon.com/textract/latest/dg/how-it-works-analyzing.html**
15. **https://aws.amazon.com/textract/**
16. **https://aws.amazon.com/ai/generative-ai/use-cases/document-processing/**
17. **https://aws.amazon.com/blogs/architecture/category/artificial-intelligence/amazon-textract/**
18. **https://docs.aws.amazon.com/textract/latest/dg/how-it-works-tables.html**
19. **https://aws.amazon.com/blogs/machine-learning/build-a-receipt-and-invoice-processing-pipeline-with-amazon-textract/**

CHAPTER 10
Designing and Deploying AI Applications on AWS

Introduction

In this part of the book, we move from using **artificial intelligence** (**AI**) services to actually operationalizing your own machine learning on AWS. Amazon SageMaker **Machine Learning** (**ML**) Pipelines Design gives you a way to treat ML work as an engineered process instead of a collection of ad hoc notebooks. You define steps for data preparation, feature engineering, training, evaluation, and approval as a pipeline, so every new model run follows the same path with versioning, lineage, and automation built in. That means experiments are easier to reproduce, models are easier to audit, and collaboration between data scientists and engineers becomes much smoother.

On top of that foundation, we explore how to build modern, intelligent applications with **retrieval-augmented generation** (**RAG**) architecture and Vector Search Integration, using large language models alongside your own data so responses are grounded in reality, not just a model's internal knowledge. You will see how vector stores, embeddings, and retrieval steps fit into an AWS design and how to wire all of this into production using SageMaker Endpoints. Deploying and scaling models with SageMaker endpoints will show you how to expose models as managed, autoscaling **application programming interfaces** (**APIs**), roll out new versions safely, and monitor realworld behavior, so ML becomes a reliable, observable component of your architecture rather than an experimental sidecar.

Structure

In this chapter, we will discuss the following topics:

- Amazon SageMaker ML pipelines design
- RAG architecture and Vector Search Integration
- Deploying and scaling models with SageMaker endpoints

Objectives

In this section, the goal is to show you how to treat machine learning as a firstclass, engineered part of your **Amazon Web Services** (**AWS**) architecture, rather than as a collection of isolated experiments. With **Amazon SageMaker** ML Pipelines Design, you will learn how to break down the ML lifecycle into clear, repeatable steps, data preparation, feature engineering, training, evaluation, and approval, and then automate those steps so every new model follows the same path. The objective is to make your pipelines reproducible, auditable, and easy to integrate with the rest of your **continuous integration/continuous delivery** (**CI/CD**) processes, so models can move from idea to production in a controlled way.

You will also learn how to design applications that combine powerful language models with your own data using RAG architecture and Vector Search Integration, and then serve those models reliably with SageMaker endpoints. The aim is to give you practical patterns for storing embeddings, retrieving relevant context, and feeding that into your models, as well as strategies for deploying and scaling endpoints, handling autoscaling, versioning, canary rollouts, and monitoring. By the end of this chapter, you should be able to design ML systems that are robust, observable, and aligned with the same architectural principles you already use for the rest of your AWS workloads.

Amazon SageMaker ML pipelines design

Amazon SageMaker Pipelines transform ML projects into repeatable, production-grade pipelines instead of one-off notebooks. It enables defining end-to-end ML workflows as code, including data preparation, training, evaluation, conditional approvals, registration, and batch or real-time deployment. It also tracks lineage and integrates with the SageMaker platform. For AWS Solutions Architects, Pipelines are the core of ML CI/CD: design once, parameterize, and reliably trigger across development, staging, and production.

SageMaker Pipelines is built around a small set of core ideas:

- **Pipelines**: A pipeline is an ordered graph of steps with defined dependencies.
- **Steps**: Each step represents a unit of work or task, ProcessingStep, TrainingStep, TransformStep, ConditionStep, RegisterModel, LambdaStep, and others.
- **Parameters**: Runtime inputs like S3 path, instance types, environment, or approval flags that enable the same pipeline definition to run across multiple environments.
- **PipelineSession**: A context linking steps to SageMaker resources and supporting lazy evaluation; execution begins only when the pipeline starts.
- **Integration with experiments and Model Registry**: Pipeline runs can automatically create experiment trials and register trained models for later deployment and governance.

This structure provides a consistent method for orchestrating SageMaker jobs, tracking artifacts, and embedding decision logic, such as registering or deploying only when metrics meet thresholds.

Typical pipeline design and detailed steps

A typical SageMaker Pipeline for supervised learning follows this pattern:

preprocess | train | evaluate | condition | register | deploy | batch transform(optional)

The detailed steps are as follows:

1. **Define pipeline parameters**: You start by declaring parameters for anything likely to vary:
   - S3 Path for input and batch data.
   - Instance types and counts for processing, training, and inference.
   - Model approval status (for example, *PendingManualApproval* vs. *Approved*).
   - Training hyperparameters or flags for specific behaviors.

   These parameters enable reusing the same pipeline definition across environments by changing values at runtime.
2. **Data preprocessing (ProcessingStep)**: Use a ProcessingStep backed by a SageMaker Processing job (for example, SKLearnProcessor or ScriptProcessor) to:
   a. Read raw data from S3.
   b. Clean and join datasets, handle missing values and null values, and engineer features.
   c. Split into train/validation/test data sets and write them back to S3.

   Outputs from this step become pipeline artifacts referenced by later steps (for example, step_process.properties.ProcessingOutputConfig[...]).
3. **Model training (TrainingStep)**: Define an Estimator (built-in algorithm or framework container) and create a TrainingStep that:
   a. Use the processed training and validation data from the previous step.
   b. Use parameterized hyperparameters and resource settings.
   c. When the pipeline runs, SageMaker launches training jobs on demand, saves model artifacts to S3, and exposes ModelArtifacts.S3ModelArtifacts to downstream steps.
4. **Model evaluation (ProcessingStep)**: Create another ProcessingStep to run an evaluation script that:
   - Loads the trained model artifacts.

- Scores the validation or test dataset.
- Compute metrics such as accuracy, F1, **root mean squared error** (**RMSE**), or **area under the curve** (**AUC**).

  This step writes metrics to an evaluation report (e.g., JSON file) on S3. Its properties, such as metric values, are used later in conditional logic.

5. **Conditional step for quality gates (ConditionStep)**: Use a ConditionStep to implement quality gates:
   a. Read a metric from the evaluation output. Metrics generated in a ProcessingStep are accessed in a ConditionStep using JsonGet property files. The evaluation script must write metrics to a JSON file in S3. The pipeline then uses JsonGet to parse this file and extract specific values for threshold comparison, instead of reading directly from ProcessingOutputConfig.
   b. Apply conditions (lessthan or greaterthan thresholds).
   c. If the model meets criteria, run the *happy path* steps (register, create model, transform). Otherwise, skip registration and deployment, ending the run.
6. **Model registration (RegisterModel):** Inside the if_steps branch of the ConditionStep, add a RegisterModel step to:
   a. Register the trained model with the SageMaker Model Registry.
   b. Attach metadata such as model package group name, approval status (for example, PendingManualApproval), and metrics.

   This creates versioned model packages that downstream CI/CD systems (such as SageMaker Projects or external pipelines) can promote to staging or production.
7. **Create model and batch transform (CreateModelStep and TransformStep)**:
   a. Optionally, define a CreateModelStep to construct a SageMaker model object from the trained artifacts and container image.
   b. Then define a TransformStep that uses a Transformer configured with the model name and S3 input/output locations to run Batch Transform for offline scoring.

      These steps run under the ConditionStep and execute only if the model meets quality criteria.
8. **Realtime deployment (optional): Realtime deployment is often handled by a separate** CI/CD pipeline, but you can include a LambdaStep that, on successful registration, triggers an external deployment workflow (for example, via CodePipeline, Step Functions, or an internal API).
9. Create and run the pipeline:
   a. Finally, instantiate the Pipeline with:

- A unique name.
- The list of parameters.
- The ordered list of steps [step_process, step_train, step_eval, step_cond] (with conditional branches containing registration and transform).

b. You then upsert and start pipeline runs from Studio, the SDK, or CI/CD, supplying parameter values as needed.

This design delivers a robust, repeatable ML workflow with explicit dependencies and quality gates.

Example of architecture of CI/CD for tabular ML model

In this section, we will see the steps involved as an example of the architecture of CI/CD for a tabular ML model.

A practical workflow using SageMaker Pipelines for a tabular model might look like this:

1. **Trigger**: A CodePipeline or EventBridge rule triggers the SageMaker Pipeline when new training data arrives in S3 or when code changes are merged.
2. **Pipeline run**: The pipeline executes the steps described above: processing, training, evaluation, condition, registration, and optional batch transform.
3. **Model Registry and approval**:
   - At the end of the run, a new model package version appears in Model Registry with metrics and *PendingManualApproval* status.
   - A human reviewer reviews metrics and metadata, then changes the status to *Approved*, triggering a downstream deployment pipeline.
4. **Deployment**: A deployment pipeline (often another SageMaker Project or CodePipeline) detects the approved package and:
   - Deploys it to a staging endpoint.
   - Runs smoke tests and load tests.
   - Promotes to production endpoint with blue/green or canary strategy.
5. **Monitoring and feedback**:
   - Model Monitor jobs detect data drift and performance degradation, publishing metrics to CloudWatch.
   - If issues are detected, the system can automatically trigger a new pipeline run with fresh data.

This integration connects Pipelines with Model Registry, deployment tools, and monitoring for comprehensive ML lifecycle management.

Best practices for SageMaker pipeline design

In this section, we will see the best practices for SageMaker pipeline design. Several design patterns and best practices enhance reliability, security, and usability:

- **Design for reusability and parameterization**:
  - Use pipeline parameters for all environment-specific settings (S3 paths, instance types, **Virtual Private Cloud** (**VPC**) settings, approval flags instead of hard-coding.
  - Keep your pipeline definition generic and environment-agnostic; let CI/CD or environment config supply parameter values.
- **Use PipelineSession and local mode during development**:
  - Define pipelines using PipelineSession to enable lazy loading and ensure consistent interactions with SageMaker resources.
  - Use LocalPipelineSession for fast, cost-effective testing of pipeline code on small subsets of data before running at scale.
- **Integrate with experiments and lineage**:
  - Configure PipelineExperimentConfig to link each pipeline run to a SageMaker Experiment and trial, aiding metric tracking, artifact management, and run comparisons over time.
  - Use built-in lineage tracking to identify which code, data, and parameters produced specific model versions, supporting audit and reproducibility.
- **Version pipelines and manage changes**:
  - Use naming patterns or tags (such as timestamps or Git commit hashes) to version pipeline definitions, especially during rapid iteration.
  - Manage pipeline definitions as code in a repository, reviewed via pull requests and promoted through environments using infrastructure as code and CI/CD.
- **Secure pipelines in a private VPC**:
  - Run processing, training, and transform jobs in private subnets with VPC endpoints for S3 and required services instead of over the public internet.
  - Enforce network isolation where appropriate, especially for sensitive or regulated data, and restrict the pipeline execution role via least-privilege IAM policies.
- **Keep steps focused and modular**:
  - Each step should focus on a single task (preprocess, train, evaluate, register). Avoid overloading steps with multiple responsibilities to simplify debugging and reuse.

  - For complex workflows or branching scenarios, consider splitting into multiple pipelines triggered from a LambdaStep or external orchestrator (Step Functions) rather than forcing everything into a single, deeply nested pipeline graph.
- **Build robust quality gates and fail-fast behavior**:
  - Use ConditionStep to enforce metric thresholds and prevent auto-promotion of poor models.
  - Emit clear failure reasons in evaluation outputs and logs, so teams can quickly diagnose why a run did not pass.
- **Align pipelines with MLOps and CI/CD**:
  - Integrate SageMaker Pipelines with SageMaker Projects or external CI/CD systems to manage triggers, environment promotion, and deployment approvals.
  - Use events (such as pipeline state changes) to connect with notification systems or ticketing tools when runs succeed or fail.

Applying these patterns makes *Amazon SageMaker ML Pipelines Design* less about individual jobs and more about a repeatable, opinionated process to move models from data to production. The pipeline definition serves as a living contract among data scientists, engineers, and operators, codifying how models are built, evaluated, and deployed within the AWS architecture.

RAG architecture and Vector Search Integration

RAG combines a large language model with live data from your systems to ensure responses are grounded in reality rather than relying solely on pretraining. On AWS, RAG typically pairs foundation models (for example, via Amazon Bedrock) with a vector search layer like Amazon OpenSearch Service, Amazon S3 Vector, or Aurora PostgreSQL with pgvector. A fully managed Amazon Bedrock Knowledge Base leverages these storage and indexing services to provide an abstraction layer that streamlines ingestion, embedding, and retrieval workflows. A RAG system has two distinct phases: an offline ingestion/indexing pipeline and a runtime query pipeline.

During the ingestion phase, you:

- Collect documents or records from S3, databases, wikis, CRMs, and so on.
- Normalize them to text, split them into *chunks,* generate vector embeddings, and store those vectors plus metadata in a vector index.

During the runtime phase, you:

- Convert the user's question into the embedding (similar to the embedding above).
- Use vector search to retrieve the most similar chunks.

- Augment the LLM prompt with those chunks and let the model generate an answer grounded in that context.

On AWS, you can implement this in several ways:

- **Fully managed**: Amazon Q Business or Bedrock knowledge bases manage ingestion, chunking, embeddings, and vector storage for you.
- **Semi-managed**: Bedrock knowledge bases with your own OpenSearch vector cluster as the store.
- **Custom**: You own all ingestion and retrieval logic using OpenSearch, Aurora pgvector, MemoryDB, Neptune Analytics, or S3 Vector.

Detailed ingestion and indexing pipeline

This section assumes a custom or semi-custom design using Bedrock embeddings with OpenSearch or another AWS vector store. The same steps apply if Bedrock knowledge bases manage them. The steps involved in the ingestion and indexing pipeline are as follows:

1. **Source data discovery and selection**:
    a. Identify which systems contain the truth you want the model to use: S3 document buckets, Confluence/SharePoint exports, database tables, logs, knowledge articles.
    b. Filter for stable, high-quality content. Avoid adding raw, noisy logs to the RAG index unless strong filtering is in place.
2. **Document ingestion and normalization**:
    - For unstructured content (PDF, **Document** (**DOCX**), **Hyper Text Markup Language** (**HTML**)), use existing pipelines such as Amazon Textract or HTML extraction to convert it to clean text.
    - Normalize encodings, remove boilerplate, and attach metadata like source system, document type, creation/update time, tenant, and access labels.
3. **Chunking strategy**: Split documents into chunks, sections of text that the model can process. AWS guidance recommends manageable chunk sizes and preserving links to the source document. Common patterns are:
    - Fixed-size chunks (for example, 500–1,000 tokens) with overlap to maintain context.
    - Semantic or structural chunks based on headings, paragraphs, or table boundaries to improve coherence.
4. **Embedding generation**:
    - Use an embedding model (for example, a Bedrock embedding FM) to convert each chunk into a high-dimensional vector representing its meaning.

- In a Bedrock knowledge base, this step is fully managed; you configure the embedding model and data source, and Bedrock runs chunking and embedding for you.

5. **Vector index creation and storage**: Select a vector store based on your requirements:
   - **Amazon OpenSearch Service** with kNN/HNSW for general vector search and metadata filtering.
   - **Amazon Aurora PostgreSQL with pgvector** if you want vectors alongside transactional data.
   - **Amazon S3 Vector** for a serverless, lowcost index over S3 objects (check current regional availability). It is worth noting for production RAG at scale that OpenSearch and Aurora pgvector have significantly more operational history and documented performance benchmarks.
   - **MemoryDB or Neptune Analytics** for low-latency or graph-plus-vector use cases.

   For OpenSearch, create a kNN index including fields for:
     - Embedding vector.
     - Text chunk.
     - Metadata (document ID, source, tenant, **access control list** (**ACL**) labels).
6. **Metadata and security tagging:**
   - Store access control and tenancy information in metadata fields to enable filtering by tenant or role before similarity search, especially in multi-tenant designs.
   - For multi-tenant RAG with OpenSearch, AWS guidance recommends metadata filtering on tenant and domain, plus IAM or fine-grained access control on the index.
7. **Incremental sync and reindexing**:
   - Implement ongoing sync jobs (for example, scheduled Lambda or Step Functions) to detect new, changed, or deleted documents and update the vector index accordingly.
   - If you use Bedrock knowledge bases, *steps 3-7* are largely handled for you: you connect the data source (for example, S3 or OpenSearch), and Bedrock manages chunking, embeddings, and index updates.

Detailed runtime RAG pipeline

At query time, the system moves through a repeatable sequence. The steps involved at runtime in the RAG pipeline are as follows:

1. **User query intake**: A client (web UI, API, chat widget, agent) sends a natural-language question plus context (user ID, tenant ID, conversation history) to your backend.

2. **Query understanding and enrichment (optional)**: Optionally, a Bedrock model or rule layer rewrites or classifies the query, such as expanding acronyms or inferring relevant products or domains.
3. **Query embedding**: Use the same embedding model you used at ingestion to convert the query into a vector.
4. **Vector search with metadata filters**:
   - Query the vector index with kNN or a similar algorithm to find the topK semantically similar chunks.
   - Apply filters on tenant, access labels, and document types to ensure users see only authorized content within the correct domain.
5. **Context selection and prompt construction**: Select the most relevant chunks (for example, top 5 to 10) and build a prompt including:
   - System and task instructions.
   - The user's question.
   - Retrieved chunks formatted clearly (for example, as *Context 1… Context 2…*).
6. **LLM call and answer generation**:
   - Call your chosen generator (for example, an FM on Bedrock) with the augmented prompt.
   - The model generates an answer grounded in the provided context. Optionally, it includes references or IDs for the chunks used.
7. **Postprocessing and safety checks**:
   - Apply guardrails or moderation to enforce permitted topics, tone, and redaction policies.
   - Optionally, run verification checks such as asking the model to answer *based only on the context* or performing a second pass to detect hallucinations.
8. **Response and telemetry**:
   - Return the answer along with citations linking back to the original documents.
   - Log queries, retrieved documents, and model output (with redaction as needed) for observability and offline evaluation.

With Bedrock knowledge bases, steps 3 to 6 are mostly managed via API: Bedrock embeds the query, performs vector search on your configured store, augments the prompt, and calls the FM.

Example of workflow for RAG with Bedrock

AWS provides a common reference pattern for RAG that integrates Bedrock knowledge bases with Amazon OpenSearch Service. The steps involved in the workflow for RAG with the Bedrock knowledge base with Amazon OpenSearch are as follows:

- **Vector store setup**:
  - o Create an OpenSearch Service domain with kNN enabled and fine-grained access control.
  - o Configure a vector index with fields for embedding, text chunk, and metadata, including tenant and document IDs.
- **Knowledge base configuration**:
  - o In Bedrock, create a knowledge base, point it at an S3 bucket with your documents, and choose OpenSearch as the vector store backend.
  - o Bedrock automatically handles chunking, embedding, and indexing vectors in OpenSearch.
- **Runtime flow**:
  - o A user's question is received by an API or a Bedrock agent.
  - o Bedrock knowledge base:
    - ▪ Embeds the query with a Bedrock embedding model.
    - ▪ Queries OpenSearch for top-K similar chunks, optionally applying metadata filters for tenant or domain.
    - ▪ Builds an augmented prompt with those chunks as context.
    - ▪ Calls a chosen Bedrock FM to generate the answer.
  - o The response is returned to the caller, often with references such as source URLs or document titles.
- **Multitenant extension**: For multi-tenant **software as a service** (**SaaS**), AWS recommends storing tenant and index metadata in DynamoDB, then using these attributes to route vector queries to the correct OpenSearch index or collection and filter results by tenant ID.

This design provides a managed RAG flow while allowing control over OpenSearch topology, security, and performance.

Best practices for RAG and vector search on AWS

The following are the best practices for RAG and vector search on AWS. AWS prescriptive guidance and Bedrock documentation highlight best practices worth incorporating into solution designs:

- **Choose the right RAG option for your needs**:
  - Choose Amazon Q Business for a turnkey enterprise assistant across multiple data sources.
  - Use Bedrock knowledge bases for managed RAG when you want to select your foundation model or vector store.
  - Build a custom RAG when you require full control over chunking, retrieval, latency, or vector database choice (OpenSearch, Aurora pgvector, S3 Vector, etc.).
- **Design chunking and embeddings carefully**:
  - Keep chunks small enough to include multiple in your prompt but large enough to maintain local context.
  - Use overlapping chunks to avoid splitting critical information across boundaries.
  - Use the same embedding model for indexing and querying; changing models requires re-embedding your corpus.
- **Use metadata filtering and hybrid search**:
  - Always store metadata fields such as tenant, document type, recency, and access labels to filter candidates before similarity search.
  - Consider hybrid retrieval (vector plus keyword) when precise term matching matters, such as identifiers or API names.
- **Secure the vector store and RAG endpoints**:
  - Restrict vector index access using IAM, VPC, and, for OpenSearch, fine-grained access control.
  - Enforce tenant isolation via separate indexes or collections per tenant, or strict metadata filters and permission checks.
  - Encrypt data at rest and in transit across all RAG components, including S3, OpenSearch, and Aurora.
- **Implement evaluation and feedback loops**:
  - Use offline test sets and human evaluation to measure retrieval quality and answer quality (relevance, faithfulness).
  - Log queries, retrieved chunks, and answers, and sample regularly for manual review and labeling.
  - Iterate on chunking, embeddings, and prompt templates based on evaluation results.
- **Control hallucinations and enforce grounding**:
  - Structure prompts to instruct the model to answer only using the provided context and to respond `I do not know` when context is insufficient.

    - Use guardrails and content filters, such as via Bedrock, to block disallowed topics and prevent sensitive data leakage.
    - Consider secondary checks: ask the model to justify which context segments support its answer, or run a *factchecking* pass that crosschecks statements against retrieved chunks.
- **Optimize cost and performance**:
    - Use serverless or managed vector options like S3 Vector or OpenSearch Serverless when appropriate to avoid overprovisioning.
    - Cache frequent query results at the application layer to reduce repeated vector searches and foundation model calls.
    - Adjust index parameters, such as HNSW settings in OpenSearch, to balance recall and latency according to your SLAs.

Designing *RAG architecture and Vector Search Integration* this way creates a layered AWS environment: durable data sources at the base; vector search and retrieval in the middle; and foundation models and assistants at the top that use retrieved context to produce grounded, auditable answers integrated into your existing solutions.

Deploying and scaling models with SageMaker endpoints

Deploying and scaling models with SageMaker endpoints involves making trained model artifacts available for real-time or batch inference at production scale. SageMaker Hosting offers three options: real-time endpoints for low-latency predictions, serverless inference for spiky workloads, and batch transform for offline scoring of large datasets. AWS Solutions Architects focus on designing endpoints that balance latency, throughput, cost, and resilience while integrating with the broader application architecture.

SageMaker offers three inference options:

- **Realtime endpoints**: Provisioned instances that host one or more models and serve predictions over HTTPS. Supports **multimodel endpoints** (**MMEs**) for hosting dozens of models on a single fleet.
- **Serverless inference**: Fully managed, autoscaling compute that scales to zero when idle; ideal for sporadic or unpredictable workloads. While serverless inference eliminates idle costs by scaling to zero, architects must consider cold start latency, which can range from milliseconds to several seconds for large models. This variability makes serverless inference unsuitable for latency-sensitive production workloads that require consistent response times.
- **Batch transform**: On-demand jobs that process entire datasets from S3 and write predictions back to S3; no persistent endpoint needed.

Most architectures combine options: real-time for interactive apps, batch transform for ETL and analytics, and serverless for experimental or edge workloads.

Detailed deployment pipeline

A typical end-to-end pipeline for deploying a model to a real-time endpoint includes:

1. **Model preparation and registration**:
   a. Register your trained model in SageMaker Model Registry with metadata such as accuracy metrics, lineage, and a model card.
   b. Use the RegisterModel step in SageMaker Pipelines to create a model package version with an approval status. In newer SDK patterns, model creation and registration can also be handled together (for example, via ModelStep or related abstractions), but the exact approach depends on the SageMaker SDK version and pipeline design.
2. **Run inference recommender**:
   a. Use SageMaker Inference Recommender to benchmark your model against multiple instance types (CPU, GPU, Inferentia, Trainium) and configurations.
   b. Provide a sample payload (S3 URL with representative inputs) and optionally specify supported instance types. Inference Recommender runs load tests and recommends the optimal configuration for your latency and throughput requirements.

   Output: A report with metrics (latency percentiles, throughput, cost) and recommended instance types (for example, ml.c5.2xlarge or ml.g5.xlarge).
3. **Create a SageMaker model object**: Use the CreateModel API or CreateModelStep with the following:
   - Model artifacts (S3 **Uniform Resource Identifier** (**URI**) from training).
   - Container image (built-in algorithm, framework image, or custom Docker).
   - Environment variables (for example, model cache size, batching settings).

   For multi-model endpoints, the model object is one of many stored in S3 that the endpoint loads on demand.
4. **Deploy to endpoint**:
   a. **Create endpoint configuration** by specifying production variants, instance types, initial instance count, and optional multi-model settings:

```
json
{
  "ProductionVariants": [
    {
```

```
      "VariantName": "Prod",
      "ModelName": "my-model",
      "InitialInstanceCount": 2,
      "InstanceType": "ml.c5.xlarge"
    }
  ]
}
```

   b. **Create endpoint**: Create an endpoint by pointing it to the endpoint configuration. SageMaker provisions instances, downloads model artifacts, and reports status.

   c. **Traffic routing**: For blue/green deployments, use a production variant with a percentage split to gradually shift traffic from old to new models.

5. **Configure autoscaling**:

   a. Register the endpoint variant with the Application Auto Scaling service.

   b. Use the **`SageMakerVariantInvocationsPerInstance`** predefined metric (recommended for multimodel endpoints):

```
json
{
  "TargetValue": 65.0,  // invocations per instance per minute
  "PredefinedMetricSpecification": {
    "PredefinedMetricType": "SageMakerVariantInvocationsPerInstance"
  }
}
```

   Note: **A `TargetValue` of 65.0 is just an example; the correct `TargetValue` depends heavily on model inference latency, instance type, and payload size.**

   c. Use custom metrics such as CPU/GPU utilization and queue length for specialized workloads. Set cooldowns for scale-in and scale-out (e.g., 5 minutes for scale-out, 10 minutes for scale-in).

   For multimodel endpoints, scaling is based on aggregate load across all models.

6. **Invoke the endpoint**:

   - Send inference requests via **`InvokeEndpoint`** with JSON payloads.
   - SageMaker supports streaming for long responses (LLMs) and multi-record batching to improve throughput.

7. **Monitor and optimize**:

   - **CloudWatch metrics**: **`InvocationsPerInstance`**, latency percentiles, model loading time (for MMEs).

- SageMaker Model Monitor for data quality, bias, and drift detection.
- Inference Recommender's Load Test job type to validate scaling under production-like load.

Example of deploying a fraud detection model

Here is a concrete pipeline for deploying a tabular fraud model from Model Registry to a production endpoint:

- **Trigger**: CodePipeline detects a new *Approved* model package in the Model Registry.
- **Inference recommender**: Runs a default job on the model package ARN using sample transaction payloads and recommends ml.c5.2 times larger for low latency and high throughput.
- **Create model**: Register the model with the recommended container and optimized environment variables (e.g., batch size).
- **Endpoint configuration**: Define production variants for v1 (current) and v2 (new), with initial traffic set to 100% v1 and 0% v2; configure autoscaling (min 1, max 10, target `InvocationsPerInstance = 100`).
- **Deploy**: Update the endpoint to add v2 alongside v1 without shifting traffic initially (blue/green or canary setup).
- **Traffic shifting**: Gradually shift traffic from v1 to v2 (for example, 10% → 50% → 100%) while monitoring latency and error rates.
- **Validation**: Load tests and live metrics confirm p95 latency below 100 ms at target throughput.
- **Go live**: Route 100% traffic to v2 and optionally decommission v1; the endpoint serves production traffic via API Gateway or direct client calls.

Best practices for SageMaker endpoints

Best practices for Amazon SageMaker AI endpoints focus on optimizing for performance, cost, and security to ensure production-grade inference. The best practices for SageMaker endpoints are as follows:

- **Always run the inference recommender first**: It eliminates guesswork on instance types. Test with realistic payloads and traffic patterns.
- Use **multi-model endpoints (MMEs)** to support model diversity:
    - Host tens to hundreds of models on a single fleet, loading them into memory on demand. This is ideal for A/B testing, personalization, or microservices with many small models.

  - Monitor model-loading latency and cache frequently used models using `ModelCacheSetting`.
- **Configure intelligent autoscaling**:
  - Use `InvocationsPerInstance` for most cases; it normalizes for instance size and model complexity.
  - Set a conservative initial capacity and let autoscaling handle spikes. Load testing with Inference Recommender is strongly recommended to determine the appropriate `TargetValue`.
  - Enable warm pools to reduce cold-start latency during scale-out. It is also worth noting that maintaining warm instances increases costs even when idle. Warm pools are not available for all instance types, so verify compatibility and include these costs in your endpoint budget before enabling this feature.
- **Design for resilience**:
  - Deploy across two or more Availability Zones with a minimum of two instances.
  - Use blue/green traffic shifting to enable zero-downtime deployments.
  - Implement retry logic with exponential backoff in client applications.
- **Optimize inference performance**:
  - **Container optimization**: Use optimized frameworks such as Triton and Deep Learning Containers, enable batching, and tune payload size.
  - **Instance selection**: Match compute type to model, ml.c5 and ml.m5 for CPU, ml.g4dn and ml.g5 for GPU, ml.inf1 and ml.trn1 for Inferentia and Trainium.
  - **Use serverless inference**: For workloads with unpredictable or sporadic demand where cost efficiency matters. This works fine for applications that can tolerate occasional latency spikes from cold starts, rather than those requiring consistently low latency.
- **Security and networking**:
  - Deploy endpoints in a private VPC with VPC endpoints for S3 and model artifacts.
  - Use IAM authentication or API Gateway with Cognito to secure production traffic.
  - Data encryption in transit with TLS 1.2+ and at rest using KMS.
- **Cost optimization**:
  - Use Spot instances for non-critical batch transform jobs.
  - Multi-model endpoints to share infrastructure across models.
  - Scale to zero using serverless inference or scheduled shutdowns for development endpoints.
  - Monitor costs using Cost Explorer and Inference Recommender's cost metrics.

- **Monitoring and observability**:
  - o Enable Model Monitor to detect input/output drift and bias.
  - o Use CloudWatch dashboards to track `InvocationsPerInstance`, latency, and error rates.
  - o Use CloudWatch Logs and X-Ray to debug cold starts and model loading.

Following these patterns makes deploying and scaling models with SageMaker endpoints a repeatable process integrated into your CI/CD pipeline. Endpoints become observable, scalable components of your production architecture, ready to serve predictions reliably at any scale.

Conclusion

This chapter showed how to treat machine learning as a well-engineered part of AWS architectures rather than a loose collection of notebooks and ad hoc scripts. Amazon SageMaker ML Pipelines Design breaks the ML lifecycle into clear, automated steps: data preparation, training, evaluation, and approval, ensuring every model follows a consistent, auditable path. We explored how RAG architecture and Vector Search Integration connect powerful language models with your data, retrieving relevant context through vector search so responses are grounded in real business knowledge rather than generic model memory.

Finally, we covered deploying and scaling models with SageMaker endpoints, turning trained models into managed, autoscaling APIs that can be versioned, rolled out safely, and monitored like any other production service. Together, these components provide a practical blueprint for building ML-powered systems that are reliable, observable, and easy to evolve over time.

In the next chapter, we will take the machine learning capabilities we have built and make them truly productionready by surrounding them with robust operational practices. You will learn how to automate model deployment with CI/CD pipelines, treating models like any other code artifact that moves through testing, approval, and rollout stages. We will explore integrating generative AI using Amazon Bedrock to add powerful foundation models to your workflows with enterprisegrade security and customization, alongside using Serverless for AI workflow orchestration to coordinate complex inference pipelines without managing servers. Finally, we will cover monitoring and maintaining AI models to catch drift and performance issues early, plus cost optimization strategies for AI applications to keep your intelligent systems efficient at scale. These patterns complete the picture, turning experimental ML into a reliable, costaware architecture that evolves with your business.

References

1. **https://docs.aws.amazon.com/sagemaker/latest/dg/batch-transform.html**
2. **https://docs.aws.amazon.com/sagemaker/latest/dg/endpoint-Auto Scaling.html**

3. **https://docs.aws.amazon.com/sagemaker/latest/dg/inference-recommender.html**
4. **https://docs.aws.amazon.com/sagemaker/latest/dg/multi-model-endpoints-autoscaling.html**
5. **https://docs.aws.amazon.com/sagemaker/latest/dg/deployment-best-practices.html**
6. **https://docs.aws.amazon.com/sagemaker/latest/dg/whatis-features.html**
7. **https://docs.aws.amazon.com/prescriptive-guidance/latest/retrieval-augmented-generation-options/choosing-option.html**
8. **https://docs.aws.amazon.com/prescriptive-guidance/latest/choosing-an-aws-vector-database-for-rag-use-cases/introduction.html**
9. **https://docs.aws.amazon.com/en us/bedrock/latest/userguide/kb-how-it-works.html**
10. **https://aws.amazon.com/blogs/machine-learning/dive-deep-into-vector-data-stores-using-amazon-bedrock-knowledge-bases/**
11. **https://docs.aws.amazon.com/bedrock/latest/userguide/kb-how-it-works.html**
12. **https://aws.amazon.com/bedrock/**
13. **https://aws.amazon.com/blogs/machine-learning/amazon-bedrock-knowledge-bases-now-supports-amazon-opensearch-service-managed-cluster-as-vector-store/**
14. **https://docs.aws.amazon.com/pdfs/prescriptive-guidance/latest/writing-best-practices-rag/writing-best-practices-rag.pdf**
15. **https://aws.amazon.com/blogs/machine-learning/multi-tenant-rag-implementation-with-amazon-bedrock-and-amazon-opensearch-service-for-saas-using-jwt/**
16. **https://aws.amazon.com/q/business/**
17. **https://docs.aws.amazon.com/sagemaker/latest/dg/workflows.html**
18. **https://docs.aws.amazon.com/sagemaker/latest/dg/define-pipeline.html**
19. **https://docs.aws.amazon.com/sagemaker/latest/dg/build-and-manage-steps.html**
20. **https://aws.amazon.com/blogs/machine-learning/best-practices-and-design-patterns-for-building-machine-learning-workflows-with-amazon-sagemaker-pipelines/**
21. **https://docs.aws.amazon.com/sagemaker/latest/dg/best-practices.html**

CHAPTER 11
Scaling and Automating AI Applications

Introduction

This section covers running **artificial intelligence** (**AI**) and **machine learning** (**ML**) in production on **Amazon Web Services** (**AWS**) like any other critical workload. Automating model deployment with **continuous integration** (**CI**)/**continuous deployment** (**CD**) pipelines treats models like application code: changes are tested, reviewed, and promoted through controlled, repeatable environments. Rather than manually copying artifacts or using ad hoc scripts, you connect training outputs to pipelines that manage packaging, validation, deployment, and rollback, making new model releases safe and routine instead of risky and one-off.

Next, we explore the integration of modern AI into real systems. Integrating generative AI using Amazon Bedrock explains how to securely access foundation models, customize them with your data, and embed them into applications for tasks such as summarization, content generation, and intelligent search. Using serverless for AI workflow orchestration covers coordinating data preparation, retrieval, model calls, and post-processing without managing servers, enabling scalable, complex workflows on demand. Finally, we address monitoring and maintaining AI models and cost optimization strategies for AI applications, showing how to track model quality and performance, detect drift, and control inference costs to keep AI features reliable and cost-effective.

Structure

In this chapter, we will discuss the following topics:

- Automating model deployment with CI/CD pipelines
- Integrating generative AI using Amazon Bedrock
- Using serverless for AI workflow orchestration

- Monitoring and maintaining AI models
- Cost optimization strategies for AI applications

Objectives

This section shows how to run AI and ML in production with the same discipline applied to your AWS workloads. Automating model deployment with CI/CD pipelines helps you treat models as deployable artifacts: versioned, tested, and promoted through pipelines instead of ad hoc scripts. You will learn what to automate, from packaging and validation to rollout and rollback, so deploying a new model becomes a safe, routine process rather than a risky manual task.

You will also learn how to systematically integrate modern AI into your architectures. Integrating generative AI using Amazon Bedrock covers adding foundation models with clear patterns for security, customization, and integration. Using serverless for AI workflow orchestration provides patterns to coordinate model steps, retrieval, enrichment, inference, and post-processing, without managing servers. Finally, monitoring and maintaining AI models and cost optimization strategies for AI applications focus on keeping systems healthy and sustainable by tracking model quality and latency, detecting drift, and designing inference patterns that deliver value without high costs. By the end, you will be able to design AI features that are automated, observable, and cost-aware from day one.

Automating model deployment with CI/CD pipelines

Automating model deployment with CI/CD pipelines transforms releases into repeatable, auditable processes rather than manual, one-off tasks. You integrate source control, SageMaker pipelines, model registry, and deployment tools (CodePipeline/CodeBuild/CodeDeploy or external CI) so every code or model change passes through consistent build, test, and deploy stages with automated checks and controlled promotion to production.

Core ideas of CI/CD for ML on AWS

Traditional CI/CD targets application code, but ML involves additional components: data, training jobs, models, and evaluation metrics. A robust ML CI/CD design on AWS typically includes the following:

- **Model build pipeline**: It automates data preparation, training, evaluation, and model registration using SageMaker pipelines and model registry.
- **Model deployment pipeline**: It automates promotion of approved model packages to staging and production endpoints, applying deployment strategies (all-at-once, canary, linear) and rollback.

- **Infrastructure as code (IaC)**: Use CodePipeline/CodeBuild, CloudFormation/SAM/CDK, or Terraform to version and reproduce all infrastructure.
- **Observability and guardrails**: Implement model monitoring, CloudWatch metrics and alarms, and automated rollback if quality or SLA thresholds are breached.

The rest of this section walks through a detailed, end-to-end design.

Detailed CI/CD pipeline

A common pattern that aligns with the AWS ML Lens is a two-pipeline setup: a build pipeline and a deploy pipeline.

Model build pipeline

This pipeline is usually triggered by changes in the model repo (code, config) or periodic schedules when new data arrives. Typically, the flow looks like (data → trained model → registry)

1. **Source stage**:
   a. **Source**: Git repository (CodeCommit, GitHub, GitLab) containing training code, pipeline definition, and IaC.
   b. A commit to the main or development branch, or a tag, triggers CodePipeline or GitHub Actions/Jenkins integrated with SageMaker.
2. **Build and unit-test stage (CodeBuild)**:
   a. Install dependencies, run unit tests on feature engineering and model code.
   b. Lint and static analysis of training scripts and pipeline definition.
   c. Build and push custom training/inference container images to Amazon ECR if you use custom containers.
3. **Training and evaluation (SageMaker pipelines)**:
   a. CodeBuild or the orchestrator initiates a SageMaker Pipeline run with parameters such as data location and hyperparameters.
   b. **The pipeline runs**:
      i. **ProcessingStep** for data prep and split.
      ii. **TrainingStep** to train the model.
      iii. **ProcessingStep** to evaluate metrics.
      iv. **ConditionStep** to enforce quality thresholds.
      v. **RegisterModel** to push a model package into SageMaker Model Registry if metrics pass.

   c. The pipeline's run status and metadata are tracked as experiments for traceability.

4. **Model registration and approval gating**:

   a. The pipeline registers a new model package in a model package group with status PendingManualApproval or Approved for lower environments.

   b. Optionally, CodePipeline includes a **manual approval stage** where an ML lead reviews metrics, plots, and model cards before approving or rejecting.

5. **Trigger deploy pipeline**:

   a. Once a model package is approved, an EventBridge rule or CodePipeline action triggers the deployment pipeline, using the model package **Amazon Resource Name** (**ARN**) as an input artifact.

Model deployment pipeline

This pipeline standardizes deployment to SageMaker endpoints and applies guardrails and traffic-shifting strategies. Typically, the workflow looks like (approved model → staging → production)

1. **Source stage:**

   a. Input includes a model package ARN and deployment configuration (IaC templates or CDK stack) from the previous pipeline.

2. **Build/deploy infra stage (CodeBuild + CloudFormation/CDK)**:

   a. **Use IaC to define**:

      i. Endpoint configuration (instance types/counts, variants).

      ii. Blue/green/canary deployment settings via SageMaker deployment guardrails (BlueGreenUpdatePolicy).

      iii. Model Monitor schedules and alarms.

   b. CodeBuild deploys or updates the stack to create/update the SageMaker endpoint pointing at the new model package.

3. **Deploy to staging**:

   a. First, create or update the *staging endpoint*.

   b. **Run smoke tests and integration tests**:

      i. Check basic functionality with representative payloads.

      ii. Validate contract with calling applications (schemas, error handling).

   c. Optionally, use SageMaker Inference Recommender at this stage to revalidate latency and throughput for the new model package and adjust instance types if needed.

4. **Automated tests and quality checks**:
    a. **Execute automated tests as CodeBuild actions, including**:
        i. Data-quality checks against live/staging traffic (feature ranges, missing fields).
        ii. Backtest model performance on a hold-out set.
        iii. API/contract tests to ensure stability.
    b. If tests fail, the pipeline stops and no production rollout occurs.
5. **Production deployment with traffic shifting**:
    a. Use SageMaker deployment guardrails to configure a **blue/green** strategy with one of the following:
        i. **All-at-once**: Switch all traffic once tests pass (for low-risk, low-traffic models).
        ii. **Canary**: Send a small percentage (for example, 10%, *The canary size should be less than or equal to 50% of the new fleet's capacity*) of traffic to the new model, monitor metrics for a window, then complete or roll back.
        iii. **Linear**: Gradually shift traffic in steps (for example, 10% every 5 minutes) while monitoring metrics; stop or rollback if issues arise.
        iv. **Rolling deployments**: In this, you can update your endpoint incrementally, provision capacity, and shift traffic to a new fleet in steps of a particular batch size.
    b. These strategies are configured declaratively (BlueGreenUpdatePolicy with CANARY or LINEAR) and integrated into the pipeline to ensure consistent deployments.
6. **Postdeployment verification and monitoring hooks**:
    a. After the new model receives production traffic, CloudWatch/Model Monitor dashboards and alarms watch:
        i. Latency and error rates.
        ii. Data drift, Model Quality Monitoring (where available), bias metrics.
        iii. Business KPIs (conversion rate, fraud catch rate, etc.).
    b. If thresholds are breached, automated rollback policies restore the previous endpoint version and mark the deployment as failed.
7. **Notification and audit**:
    a. Integrate with SNS, Slack, or Teams to notify teams of success or failure, including model version and metrics.
    b. CloudTrail and CodePipeline history provide an audit trail of who approved what and when.

Example workflow of CI/CD for a recommendation model

To make this concrete, consider a recommendation model powering a retail site:

- **Build pipeline**:
  - The data scientist commits updated training pipeline code and feature schema.
  - CodePipeline and CodeBuild run unit tests and start a SageMaker Pipeline training and evaluation run.
  - SageMaker Pipeline trains the model, evaluates NDCG/precision, and if above threshold, registers a new model package with PendingManualApproval.
  - An approver reviews metrics and model card, then approves; this fires the deployment pipeline.
- **Deploy pipeline**:
  - CodePipeline uses CloudFormation/CDK to create/update a staging endpoint and Model Monitor schedule.
  - CodeBuild runs smoke tests and a small offline A/B comparison between the current and the new model on a golden dataset.
  - If tests pass, the pipeline configures a **canary deployment directing** 10% of production traffic to the new model variant and 90% to the old.
  - After 30 to 60 minutes, if business and technical metrics are satisfactory, traffic shifts automatically to 100% new model. Otherwise, deployment guardrails and pipeline logic roll back to the old variant and raise an incident.

From the team's perspective, *deploying the new recommender is now as simple as merging to main and approving the model* with automation handling the rest.

Best practices for automating model deployment

AWS prescriptive guidance and MLOps patterns highlight key practices for reliable CI/CD:

- **Separate build and deploy concerns**:
  - Use one pipeline (or set of pipelines) for training/evaluation and model registration, and another for deployment.
  - This approach simplifies frequent retraining while promoting only select models to production.
- **Use the Model Registry as the contract between data science and operations**:
  - Treat a model package with its metrics, schema, and artifacts as the unit of deployment.
  - Only deploy models that have been registered and (optionally) manually approved.

- **Adopt IaC throughout**:
  - Define SageMaker endpoints, variants, monitors, alarms, and IAM roles as code (CDK/CloudFormation/Terraform) and version them with your repository.
  - Avoid manually configuring endpoints in the console; all changes should flow through Git-backed pipelines.
- **Include ML-specific tests in your pipelines**:
  - **Automated tests should cover**:
    - Data quality (feature ranges, missingness, drift).
    - Model quality (offline metrics vs. baselines).
    - Inference API behavior (schema, latency, error handling).
  - Fail fast if a new model underperforms or violates contracts.
- **Standardize deployment strategies and rollback**:
  - Use SageMaker's deployment guardrails with blue/green, canary, or linear shifting for all production endpoints.
  - Combine this with CloudWatch alarms and automated rollback logic within the pipeline.
- **Design for multienvironment promotion**:
  - Use separate AWS accounts or at least separate VPCs and endpoints for dev, staging, and prod.
  - Pipelines should promote the same model package across environments rather than retraining separately in each.
- **Integrate monitoring and feedback loops**:
  - Incorporate model monitoring and logging into deployment templates; no endpoint should be deployed without Model Monitor and essential CloudWatch metrics and alarms.
  - Integrate monitoring results into planning; if drift is detected, automatically trigger a new training run.
- **Clarify roles and governance**:
  - Document ownership of code, data, and deployment approvals.
  - Use CodePipeline approval stages and IAM to enforce that only authorized roles can approve production deployments.

Applying these patterns makes *automating model deployment with CI/CD pipelines* a natural extension of your DevOps practices. Models progress from idea to production through a governed, observable pipeline, providing your AWS architecture with a reliable foundation for continuous ML delivery.

Integrating generative AI using Amazon Bedrock

Integrating generative AI with Amazon Bedrock means treating foundation models as governed, first-class services within your AWS architecture rather than ad-hoc **application programming interface** (**API**) calls on individual applications. Bedrock provides managed access to text, chat, image, and embedding models, along with higher-level components like knowledge bases and agents. This lets you embed generative AI into web applications, backends, and workflows while maintaining control over security, costs, and operations.

Core integration patterns with Bedrock

At a high level, Bedrock integrates in three main ways:

- **Direct model calls from applications**: Your API or backend uses InvokeModel or InvokeModelWithResponseStream via the AWS SDK to generate text, images, or embeddings on demand.
- **Knowledge bases for RAG**: Bedrock knowledge bases handle chunking, embeddings, and vector search over your content, augmenting prompts with retrieved context to ground answers in your data.
- **Agents and Step Functions workflows**: Bedrock Agents and Step Functions integrations orchestrate multi-step tasks, tool calls, and batch jobs, combining foundation models with your APIs and other AWS services.

Typical solutions combine these patterns, such as a chat application backed by a knowledge base, with long-running or multi-step tasks orchestrated by Step Functions, all within a secure, VPC-integrated Bedrock *landing zone.*

End-to-end pipeline

A robust Bedrock integration typically follows a repeatable pipeline. The following is a common pattern for a text-centric application, such as an internal knowledge assistant or customer support copilot:

1. **Prepare and govern your data**:
    a. **Identify sources**:
        i. Select repositories to feed your generative app, such as S3 document buckets, Confluence or SharePoint exports, wikis, ticketing systems, and other knowledge stores.

ii. Filter sources by confidentiality, freshness, and quality; exclude noisy or sensitive content you do not want surfaced.

b. **Normalize content**:

i. Convert documents to clean text (HTML stripping, PDF/OCR via Textract if needed) and store them in S3 with metadata for source, document type, timestamps, and access labels.

ii. Define data retention and re-indexing policies within your governance model.

2. **Build a knowledge base (RAG layer)**: For most practical use cases, use RAG so the model can reference your latest content. Bedrock knowledge bases largely manage this process:

1. **Create a knowledge base**:

i. In Bedrock, define a knowledge base, link it to an S3 data source, select an embedding model, and configure a vector store such (refer to the mentioned supported options). *As of this writing, supported vector stores include OpenSearch Serverless, OpenSearch Managed Clusters, Aurora PostgreSQL (pgvector), Amazon S3 Vectors, Pinecone, Redis Enterprise Cloud, and MongoDB Atlas*

ii. Configure chunk size and overlap. AWS recommends tuning these based on the model's context window and document structure.

2. **Ingestion and sync**:

i. Trigger a data ingestion job for Bedrock to parse, chunk, and embed your documents, then write vectors into the configured store.

ii. Set up periodic sync or event-driven ingestion to keep the knowledge base current as documents change.

3. **Access control and tenancy**:

i. Use metadata and IAM to ensure retrieval respects tenant and role boundaries, such as filtering by team, region, or classification.

3. **Design the runtime request flow**: For A typical chat or Q and A backend runtime flow includes the following steps:

a. **User request intake**: A web / mobile client sends a prompt (for example, *summarize our incident runbook for SEV-1 and SEV-2 outages*) to your API, along with identity and context (user id, tenant, channel).

b. **Call a Bedrock knowledge base/custom RAG**:

- **For knowledge bases**: Your backend calls the Bedrock knowledge base API, which embeds the query, retrieves the top-K relevant chunks from your vector store, and augments the prompt.

- **For custom RAG**: You embed the query with Bedrock, query OpenSearch, or S3 Vector directly, and construct the augmented prompt manually.

c. **Invoke a foundation model**:

- Use the Bedrock runtime client (bedrock-runtime) and InvokeModel or streaming APIs to call your chosen text or chat model with system instructions and retrieved context.
- **Prompt structure typically includes**:
  - o System message defining role, tone, and constraints.
  - o Context section with retrieved passages.
  - o User question and any tool output.

Note: **this is a direct call to a Bedrock foundation model, separate from invoking a custom model hosted on a SageMaker endpoint (see Chapter 10, Designing and Deploying AI Applications on AWS).**

d. **Post-processing and response**:

- Apply guardrails such as redaction or topic filters, add citations from source documents, and return the answer to the client.
- Log interactions with appropriate redaction for monitoring, evaluation, and tuning.

4. **Orchestrate complex workflows with Step Functions and agents**: When tasks span multiple calls or services, orchestrate them rather than handling everything in a single API call. Two main patterns include:

a. **Step Functions + Bedrock**:

i. Use the Step Functions optimized integration with Bedrock to call models, chain prompts, and branch logic without Lambda wrappers.

ii. **A typical state machine for batch or multistep tasks**:

- Preprocess input (format prompts, split batch).
- Parallel Map state to submit multiple Bedrock jobs or model invocations.
- Wait for completion using callback patterns and DynamoDB to track job status.
- Postprocess outputs (parse JSON, store summaries in S3 or databases).

b. **Bedrock Agents**:

i. To create an *agentic* assistant that autonomously calls APIs or knowledge bases, configure a Bedrock Agent with:

- Instructions (what it can do, constraints).
- Action groups with OpenAPI schemas for your internal services.
- Optional knowledge base attachments.

ii. The agent uses ReAct-style reasoning (Reason Act Observation) to break requests into steps, call tools, review results, and iterate before responding.

Both approaches keep control flow, retries, and branching outside the model and integrate naturally into event-driven AWS architectures.

Example of Internal Cloud Architecture Assistant

Consider integrating Bedrock as an *architecture copilot* for your AWS platform team:

- **Data layer**:
  - o Store design docs, runbooks, well-architected reviews, and Terraform/CDK patterns in S3.
  - o Build a Bedrock knowledge base over this content using OpenSearch as the vector store.
- **Runtime flow**:
  - o Engineers ask questions via a web UI or Slack integration (for example, *Design a multiAZ serverless API for this use case*).
  - o The backend calls the knowledge base to retrieve relevant patterns and guidance, then uses a Bedrock text model to draft an answer including diagrams (as text), pros and cons, and references.
  - o For *take action* requests (e.g., *generate a CDK stack for this pattern*), a Bedrock Agent calls code-generation APIs or template services, returning ready-to-review IaC snippets.
- **Orchestration and guardrails**:
  - o Step Functions orchestrates longer tasks such as batch refactoring suggestions or Well-Architected review summaries, invoking Bedrock in multiple steps.
  - o Guardrails ensure the assistant cannot directly change infrastructure but only suggest changes via PRs or tickets, enforced through IAM and action-group design.

Best practices for integrating Amazon Bedrock

AWS guidance highlights several best practices for building Bedrock-based systems.

1. **Align with the Well-Architected generative AI guidance**:

- Apply the AWS Well-Architected Framework to your generative AI workloads, focusing on operational excellence, security, reliability, performance, and cost optimization.
- Treat Bedrock as part of a landing zone with dedicated accounts, centralized logging, and clear blast-radius boundaries.

2. **Start with RAG, not just raw prompts**:
   - Implement retrieval-augmented generation using knowledge bases or custom RAG so the model answers based on your up-to-date data.
   - Design chunking, embedding, and metadata carefully to improve retrieval quality and enforce access control.
3. **Choose models intentionally and evaluate them**:
   - Experiment with multiple foundation models to balance cost, latency, and quality. Use smaller, cheaper models for simple tasks and stronger models for complex reasoning.
   - Build evaluation pipelines, both automatic and human-in-the-loop, to compare models and prompt variants using real workloads.
4. **Use IaC and CI/CD**:
   - Define Bedrock resources, knowledge bases, agents, Step Functions workflows, VPC endpoints, and IAM roles, using CDK or CloudFormation for repeatable, versioned deployments.
   - Integrate Bedrock usage into CI/CD pipelines, including tests for prompts, workflows, and guardrails before production deployment.
5. **Secure access and network paths**:
   - Use VPC endpoints (AWS PrivateLink) to keep Bedrock API traffic private within your VPC, avoiding exposure to the public internet.
   - Tighten IAM policies to control which workloads can access models, knowledge bases, and agents, and log all access via CloudTrail.
6. **Implement guardrails and output controls**:
   - Use Bedrock's safety and guardrail features to:
     - Block disallowed topics and PII.
     - Enforce response styles and formats.
     - Limit actions agents can take.
   - Consider secondary validation steps for sensitive workflows, such as approval processes or a *verification model* that checks outputs against context.

7. **Design for cost and performance**:
   - Cache frequent responses and intermediate results when appropriate.
   - Batch or parallelize requests with Step Functions for large-scale generation jobs.
   - Right-size models by using cheaper, faster options for drafting or simple tasks and reserving more capable models for complex needs.

Treat *integrating generative AI using Amazon Bedrock* as an architectural concern, covering data pipelines, RAG, workflows, security, and IaC, rather than just API calls. This approach delivers reliable, governable, and reusable generative capabilities across your AWS environment.

Using serverless for AI workflow orchestration

Using serverless for AI workflow orchestration lets managed services like AWS Step Functions and AWS Lambda handle data preparation, model calls, and post-processing, eliminating the need for custom workflow engines or long-running servers. In a nutshell, Step Functions remains the better fit for cross-service orchestration spanning many AWS services, while Lambda durable functions (covered next) suit workflows that are mostly within a single function's logic but need to pause and resume. This approach suits AI and ML workloads well, as they are often bursty, multi-step, and integrate with various AWS services and external APIs.

Why serverless for AI workflows

Serverless orchestration with Step Functions and Lambda brings several advantages:

- **No servers to manage**: Focus on workflow logic while AWS handles scaling, patching, and availability.
- **Built-in integration**: Step Functions offers optimized connections to Amazon Bedrock and over 220 AWS services, enabling direct calls from state machines without boilerplate Lambdas.
- **Visual and auditable workflows**: Each execution is tracked with a visual graph, input/output histories, and error paths for debugging and compliance.
- **Cost-aligned**: Pay per state transition and Lambda invocation, matching AI workloads that run in bursts or batch windows.

Architecturally, Step Functions acts as the *conductor*, Lambda manages glue code and custom logic, and AI services like Bedrock or SageMaker handle heavy model processing.

Note: **AWS launched Lambda Durable Functions in 2025 as a new capability specifically for multi-step AI workflows. It provides built-in state management for long-running Lambda executions.**

Typical AI orchestration architecture

A typical serverless AI workflow architecture on AWS includes:

- **Event sources**: API Gateway, EventBridge, S3 events, or scheduled triggers initiate a Step Functions state machine.
- **Step Functions**: Orchestrate the pipeline - branching, retries, parallelism, and waiting for long-running jobs.
- **Lambda**: Implements business logic, data transformation, and integrations with external systems.
- **AI services**: Amazon Bedrock for foundation models, SageMaker for custom models, or other AI APIs invoked directly from Step Functions.
- **State and results**: S3 for bulk input/output, DynamoDB for execution state and job inventory (see the following batch workflow example for a concrete illustration), CloudWatch for logs and metrics.

You can apply this pattern to generative AI (prompt chaining, RAG), batch embedding or summarization jobs, model evaluation pipelines, or even multi-agent workflows.

Example of serverless Bedrock batch workflow

AWS offers a reference pattern for a serverless workflow that orchestrates large-scale batch inference with Amazon Bedrock using Step Functions, Lambda, S3, and DynamoDB. A generalized pipeline includes:

1. **Phase 1, ingestion and preprocessing**:
    a. **Job submission**:
        i. A user uploads a configuration file and input dataset (for example, prompts to embed or documents to summarize) to S3 or submits a request via API Gateway.
        ii. This event triggers a Step Functions state machine with metadata including S3 locations, model choice, batch size, and other options.
    b. **Preprocessing Lambda**:
        i. A Lambda function reads the configuration and input dataset, validates them, and splits the data into manageable batches (e.g., 1,000 records per batch).
        ii. It writes per-batch manifests to S3 and records batch job metadata (job ID, batch IDs, status) in DynamoDB.
2. **Phase 2, parallel batch inference**:
    1. **Map state orchestration**:

i. Step Functions uses a Map state to iterate over batches in parallel, controlling concurrency to respect Bedrock or model-specific job limits.

ii. **For each batch, it starts a branch that**:

- Submits a Bedrock batch inference job (e.g., embedding or text generation) or runs synchronous InvokeModel calls.
- Stores job IDs or tokens in DynamoDB for tracking.

2. **Asynchronous job tracking**:

i. Bedrock emits events when batch jobs complete. A separate mechanism (EventBridge and Lambda) updates job status in DynamoDB and, for callback patterns, notifies Step Functions via a *wait for task token* to resume execution upon job completion.

ii. This enables the state machine to handle long-running jobs without blocking or timeouts.

3. **Phase 3, post-processing and aggregation**:

1. **Post-processing Lambda**: After a batch job completes, a Lambda function processes the output JSON files in S3:

i. Parses model outputs.

ii. Maps outputs back to original inputs (for example, embedding vectors to text, summaries to document IDs).

iii. Writes cleaned and enriched results to finalized S3 locations or indexes (e.g., a vector database).

2. **Aggregation and completion**:

i. After all Map branches are complete, a final state aggregates metadata, writes a summary record (e.g., total records processed, errors, output locations) to DynamoDB, and sends a notification via SNS or EventBridge.

ii. The state machine ends with a clear success or failure status and logs each batch to CloudWatch.

This fully serverless pattern requires no EC2, containers, or custom schedulers. It scales to large workloads while respecting service quotas and providing robust observability.

Example serverless prompt chaining for generative applications

For interactive generative AI applications, AWS demonstrates how to combine Step Functions and Bedrock using prompt chaining:

1. **User request**: A client calls an API (API Gateway and Lambda) with a complex task such as *Generate a personalized 5-day travel itinerary with activities and packing list.*
2. **State machine with multiple Bedrock steps**:
   a. **Step Functions runs a state machine where each state**:
      - Calls Bedrock with a specific, smaller prompt (e.g., extract preferences, propose itineraries, then create a packing list).
      - Uses the result as input to the next state.

   b. A parallel state can run sub-tasks (e.g., hotel and restaurant suggestions) concurrently to reduce latency.
3. **Lambda for aggregation and formatting**: A final Lambda step merges intermediate outputs into a single response, formats it (e.g., Markdown or PDF), stores it in S3, and returns a signed URL to the client.

Step Functions' optimized Bedrock integration lets you call InvokeModel directly from the workflow without extra Lambda wrappers, simplifying code and reducing costs.

Best practices for serverless AI orchestration

AWS guidance and real-world patterns recommend best practices for serverless AI workflows:

1. **Keep workflows modular and composable**:
   - Break complex AI pipelines into smaller, reusable state machines and Lambda functions (e.g., separate preprocessing, inference, post-processing) instead of one monolithic workflow.
   - Reuse generic steps across projects (prompt formatting, JSON validation, S3 I/O) through shared Lambda libraries or Step Functions nested workflows.
2. **Use Step Functions' optimized integrations where possible**:
   - Prefer direct service integrations (Bedrock, SageMaker, DynamoDB, SQS, SNS, Glue, etc.) over wrapping every call in Lambda; this reduces code and improves observability.
   - Use callback patterns and task tokens for long-running or asynchronous jobs (e.g., Bedrock batch inference, SageMaker training).
3. **Control concurrency and quotas**:
   - Use Map state concurrency controls and job-inventory tables (DynamoDB) to stay within upstream quotas (e.g., max concurrent Bedrock batch jobs).
   - Implement exponential backoff and retries for transient errors. Rely on Step Functions' retry/catch semantics instead of custom loops in Lambda.

4. **Design for idempotency and resilience**:
    - Make Lambda functions idempotent so replays or retries do not duplicate work (e.g., check DynamoDB or S3 markers before reprocessing).
    - Use **dead-letter queues** (**DLQs**) or failure branches in Step Functions to handle irrecoverable errors and trigger alerts.
5. **Secure by design**:
    - Use least-privilege IAM roles for each Lambda and state machine; avoid broad wildcards over AI services.
    - Keep AI traffic private with VPC endpoints (for Bedrock, SageMaker, and data stores) where applicable, and enforce encryption in transit and at rest.
6. **Observe, log, and trace**:
    - Standardize logging using Powertools for AWS Lambda and CloudWatch log groups per workflow. Log prompt/response metadata with redaction for sensitive content.
    - Use CloudWatch metrics and alarms on Step Functions executions (success, failure, duration) and Lambda errors, plus X-Ray tracing for end-to-end visibility.
7. **Cost and performance optimization**:
    - Prefer Step Functions direct integrations over Lambda where possible to reduce extra invocations.
    - Tune Map state concurrency to balance throughput and cost. Avoid unnecessary intermediate writes when data volumes are large.
    - For batch workloads, plan scheduling and grouping to keep workflows within execution limits and minimize per-state overhead.

Adopting these patterns makes *using serverless for AI workflow orchestration* a core architectural advantage rather than an implementation detail. Your AI workloads become easier to manage, automatically scalable, auditable, and faster to evolve as new models and use cases emerge.

Monitoring and maintaining AI models

Monitoring and maintaining AI models means treating them as living systems rather than one-time deployments. Continuous visibility into data, predictions, behavior, and cost helps catch issues early, retrain safely, and ensure AI remains accurate, fair, and compliant over time. What *monitoring* means for AI models. For traditional ML models, monitoring focuses on the following:

- **Data quality and drift**: Are production features consistent with training data? Check for missing values, schema changes, or distribution shifts.

- **Model quality and drift**: Are accuracy, precision/recall, or business KPIs declining over time due to changing conditions?
- **Bias and explainability**: Are predictions showing bias against groups or unexpected shifts in feature attributions?
- **Operational health**: Latency, error rate, throughput, and cost per prediction.

For LLMs and generative models, you add:

- **Grounding and hallucination**: Are responses aligned with the provided context, or is hallucination increasing?
- **Prompt/response quality**: Are prompts remaining effective as data and use cases evolve?
- **Token usage and cost**: Are token counts and total spend aligned with expectations and budgets?

On AWS, core building blocks for this include SageMaker Model Monitor for classic ML, CloudWatch metrics and logs, XRay, and specialized guidance for LLMs and serverless AI flows.

Reference pipeline for monitoring SageMaker model

SageMaker Model Monitor offers a structured approach to monitor data and model quality for models hosted on SageMaker endpoints or batch jobs. A typical monitoring pipeline includes these steps:

1. **Enable data capture**:
    a. For real-time endpoints, enable data capture to store inference requests and responses (features and predictions) in S3. The sampling percentage can be adjusted to control volume.
    b. For batch transform, configure capture of batch inputs and outputs in S3.
2. **Create a baseline**:
    a. Use the training dataset or a high-quality validation set to compute baseline statistics and constraints, such as distributions, ranges, and category frequencies.
    b. Model Monitor can generate these automatically and suggest thresholds for comparing production data.
3. **Configure monitoring schedules**:
    a. Define scheduled monitoring jobs, such as data quality, model quality, bias drift, and feature-attribution drift, that run hourly or daily.
    b. **Each schedule specifies**:

i. Which captured data to analyze, including S3 locations and time windows.

ii. Which baseline and constraints to use for comparison.

iii. Where to store analysis reports.

4. **Analyze and report**:

   a. Monitoring jobs, computing metrics, and flagging constraint violations, such as feature distribution divergence or prediction error exceeding limits.

   b. Reports are stored in S3, and metrics can be sent to CloudWatch for dashboards and alarms.

5. **Alerting and remediation**:

   a. CloudWatch alarms detect when violations or drift metrics exceed thresholds.

   b. **Typical responses include**:

      i. Trigger a retraining pipeline with fresh data.

      ii. Audit upstream data sources for errors.

      iii. Roll back to a prior model version or adjust decision thresholds.

This pipeline can be adapted for batch-only models, in which outputs from batch transform jobs are monitored on a schedule rather than through a live endpoint.

Reference pipeline for monitoring LLM and RAG systems

Monitoring generative AI and RAG systems requires additional layers, since traditional accuracy metrics often miss issues such as hallucinations or unsafe content. AWS guidance for serverless AI observability recommends tracking the full request path through your pipeline:

1. **Trace the full workflow**:

   - **Capture metrics and logs at each stage**:

     a. **API or UI entry point**: response time, 4xx/5xx errors.

     b. **Preprocessor Lambda**: parsing failures, validation errors, cold starts.

     c. **RAG retrieval**: hit/miss ratio, relevance scores, retrieval latency.

     d. **Model invocation (Bedrock or SageMaker)**: latency, tokens, model name, prompt, and response IDs.

     e. **Postprocessor**: schema validation, hallucination, or fallback triggers.

   - Use CloudWatch Logs, metrics, and X-Ray traces to correlate data via request or session IDs.

2. **Monitor key LLM-specific KPIs**: According to AWS guidance, useful metrics include:

a. **Inference latency per model**: Per-provider/Per-model p95/p99.

b. **Grounding relevance**: RAG hit rate, retrieval relevance scores, ratio of answers that use retrieved context vs none.

c. **Prompt and response quality**: Hallucination rate, fallback rate, answer completeness scores.

d. **Token usage and cost**: Total input/output tokens per session and feature; spikes may indicate prompt bloat or misuse.

e. **Security and access**: Model/agent usage by IAM role, tool call frequency.

3. **Centralize observability**: Use CloudWatch Logs and metrics for operational monitoring, OpenSearch to index logs and responses for deeper analysis, and CloudWatch Synthetics canaries to send predefined prompts that detect regressions over time (*CloudWatch Synthetics canaries can be scheduled to run a script that sends fixed prompts to the model and checks the response against expected output, surfacing regressions the same way a canary would catch a broken web endpoint*).

4. **Governance and compliance**: Apply frameworks such as the AWS Generative AI Best Practices Framework to document regular model evaluations and monitoring for bias and unsafe outputs, using CloudWatch and Audit Manager to collect artifacts.

Example, end-to-end monitor and maintain loop

To illustrate, consider an e-commerce fraud model alongside a support copilot LLM:

1. **Deploy and instrument:**
   - Deploy the fraud model on a SageMaker endpoint with data capture and Model Monitor schedules for data quality, model quality, and bias drift.
   - Deploy the support copilot using Bedrock with structured logging, X-Ray tracing, and metrics for latency, token usage, and hallucination signals.
2. **Continuous monitoring**: CloudWatch dashboards display:
   - **Fraud model**: feature drift vs. baseline, accuracy over labeled samples, error rate, endpoint latency.
   - **Copilot**: RAG hit rate, fallback rate, token cost per session, and user satisfaction scores when available.
3. **Alert and diagnosis:**
   - A CloudWatch alarm triggers when fraud model data drift metrics exceed thresholds. Model Monitor reports reveal a new pattern in transaction origin country distribution.
   - For the copilot, anomaly detection flags a surge in long prompts, causing higher costs. Logs indicate a recent application feature change altered prompt construction.

4. **Remediation and improvement:**
   - **Fraud model:**
     - Trigger a SageMaker training pipeline with recent data, evaluate metrics, register a new model version, and deploy it through your CI/CD pipeline after approval.
     - Update feature engineering to accommodate the new country distribution.
   - **Copilot:**
     - Correct prompt construction logic and enforce stricter length constraints.
     - Adjust RAG chunking or retrieval configuration to improve relevance, then re-evaluate hallucination and fallback metrics.
5. **Governance**: Document changes, metrics, and approvals in the Model Registry, ticketing systems, and, for generative AI, in your best-practices framework to enable audit trails of model modifications.

This closes the loop: monitoring not only detects issues but also informs retraining and improvements to prompts and architecture.

Best practices for monitoring and maintaining AI models

AWS documentation and guidance highlight several best practices:

1. **Define clear KPIs up front**:
   - Business KPIs (fraud loss, conversion rate, CSAT), model metrics, and operational metrics (p95 latency, error rate, cost per 1,000 predictions).
   - **For LLMs**: add grounding quality, hallucination rate, and token cost KPIs.
2. **Use structured, correlated telemetry**:
   - Log prompts, responses, and metadata in structured formats (e.g., JSON with session ID, user ID, model ID, prompt template version) to correlate issues across components.
   - Tag logs and metrics by environment, version, region, and feature flag to enable segmented analysis.
3. **Automate drift and quality monitoring**:
   - Use Model Monitor to continuously compare live data and predictions against training baselines for data, model, bias, and feature-attribution drift.
   - Set CloudWatch alarms on drift metrics and business KPIs, beyond infrastructure metrics.

4. **Combine online monitoring with offline evaluation**:
    - Conduct periodic offline re-evaluation of models and LLM prompts using curated test sets, including *golden* edge cases and safety-critical scenarios.
    - Use these evaluations to validate model updates before deployment and detect subtle degradations that online metrics may miss.
5. **Implement human-in-the-loop where needed**:
    - For high-risk tasks such as credit decisions, medical suggestions, or policy changes, incorporate human review queues, random sampling, or approval workflows.
    - Capture reviewer feedback as labels to enhance future models and prompts.
6. **Monitor cost and usage explicitly**:
    - Track inference cost per request, user, and feature. For Bedrock, monitor token usage and cost trends.
    - Use anomaly detection to identify sudden cost spikes, often caused by prompt bloat, runaway loops, or misuse.
7. **Tie monitoring to governance controls**:
    - Use frameworks such as AWS Generative AI Best Practices and AWS Config conformance packs for AI/ML to ensure regular model evaluation, bias monitoring, and least-privilege access.
    - Treat monitoring artifacts, reports, dashboards, and evaluation logs as evidence for compliance and internal risk management.

Embedding these practices into your architecture makes monitoring and maintaining AI models a core, automated part of running AI systems on AWS, delivering reliability, safety, and business value well beyond initial deployment.

Cost optimization strategies for AI applications

Cost optimization for AI applications means aligning model power and infrastructure with business value instead of defaulting to the fastest or largest options. It involves model selection, prompt and token design, infrastructure patterns, and governance to ensure AI workloads scale cost-effectively without unnoticed cost increases.

Where AI costs come from

AI applications on AWS incur costs in several layers:

- **Inference layer**: Per-request or per-token charges for foundation models (for example, Amazon Bedrock), and instance-hour costs for SageMaker endpoints or custom inference services.

- **Training and tuning**: One-off or periodic training jobs, fine-tuning runs, and continued pre-training on GPUs or accelerators. These can be some of the largest but also easiest to schedule and right-size.
- **Orchestration and glue**: Serverless runtimes (Lambda, Step Functions), queues, and event buses, all billed per invocation or state transition.
- **Data and vector stores**: Storage and I/O for S3, vector indices, OpenSearch, databases, and logs that grow with usage and retention.

Effective cost optimization means addressing each layer with targeted techniques, not just looking at compute in isolation.

Strategy 1, right-size models and infrastructure

Let us have a look at the components of the first strategy:

- **Tiered model selection**: In generative AI, overspending often occurs when all requests are routed to large, costly foundation models, even when many tasks require only small or mid-tier models. The recommended approach is:
  - o Route simple, frequent tasks (FAQs, formatting, light summarization) to smaller, cheaper models.
  - o Reserve larger models for complex reasoning, multi-tool orchestration, or high-value interactions, ideally behind confidence or *escalation* logic.

  AWS guidance for Bedrock outlines a decision flow: first, determine if customization is needed, then try light techniques like prompting and RAG before advancing to fine-tuning or continued pre-training, as each step raises costs.
- **Right-sizing compute**: For custom models (for example, on SageMaker), apply classic cloud cost practices with AI specifics:
  - o Select instance families based on workload (CPU, GPU, Inferentia, Trainium) and use Inference Recommender benchmarking to identify the smallest instance that meets latency and throughput requirements rather than guessing.
  - o Right-size regularly; AI workloads drift over time, so capacity that once fit may become over-provisioned as traffic or models change.
- **Commitment and pricing models**: Use Savings Plans or Reserved Instances for steady baseline workloads, and on-demand or Spot instances for bursty or non-critical jobs like experimentation, batch training, or offline evaluation.

Strategy 2, control prompts, tokens, and workflows

Let us have a look at the components of the second strategy:

- **Prompt engineering for cost, not just quality**: Token usage is one of the biggest levers in generative AI cost. AWS guidance recommends:

- Trim prompts and context by using concise instructions and avoiding embedding entire documents. Summarize or chunk context before inclusion.
- Cap lengths by enforcing maximum sizes for prompts and outputs (e.g., 400–800 tokens for context, limited response lengths) within templates and code.
- Reuse system prompts by centrally storing templates to enable evolution and auditing of their impact on quality and cost.

- **RAG and light customization first**: Rather than immediately opting for costly fine-tuning, follow AWS Bedrock's recommended optimization sequence:

  a. **Prompt engineering**: Zero infrastructure cost beyond existing inference.

  b. **RAG**: Use knowledge bases to bring your data to the model instead of retraining.

  c. **Fine-tuning**: Only when prompts + RAG can't meet quality needs.

  d. **Continued pre-training**: Only for highly specialized, large-scale tasks due to high compute and operational costs.

  This approach ensures you only pay for additional training capacity when it clearly adds value.

- **Cache repeated results**: Caching is a direct cost lever for AI calls:
  - Cache frequent prompts and their responses (or embedding results) in memory stores like Redis or application caches.
  - Check the cache before calling foundation models or inference endpoints; higher cache hit rates directly reduce billable AI calls.

For RAG, caching retrieval results (top-K document chunks) separately from generation improves efficiency by reusing context while generating fresh responses as needed.

Strategy 3, architect efficient serverless and inference workflows

Serverless AI workloads introduce additional cost dimensions: per-call, per-state, and per-event billing. Tune orchestration; prescriptive guidance for serverless AI suggests:

- Avoid unnecessary steps in Step Functions Standard workflows, since each state transition incurs a cost (*Express workflows are priced by duration and number of executions instead*). Combine trivial transformations or use service integrations instead of additional Lambdas.
- Manage parallelism and concurrency in Map states to balance performance and cost, avoiding large parallel branches for small tasks.
- Use asynchronous patterns like callbacks and event-driven designs for long-running jobs to avoid paying for idle orchestrator time.

Optimize Lambda usage; for Lambda in AI glue code:

- Right-size memory and timeouts since over-provisioning or long timeouts increase costs without benefits.
- Optimize functions by reusing network clients and avoiding heavy initialization to reduce execution time and cold-start overhead.
- Offload heavy loops to batch jobs or dedicated compute resources when running at high volume.

Make endpoints elastic; for hosted models:

- Enable autoscaling on SageMaker endpoints with multi-AZ for resilience, scaling based on invocations per instance or custom model-aware metrics.
- Use serverless inference or multi-model endpoints for low-throughput or many small-model scenarios to avoid paying for idle dedicated instances.

Strategy 4, data, storage, and logging discipline

AI applications generate lots of data, requests, responses, embeddings, and logs, which can quietly dominate your bill if left unchecked:

- Apply S3 lifecycle policies to move old logs, inference data, and intermediate artifacts to cheaper storage like Glacier or Glacier Deep Archive, or delete them when no longer needed.
- Use S3 Intelligent-Tiering or storage classes aligned with access patterns; right-size databases and indexes (e.g., OpenSearch, vector stores) and remove stale embeddings.
- Log sufficiently to debug and monitor quality, but avoid excessive verbosity for every token or step. Use sampling when possible.

This is especially important for vector search: embedding and indexing every possible field or temporary artifact can explode storage and I/O costs without improving retrieval quality.

Strategy 5, cost-aware governance and pipelines

Start with visibility; multiple guides emphasize that cost optimization begins with tagging and visibility:

- Tag AI resources (endpoints, models, vector stores, serverless functions) by team, project, environment, and feature..
- Use cost allocation reports and budgets to attribute spend and set alerts when AI services exceed expected thresholds.

Cost-aware CI/CD; deployment pipelines can enforce cost discipline:

- Evaluate resource changes such as instance sizes and concurrency limits before deployment, flagging or blocking those that exceed monthly cost thresholds.
- Incorporate cost checks into PR reviews with messages like *this change increases inference cost by ~X% at current volume.*

Automated anomaly detection: Use cost anomaly detection to identify sudden spikes, often caused by misconfigured prompts, loops, or runaway batch jobs, early, and set guardrails to automatically respond, such as disabling feature flags or scaling down problematic endpoints.

Best practices

Several consistent themes emerge across sources for *Cost Optimization Strategies for AI Applications*:

- Start with visibility: tagging, allocation, and dashboards.
- Right-size models, instances, and storage; revisit sizing regularly.
- Use tiered model routing and prefer prompt/RAG improvements before expensive tuning.
- Be token-disciplined: trim prompts, cap outputs, and cache aggressively.
- Architect elastic, serverless workflows to match real demand instead of peak.
- Bake cost checks into governance and CI/CD, and use anomaly detection for early warning.

Designing AI solutions on AWS with these strategies enables scalable experimentation and production while keeping costs predictable and aligned with business outcomes.

Conclusion

In this section, we brought AI and ML into the same disciplined engineering world as the rest of your AWS architecture. You saw how automating model deployment with CI/CD pipelines turns models into versioned, testable artifacts that move through environments predictably, and how integrating generative AI using Amazon Bedrock lets you plug powerful foundation models into real applications with clear security and integration patterns. We looked at using serverless for AI workflow orchestration to coordinate all the steps around inference, data prep, retrieval, calls to models, and post-processing, without managing servers, and we highlighted the importance of monitoring and maintaining AI models to catch drift, performance regressions, and failures early. Finally, we discussed cost optimization strategies for AI applications, showing how choices like batching, caching, right-sizing, and selecting the right interaction patterns keep intelligent features both effective and affordable; together, these ideas give you a practical blueprint for running AI solutions that are reliable, observable, and cost-aware in production.

In the next chapter, we will turn our attention from running intelligent applications to the foundations that support them: how we define, deploy, and operate the underlying cloud infrastructure. We will start with an introduction to IaC concepts and an overview of AWS CloudFormation, Terraform, and the AWS CDK, treating them as different ways to describe the same architectural intent in code. From there, we will look at how to design modular and reusable IaC templates and code, and how to wire them into CI/CD pipelines for infrastructure deployment so environments are created and updated through repeatable, automated workflows instead of manual console changes. We will also explore GitOps and continuous delivery best practices, security and compliance automation in IaC, drift detection and state management, and monitoring and alerting for infrastructure health, so that your infrastructure changes are auditable, policy-aware, and observable by default. Together, these topics will give you a toolkit for managing AWS architectures as living codebases that evolve safely and consistently over time.

References

1. **https://docs.aws.amazon.com/wellarchitected/latest/machine-learning-lens/mlops04-bp01.html**
2. **https://aws.amazon.com/blogs/machine-learning/mlops-deployment-best-practices-for-real-time-inference-model-serving-endpoints-with-amazon-sagemaker/**
3. **https://aws.amazon.com/blogs/machine-learning/build-an-end-to-end-mlops-pipeline-using-amazon-sagemaker-pipelines-github-and-github-actions/**
4. **https://aws.amazon.com/blogs/machine-learning/build-a-ci-cd-pipeline-for-deploying-custom-machine-learning-models-using-aws-services/**
5. **https://docs.aws.amazon.com/sagemaker/latest/dg/deploy-model.html**
6. **https://docs.aws.amazon.com/sagemaker/latest/dg/inference-recommender.html**
7. **https://docs.aws.amazon.com/prescriptive-guidance/latest/patterns/build-an-mlops-workflow-by-using-amazon-sagemaker-and-azure-devops.html**
8. **https://aws.amazon.com/blogs/machine-learning/model-hosting-patterns-in-amazon-sagemaker-part-1-common-design-patterns-for-building-ml-applications-on-amazon-sagemaker/**
9. **https://aws.amazon.com/blogs/architecture/category/artificial-intelligence/amazon-machine-learning/amazon-bedrock/**
10. **https://aws.amazon.com/bedrock/**
11. **https://aws.amazon.com/video/watch/d1efa0d9a89/**
12. **https://docs.aws.amazon.com/bedrock/latest/userguide/kb-how-it-works.html**
13. **https://aws.amazon.com/blogs/machine-learning/dive-deep-into-vector-data-stores-using-amazon-bedrock-knowledge-bases/**
14. **https://docs.aws.amazon.com/step-functions/latest/dg/connect-bedrock.html**

15. https://aws.amazon.com/blogs/aws/build-generative-ai-apps-using-aws-step-functions-and-amazon-bedrock/
16. https://docs.aws.amazon.com/bedrock/latest/userguide/agents-how.html
17. https://aws.amazon.com/blogs/dotnet/building-ai-ready-applications-with-amazon-bedrock-and-net-aspire/
18. https://docs.aws.amazon.com/prescriptive-guidance/latest/retrieval-augmented-generation-options/choosing-option.html
19. https://aws.amazon.com/blogs/machine-learning/amazon-bedrock-knowledge-bases-now-supports-amazon-opensearch-service-managed-cluster-as-vector-store/
20. https://docs.aws.amazon.com/pdfs/prescriptive-guidance/latest/writing-best-practices-rag/writing-best-practices-rag.pdf
21. https://aws.amazon.com/blogs/machine-learning/multi-tenant-rag-implementation-with-amazon-bedrock-and-amazon-opensearch-service-for-saas-using-jwt/
22. https://aws.amazon.com/blogs/machine-learning/best-practices-for-building-robust-generative-ai-applications-with-amazon-bedrock-agents-part-2/
23. https://aws.amazon.com/blogs/machine-learning/build-a-serverless-amazon-bedrock-batch-job-orchestration-workflow-using-aws-step-functions/
24. https://aws.amazon.com/blogs/aws/build-generative-ai-apps-using-aws-step-functions-and-amazon-bedrock/
25. https://docs.aws.amazon.com/step-functions/latest/dg/connect-bedrock.html
26. https://aws.amazon.com/blogs/machine-learning/build-modern-serverless-solutions-following-best-practices-using-amazon-q-developer-cli-and-mcp/
27. https://aws.amazon.com/blogs/aws/build-multi-step-applications-and-ai-workflows-with-aws-lambda-durable-functions/
28. https://docs.aws.amazon.com/prescriptive-guidance/latest/agentic-ai-serverless/observability-and-monitoring.html
29. https://docs.aws.amazon.com/sagemaker/latest/dg/model-monitor.html
30. https://aws.amazon.com/blogs/machine-learning/techniques-and-approaches-for-monitoring-large-language-models-on-aws/
31. https://docs.aws.amazon.com/audit-manager/latest/userguide/aws-generative-ai-best-practices.html
32. https://docs.aws.amazon.com/sagemaker/latest/dg/best-practices.html
33. https://docs.aws.amazon.com/config/latest/developerguide/operational-best-practices-for-AI-and-ML.html
34. https://docs.aws.amazon.com/sagemaker/latest/dg/batch-transform.html

CHAPTER 12
Infrastructure as Code and DevOps Automation

Introduction

This section shifts focus from running workloads on AWS to defining and managing the cloud foundation. **Infrastructure as code** (**IaC**) lets you describe resources, **Virtual Private Clouds** (**VPCs**), subnets, security groups, load balancers, and databases as code. This code can be reviewed, versioned, tested, and reused like application code. We will examine how **AWS CloudFormation**, **Terraform**, and the **Amazon Web Services** (**AWS**) **Cloud Development Kit** (**CDK**) express this intent differently through declarative templates, multi-cloud configurations, or programming languages. The goal is to make environments reproducible and predictable, whether deploying a single dev stack or multiple standardized accounts. In this chapter, we will also learn drift detection, state management, and health monitoring. Drift detection and state management keep your IaC definitions aligned with the actual AWS environment, while monitoring and alerting for infrastructure health shifts, and focus from configuration correctness to operational behavior

Next, we cover operational practices that unlock IaC's full potential in teams. You will learn to design modular, reusable templates and constructs to avoid duplicating VPC or **Elastic Container Service** (**ECS**) service definitions. We will show how to integrate these modules into **continuous integration/continuous deployment** (**CI/CD**) pipelines so infrastructure changes follow the same build-test-deploy process as applications. We will explore GitOps and continuous delivery, where Git serves as the source of truth and changes apply automatically upon pull request merges. Finally, we will link IaC to security, compliance, and operations by embedding guardrails and policy checks, detecting and correcting drift from manual changes, and setting up monitoring and alerting to keep infrastructure health visible and actionable. These practices help you manage AWS architectures as living codebases that evolve safely and consistently with less manual effort.

Structure

This chapter covers the following topics:

- Understanding infrastructure as code
- Infrastructure as code tools
- Modular and reusable IaC templates and code
- CI/CD pipelines for infrastructure deployment
- GitOps and continuous delivery best practices
- Security and compliance automation in IaC
- Other IaC concepts

Objectives

This section explains how to manage AWS infrastructure, such as application code: describing, reviewing, versioning, and safely rolling changes forward or backward. IaC means defining VPCs, networks, security groups, compute, and databases in files rather than in the console. We will examine how AWS CloudFormation, Terraform, and the AWS CDK express these definitions differently, from declarative templates to higher-level constructs in familiar programming languages. The goal is reproducible, consistent environments, whether for a single dev stack or dozens of standardized accounts.

Next, we explore how to operationalize IaC to scale with teams and complexity. You will learn how modular, reusable templates or CDK constructs prevent redundant VPC or ECS service definitions. CI/CD pipelines can automate infrastructure changes by testing and approving them, avoiding manual console updates. We will address day-two concerns by applying GitOps and continuous delivery to treat Git as the source of truth, embedding security and compliance checks, detecting and correcting drift, and enabling monitoring and alerting for visible, actionable infrastructure health. These topics offer a practical guide to managing AWS architectures as living codebases that evolve safely and transparently.

Understanding infrastructure as code

IaC defines and manages infrastructure using machine-readable configuration files rather than manual console actions or ad hoc scripts. In AWS Solutions Architecture, IaC converts VPCs, subnets, security groups, load balancers, databases, serverless resources (Lambda, API Gateway), containers (ECS, EKS), and entire application stacks into versioned artifacts that can be reviewed, tested, and deployed like application code. This approach ensures consistent, repeatable environments across development, testing, and production, enabling safe collaboration at scale.

Significance of IaC in AWS architectures

IaC addresses three key challenges: drift, repeatability, and speed. Manual console setups cause environments to diverge (see drift detection and state management later in this chapter), complicating debugging and compliance. IaC stores the truth in code, creating environments from consistent templates that reduce drift and unexpected issues. Changes appear as code diffs, allowing review, testing, and rollback with a clear audit trail aligned with best practices. IaC also speeds up delivery by provisioning multi-tier architectures with a single command or pipeline, rather than days of manual work.

Declarative vs. imperative IaC

There are two main IaC styles in AWS ecosystems. Declarative approaches specify the desired end state, such as *a VPC with these Classless Inter-Domain Routing (CIDR) blocks and three subnets*, with an engine determining how to achieve it; this is used by template-driven tools like CloudFormation. Imperative approaches are procedural, requiring explicit commands such as *create this VPC, then these subnets, then attach this gateway*, often in a general-purpose language. Modern AWS solutions often combine both, using higher-level, code-like interfaces while converging resources toward a declared target state.

Core IaC building blocks

Every IaC design includes key concepts regardless of tooling. You define resources (e.g., **Elastic Compute Cloud** (**EC2**) instances, S3 buckets, **Relational Database Service** (**RDS**) databases) and their properties, and specify dependencies to ensure correct creation, update, and deletion order. Templates are parameterized to work across environments by supplying values such as **Virtual Private Clouds** (**VPC**) IDs, CIDR ranges, instance sizes, and feature flags at deployment time. Code is organized into reusable modules or stacks, separating concerns such as network foundation, application layer, and observability, allowing teams to evolve infrastructure parts independently while composing complete systems.

IaC significance in the SDLC and DevOps practices

In mature AWS solutions, IaC code resides alongside application code in version control, following the same development lifecycle: branch, review, test, merge, and deploy. Feature teams can add a microservice and define its load balancer, target group, **Identity and Access Management** (**IAM**) roles, and alarms within the same pull request using IaC. Pipelines validate templates, perform security and compliance checks, and deploy to lower environments before production. This integration supports DevOps goals by enabling developers to self-service infrastructure changes within guardrails, providing operations teams with predictable, traceable deployments, and allowing security and compliance teams to manage infrastructure through code rather than ad hoc documentation.

Infrastructure as code tools

AWS CloudFormation, Terraform, and AWS CDK all address provisioning and managing infrastructure as code, but use different approaches and target distinct audiences. CloudFormation is the AWS-native baseline, Terraform is the multi-cloud universal remote, and CDK is a developer-friendly, higher-level tool that generates CloudFormation using programming languages.

AWS CloudFormation

CloudFormation is AWS's native IaC service. You define AWS resources in declarative YAML or JSON templates, which CloudFormation manages as stacks. It integrates tightly with AWS, supports nearly all services, and handles state, rollback, and dependency ordering automatically. Here is how CloudFormation works:

- You write a template that declares resources (VPCs, subnets, IAM roles, Lambda functions, etc.) and their properties.
- You submit the template to CloudFormation as a stack.
- CloudFormation compares the template to the current stack state and:
  - Figures out which resources to create, update, or delete.
  - Orders operations based on implicit and explicit dependencies.
  - Applies changes and rolls back if something fails.
- State (what was created, with which IDs) lives in AWS and is fully managed by CloudFormation.

CloudFormation is a purely declarative, AWS-native desired-state engine. Its key components include:

- **Templates**: YAML/JSON documents describing resources, parameters, mappings, conditions, outputs.
- **Resources**: Individual AWS resources (AWS::EC2::Instance, AWS::S3::Bucket, etc.).
- **Parameters and outputs**: Inputs to a stack and exported values that other stacks can consume.
- **Stacks**: Deployed instances of templates. A stack is the unit of deploy/rollback.
- **StackSets**: Mechanism to roll out stacks across multiple accounts and regions.

Note: **AWS CloudFormation introduced git sync in late 2023, which allows CloudFormation stacks to sync automatically from a Git repository.**

Terraform by HashiCorp

Terraform by HashiCorp is a cloud-agnostic IaC tool using its declarative language, **HashiCorp Configuration Language** (**HCL**), and a broad provider ecosystem to manage infrastructure across AWS, other clouds, on-premises, and SaaS APIs. You define a desired state; Terraform plans and applies changes by calling provider APIs directly. It is ideal for managing multiple environments and vendors with a single tool and workflow. Here is how Terraform works:

- You write `.tf` files in HCL describing resources, data sources, variables, and outputs.
- Terraform builds an internal state snapshot that tracks what has been created and its attributes.
- When you run terraform plan, it:
  - Reads the current real infrastructure via provider APIs.
  - Compares it to the desired configuration.
  - Produces a plan of adds/changes/deletes.
- Terraform applies and then executes that plan by calling provider APIs directly.
- State is stored in a state file (State is stored in S3 with native S3 locking (recommended, available since Terraform v1.10) or DynamoDB locking (deprecated, legacy approach as of Terraform 1.11+) or in Terraform Cloud) and must be managed carefully.

Terraform is declarative but operates outside AWS, interacting with AWS and other systems via providers. Its key components include:

- **Configuration files**: `.tf` modules written in HCL with resource, data, variable, and output blocks.
- **Providers**: Plugins that know how to speak to specific APIs (AWS, Azure, etc.).
- **State**: A JSON state file tracking real resources vs configuration, often stored remotely (S3, Terraform Cloud).
- **Modules**: Reusable configuration units; encourage composable, shared patterns.
- **Plan and apply**: Two-phase workflow, review planned changes, then apply them.

AWS Cloud Development Kit

AWS CDK is a higher-level framework for defining AWS infrastructure using familiar programming languages such as TypeScript, Python, Java, or C#. You write standard code, classes, functions, and loops that describe infrastructure using constructs. CDK synthesizes this code into CloudFormation templates and uses CloudFormation as the deployment engine. It offers a developer-centric interface on the same platform. Here is how CDK works:

- You write code using CDK libraries. For example, a VPC construct, then an `ApplicationLoadBalancedFargateService`, etc.

- CDK builds a construct tree in memory representing your infrastructure design.
- When you run `cdk synth`, CDK synthesizes the construct tree into one or more CloudFormation templates.
- CDK deploys and then uploads those templates to AWS, and CloudFormation executes them just as if you had written the templates by hand.
- State and lifecycle are therefore managed by CloudFormation; CDK is a higher-level authoring layer.

This provides abstractions, reuse, and standard programming features on top of CloudFormation's engine. Key CDK components include:

- **Constructs**: The core building block; classes that represent one or more underlying resources, from low-level (L1) to high-level patterns (L3). L1 constructs map 1:1 to CloudFormation resources (prefixed with Cfn); L2 constructs are curated abstractions with sensible defaults and built-in security practices; L3 constructs are high-level patterns that compose multiple resources into complete, opinionated architectures.
- **Stacks**: CDK Stack classes that model a deployable unit; each stack synthesizes to a CloudFormation stack.
- **Apps**: A CDK app is a collection of stacks/constructs, an entry point for synthesis and deployment.
- **Context and environment**: Configuration and environment-specific values are resolved at synthesis time.
- **CDK Command Line Interface (CLI)**: Compiles your code (synth), deploys stacks, and manages diff/rollback via CloudFormation.

Comparison between CloudFormation, Terraform, and CDK

There is no absolute winner; the best choice depends on your organization, scope, and constraints. We use AWS CloudFormation when:

- You want AWS-native, managed IaC with minimal extra tooling.
- Your organization already standardizes on AWS services and values tight integration, StackSets, and service-level support.
- You are building straightforward stacks, often serverless or reference architectures, where declarative YAML/JSON is acceptable.
- Compliance and audit prefer tools entirely under AWS's control.

  Trade-offs: templates can become verbose; reuse and abstraction are limited compared to full programming languages; and multi-cloud is out of scope.

We use Terraform when:

- You need multi-cloud or multi-provider IaC. AWS plus other clouds, on-prem systems, SaaS APIs, and shared workflows across all of them.
- Platform / DevOps teams want a single tool and language (HCL) to manage everything, not just AWS.
- You need a mature ecosystem of providers and modules and be comfortable managing Terraform state and lifecycle.
- You want the plan/apply experience decoupled from any one cloud provider, perhaps integrated into an existing CI toolchain or Terraform Cloud.

  Tradeoffs: AWS integration is via the provider, not native; you must manage state backends, locking, and upgrades. CDK-style high-level constructs are available only through third-party wrappers or CDK for Terraform, adding complexity.

We use AWS CDK when:

- You are AWS-centric, and your teams are mostly application developers comfortable in TypeScript/Python/Java more than declarative YAML.
- You want to co-locate app and infra code, use the same language, and benefit from loops, conditions, and reusable classes.
- You value high-level construct libraries that encode AWS best practices.
- You are okay with CloudFormation as the underlying engine (state, limits, StackSets, etc.), and you want to build your own internal abstractions.

  Tradeoffs: AWS-only; very large stacks can produce large templates; debugging may require inspecting generated CloudFormation. For multi-cloud or non-AWS targets, Terraform over CDK is usually preferred.

Putting it together:

- **Pure AWS, ops-driven, compliance-sensitive**: CloudFormation is a solid baseline; CDK can be layered on later as development practices mature. CloudFormation's state is managed by AWS.
- **AWS-only, developer-heavy product teams**: CDK often provides the best experience, rich abstractions, shared constructs, and infra alongside service code. CDK's state is managed by AWS.
- **Multi-cloud or lots of non-AWS dependencies**: Terraform is usually the most pragmatic choice, giving you one IaC toolchain across everything. Terraform's state lives outside AWS

Many architectural mix tools. Terraform for global, cross-cloud foundations, and CDK or CloudFormation for AWS-specific application stacks. As a solutions architect, standardize by domain and team to minimize fragmentation and select tools that best fit each platform area's scope and skill set.

Modular and reusable IaC templates and code

Modular and reusable IaC means build once, reuse everywhere for infrastructure components. Instead of one large template, break infrastructure into small, well-named modules that each solve a single problem, then assemble them like LEGO bricks across environments and workloads.

IaC concept

Modular and reusable IaC treats infrastructure definitions like a library rather than one-off scripts. Instead of a large template covering everything from VPCs to Lambda functions, break your design into smaller, well-scoped blocks such as network, app tier, data tier, and observability. Each block has defined inputs and outputs and can be composed into larger systems. This approach simplifies change management, promotes pattern sharing between teams, and prevents copy-paste drift across projects.

Think in layers. Foundational modules cover accounts, VPCs, subnets, and shared security controls. Above the foundational layer sit reusable patterns for application components like web service stacks, serverless APIs, or batch jobs. At the top, assemble these modules into environment stacks (dev, test, prod), passing environment-specific configurations while keeping structure and code consistent. New environments or applications are created by assembling and parameterizing existing modules rather than starting from scratch.

Apply these rules: keep modules small and focused on a single responsibility with clear, documented inputs and outputs. Avoid hard-coding environment-specific values; pass them in to enable reuse across accounts and regions. Maintain consistent layout and naming conventions across repositories, and publish blessed modules for common patterns to prevent reinvention. AWS Service Catalog and the CDK Construct Hub provide native mechanisms to publish and distribute approved IaC modules across teams and accounts. Route all changes through version control and CI/CD, treating modules like any code library with reviews, semantic versioning, and changelogs to ensure predictable AWS architecture evolution without breaking dependent stacks.

Example of modular and reusable IaC templates

A simple example is a standard VPC module that creates a VPC with public and private subnets across three Availability Zones, **Network Address Translation** (**NAT**) gateways, route tables, and basic flow logs. Inputs include CIDR ranges, environment name, and a flag for with or without NAT. Each new workload, such as the orders service, payments service, or internal tools, calls this module instead of recreating the networking. If you update the module, such as by adding VPC flow logs or changing the NAT design, all new environments benefit from the change.

Another common pattern is a service stack module for compute. For example, a reusable definition for an ECS or **Elastic Kubernetes Service** (**EKS**) backed microservice might include an Auto Scaling group or Fargate service, an **Application Load Balancer** (**ALB**) with standard listeners and health checks, CloudWatch alarms, and log configuration. Inputs include container image URI, CPU/memory settings, desired count, and domain/paths. Each microservice uses this module with different parameters, ensuring consistent security groups, logging, and scaling rules. Similarly, a reusable RDS or Aurora module enforces encryption at rest, backup retention, multi-AZ, parameter groups, and standard alarms while allowing teams to select engine version and instance size.

You can extend this approach with cross-cutting modules. A central logging module creates log groups, metric filters, and subscriptions to a log-processing Lambda. A monitoring baseline module attaches standard CPU, latency, and error alarms to any load balancer or Auto Scaling group. A security baseline module defines IAM roles, SCPs, and Config rules applied to every new account or environment. In all cases, you capture best practices once in IaC, provide teams with simple parameters to customize, and avoid building each environment as a unique snowflake.

CI/CD pipelines for infrastructure deployment

CI/CD pipelines bring software delivery discipline to AWS environments by routing every VPC, subnet, IAM role, or ECS cluster change through version control, automated checks, and controlled promotion instead of manual console edits. This approach treats infrastructure as a product with its own lifecycle, tests, and approvals, significantly reducing drift and surprises while enabling safe evolution of complex architectures. This description focuses on general patterns and workflows without referencing specific service screenshots.

CI/CD pipeline for infrastructure

At a high level, an infrastructure CI/CD pipeline follows the same stages as an application pipeline: source, build/validate, test, and deploy (dev to test to prod). The key difference is the artifacts: instead of binaries or container images, the primary artifacts are IaC templates or code (CloudFormation/CDK, Terraform, etc.) plus generated plans or change sets. Every infrastructure change starts with a commit to a Git repository. The pipeline then:

- Pulls the new version of the templates or CDK/Terraform code.
- Runs static checks and security/compliance scans.
- Generates a plan or diff showing proposed resource changes.
- Deploys to a lower environment and runs post-deployment checks.
- Promotes the same artifact (same commit) to higher environments once checks pass, in case of CDK/CloudFormation, for Terraform, this means promoting the same configuration code, with only environment-specific variables changing.

This creates a single, auditable path from design to production for your AWS foundation and application stacks.

Example workflow with detailed pipeline steps

Assume you are using Git with an AWS-native pipeline (for example, CodePipeline with CodeBuild) and CloudFormation/CDK for IaC. The same pattern translates almost directly if you swap in Terraform or another engine. The workflow is as follows:

1. **Source stage**:
   - All infrastructure definitions live in a Git repository (often separate repos or folders for platform vs application stacks).
   - A push to the main branch or a merge of a pull request triggers the pipeline.
   - Branch protection and code review ensure that at least one other engineer has looked at the change.

   Outcome: The pipeline has a specific commit of your IaC code as input.

2. **Build and validation stage**: In this stage, the pipeline treats IaC as code and performs non-destructive checks:
   - **Syntax and linting**: Validate YAML/JSON; run formatters and linters for CDK/Terraform modules.
   - **Unit or structural tests**: For CDK, synthesize templates and run assertions; for Terraform, run terraform validate and module tests.
   - **Security and compliance checks**: Scan for risky patterns (public S3 buckets, overly broad IAM, missing encryption, etc.) using policy-as-code tools.

   If any check fails, the pipeline stops and no deployment occurs.

   Outcome: Only templates/code that pass basic quality and security gates progress.

3. **Plan/changeset stage**: Before modifying infrastructure, generate a preview of the proposed changes:
   - **For CloudFormation/CDK**: create a change set that shows which resources will be created, modified, or deleted.
   - **For Terraform**: run a plan and capture the output.
   - Display this diff in the pipeline UI or PR comments so reviewers can assess the exact impact.

   This what-if step helps catch unintentional deletions, large destructive changes, or mis-scoped updates before deployment.

   Outcome: A human-readable plan/change set that reviewers and approvers can inspect.

4. **Deploy to development (or sandbox) environment**: Once the plan is verified, the pipeline automatically applies the change to a non-production environment:

- **Apply IaC**: Execute the CloudFormation change set, CDK deploy, or Terraform apply for the dev environment.
- **Run smoke tests**:
    - Can new resources be reached (for example, a connection to the database is present)?
    - Are health checks on ALBs/**Network Load Balancers** (**NLBs**) passing?
    - Do basic permissions (IAM, security groups, **Network Access Control Lists** (**NACLs**) behave as expected?

If deployment or tests fail, the pipeline stops and rolls back (for CloudFormation) or requires a manual fix and new commit.

Outcome: The new infrastructure definition is proven to work in at least one environment.

5. **Promotion to test/staging**: If the development environment deploys successfully, the same artifact (commit and templates) is promoted to test or staging:
    - The pipeline parameterizes environment-specific details (account IDs, VPC IDs, instance sizes) but does not change the IaC code itself.
    - Deploys to staging via the same mechanism.
    - **Runs more thorough validation**:
        - Integration tests with dependent services.
        - Load or performance tests for critical components.
        - Security tests (for example, dynamic checks, penetration scans).

    Some organizations require manual approval at this stage, where an architect or platform owner reviews test results and the change plan before promoting to production.

    Outcome: The change is validated under production-like conditions and signed off.

6. **Production deployment**: Finally, the pipeline deploys to production, again with the exact same templates and code:
    - Use blue/green or rolling deployment strategies for supported components (e.g., ECS services, Lambda aliases, **Auto Scaling groups** (**ASGs**) behind load balancers):
        - Stand up a new stack or resource set.
        - Shift traffic gradually and monitor metrics.
        - Roll back automatically on failure or unacceptable health signals.
    - **Implement strict safety checks**:
        - Require production-only approvals.
        - Enforce extra checks for certain resource types (databases, IAM, networking).

After deployment, the pipeline runs production smoke tests and sends notifications via Slack or email with a link to the change record.

Outcome: Production is updated in a controlled, repeatable way, with clear traceability back to code and reviews.

Best practices for infrastructure CI/CD

Several patterns consistently improve pipeline safety and maintainability:

- Treat IaC as first-class code:
  - Keep it in Git with code review, branching strategies, and semantic versioning for modules or stacks.
  - Use clear directory structure and naming conventions for environments and components.
- Separate concerns and scopes:
  - Have distinct pipelines (or at least distinct stages) for:
    - Platform / landing-zone infrastructure (accounts, orgs, baseline networking).
    - Shared services (central logging, security tooling, CI infrastructure).
    - Application specific stacks.
  - This limits the blast radius and simplifies rollbacks.
- Enforce least privilege and guardrails:
  - Pipeline roles should only be able to affect the stacks and resources they manage, not the entire account.
  - Use policies to prevent direct, unmanaged console changes on critical stacks where possible to minimize drift.
- Make plans and diffs mandatory:
  - Never apply changes blindly. Always generate and review a plan or change set, especially for production.
  - For high-risk environments, require human approval that includes both code and infrastructure diffs.
- Promote artifacts, not re-runs:
  - Do not retrain or re-synthesize infrastructure independently per environment. Build once and promote the same artifact through dev, test, and prod.
  - Only environment parameters (e.g., account IDs, CIDR ranges) should differ.
- Integrate testing and observability:
  - Embed automated tests into the pipeline: connectivity checks, synthetic transactions, or simple *does this endpoint respond?* probes.

- After deployment, monitor metrics, logs, and alarms to detect regressions and consider blocking deployments that degrade key **service level agreements** (**SLAs**).
- Design for rollback and disaster recovery:
  - Ensure you can roll back to a previous version of IaC quickly (for example, by redeploying the previous commit).
  - For stateful resources (databases, S3), combine infrastructure rollbacks with snapshots and data recovery plans.
- Document and socialize the pipeline:
  - Make the pipeline the default path for any infrastructure change, and train teams to use it instead of manual edits.
  - Provide clear runbooks for handling failed deployments, rollbacks, and emergency fixes via the same pipeline.

When you set up CI/CD pipelines for infrastructure deployment this way, your AWS architectures become not just welldesigned on paper, but consistently realized in practice. Every change is reviewed, tested, and tracked; environments stay in sync; and teams can rapidly evolve the platform without sacrificing safety or predictability.

GitOps and continuous delivery best practices

GitOps and continuous delivery move the deployment pipeline into Git: the desired state resides in repositories, and automated agents reconcile the running environment to match the main branch. For an AWS Solutions Architect, this shifts the mindset from CI/CD pushing artifacts into clusters or accounts to clusters and platforms continuously pulling and converging to Git's declared state, providing strong auditability, easy rollbacks, and consistent multi-environment behavior. On Amazon EKS, the two most widely used GitOps controllers are Flux and ArgoCD, both of which are supported by AWS prescriptive guidance and can be configured to authenticate with ECR and assume IAM roles via IRSA.

GitOps concept in practice

In GitOps, Git serves as the single source of truth for application and often environment configuration. Kubernetes manifests, Helm charts, Kustomize overlays, or other declarative specs are stored in one or more repositories. A GitOps controller, such as one running in Amazon EKS, monitors these repos, detects changes, and reconciles the live cluster state accordingly. Rather than humans or CI jobs applying kubectl commands, the platform continuously pulls the desired state from Git to maintain synchronization.

Continuous delivery under GitOps is essentially merge to deploy: once a change is reviewed and merged into the appropriate branch or directory (for example, **`environments/prod/`**), the system ensures that the environment converges to that version. Rollback becomes a git revert or a promotion of a previous tag; disaster recovery becomes recreating the cluster and letting the GitOps controller reconcile it from scratch.

Example of GitOps workflow on AWS

A typical GitOps continuous delivery flow for workloads on Amazon EKS looks like this:

1. **Source and structure**:
   - **You maintain at least two repos**:
     - An app repo with code, Dockerfiles, tests, and CI workflows.
     - An environment/config repo with Kubernetes manifests, Helm charts, or Kustomize overlays for dev, staging, and prod.
   - Each environment has its own path or branch (for example, **`envs/dev`**, **`envs/stage`**, **`envs/prod`**).
2. **Application CI**:
   - A conventional CI pipeline builds your container image from the app repo, runs unit and integration tests, and pushes the image to Amazon ECR.
   - Upon success, CI updates the environment repo, such as bumping the image tag in a Helm values file for dev, via an automated pull request.
3. **Change review and merge**:
   - Platform or app engineers review the environment repo pull request, examining changed manifests such as image tags, resource limits, and configuration.
   - Once approved and merged into the dev environment path/branch, Git becomes the new desired state for dev.
4. **GitOps reconciliation (dev)**:
   - A GitOps controller running in the dev EKS cluster continuously watches the environment repo.
   - It detects the new commit in **`envs/dev`**, pulls the latest manifests, compares them to live cluster objects, and applies the changes.
   - The new version rolls out in dev according to the deployment strategy defined (for example, rolling update, canary, or blue/green).
5. **Promotion to higher environments**:
   - If dev tests look good, you promote the same version to staging and production by:
     - Update the image tag in **`envs/stage`** and **`envs/prod`**, often via a promotion pull request or tagging mechanism.

    - Use automation to copy the dev configuration into other environment folders.
  - Merge into stage or prod triggers the same reconcile loop in those clusters: they pull the change and converge.

6. **Rollback**:
   - If a deployment fails, revert the problematic commit in the environment repo or reset to a previous tag. The GitOps controllers then reconcile, rolling the cluster back to the last known good state.

Architecturally, the delivery pipeline for clusters is now Git | controller | cluster, with CI responsible only for building artifacts and updating the desired state in Git.

Detailed end-to-end pipeline steps

You can think of GitOps continuous delivery as two linked pipelines:

1. **CI pipeline (artifact pipeline)**:
   - **Trigger**: Code pushed to application repository.
   - **Steps**:
     a. Build container image.
     b. Run tests and security scans.
     c. Push image to ECR.
     d. Open or update a pull request in the environment repo with the new image tag for the target environment.
2. **GitOps CD pipeline** (**environment pipeline**):
   - **Trigger**: PR merged in the environment repo.
   - **Steps**:
     a. Environment repo updated (for example, **`envs/dev`** now refers to **`app:v1.2.3`**).
     b. GitOps controller in the corresponding cluster detects a repo change.
     c. Controller fetches manifests/Helm chart and computes desired vs. actual cluster state.
     d. Controller applies changes: updates Deployments, ConfigMaps, Services, etc., following the configured rollout strategy.
     e. Observability tools, metrics, logs, and alerts confirm or reject health. If a progressive deployment tool is used, it can automatically roll back when health checks fail.

The key difference from traditional push-based CD is that the cluster pulls and reconciles, eliminating direct kubectl or cluster access from CI systems.

Best practices for GitOps and CD in AWS

In this section, we will discuss various best practices for GitOps and CD in AWS, and we can opt for building an efficient and robust system:

- Git as the single source of truth:
  - Treat Git, not the cluster or CI jobs, as the authoritative record of what should be running.
  - Avoid manual kubectl changes. If a hotfix is necessary, codify and commit it promptly.
- Separate app and environment repos:
  - Keep application code and environment definitions decoupled. App teams can iterate freely while environment repos capture deployments and promotion history.
  - This approach encourages clear promotion flows and precise access control, such as stricter permissions on production environment repos.
- Use declarative specs everywhere:
  - Prefer declarative manifests (Kubernetes YAML, Helm, Kustomize, or similar) that represent the full desired state.
  - Avoid imperative scripts in the environment repo, as they can cause drift or unpredictable side effects.
- Design clear environment promotion flows:
  - Make promotion explicit: dev, staging, and prod should be separate merges, often requiring different approvals.
  - Use tags or branches to represent versions (for example, v1.2.3 is now the desired prod version) and rely on Git history for traceability.
- Apply least privilege and robust **role-based access control** (**RBAC**):
  - Restrict who can merge to the environment repos, especially for production.
  - Lock down cluster roles so the GitOps controller has the necessary permissions to reconcile resources, while CI and human operators have limited direct write access.
- Integrate progressive delivery:
  - Combine GitOps with canary or blue/green strategies where possible. The controller applies a new configuration; rollout controllers or service meshes handle the gradual shift in traffic.
  - Use metrics and alerts integrated into rollouts to automatically trigger rollbacks when error rates or latency exceed thresholds.

- Observability and drift detection:
  - Monitor reconciliation status to track how often clusters are out of sync and identify the causes.
  - Build dashboards displaying the current desired version per environment, sync status, and rollout health, enabling operators to quickly verify alignment between Git and the live environment.
- Multi-cluster and multi-tenant considerations:
  - For SaaS on EKS or multi-cluster setups, standardize a pattern, such as one environment repo with per-cluster directories or one repo per tenant, and adhere to it to avoid confusion.
  - Use templating tools like Helm or Kustomize so shared services and tenants maintain a base configuration with minimal environment-specific overlays.

Implementing GitOps and continuous delivery this way in AWS makes your clusters and platforms self-healing regarding configuration. If a resource is changed manually, the controller detects and corrects drift. When reconstructing an environment, you can create new clusters and let Git drive them to the correct state. For a Solutions Architect, the real benefit is predictable, auditable Git events and runtime infrastructure that faithfully reflect your repositories.

Security and compliance automation in IaC

Security and compliance automation in IaC means embedding guardrails directly into the cloud-defining code rather than adding them later. When every VPC, subnet, role, and database is created from templates or constructs, you have a single place to enforce rules such as that everything must be encrypted, only these ports are allowed, or logs must go to a central account. The principle is simple: if infrastructure is created only through IaC that includes security and compliance rules, every new environment starts closer to compliance by default.

This begins with secure defaults. Base modules, such as a VPC, ECS service, or RDS instance, should always enable encryption at rest, enforce **Transport Layer Security** (**TLS**) where applicable, restrict security groups to the minimum required, and send logs to CloudWatch or a centralized logging solution. Teams use these modules instead of raw building blocks, inheriting controls without extra effort. Over time, these golden modules become internal standards, ensuring workloads align with baseline security posture.

You can go a step further by shifting checks left into the IaC workflow. That means running automated policy checks whenever someone proposes a change: static analysis on templates, policy-as-code tools (like AWS CloudFormation Guard (cfn-guard), AWS Config conformance packs, Open Policy Agent/ Rego, or similar) that enforce rules such as no public S3 buckets, no wide-open security groups, and all IAM roles must have tags. These checks run in pull requests or pipeline stages, so insecure or non-compliant changes fail before they ever reach AWS.

Instead of security teams manually reviewing every change, they codify their expectations once, and the pipeline enforces them consistently.

Compliance frameworks like **Payment Card Industry Data Security Standard** (**PCI DSS**), **Health Insurance Portability and Accountability Act** (**HIPAA**), and internal standards benefit from this approach. Many requirements, such as mandatory logging, retention periods, restricted network paths, encryption, and backup policies, can be codified. Account-level controls, such as multi-factor access requirements, can be enforced via **Service Control Policies** (**SCPs**), which are also manageable as code. Encoding these into IaC modules and automated checks simplifies evidence generation: every RDS instance is created via this module, enforcing encryption, backups, and logging, and every change passes through a reviewed pull request and a recorded pipeline run. This shifts audits from console searches to code, configuration, and pipeline history review.

Automation in IaC supports ongoing enforcement beyond initial deployment. If someone makes an out-of-band console change, drift detection identifies it, which can then be remediated through IaC re-deployment or AWS Config auto-remediation rules. Combined with monitoring and alerting on critical changes, such as a bucket becoming public or a security group opening, your architecture gains a feedback loop: detect deviations, alert, and either auto-correct via IaC or require a reviewed code change. This makes security and compliance continuous, automated parts of building and evolving AWS infrastructure.

Other IaC concepts

Apart from various IaC concepts we discussed earlier, we are going to cover a few other key IaC concepts, such as drift detection, state management, and monitoring and alerting for infrastructure health. Drift detection and state management keep your IaC definitions aligned with the actual AWS environment, while monitoring and alerting for infrastructure health shifts, and focusing on configuration correctness for operational behavior.

Drift detection and state management

Drift detection and state management keep your IaC definitions aligned with the actual AWS environment. Console changes, like opening a security group or adjusting auto scaling, can cause discrepancies between your templates or CDK stacks and live resources. Drift detection identifies these differences by comparing the declared state with the live state and flags mismatches. Effective state management treats IaC definitions and state files as the single source of truth, applies changes only through code, and uses drift reports to decide whether to roll back manual edits, codify them, or investigate misconfigurations.

Monitoring and alerting for infrastructure health

Monitoring and alerting for infrastructure health shifts focus from configuration correctness to operational behavior. Even with perfectly synced stacks, you must ensure resources are healthy: instances and containers stay within CPU and memory limits, databases respond, load balancers avoid unusual errors, and queues do not back up. This is achieved by integrating metrics, logs, and traces into dashboards and alarms, turning issues into clear signals rather than vague complaints. In a well-designed AWS architecture, alerts cover both application and platform layers, notifying you of unhealthy services, stressed Availability Zones, or critical resources nearing limits. Together, drift detection, state management, and health monitoring provide continuous feedback that the infrastructure is both correctly defined and reliably running in production. **Amazon CloudWatch**, **AWS Health Dashboard**, and **AWS Systems Manager OpsCenter** to aggregate and triage the operational issues (OpsItems) that CloudWatch and Config alarms generate.

Conclusion

This chapter presents infrastructure as code for designing, reviewing, and evolving infrastructure rather than creating it instantly. We introduced the fundamentals of IaC and how AWS CloudFormation, Terraform, and AWS CDK offer different ways to describe VPCs, security, compute, and data services consistently. We then covered modular, reusable templates that capture common patterns, standard VPCs, service stacks, and database baselines, enabling teams to build architectures from trusted components instead of reinventing them. Finally, we integrated these with CI/CD pipelines and GitOps, where changes pass through pull requests, automated checks, and staged deployments, ensuring environments are auditable and changes predictable.

We also linked IaC to day-two concerns: security, compliance, and operational health. Embedding guardrails and policies into modules and pipelines automates security and compliance, ensuring new environments start closer to right and catching non-compliant changes early. Drift detection and state management keep declared states aligned with reality, exposing manual edits and configuration drift before issues arise. Monitoring and alerting extend feedback from configuration to behavior, indicating when resources are stressed or failing, not just if they are defined correctly. Together, these practices enable running AWS architectures as living codebases that are consistent, safe to change, observable, and easier to manage as they grow.

The next chapter shifts focus from building and automating architectures to ensuring they are secure and well-governed. We will cover layering security across identities, networks, data, and applications, and use AWS-native controls to enforce least privilege and strong isolation without hindering teams. We will also explore governance patterns such as multi-account strategies, guardrails, and policy-as-code that help large organizations align workloads with shared standards. The goal is to demonstrate how to design AWS architectures that are scalable, efficient, secure, compliant, and manageable as they grow.

References

1. **https://aws.amazon.com/solutions/guidance/building-saas-applications-on-amazon-eks-using-gitops/**
2. **https://docs.aws.amazon.com/prescriptive-guidance/latest/eks-gitops-tools/best-practices.html**
3. **https://docs.aws.amazon.com/prescriptive-guidance/latest/eks-gitops-tools/introduction.html**
4. **https://docs.aws.amazon.com/pdfs/prescriptive-guidance/latest/eks-gitops-tools/eks-gitops-tools.pdf**
5. **https://www.pulumi.com/blog/gitops-best-practices-i-wish-i-had-known-before/** *-Third-party perspective*
6. **https://docs.aws.amazon.com/prescriptive-guidance/latest/patterns/set-up-a-ci-cd-pipeline-by-using-aws-codepipeline-and-aws-cdk.html**
7. **https://docs.aws.amazon.com/cdk/v2/guide/cdk-pipeline.html**
8. **https://docs.aws.amazon.com/codepipeline/latest/userguide/pipelines-create.html**
9. **https://docs.aws.amazon.com/prescriptive-guidance/latest/strategy-cicd-litmus/understanding-cicd.html**
10. **https://docs.gitlab.com/ci/cloud_deployment/**
11. **https://docs.aws.amazon.com/cloudformation/**
12. **https://docs.aws.amazon.com/cdk/**
13. **https://developer.hashicorp.com/terraform/cloud-docs/recommended-practices**

CHAPTER 13
Securing and Governing AWS Architectures

Introduction

This chapter shifts focus from individual services to securing, managing, and sustaining entire **Amazon Web Services** (**AWS**) environments. We use the AWS Well-Architected Framework pillars as a practical model for cloud best practices. Each pillar addresses specific risks or inefficiencies: system operation and improvement, data and identity protection, workload resilience, resource efficiency, cost control, and responsible energy use. Instead of abstract checklists, these pillars guide everyday design and operational decisions, becoming integral to your architectural approach.

Next, we translate these principles into automated practices. We demonstrate how AWS Security Hub and AWS Config continuously monitor your accounts against security and compliance baselines, proactively detecting issues. We link this to monitoring, logging, and incident response workflows, where metrics, logs, and traces trigger alerts and runbooks to guide your response. The goal is to build AWS architectures that perform reliably every day, supported by active monitoring, continuous improvement, and governance through code and processes rather than reliance on memory or intent.

Structure

This chapter covers the following topics:

- AWS Well-Architected Framework's pillars
- Operational excellence and continuous improvement
- Automating security and compliance with AWS Security Hub and Config
- Monitoring, logging, and incident response workflows

Objectives

Securing and managing AWS architectures begins with a clear understanding of the AWS Well-Architected Framework. Its pillars offer a practical approach to evaluating designs for security, reliability, operational excellence, performance efficiency, cost optimization, and sustainability. These principles enable architects to create systems that are functional, secure, resilient, and manageable over time.

Operational excellence involves disciplined system management and ongoing improvement. In AWS, this includes automation, outcome reviews, incident analysis, and process refinement as environments evolve. Well-governed architectures adapt through continuous feedback and improvement.

Automating checks and controls enhances security and compliance. AWS Security Hub centralizes security findings, while AWS Config monitors resource configuration changes and evaluates them against defined rules. These tools help identify drift, reduce manual effort, and maintain consistent standards across accounts and workloads.

Monitoring, logging, and incident response are essential components. Effective architectures collect relevant logs, generate actionable alerts, and support clear response workflows. This visibility enables teams to detect issues early, assess impact, and recover confidently.

AWS's Well-Architected Framework's pillars

The pillars of AWS's Well-Architected Framework define the essential qualities that a robust cloud architecture should uphold throughout its lifecycle. These pillars function as both a comprehensive checklist and a standardized language for design and review processes. They address operational excellence, which focuses on the continuous improvement of systems; security, which involves the protection of identities, data, and workloads; and reliability, which ensures system resilience in the event of component failures. Additionally, the pillars guide the efficient use of compute, storage, and networking resources (performance efficiency), promote cost control by minimizing waste (cost optimization), and encourage responsible management of energy and resources (sustainability). Evaluating architectures against these pillars enables the development of solutions that are not only functional but also secure, efficient, resilient, and scalable to meet evolving business requirements.

Note: **AWS's Well-Architected Tool, available at no cost in the AWS console, offers a structured review of your workloads against framework best practices and generates a prioritized improvement plan. Also, Well-Architected Lenses, which are domain-specific extensions of the framework (ML Lens, Serverless Lens, SaaS Lens, GenAI Lens, etc.) extend the framework for specific domains.**

Pillars of AWS's Well-Architected Framework

The AWS Well-Architected Framework describes six core pillars that guide how we design systems on AWS.

Security pillar

The security pillar is about protecting your systems, data, and people. It covers how you control who can do what, how you protect data at rest and in transit, how you detect bad behavior, and how you respond when something goes wrong.

Modern AWS security design increasingly adopts Zero Trust principles, which require explicit verification of every request, regardless of network location, instead of assuming internal network traffic is safe.

Uses

You apply the security pillar in every design discussion, not as an afterthought. Whether building a small serverless API or a multi-account enterprise platform, you determine:

- How identities (users, apps, services) authenticate and what they can access.
- How data is encrypted and where keys live.
- How you log, monitor, and alert on suspicious activity.

On AWS, this includes using **Identity and Access Management** (**IAM**) roles and policies instead of long-lived access keys, private subnets and security groups, **key management service** (**KMS**) encrypted storage, centralized logging, and services like AWS **Web Application Firewall** (**WAF**) and Shield to protect public endpoints. **Amazon Macie** specializes in discovering and classifying sensitive data, such as PII, within **Amazon S3**. Although it offers some visibility into S3 bucket access and security posture, comprehensive bucket-level policy monitoring is better handled by S3 Block Public Access, IAM Access Analyzer, and **AWS Config**.

Significance

Effective security design enables fast progress without recklessness. It limits impact during incidents and simplifies compliance for auditors and customers. For Solutions Architects, security is the guardrail that supports safe innovation.

Example

A payment-processing API is deployed in private subnets within a **Virtual Private Cloud** (**VPC**) and fronted by an internal **Application Load Balancer** (**ALB**). Amazon CloudFront serves as the public entry point, providing TLS termination, caching, and AWS WAF protection, and forwards requests to the ALB over private connectivity. The application uses IAM roles to securely access DynamoDB and S3, enforces encryption with AWS KMS, and streams logs to a centralized logging account for analysis. IAM policies and security group rules are reviewed as rigorously as application code to maintain a strong security posture.

Reliability pillar

The reliability pillar is about making sure your system works as expected, even when individual parts fail. It focuses on fault tolerance, automatic recovery, and the ability to handle changes in load or infrastructure. AWS Resilience Hub enables you to set resilience targets, evaluate workloads against the reliability pillar, and monitor progress over time.

Uses

You apply the reliability pillar when you decide:

- How many **Availability Zones** (**AZs**) to use.
- How workloads recover from instance or AZ failures.
- How you perform backups, restores, and disaster recovery.

On AWS, this involves using multiple Availability Zones for stateless services, managed databases with automated backups and multi-AZ replicas, load balancer health checks, and services like Auto Scaling and Route 53 for failover.

Significance

Reliable systems minimize downtime and protect your reputation. They also improve on-call experiences. For Solutions Architects, reliability transforms proofs of concept into trusted solutions for critical workloads.

Example

Consider an ecommerce website. You deploy stateless application containers across at least two AZs behind a load balancer, store product data in a **Relational Database Service** (**RDS**) database with multiAZ enabled, and cache hot data in ElastiCache. Auto Scaling replaces unhealthy instances automatically. You also have a tested runbook and scripts to restore from RDS snapshots if something catastrophic happens.

Performance efficiency pillar

The performance efficiency pillar is about using computing resources efficiently so your system can meet demand and respond quickly. It covers how you choose instance types, database engines, caching strategies, and patterns that keep latency low and throughput high.

AWS Graviton processors deliver significantly better price-performance for many workloads, and AWS Inferentia offers optimized inference for ML workloads. Both are key to improving performance efficiency in modern AWS architectures.

Uses

You apply this pillar when you:

- Size instances or choose between CPU, GPU, and specialized chips.
- Decide whether to use serverless, containers, or traditional servers.
- Introduce caches, **content delivery networks** (**CDNs**), and asynchronous processing.

On AWS, this may involve using Lambda or Fargate for bursty workloads, CloudFront to cache content near users, DynamoDB for high-throughput key-value access, and autoscaling policies to automatically handle spikes.

Significance

Performance issues often manifest as slow apps or laggy search, directly affecting user satisfaction and revenue. Thoughtful performance design enables smooth growth without constant firefighting.

Example

Take a video streaming service. You store video files in S3 and serve them through CloudFront so content is cached at edge locations. Metadata and user preferences sit in DynamoDB. Transcoding happens asynchronously using EventBridge, Lambda, and Step Functions, so upload actions do not block on heavy processing. The result is fast playback and a responsive UI even during peak hours.

Cost optimization pillar

The Cost optimization pillar focuses on delivering business value at the lowest reasonable cost. It emphasizes intentional spending where it matters and avoiding waste, not simply minimizing expenses. AWS Cost Anomaly Detection automatically identifies unusual spending patterns. AWS Compute Optimizer offers ML-driven right-sizing recommendations for EC2, Lambda, ECS, and other services. Both are essential for ongoing cost optimization.

Uses

You apply this pillar whenever you:

- Choose between instance families and serverless.
- Decide whether to use on-demand, savings plans, or spot.
- Design data retention policies, logging levels, and scaling rules.

On AWS, this often involves right-sizing instances, using auto scaling to avoid paying for idle capacity, selecting storage tiers based on access patterns, and tagging resources to track costs by team or project.

Significance

Uncontrolled cloud costs can undermine the benefits of migrating to AWS. Designing with cost in mind maintains business support for cloud initiatives and frees budget for innovation rather than waste.

Example

Imagine an analytics pipeline that processes logs once per day. Instead of a large, always-on cluster, you use **S3** for storage, **Glue** or **Elastic MapReduce** (**EMR**) on Spot instances for batch processing, and Athena for adhoc queries. You store older data in cheaper S3 tiers and down-sample metrics. The system still provides the insights the business needs, but at a fraction of the cost.

Sustainability pillar

The sustainability pillar minimizes the environmental impact of cloud workloads by using resources efficiently, avoiding unnecessary work, and designing systems that achieve more with less. The AWS Customer Carbon Footprint Tool delivers emissions data by service, region, and time period to support architects in making informed sustainability decisions.

Uses

You use this pillar when you:

- Choose regions (considering AWS's sustainability data and energy mix).
- Optimize workloads to run on fewer, more efficient resources.
- Remove idle or orphaned resources and reduce waste in data processing.

In AWS, sustainability involves preferring managed, shared services over always-on custom fleets, using auto scaling and serverless to reduce idle capacity, compressing and archiving data, and optimizing code to use fewer CPU cycles per request.

Significance

Sustainability is increasingly a business requirement, not just a nice-to-have. Efficient workloads reduce carbon footprint and cost while often improving performance. For Solutions Architects, the Sustainability Pillar frames efficiency as both a technical and ethical priority.

Example

Consider a nightly reporting job that previously ran on a fleet of EC2 instances. You redesign it using serverless: data lands in S3, Athena queries transform it, and a Lambda/Step Functions workflow orchestrates the process. Resources run only when needed, scale with data size, and shut down afterward. This reduces energy use, simplifies operations, and likely lowers costs without sacrificing functionality.

These pillars are not separate checklists applied at the end, but lenses to guide design. A single architecture decision, such as choosing serverless over fixed instances, often impacts security, reliability, performance, cost, and sustainability simultaneously. As an AWS Solutions Architect, your role is to balance these pillars to align with your organization's goals and constraints.

Note: **Sixth Pillar Operational excellence and continuous improvement is covered separately in the next section.**

Operational excellence and continuous improvement

Operational excellence means running systems as well as designing them. AWS Solutions Architecture involves building habits, tools, and culture to operate safely daily, respond quickly to issues, and continuously improve. Rather than relying on heroic efforts, you use runbooks, clear dashboards, and automated responses to ensure predictable system behavior at any time.

Operational excellence manifests in practical choices. You standardize deployments, such as using CI/CD, and avoid manual console changes. Logs, metrics, and traces are easy to access, so engineers can quickly understand system status. You create and test playbooks for common incidents. Operations considerations like health checks, timeouts, retries, and fallback behaviors are integrated into the architecture from the start.

Continuous improvement is the learning aspect of operational excellence. Every incident, deployment, or new requirement provides system feedback. When issues occur, conduct blameless post-incident reviews to identify failures, missed detections, and design or process changes to prevent recurrence. Recurring manual tasks, such as repeated configuration updates, are automated. Over time, this cycle transforms one-off fixes into systemic improvements.

Operational excellence and continuous improvement form a cycle. You design and deploy with operations in mind, observe real-world system behavior, and regularly refine both architecture and operations. For an AWS Solutions Architect, the goal is a system and operating model that adapts, learns, and remains healthy as the platform, team, and business evolve.

AWS Systems Manager and AWS OpsCenter, which is a capability of AWS Systems Manager, are the primary AWS services for implementing operational excellence practices, including runbook automation, patch management, and incident tracking.

Automating security and compliance with AWS Security Hub and Config

Automating security and compliance on AWS means transforming checklists and audits into continuous, integrated processes. AWS Security Hub and AWS Config complement each other well: one monitors configuration over time, and the other consolidates findings into a prioritized dashboard. In this section, we will understand the goals, uses, and significance of these services. We will also look at a typical workflow for automating security and compliance with these services. At the end, we will take a simple example scenario to understand this further in a better way.

Security Hub has evolved from a findings dashboard into an active risk prioritization engine. It now correlates signals across GuardDuty, Inspector, Macie, and Security Hub misconfigurations, delivering near-real-time risk scoring and automatic finding correlation.

AWS Firewall Manager centrally enforces security policies such as WAF rules, security group configurations, and Shield Advanced protections across your organization. AWS Security Hub aggregates and correlates security findings. Together, Firewall Manager delivers consistent preventive controls, while Security Hub provides centralized visibility and monitoring of your security posture.

Understanding goals

AWS Security Hub provides a central dashboard for your security posture. It aggregates findings from AWS services such as GuardDuty, Inspector, Macie, and IAM Access Analyzer, as well as partner tools, and then evaluates your environment against standards such as **AWS Foundational Security Best Practices** (**FSBP**), **Center for Internet Security** (**CIS**) Benchmarks, and **Payment Card Industry** (**PCI**) best practices. This unified view lists security issues with severity and affected resources, eliminating the need to access multiple consoles.

AWS Config records your AWS resource configurations over time and evaluates them against defined rules. It shows your current environment, tracks changes, and flags compliance issues. For example, it identifies public S3 buckets, security groups allowing 0.0.0.0/0 on specific ports, or missing required encryption.

Uses and significance

Use these services whenever consistent security and compliance across multiple accounts and regions matter, which is nearly always. In small environments, they prevent accidental misconfigurations. In large enterprises, they provide security and compliance teams with near-real-time visibility, replacing periodic manual reviews.

Their value lies in automation and scale. Instead of relying on teams to remember to configure things securely, you codify expectations as rules and standards. Security Hub continuously evaluates accounts and highlights deviations; AWS Config tracks configurations and flags non-compliance. Together, they enable early issue detection and prioritization and demonstrate ongoing controls to auditors beyond point-in-time audits.

Narrative workflow

A typical workflow for automating security and compliance with these services includes:

1. **Set a baseline**: In your landing zone or shared services account, define relevant security standards such as CIS AWS Foundations or your internal baseline. Enable AWS Config to record resource configurations across accounts and activate Security Hub with the selected standards.
2. **Define rules and controls**: In AWS Config, enable managed rules or create custom ones that reflect your policies:
   - All S3 buckets must block public access.
   - All **Elastic Block Store** (**EBS**) volumes must be encrypted.
   - IAM root accounts must not have access keys.

   These rules continuously evaluate resources and classify them as compliant or non-compliant.
3. **Aggregate findings centrally**: Security Hub ingests and normalizes findings from AWS Config and other security services. Instead of reviewing raw rules per account, you see aggregated findings, such as these 10 buckets in these three accounts violate your public access policy, with standardized severity levels.
4. **Alert and respond**: Connect Security Hub findings to your incident and workflow tools via EventBridge. When a high-severity issue arises, such as a new public S3 bucket, an event can automatically create a ticket, send a message to Slack or Teams, or trigger a Lambda function to remediate the issue by disabling public access and tagging the bucket for follow-up.
5. **Remediation and continuous improvement**: Over time, add automated remediation where safe, such as closing open ports, enforcing encryption, or removing unused IAM permissions. For sensitive cases, keep humans involved while relying on automatic detection and ticket creation. Refine rules to reduce false positives and improve signal-to-noise ratio.

The following figure demonstrates the flowchart showing the security automation pipeline from Config rules through to remediation discussed in this section:

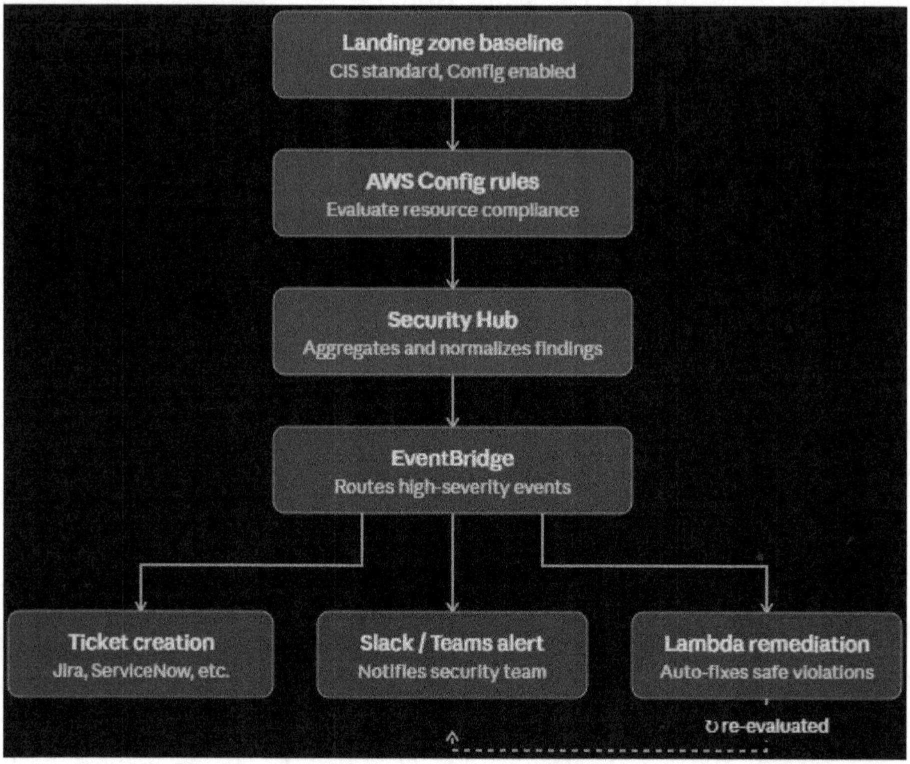

***Figure 13.1:** Security automation pipeline from Config rules through to remediation*

Simple example scenario

Imagine you are responsible for a set of production accounts hosting customer data:

- Enable AWS Config across all accounts with rules requiring encryption on all databases and storage and forbidding public S3 buckets.
- Activate Security Hub and enable the CIS benchmark. It immediately runs checks and highlights deviations from best practices, such as unencrypted snapshots and buckets with public read access.
- Integrate Security Hub with EventBridge so that any new public S3 bucket finding automatically triggers a Lambda function. The function removes public access, tags the bucket with a warning, and posts a message in your team's channel detailing the fix.
- Over time, your dashboards show fewer and fewer recurring issues, and audits become easier because you can demonstrate ongoing, automated controls instead of manually collected screenshots.

Thus, *Automating Security and Compliance with AWS Security Hub and Config* shifts from occasional projects to a continuous safety net integrated into your AWS platform. As a solutions architect, you can design workloads assuming this safety net detects, surfaces, and often resolves misconfigurations before they cause incidents.

Monitoring, logging, and incident response workflows

Monitoring, logging, and incident response form the nervous system of a secure AWS architecture. Designing for security and governance involves not only defining VPCs and IAM roles but also determining how to observe, record, and respond to events. This creates a clear process: an event occurs in the cloud, we detect it quickly, understand it, and then resolve and learn from it.

Monitoring the health and security of your systems

Monitoring is about answering, Is the system behaving as expected right now? For AWS solutions, you typically watch three broad categories:

- **Infrastructure health**: CPU, memory, latency, error rates, and other metrics for instances, containers, databases, and serverless functions.
- **Application behavior**: Request rates, response times, failed logins, and business KPIs like orders per minute or failed payment percentage.
- **Security signals**: Unusual API activity, spikes in denied requests, changes to critical resources, or suspicious network patterns.

In a secure architecture, define these signals upfront. For example, create standard dashboards for every internet-facing workload: panels for 4xx/5xx errors, latency, authentication failures, and key security findings. Deploying a new service automatically includes these dashboards, ensuring consistent visibility for operations and security teams. Amazon CloudWatch offers metrics, logs, and alarms for monitoring infrastructure and applications. AWS X-Ray enables distributed tracing across microservices. Together, they form the observability foundation of a well-monitored AWS architecture.

Creating reliable security record by logging

Logging is your memory. It lets you go back in time to see what actually happened when something looks suspicious or breaks. On AWS, you usually think about logs in a few layers:

- **AWS service logs**: API calls, configuration changes, network flows, and managed service events.
- **Application logs**: What your code writes, errors, warnings, audit trails, and custom security events.

- **Access and audit logs**: Who accessed what, from where, and with which permissions (for example, admin actions, changes to IAM, or data access).

In secure, governed architectures, centralize key logs in a dedicated logging account or shared platform to ensure:

- Logs are harder to tamper with when the workload is compromised.
- Security teams have one place to search when investigating incidents.
- Retention, encryption, and access policies can be managed consistently.

Typically, each AWS account streams key logs (API activity, configuration changes, critical application logs) into a central log store. This enables indexing, searching, and alerting without accessing each account individually. AWS CloudTrail is the primary audit trail service, capturing all API calls across accounts and regions. It should be enabled in every account, with logs delivered to a central, protected S3 bucket.

Incident response workflows

Incident response guides your actions when issues arise. A good workflow is a repeatable, well-understood sequence rather than relying on ad hoc decisions. A typical AWS security incident workflow includes:

1. **Detection**:
   - An alert triggers when a metric or log pattern crosses a threshold, such as a spike in failed logins, a critical resource configuration change, or a new public S3 bucket.
   - The alert appears in a shared channel (email, chat, ticketing system) with context: what happened, when, which account and region, and the affected resource.
2. **Triage**: An on-call engineer or security analyst promptly addresses two questions:
   - Is this a real or a false alarm?
   - How severe is it?

   They review dashboards and logs to confirm the situation. For high-severity incidents, such as potential credential compromise or data exposure, they escalate immediately and follow a predefined playbook.
3. **Containment**: The goal is to contain the incident. Depending on the situation, this may involve:
   - Disabling an access key or role.
   - Isolating an instance or container in a quarantine security group.
   - Reverting a risky security group or bucket policy to a safe baseline.

   In well-designed architectures, many actions are scripted or automated. The playbook directs running tools instead of manual console steps.

4. **Eradication and recovery**: Once the immediate risk is contained, you clean up and restore normal operations:
   - Remove malicious code or configuration.
   - Rotate secrets and credentials.
   - Rebuild or redeploy compromised resources from known-good templates.

   Using IaC, rebuilding typically involves redeploying the stack from Git instead of manually recreating resources.
5. **Post-incident review and improvement**: After things are stable, the team runs a blameless review:
   - What exactly happened?
   - Why did it happen?
   - How did we detect it?
   - What helped, and what slowed us down?

   The team translates lessons into concrete improvements: new or refined alerts, enhanced dashboards, updated runbooks, or architectural changes such as stricter network boundaries or automated guardrails.

Over time, this loop transforms your incident response from chaotic to professional. Each incident makes the system and your response better. Amazon Detective supports in-depth security incident investigations by automatically correlating and visualizing data from CloudTrail, VPC Flow Logs, and GuardDuty findings. It complements Security Hub's detection capabilities by providing greater investigative detail.

Putting it together with an example scenario

Imagine you are securing a multi-account AWS environment with a customer-facing API:

- **Monitoring**:
  - You track error rates and latency for the API, database, and cache.
  - You also watch for security-specific patterns: spikes in 401/403 responses, unusual request rates from a single IP, or unexpected configuration changes in the API's account.
- **Logging**:
  - All API access logs, load balancer logs, and application logs flow into a central logging account.
  - Configuration and access logs from each account are also centralized and retained for a longer period for audits and investigations.

- **Incident response**:
  - One night, alerts trigger due to spikes in API error rates and failed logins. Simultaneously, configuration logs reveal a recent change to an identity provider setting.
  - The on-call engineer follows the runbook: verifies the pattern, temporarily reduces API privileges or rate limits, rolls back the risky configuration change, and updates stakeholders.
  - The review reveals that a misconfigured automation altered an auth setting. A guardrail is added: a rule that blocks or auto-reverts similar changes and triggers an earlier alert if the setting drifts again.

For a Solutions Architect, monitoring, logging, and incident response workflows are integral to design, not just operations. When proposing a new architecture, describe how it will be observed, where logs will be stored, and how the team will respond to incidents. This approach transforms a secure design on paper into a secure, governable production system.

Conclusion

This chapter applies a practical approach to securing and governing AWS environments. Using the AWS Well-Architected Framework's pillars, we showed how operational excellence, security, reliability, performance efficiency, cost optimization, and sustainability guide daily design and operational decisions. We also used the operational excellence, security, reliability, performance efficiency, cost optimization and sustainability pillars to review architectures and identify risks, trade-offs, and opportunities for improvement.

We emphasized that effective security and governance depend on automation and observability. Services such as **AWS Security Hub** and **AWS Config** continuously assess accounts against security and compliance baselines, detecting misconfigurations and drift early. Integrating these tools with monitoring, logging, and incident response workflows creates a feedback loop. Metrics, logs, and traces reveal activity. Alerts and playbooks guide responses. Post-incident reviews strengthen controls and designs. These practices support AWS architectures that are functional, scalable, secure, compliant, efficient, and able to improve as workloads and organizations grow.

The next chapter covers AWS Fargate and Amazon ECS, which allow you to package services into containers and run them on a managed platform. The **Serverless Application Model** (**SAM**) enables you to define event-driven applications, often using Lambda, API Gateway, and other managed services, in a compact, easily deployable template.

References

1. **https://docs.aws.amazon.com/wellarchitected/latest/migration-lens/well-architected-framework-pillars.html**
2. **https://aws.amazon.com/video/watch/883325fcd08/**
3. **https://docs.aws.amazon.com/wellarchitected/latest/framework/the-pillars-of-the-frmework.html**
4. **https://aws.amazon.com/blogs/apn/the-6-pillars-of-the-aws-well-architected-framework/**
5. **https://aws.amazon.com/architecture/well-architected/**
6. **https://aws.amazon.com/security-hub/**
7. **https://aws.amazon.com/config/**
8. **https://docs.aws.amazon.com/pdfs/whitepapers/latest/aws-security-incident-response-guide/aws-security-incident-response-guide.pdf**
9. **https://docs.aws.amazon.com/emr/latest/ManagementGuide/emr-what-is-emr.html**
10. **https://docs.aws.amazon.com/security-ir/latest/userguide/introduction.html**
11. **https://docs.aws.amazon.com/awscloudtrail/latest/userguide/cloudtrail-user-guide.html**
12. **https://docs.aws.amazon.com/config/latest/developerguide/managed-rules-by-aws-config.html**

CHAPTER 14
AWS Fargate, ECS, and SAM

Introduction

This chapter shifts focus from individual **Elastic Compute Cloud** (**EC2**) instances to platforms that run your code. **Amazon Elastic Container Service** (**ECS**) and **Amazon Web Services** (**AWS**) **Fargate** let you package applications into containers while AWS handles much of the underlying work. Instead of managing servers and **Amazon Machine Images** (**AMIs**), you manage tasks, services, images, and scaling. Fargate eliminates the need to manage cluster instances, while ECS offers flexible control over container scheduling. Together, they provide a new approach: you specify what to run and how it should behave, and the platform manages capacity and placement.

We also explore the **Serverless Application Model** (**SAM**), which applies the **infrastructure as code** (**IaC**) concept to event-driven, serverless applications. With SAM, you define Lambda functions, **application programming interfaces** (**APIs**), event sources, and permissions in a compact template, then use simple commands to build, test, and deploy them. This chapter guides you up the stack: from managing machines to containers to focusing solely on functions and events. By the end, you will understand how ECS, Fargate, and SAM offer a range of options for running modern AWS applications, each balancing control, simplicity, and operational effort differently.

Structure

This chapter covers the following topics:

- AWS Fargate
- Amazon Elastic Container Service
- Serverless Application Model

Objectives

This chapter aims to help you design and run AWS applications without managing individual servers. You will learn to use Amazon ECS and AWS Fargate to package workloads into containers, define their operation, and let the platform manage placement, scaling, and routine tasks. You will also explore how the SAM enables concise, repeatable deployment of event-driven, function-based applications. By the chapter's end, you will be able to assess when to use ECS/Fargate containers, when a SAM-based serverless approach is preferable, and how to combine both in a clean, cloud-native architecture.

AWS Fargate

AWS Fargate helps you to run containers in the cloud without managing underlying servers. As an AWS cloud architect, you can focus on task definitions, scaling, and security while AWS handles EC2 instances, patching, and cluster capacity. This makes it ideal for teams seeking container benefits without the operational overhead of cluster management.

Understanding AWS Fargate

AWS Fargate is a serverless computing engine for containers. You define containers and their runtime, and Fargate automatically provides CPU, memory, and networking. You do not select instance types, manage auto scaling groups, or access hosts directly.

You typically use Fargate with the following:

- **Amazon ECS**
- **Amazon Elastic Kubernetes Service** (**EKS**)

In both cases, you define workloads as tasks or Pods, and Fargate runs them on a fully managed fleet.

Fargate's role in architecture

In a typical AWS architecture, Fargate sits in the application compute layer. It is especially useful when:

- You are containerizing microservices and APIs.
- You want consistent deployment packaging (Docker images) but do not want to manage worker nodes.
- You expect variable or bursty load and want to scale quickly without capacity planning.

A common narrative pattern looks like this:

- A client calls your API through Amazon API Gateway or an **Application Load Balancer** (**ALB**).

- The request is routed to one of several containers running on Fargate in private subnets.
- Those containers talk to services like **Relational Database Service** (**RDS**), **DynamoDB**, **S3**, or external APIs.
- Fargate automatically scales the number of running tasks up or down based on traffic.

Externally, it resembles a standard microservices architecture. Internally, it eliminates operational overhead by removing the need to patch or size EC2 nodes.

Core building blocks with ECS + Fargate

When you use **Fargate** with **Amazon ECS**, you work with a few core concepts:

- **Task definitions**: A task definition specifies how containers run: image, CPU and memory allocation, environment variables and secrets, exposed ports, and logging configuration.
- **Services**: An ECS service keeps a certain number of tasks running. For example, you might say, *I want three copies of this API task running at all times*. The service integrates with a load balancer and can scale based on **CloudWatch** metrics.
- **Clusters (logical only)**: On Fargate, AWS provides the compute behind the cluster, whereas on EC2, we provide the instances.
- **Networking and security**: You select subnets and security groups for tasks. Typically, tasks run in private subnets and receive traffic through an ALB or internal services. Security groups regulate network access, similar to EC2 instances.

For EKS + Fargate, the ideas are similar, but expressed in Kubernetes language: you define Pods and namespaces, then configure Fargate profiles to tell AWS which Pods should run on Fargate rather than on your own worker nodes.

Note: **EKS is out of the scope of this chapter; we will learn more about EKS in the upcoming chapters.**

Simple Fargate-backed Web API

Consider building a simple REST API for a product catalog:

1. Containerize your application and push the image to **Amazon Elastic Container Registry** (**ECR**).
2. Create an ECS task definition referencing this image, allocating 0.5 **virtual Central Processing Unit** (**vCPU**) and 1 GB memory, exposing port 8080, and configuring logs to CloudWatch Logs.
3. Define an ECS service to maintain three tasks running across two private subnets in your **Virtual Private Cloud** (**VPC**).

4. Attach the service to an ALB that listens on HTTPS, terminates **Transport Layer Security** (**TLS**), and forwards traffic to the tasks.
5. Add auto scaling rules so that if the average CPU usage exceeds 60% for several minutes, Fargate launches more tasks; if it drops, it scales down.

You have built a resilient, Auto Scaling API without selecting EC2 instance sizes or patching operating systems.

Use cases of Fargate

Fargate is usually a strong fit when:

- You want simplified operations and accept slightly higher compute costs in exchange for not managing servers.
- You have spiky or unpredictable workloads where automatic scaling prevents over-provisioning.
- You are building new containerized services and want a streamlined deployment without full cluster administration.

Consider EC2-backed ECS or EKS nodes when:

- You need very finegrained cost tuning at scale and are willing to manage instances.
- You run specialized workloads that need custom kernel modules or configurations not available in Fargate.
- You want to pack many small containers onto large nodes for cost efficiency and have the operational maturity to manage this.

For many application teams, Fargate offers a balance of container portability, ECS/EKS integration, and serverless operational simplicity. It is the natural next step after adopting containers and before managing full clusters.

Difference between EC2 and Fargate

EC2 provides virtual servers where you select instance types, AMIs, storage, and networking. You are responsible for patching, scaling, and lifecycle management. EC2 supports containers, traditional apps, databases, custom networking appliances, and experimental stacks, provided you manage the **operating system** (**OS**) and runtime.

Fargate is serverless compute for containers. You define a task or Pod (image, CPU, memory, environment variables), and AWS runs it without exposing underlying instances. Typically used via ECS or EKS, you do not patch nodes, manage auto scaling groups, or bin-pack (*pack many small containers onto large nodes*) containers onto instances; you simply run workloads.

The following table shows the tabular summary of the differences between Amazon EC2 and Fargate services as follows:

Aspect	Amazon EC2	AWS Fargate
Compute model	Virtual machines you manage	Serverless containers (no servers to manage)
What you manage	OS, patches, agents, capacity, and scaling of instances	Task definitions/Pods and scaling of tasks only
Packaging	Anything (binaries, containers, scripts)	Containers only (via ECS or EKS)
Control over OS	Full (kernel params, agents, custom AMIs)	Minimal (no host access, limited lowlevel tuning)
Scaling unit	Instances (**Auto Scaling groups** (**ASGs**), node groups)	Tasks/Pods (per-task CPU/memory)
Cost pattern	Pay per instance hour, good for steady high usage	Pay per vCPU/GB per task, good for spiky workloads
Cost optimization levers	Savings plans/RIs, Spot, bin-packing containers	Right-size task resources, configure desired count to zero for workloads that can tolerate downtime.
Operational overhead	Higher: patching, node health, capacity planning	Lower: no node management, simpler operations
Multi-tenancy and isolation	Shared hosts; you design isolation via security groups	Per-task isolation (separate **Elastic Network Interfaces** (**ENIs**), strong boundaries)
Fit for non-container apps	Yes (legacy, custom databases, etc.)	No (containers required)
Best when	You need control, tuning, or mixed workloads	You want simplicity and serverless container compute

***Table 14.1**: Difference between EC2 and Fargate service*

Amazon Elastic Container Service

Amazon ECS is AWS's native solution for running and scaling containers without managing your own control plane. ECS handles scheduling, health checks, service discovery, and AWS integration, allowing you to run containers on EC2 instances or in a serverless environment with AWS Fargate.

Understanding ECS

ECS is a fully managed container orchestration service. You package your application as Docker images and define their runtime settings. ECS handles placement, restarts on failure, and scaling based on load. You can run ECS in two main ways:

- **ECS on EC2**: You manage a cluster of EC2 instances; ECS schedules tasks onto those instances.
- **ECS on Fargate**: You do not manage any instances; you define tasks, and AWS runs them for you in a serverless fashion.

In both modes, the core experience is the same: you work with tasks, services, and clusters, not with individual **virtual machines** (**VMs**).

Core building blocks in ECS

When you design with ECS, a few concepts show up repeatedly:

- **Task definitions**: A task definition is the blueprint for a unit of work. It describes:
  - Which container images to run.
  - CPU and memory for each container.
  - Environment variables and secrets.
  - Ports to expose.
  - Logging configuration (for example, send logs to CloudWatch).

  You can think of a task definition as the *deployment descriptor* for your service.
- **Tasks and services**:
  - A task is a running instance of a task definition. Running it once creates one copy of your containers.
  - A service is a long-running configuration that maintains a specified number of tasks, integrates with a load balancer, and supports auto scaling.
  - Most production workloads use services: for example, *keep 4 copies of this API task running across these subnets and attach them to this Application Load Balancer*.
- **Clusters**: A cluster is a logical grouping of resources where ECS runs tasks and services:
  - In EC2 mode, the cluster is backed by EC2 instances you provision and join to ECS with an agent.
  - In Fargate mode, the cluster is mostly logical; AWS provides the compute behind the scenes.

You can create separate clusters for different domains or environments, such as *orders-prod* or *analytics-dev*.

- **Integration with the rest of AWS**: ECS integrates tightly with the following:
  - **Networking**: VPC, subnets, security groups, private endpoints.
  - **Load balancing**: ALB/**Network Load Balancer** (**NLB**) target groups for HTTP or TCP services.
  - **Identity**: IAM roles for tasks so containers can access AWS APIs safely without embedding credentials.
  - **Observability**: CloudWatch Logs and Metrics, XRay, and AWS Distro for OpenTelemetry.

  This tight integration makes ECS attractive for organizations fully committed to AWS.

ECS fits in an AWS architecture

In a typical microservices architecture, ECS serves as the **compute layer** for containerized services. A common pattern includes:

- Clients hit Amazon API Gateway or Amazon CloudFront.
- Traffic is forwarded to an ALB.
- The ALB routes to one or more ECS services (running on Fargate or EC2) in private subnets.
- Those services talk to RDS, DynamoDB, S3, and other internal APIs.
- ECS auto-scales the number of tasks based on CPU, memory, or custom CloudWatch metrics.

Externally, this forms a modern containerized stack. ECS ensures the correct number of healthy containers run and remain connected to the network.

Migrating a monolith to ECS

Consider a monolithic web application running on EC2 instances behind a load balancer that you want to modernize without adopting Kubernetes immediately. A simple migration step with ECS might look like the following:

1. **Containerize the application**: Build a Docker image for the monolith and push it to Amazon ECR.
2. **Create a task definition**: Define a single-container task specifying the image, CPU and memory, port 8080, and environment variables for database endpoints and secrets.

3. **Set up an ECS service**:
   a. Choose Fargate (serverless) or EC2 (reuse existing capacity).
   b. Create a service that runs, say, three tasks across two private subnets.
   c. Attach the service to an ALB that terminates HTTPS and forwards traffic to the tasks.
4. **Wire in scaling and observability**:
   a. Configure auto scaling to add tasks when the average CPU or request count crosses a threshold.
   b. Send logs to CloudWatch Logs and set up basic dashboards and alarms.
5. **Cut over traffic**:
   a. Gradually redirect traffic from the old EC2 instances to the ECS-backed ALB.
   b. Once stable, retire the old instances.

You now have the same application, but running as ECS-managed containers, with clearer scaling and deployment strategies.

Choosing ECS

ECS makes sense when:

- You want **managed orchestration** tightly integrated with AWS, without the complexity of running your own Kubernetes control plane.
- Your teams are comfortable with containers and want a clear path from *Dockerfile* to *production service*.
- You like having the option to start on Fargate (no servers) and, if needed, move to EC2-backed clusters for cost tuning or special cases.

It is especially attractive in AWS-centric environments where multi-cloud portability is not a priority and focus is on application and platform behavior rather than cluster internals.

In this way, Amazon ECS serves as the backbone of your container strategy: a pragmatic solution for running microservices, background workers, and batch jobs at scale, leveraging familiar AWS building blocks for security, networking, and observability.

Serverless Application Model

AWS SAM is a shorthand language for building serverless applications on AWS. Instead of manually configuring Lambda functions, API Gateway routes, event sources, and IAM roles, you define them in a compact template that SAM expands into full CloudFormation. SAM serves as a focused framework for serverless workloads, standardizing how you define, build, test, and deploy Lambda-centric applications.

Understanding SAM

AWS SAM is an open-source framework built on CloudFormation, designed specifically for serverless applications. You write a YAML template using high-level resource types such as AWS::Serverless::Function, AWS::Serverless::Api, and AWS::Serverless::StateMachine, which SAM translates into detailed AWS resources.

Since SAM is built on CloudFormation, deployments integrate seamlessly with your AWS infrastructure. Stacks, change sets, rollbacks, and permissions function as expected.

SAM fits in architecture

SAM is primarily about the application layer when you are building with services like:

- AWS Lambda
- Amazon API Gateway
- Amazon EventBridge
- Amazon SQS, SNS, DynamoDB, and Step Functions

You typically use SAM when you are designing:

- REST or HTTP APIs backed by Lambda functions
- Event-driven backends (for example, reacting to S3 uploads or queue messages)
- Lightweight workflows orchestrated with Step Functions
- Small to medium serverless applications owned by a single team

Infrastructure like VPCs, databases, or networking baselines typically resides in separate CloudFormation or **Cloud Development Kit (CDK)** stacks. SAM focuses on the serverless business logic components built on this foundation.

Core building blocks in SAM

When you define a SAM application, you usually work with: AWS::Serverless::Function.

This is the heart of most SAM templates. A serverless function definition lets you declare:

- The Lambda handler and runtime (for example, Python, Node.js, Java)
- Memory, timeout, environment variables, and IAM policies
- Event sources that trigger the function, such as:
    - API routes (via Api or HttpApi events)
    - S3 events (object created, deleted)
    - SQS queue messages or SNS topics
    - EventBridge rules

Rather than configuring Lambda and triggers manually, you attach events directly to the function within the template:

- **AWS::Serverless::Api/HttpApi**:
  - These resources define an API Gateway API using a simple syntax.
  - You can declare routes (paths and methods) and map them to functions.
  - You can configure authorization (for example, IAM, Cognito, Lambda authorizers).
  - SAM generates the underlying API Gateway configuration automatically.
- **AWS::Serverless::StateMachine**:
  - This lets you define Step Functions workflows in the same template and bind them to Lambda functions, event sources, and other services. It is useful when you have Eventdriven serverless processes (for example, fan-out/fan-in processing, approval flows).
  - **Policies and permissions**: SAM offers policy templates to quickly grant common permissions, such as reading from S3 or writing to DynamoDB. You can also attach custom IAM policies for finer control.

Developer experience to build, test, and deploy

One of SAM's strengths is that it provides a full workflow for developers:

- **Build**: A SAM build step that compiles or packages your functions (including dependencies) and prepares them for deployment.
- **Local testing**: The SAM **command line interface** (**CLI**) can run functions locally and even emulate an API Gateway or event sources so you can test handlers on your machine.
- **Deploy**: A SAM deploy command that packages your code to S3, creates or updates the CloudFormation stack, and tracks changes over time.

For architects, this standardizes serverless application deployment; every SAM project follows a consistent pattern that integrates easily with **continuous integration** (**CI**)/**continuous deployment** (**CD**) pipelines.

Building and deploying a serverless application

The following are the steps for building and deploying a serverless application with AWS SAM:

1. **Initialize the SAM application**: Begin by creating a new SAM project, which provides a starter template and folder structure:
   a. Choose a runtime (for example, Python, Node.js, Java).

   b. SAM generates a `template.yaml` and sample function code.

   c. This serves as the place to define your Lambda functions, APIs, event sources, and other resources.

   In practice, this is where you sketch the shape of your serverless architecture in the template.

2. **Author and wire your resources**: Next, you describe your application in the SAM template:

   a. Define AWS::Serverless::Function resources for each Lambda.

   b. Attach event sources: HTTP routes (API/HttpApi), S3 events, SQS queues, EventBridge rules, etc.

   c. Declare supporting resources like DynamoDB tables, S3 buckets, or Step Functions state machines.

   d. Add IAM policies (or use SAM's policy templates) so functions can access the resources they need.

   This is where architecture decisions, what communicates to what, with which permissions, are captured as code.

3. **Build the application**: Then, you prepare the code for deployment:

   a. SAM packages each function with its dependencies.

   b. It generates a built version of the template that points to these artifacts.

   This step ensures your Lambda code is ready to run in the AWS environment and not just on your laptop.

4. **Test locally (optional but recommended)**: Before you push anything to the cloud, you can run and test pieces locally:

   a. Invoke individual functions with sample events.

   b. Start a local API to simulate the API Gateway and call endpoints from a browser or Postman.

   This tight feedback loop helps catch obvious issues early and speeds up development.

   Note: **Local SAM emulation has known limitations; it does not perfectly replicate IAM behavior, VPC networking, or certain trigger types. Readers should know not to rely on it as a full substitute for staging environment testing.**

5. **Deploy to AWS**: When you are ready, you deploy the application:

   a. SAM uploads your built artifacts (for example, zipped function code) to S3.

   b. It transforms your SAM template into a full CloudFormation template and creates/updates the stack.

   c. AWS provisions or updates all declared resources (functions, APIs, tables, roles, etc.).

   From your perspective, it is one command and a stack name; behind the scenes, it is a full infrastructure deployment.

6. **Iterate with sync (for development) and repeat**: During active development, you often:

   a. Make code/template changes.

   b. Rebuild and either redeploy or use SAM's *sync* style workflows to push changes quickly to a dev stack.

   For production changes, you usually wire these same steps into a CI/CD pipeline so that:

   a. Commits trigger the build and tests.

   b. Approved changes trigger SAM deployments to staging and then production.

7. **Operate and update**: Once deployed, your SAM stack is just another CloudFormation stack:

   - You monitor it with CloudWatch, XRay, and your usual observability tools.
   - You update it by changing the template or code and running through the same steps.
   - Rollbacks are handled by CloudFormation if something fails during an update.

In summary, the SAM service steps are: init | author | build | (local test) | deploy | iterate | operate. This provides a consistent, repeatable path from a blank project to a fully managed serverless application on AWS.

Example of a simple serverless API with SAM

Imagine you are building a small *orders* API:

1. You write a SAM template with:

   a. One AWS::Serverless::Api defining routes like POST /orders and GET /orders/{id}.

   b. Two AWS::Serverless::Function resources: CreateOrderFunction and GetOrderFunction, each triggered by its respective route.

   c. A DynamoDB table to store orders, plus a policy that lets the functions read/write that table.

2. You run the SAM build to prepare the functions and template.
3. Run sam local start-api to test the API locally, calling endpoints with curl or Postman to verify behavior.

4. When ready, run sam deploy with a stack name and environment parameters. SAM packages the code, uploads it, and creates all Lambda functions, API Gateway routes, DynamoDB tables, and IAM roles in a single operation.

From the team's point of view, they focused on code and a concise template; SAM handled the heavy lifting of wiring everything together correctly.

Use cases of SAM

SAM is a strong choice when:

- Your solution is primarily serverless, built around Lambda, API Gateway, and event-driven patterns.
- You want a lightweight, YAML-based way to define serverless stacks, with good local tooling.
- Teams value a standard, opinionated workflow: build, test, deploy in a consistent way across projects.

You might lean toward CDK or general CloudFormation when:

- You need to manage a wider range of infrastructure in the same stack (complex networking, many non-serverless resources).
- You prefer programming languages (TypeScript, Python, Java) over YAML for infrastructure.
- You are building a shared platform that spans both serverless and more traditional components.

In many organizations, SAM coexists with other IaC tools: SAM for focused serverless applications and CDK, CloudFormation, or Terraform for broader platform and networking. As an AWS cloud architect, your role is to choose SAM when it simplifies development, enabling teams building Lambda-centric services to move quickly with clear patterns and reduced risk of misconfiguration. AWS CDK offers higher-level abstractions and reusable constructs to enhance consistency and minimize duplication in large systems. In contrast, AWS SAM provides a simpler, more focused framework for serverless applications with less abstraction. Choose the tool that best matches your needs for flexibility, reuse, and architectural complexity.

Conclusion

This chapter shifted focus from managing individual servers to platforms that let you concentrate on applications rather than infrastructure. AWS Fargate and Amazon ECS enable packaging services as containers, defining how they run and delegating tasks such as placement, scaling, and daily operations to AWS. ECS offers fine-grained control over container orchestration, while Fargate eliminates the need to manage cluster instances, focusing on tasks and services. Additionally, the SAM provides a way to define event-driven applications, often using Lambda, API Gateway, and other managed services, in compact templates that are easy to version, review, and deploy.

Together, these building blocks offer a range of options for running modern workloads on AWS. Choose ECS and Fargate containers when you need control over runtime and environment, or use SAM to delegate more responsibility to AWS and focus on functions and events. Many architectures combine these approaches, such as an ECS/Fargate-based API with background processing via SAM-defined Lambda functions. Moving forward, treat ECS, Fargate, and SAM as core tools in your architectural toolbox to design systems that scale easily, operate efficiently, and align with cloud-native practices.

The next chapter will cover Kubernetes on AWS by examining Amazon EKS architecture and daily operations. You will learn how the EKS control plane functions, how worker nodes are provisioned and managed, and how cluster networking connects Pods, nodes, and AWS services flexibly and predictably. We will also cover securing cluster and workload access, setting up monitoring, logging, and observability, and leveraging advanced features and deployment models. By the end, you will have a clear, practical understanding of how to run production-grade Kubernetes clusters on AWS with EKS.

References

1. **https://docs.aws.amazon.com/step-functions/latest/dg/concepts-sam-sfn.html**
2. **https://docs.aws.amazon.com/serverless-application-model/latest/developerguide/serverless-getting-started-hello-world.html**
3. **https://docs.aws.amazon.com/serverless-application-model/latest/developerguide/serverless-deploying.html**
4. **https://docs.aws.amazon.com/serverless-application-model/latest/developerguide/serverless-getting-started.html**
5. **https://docs.aws.amazon.com/serverless-application-model/latest/developerguide/serverless-deploying-modify-pipeline.html**
6. **https://docs.aws.amazon.com/serverless-application-model/latest/developerguide/serverless-authoring.html**
7. **https://docs.aws.amazon.com/serverless-application-model/latest/developerguide/deploying-using-github.html**
8. **https://docs.aws.amazon.com/serverless-application-model/latest/developerguide/using-sam-cli-build.html**
9. **https://aws.amazon.com/ecs/**
10. **https://docs.aws.amazon.com/eks/latest/userguide/fargate.html**

Chapter 15
Amazon Elastic Kubernetes Service Architecture

Introduction

This chapter introduces the Amazon **Elastic Kubernetes Service** (**EKS**) architecture as a practical solution for running Kubernetes (also known as K8s) on **Amazon Web Services** (**AWS**) without managing every component yourself. We explain how the EKS control plane manages core Kubernetes functions, while worker nodes and node management run your containers and maintain capacity for workloads. We also cover cluster networking, showing how Pods, services, and AWS networking components work together to ensure reliable traffic flow within the cluster and to your broader environment.

We also discuss essential aspects of a production-ready EKS cluster, including security and access control, monitoring, logging, observability, and advanced features and deployment models for scaling. This chapter aims to provide a clear understanding of EKS architecture and its components, enabling you to design effective production systems. By the end, you should recognize the role and importance of each part within a well-designed AWS architecture.

Structure

In this chapter, we will discuss the following topics:

- Terminology
- EKS control plane architecture
- Worker nodes and node management
- Cluster networking
- Security and access control
- Monitoring, logging, and observability
- Advanced features and deployment models

Objectives

This chapter aims to help you understand how **Amazon EKS** (*also known as managed Kubernetes, as it is managed by the cloud provider AWS*) functions as a comprehensive Kubernetes platform on AWS and how to apply it in real-world architectures. You will learn the roles of the control plane, worker nodes, and node management, as well as how cluster networking connects Pods, services, and your AWS environment. We also cover how security and access control protect your cluster and applications, and how monitoring, logging, and observability provide insight into system health. Advanced features and deployment models will be discussed to help you design production-ready clusters. By the end, you should understand the key components of an EKS-based solution and how they support scalable, reliable applications.

Terminology

In this section, we define several basic terms frequently used in EKS and Kubernetes.

Pods

A Pod is the smallest unit in Kubernetes, typically containing one application container or a small group of closely related containers. It is where your code runs within the cluster. In EKS, Pods are scheduled on worker nodes, and Kubernetes ensures they remain available, restart if necessary, and relocate as resources change. For example, a logging sidecar and a web server container may share a Pod to use the same network space and collaborate closely.

ReplicaSet

A ReplicaSet in Kubernetes ensures application availability by maintaining the desired number of identical Pods. If a Pod stops, crashes, or is removed, the ReplicaSet automatically creates a replacement, supporting application stability and reliability. We can describe it as a background caretaker for containerized workloads on EKS, particularly for web apps and **application programming interfaces** (**APIs**) that require continuous uptime. For instance, if you specify three service instances, the ReplicaSet consistently maintains that number so users experience uninterrupted access, even during minor failures.

Deployment

In Kubernetes, a deployment defines how an application should run and be updated over time. Rather than manually managing Pods, you specify the desired number of replicas, the container image, and the update strategy. In AWS EKS, deployments are commonly used for web applications, APIs, and microservices to ensure safer and more predictable releases. For example, when rolling out a new version of a shopping application, a deployment can gradually replace old Pods, maintaining service availability during the update.

Services

A service provides Pods with a stable endpoint, allowing them to be discovered and accessed even as Pods are replaced or moved. Since Pod IP addresses can change, a service acts as a consistent entry point. In EKS, services are used to expose applications within the cluster or externally through load balancers. For example, if backend Pods are replaced during a deployment, the service maintains the same address, so frontends or users experience no disruption.

EKS control plane architecture

The control plane consists of Kubernetes management components that maintain cluster operations. In EKS, these components run in an AWS-managed environment within a dedicated **Virtual Private Cloud** (**VPC**) and are distributed across **Availability Zones** (**AZs**) for high availability. The main components include the Kubernetes API server, scheduler, controller manager, and the etcd cluster, which stores the cluster's desired and current state. The following figure illustrates the control plane components, while worker nodes include Kubelet, Pods, Kube Proxy, container runtime, and containers running inside Pods:

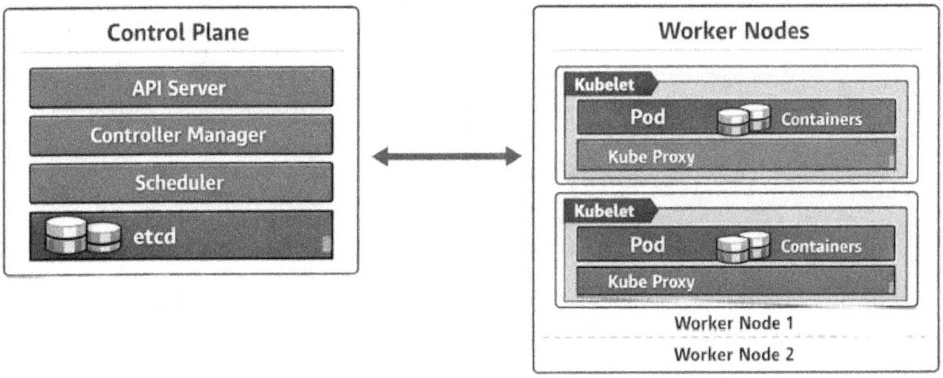

Figure 15.1: Kubernetes architecture

kubectl command

kubectl is the command-line tool for interacting with a Kubernetes cluster. It allows you to create resources, inspect workloads, debug issues, scale applications, and manage cluster operations. kubectl serves as the primary interface for managing Kubernetes.

When you run a command such as: **`kubectl apply -f filename.yaml`**

You instruct Kubernetes to apply the configuration in the file, aligning the cluster with the desired state. The control plane components then coordinate to implement these changes.

What happens when you run kubectl apply -f filename.yaml?

This is the actual flow in simple language:

1. You prepare a YAML file that describes a resource such as a Pod, Deployment, Service, or ConfigMap.
2. You run `kubectl apply -f filename.yaml`.
3. kubectl reads the file and sends the request to the Kubernetes API server.
4. The API server authenticates and authorizes your request.
5. If the request is valid, the API server stores the new desired state in etcd.
6. The controller manager notices the change and starts reconciling the actual state with the desired state.
7. If the object is a **`Deployment`**, the deployment controller creates a ReplicaSet.
8. The ReplicaSet controller creates the required Pods.
9. The Scheduler looks at the new Pods and decides which worker node should run them.
10. The assigned worker node's kubelet receives the instruction and starts the containers.
11. The Pod becomes visible as running, and your application starts serving traffic.

The key point is: kubectl does not execute workloads directly. It submits requests, after which the control plane determines the next steps, and worker nodes run the containers.

EKS control plane components

The EKS control plane is a managed service operated by AWS and includes several essential components.

Kubernetes API server

The API server is the main entry point to the cluster. Every request goes through it:

- kubectl apply
- kubectl get
- kubectl delete
- Internal requests from controllers and schedulers

The API server performs three major jobs:

- **Authentication**: *Who are you?*
- **Authorization**: *Are you allowed to do this?*
- **Validation and persistence**: *Is the request valid, and should it be stored?*

When you apply a YAML file, the API server is the first component that receives it. If the file is valid, it stores the desired state in etcd. The API server acts as the cluster's gatekeeper.

etcd

etcd serves as the cluster's database. In EKS, etcd is fully managed by AWS and not directly accessible to users, unlike self-managed Kubernetes, where operators sometimes interact with it directly. It stores all important cluster data:

- Deployments
- Pods
- Services
- ConfigMaps
- Secrets
- Node information
- Desired state of the cluster

etcd functions as the persistent memory of the cluster.

When you create or update a resource, the API server writes that information into etcd. Controllers and other control plane components keep reading from etcd to understand what the cluster should look like. Without etcd, Kubernetes would lose all cluster state information.

Scheduler

The Scheduler determines the placement of new Pods within the cluster. When a Pod is created, it usually does not yet have a node assigned. The Scheduler watches for these unscheduled Pods and looks at:

- Available CPU and memory
- Node labels
- Taints and tolerations
- Affinity and anti-affinity rules
- Availability constraints

It selects the most suitable worker node and assigns the Pod to it. For example, when you create a Deployment with three replicas, the Scheduler determines which nodes will host the Pods. The Scheduler does not start containers; it only selects their placement.

Controller manager

The controller manager is responsible for reconciliation within the cluster. Its job is to compare:

- What you want
- What actually exists

If the desired state requires three replicas but only two exist, the Controller Manager creates the missing replica. If a Pod fails, it is replaced. When a deployment changes, it updates the ReplicaSet to align the cluster with the new version. This ongoing process of checking and correcting is known as reconciliation.

The controller manager continually evaluates: *Does the cluster still match the desired state?* If the states do not match, it initiates corrective actions.

Worker nodes components

In this section, we discuss the key components of the various worker nodes in the EKS architecture.

kubelet

The kubelet is the node agent that communicates with the control plane and ensures that assigned Pods run correctly. When the Scheduler assigns a Pod to a node, the kubelet on that node:

- Pulls the container image
- Starts the container runtime
- Mounts volumes if needed
- Checks container health
- Reports status back to the control plane

The kubelet acts as the local manager for each worker node.

Container runtime

This software is responsible for running containers. The runtime starts and stops container processes according to instructions from the kubelet. EKS uses containerd as its default and primary container runtime today, and Docker-as-runtime is no longer supported. Docker was the historically dominant runtime and was deprecated as a direct Kubernetes runtime in Kubernetes 1.20 and fully removed in 1.24.

kube-proxy

kube-proxy manages networking rules on each node. It is worth noting that kube-proxy operates by managing **iptables or Internet Protocol Virtual Server** (**IPVS**) rules on each node, and importantly, in newer EKS setups, particularly with the AWS VPC **Container Network**

Interface (**CNI**) and certain networking configurations, kube-proxy can be replaced or supplemented by eBPF-based solutions like Cilium

It routes traffic to the appropriate Pod when Services are used, establishing rules to ensure traffic sent to a Kubernetes Service reaches the correct backend Pods. This enables a single service name to load-balance traffic across multiple Pods.

This is the basic Kubernetes flow: kubectl submits | API server accepts | etcd stores | controllers reconcile | Scheduler places | kubelet runs.

Worker nodes and node management

Worker nodes run applications within a Kubernetes cluster. In AWS EKS, the control plane manages decisions, while worker nodes execute tasks such as pulling container images, starting containers, handling network traffic, and maintaining application availability.

A worker node hosts Pods. When Kubernetes schedules a Pod, the node launches and maintains its containers and reports health and status to the control plane. The worker node serves as the cluster's execution layer.

Node components

A worker node consists of several key components working together:

- The operating system is usually a Linux **Amazon Machine Image** (**AMI**) optimized for Kubernetes.
- The container runtime, which actually starts and stops containers.
- The kubelet, which talks to the control plane and makes sure assigned Pods are running.
- kube-proxy or other networking components, which help route traffic to the right Pods.

These components collectively enable a compute instance to function as a Kubernetes worker node.

Understanding node management working

Node management ensures the cluster maintains sufficient healthy worker nodes to support workloads. Previously, teams manually created and maintained **Elastic Compute Cloud** (**EC2**) instances. Modern AWS architectures automate node management using managed node groups, self-managed node groups, or Fargate for serverless Pod execution.

With managed node groups, AWS manages node lifecycles, including provisioning and rolling updates. You select the instance type, scaling policies, and subnet placement, while AWS reduces operational overhead and maintenance requirements.

Joining node to cluster

When a node starts, it is configured to join the EKS cluster and register with the control plane. The scheduler then assigns workloads based on available resources and rules. The node continuously communicates with the control plane and runs assigned Pods. Effective node management matches capacity to demand. Insufficient nodes cause pending Pods and slow workloads, while excess nodes increase costs. Autoscaling addresses this balance.

A common approach is to use:

- A minimum number of nodes for baseline traffic.
- A scaling policy (through Cluster Autoscaler) to add more nodes when Pods need more room.
- A scale-in policy to remove nodes when demand falls.

This approach maintains cluster responsiveness while minimizing costs from idle capacity.

Node health significance

If a node fails, its Pods may also fail. Kubernetes can reschedule these Pods to healthy nodes if sufficient capacity is available. For production, nodes should be distributed across multiple AZs, and teams should monitor node CPU, memory, disk, and network performance closely. Node health ensures applications have stable, sufficient capacity to operate reliably and maintain uptime.

Note: **EKS Auto Mode, introduced at AWS re:Invent 2024, fully automates compute, storage, and networking management for entire clusters with a single click. It automatically provisions right-sized nodes, manages OS patching, rotates nodes every 21 days for security, and includes pre-configured load balancing and storage. For teams seeking operational simplicity, AWS now recommends EKS Auto Mode as the starting point for new clusters.**

Cluster networking

Cluster networking in Kubernetes and EKS enables communication between Pods, Services, nodes, and external systems. It serves as the cluster's communication layer, ensuring containers are accessible as required.

Each Pod in Kubernetes receives a unique IP address, allowing direct communication with other Pods. This approach simplifies communication and treats each service as a distinct unit. Cluster networking manages inbound and outbound traffic. For example, user requests may pass through a load balancer to a Kubernetes Service, which then routes traffic to the appropriate Pods.

Pod interaction within cluster

A basic flow looks like this:

1. A user sends a request to the application.
2. The request reaches an external entry point such as an Application Load Balancer.
3. The load balancer forwards traffic into the cluster.
4. Kubernetes uses Services and networking rules to find the correct Pods.
5. The Pod receives the request and sends the response back through the same path.

Within the cluster, Pods communicate directly. For example, a frontend Pod can connect to a backend Pod, which may access a database or another internal service. The networking layer enables these interactions.

Main parts of cluster networking

The following are the main parts of cluster networking:

- **Pod networking**: Each Pod receives its own IP address, allowing Pods to communicate as if they were separate machines, even on the same node. This model enhances flexibility but requires careful network design.
- **Services**: A service provides Pods with a stable network identity. While Pods may change, the Service name remains constant. If multiple Pods support a Service, traffic is load-balanced among them, ensuring consistent connectivity.
- **Ingress and load balancers**: For external traffic, an AWS load balancer or a Kubernetes Ingress resource provides a controlled entry point to the cluster. An Ingress resource requires an Ingress controller to function. In EKS, this is typically the AWS load balancer Controller, which provisions and manages Application Load Balancers on your behalf. This simplifies management, as users do not need to know individual Pod addresses.
- **Security groups and network policies**: Networking involves both connectivity and control. In AWS, security groups regulate traffic to and from nodes and load balancers. In Kubernetes, network policies provide additional control at the Pod level, helping to isolate and secure workloads.

Significance

Cluster networking directly impacts availability, performance, and security. Poor design can prevent service discovery, misroute traffic, or weaken security boundaries. Effective networking supports application scalability without altering communication models.

Example

Imagine an e-commerce application running on EKS:

- The public website receives traffic through an Application Load Balancer.
- The load balancer forwards requests to a Kubernetes Service.
- The service routes traffic to several frontend Pods.
- The frontend Pods call backend Pods through another Service.
- The backend Pods access a database in a private subnet.

To users, this appears as a single website. Within the cluster, networking reliably manages traffic among multiple components.

For AWS Solutions Architects, cluster networking integrates Kubernetes with the AWS VPC. Designing subnets, routes, security groups, and load balancers ensures the cluster aligns with the broader environment. A well-designed networking layer enhances stability, security, and operational efficiency.

In summary, cluster networking serves as the infrastructure for Kubernetes communication. Well-planned networking ensures smooth and efficient application operation.

Note: **EKS Pod Identity is AWS's recommended method for granting Pods access to AWS services. It uses a streamlined agent-based approach, enables cross-cluster role reuse without trust policy updates, and is preferred for new EKS workloads on Kubernetes 1.24 or later.**

Security and access control

Security and access control are the rules that decide who can get in, what they can touch, and what they are allowed to do. Security and access control define who can access resources and what actions they are permitted to perform. In AWS, this is critical, as every service, user, application, and workload requires clear boundaries. A robust system verifies identity, enforces least privilege, and maintains audit records.

At a simple level, security and access control answer questions like:

- *Who is the user or service?*
- *Is this person or application really who they say they are?*
- *What resources should they be allowed to use?*
- *Should they be able to read, write, delete, or just view?*
- *How do we stop accidental or malicious misuse?*

In AWS, security begins with identities and permissions. Users may authenticate through a corporate identity provider, applications may assume roles, and services require explicit permissions for resources such as **Simple Storage Service** (**S3**), DynamoDB, or queues. Architecture should clearly define these relationships.

Working in practice

A common AWS security flow looks like this:

1. A user or application tries to access a resource.
2. AWS checks the identity of the caller.
3. AWS checks the attached permissions.
4. If the request is allowed, the action proceeds.
5. If not, the request is denied and logged.

This model applies to many AWS services. For example, a Lambda function may have permission to access a specific S3 bucket, a developer may deploy to non-production, but not production, and a database administrator may manage databases without altering network rules.

Main ideas to keep in mind

With respect to security and access control, the following main ideas are worth keeping in mind.

- **Role-based access control (RBAC)**: Kubernetes's native authorization mechanism determines the actions permitted for each identity within the cluster. This is essential for effective EKS security design.
- **Secret encryption**: EKS enables envelope encryption for Kubernetes Secrets through KMS.
- **Identity**: Identity determines who or what is making a request. In AWS, this could be a user, application, container, or service. Effective identity management reduces confusion and prevents credential sharing.
- **Authentication**: Authentication is the process by which AWS verifies identity. Methods include passwords, multi-factor authentication, federated logins, or roles assumed by services.
- **Authorization**: Authorization decides what the authenticated identity can do. This is where policies, roles, and permissions matter. You might allow read-only access to a dataset, or full access to a dev environment, but only limited access to production.
- **Encryption**: Security also involves data protection. Encryption ensures that stored or transmitted data remains secure from unauthorized access.

- **Logging and auditing**: Effective security design requires visibility into access events. Tracking who accessed resources and when enables investigation and incident response.

Example

Imagine an internal application that stores customer reports in S3 and writes summary data to application hosted in **EKS Pod**. The application runs in **Lambda**. The following is the summary data:

- The Lambda function uses an **Identity and Access Management** (**IAM**) role instead of hard-coded keys.
- That role can read only the specific S3 bucket it needs.
- It can perform some actions on the application in hosted EKS Pod (e.g. create files, etc.)
- Developers can deploy changes only through a controlled pipeline.
- Administrators can view logs, but sensitive data is masked or protected.

In this design, all entities have only the access required. If the Lambda function is compromised, potential damage is limited due to restricted permissions.

As an AWS solutions architect, treat security and access control as foundational design elements. Every decision regarding networking, storage, compute, and automation should consider access: who can use it, what actions are permitted, and how safety is ensured. A secure architecture does not eliminate access but ensures it is intentional, limited, monitored, and auditable. This approach builds trust in AWS production environments.

Monitoring, logging, and observability

Monitoring, logging, and observability provide insight into system behavior after deployment. In AWS, they help assess application health, identify issues, and track changes when failures occur. Effective architectures not only operate reliably but also communicate their status clearly.

Concept

Monitoring involves tracking key indicators such as CPU usage, memory, request latency, error rates, or queue depth. It alerts you when metrics exceed normal thresholds. Logging records of system events, including errors, warnings, user actions, and backend operations. Logs are essential for investigating issues after they occur.

Observability provides a comprehensive view, enabling you to infer the system's internal state from its outputs. It helps answer not only whether a system is failing, but also why.

Significance

These concepts are essential because modern systems comprise many components, including load balancers, containers, databases, queues, serverless functions, and external APIs. When issues arise, you need to trace problems across all these elements.

Without monitoring, issues may go unnoticed until users report them. Without logging, you may detect problems but lack context. Without observability, identifying root causes becomes time-consuming. Together, these practices reduce downtime, accelerate troubleshooting, and enhance reliability.

Working together

A typical workflow includes the following steps:

1. The application runs normally and generates metrics, logs, and traces.
2. Monitoring systems watch the metrics and raise alarms if something crosses a threshold.
3. Logs provide the detailed story of what happened.
4. Observability tools correlate data across services, allowing you to trace individual requests or failures throughout the system.
5. Engineers use this information to fix issues, tune performance, and improve the design.

For example, if response times increase, monitoring may indicate high latency, logs may reveal repeated timeout errors, and observability may identify a database query as the bottleneck. This combined perspective is more valuable than any single signal.

Main parts of an AWS environment

The following main parts of an AWS environment are worth keeping in mind.

- **Metrics**: Metrics are numeric values collected over time, indicating request volume, response times, and failure rates. They are well-suited for dashboards and alarms due to their ease of aggregation and comparison.
- **Logs**: Logs are detailed event records used for debugging and auditing. They may capture user sign-ins, function failures, or service retries. Effective logs are clear, structured, and searchable.
- **Traces**: Traces track requests as they traverse multiple services, highlighting where time is spent and identifying bottlenecks. This is especially valuable in microservices and serverless architectures, where a single user action may involve many components.
- **Dashboards and alarms**: Dashboards provide a visual summary of system health, while alarms notify teams when attention is required. Together, they enable rapid response to emerging issues.

Example

Imagine an online ordering system:

- Metrics show that request latency is rising.
- Logs show repeated timeout errors from the payment service.
- Traces show that the delay begins when the application calls the order database.
- An alarm alerts the team before customers start to leave the site.

With observability, the team can trace the sequence of events and address the root cause directly, rather than relying on guesswork. As an AWS Solutions Architect, the team designs observability from the outset. Determine business priorities, identify critical signals, define log destinations, and establish alert response processes. Effective monitoring, logging, and observability transform a system into one that is trustworthy, manageable, and continuously improving.

Logging, monitoring, and observability in EKS

In Amazon EKS, monitoring, logging, and observability rely on both Kubernetes-native signals and AWS-managed services. **Amazon CloudWatch** Container Insights automatically collects metrics at the cluster, node, Pod, and container levels, including CPU, memory, disk, and network usage, and displays them in pre-built dashboards without manual setup. For logging, the Fluent Bit daemon forwards container logs from each node to CloudWatch Logs, where you can search, filter, and retain them according to your policy. Control plane logs, such as API server, audit, scheduler, and controller manager logs, can be enabled in the EKS console and are sent to CloudWatch Logs for auditing and troubleshooting.

For advanced observability, AWS supports open-source tools commonly used in production EKS clusters. **AWS Distro for OpenTelemetry** (**ADOT**) offers a vendor-neutral solution to collect traces and metrics, forwarding them to **AWS X-Ray**, **Amazon Managed Prometheus**, or third-party backends. X-Ray provides distributed tracing across EKS microservices, helping engineers identify latency issues and trace requests across Pods. Amazon Managed Grafana, often used with Amazon Managed Prometheus, delivers customizable dashboards for cluster metrics. Together, these services create a comprehensive observability stack: CloudWatch for operational metrics and logs, X-Ray for request tracing, and Prometheus with Grafana for in-depth cluster and application visibility. This layered approach enables solutions architects to manage EKS clusters confidently in production.

Advanced features and deployment models

Advanced features and deployment models elevate cloud architecture from basic to mature. Once a system is stable, the focus shifts from scaling to enhancing intelligence, safety, and adaptability. In AWS, this involves adopting patterns that minimize downtime, improve user experience, and provide greater control over software delivery.

Meaning of advanced features

Advanced features are additional capabilities that improve system performance under real-world conditions. Examples include auto scaling, blue/green deployments, canary releases, multi-AZ designs, disaster recovery strategies, and traffic shifting. These features are essential because production environments are dynamic, and teams must adapt without disrupting business operations.

For example, when launching a new application version, it is often preferable to test with a small subset of users, monitor for errors, and gradually increase traffic. This approach demonstrates the value of advanced deployment models.

Meaning of deployment models

Deployment models define how new versions of applications or infrastructure are introduced into the environment. They address the question of how to transition from old to new versions safely. Common models include:

- **Recreate deployment**: Replace the old version with the new one in one step.
- **Rolling deployment**: Update parts of the system gradually.
- **Blue/green deployment**: Keep two environments, one live and one ready, then switch traffic. These are not Native to K8s.
- **Canary deployment**: Send a small portion of traffic to the new version first.
- **Immutable deployment**: Build a new environment and replace the old one instead of changing it in place.

Each model presents trade-offs; some prioritize speed, others emphasize safety, and some facilitate easier rollback.

Significance

Advanced deployment models mitigate risk. Careful deployment allows early detection of issues and limits their impact. These models also increase development team confidence by enabling more frequent, low-risk releases.

Deployment models are also critical for operations. Well-designed models simplify rollback, improve uptime, and support greater automation in the release process. In cloud environments, this results in fewer manual steps and more controlled changes.

Example

Consider a customer-facing API serving thousands of users per minute. Deploying a new version all at once risks impacting all users if a bug exists. With a canary deployment, only a small percentage of traffic, such as 5%, is directed to the new version initially. If metrics remain stable, the rollout continues; if errors increase, the deployment is halted and rolled back before widespread impact.

This illustrates the practical value of advanced deployment models: they transform large, high-risk changes into smaller, manageable steps. As an AWS Solutions Architect, select advanced features based on system requirements, not perceived complexity. A simple internal tool may only require a rolling update, while a business-critical application may benefit from blue/green or canary releases. Highly resilient platforms may combine multi-AZ infrastructure, automated rollback, and traffic shifting.

The key principle is to design for change. Advanced features and deployment models enable systems to evolve with minimal disruption, supporting faster releases, quicker recovery, and greater operational confidence.

Frequently used kubectl commands

In this section, we will learn various kubectl commands we used in EKS for various purposes.

Inspecting resources

These commands allow you to view the current state of your cluster:

- **kubectl get <resource>**: Lists resources of a specific type (e.g., Pods, nodes, services) in the current namespace.
- **kubectl describe <resource> <name>**: Provides detailed information, including events and status, for a specific resource.
- **kubectl cluster-info**: Displays the control plane and service addresses.
- **kubectl get all**: Lists the most common resource types in the current namespace, including Pods, services, deployments, and replicasets. Note that some resource types, such as ConfigMaps and Secrets, are not included.

Managing workloads

Use these commands to create, update, or remove applications.

- **kubectl apply -f <filename.yaml>**: Creates or updates resources defined in a YAML or JSON file. This is the recommended declarative method.
- **kubectl run <Pod-name> --image=<image>**: Quickly creates a single Pod using a specific container image (In Kubernetes 1.18 and later, this creates a single Pod rather than a deployment).
- **kubectl scale deployment <name> --replicas=<number>**: Adjusts the number of running replicas for a specific deployment.
- **kubectl delete <resource> <name>**: Removes a specific resource from the cluster.

Troubleshooting and debugging

These commands help you understand why an application might be failing:

- **kubectl logs <Pod-name>**: Prints the logs from a specific Pod's container. For Pods with multiple containers, add `-c <container-name>` to specify which container's logs to retrieve.
- **kubectl exec -it <Pod-name> -- <command>**: Executes a command (like `/bin/bash` or `sh`) inside a running container for interactive debugging.
- **kubectl port-forward <Pod-name> <local-port>:<remote-port>**: Forwards a local port to a port on a Pod, allowing you to access it from your local machine.
- **kubectl top <Pod/node>**: Displays CPU and memory usage for Pods or Nodes. Requires the Kubernetes Metrics Server to be deployed in the cluster, which is not installed by default in EKS.

Configuration and contexts

Manage how kubectl connects to different clusters and namespaces:

- **kubectl config get-contexts**: Lists all available cluster contexts.
- **kubectl config use-context <context-name>**: Switches the active cluster context.
- **kubectl get namespaces**: Lists all namespaces in the cluster.
- **kubectl config set-context --current --namespace=<namespace>**: Sets the default namespace for the current context, so you do not have to append `-n <namespace>` to every command.

Conclusion

In this chapter, we summarized the core concepts of Amazon EKS and their role in a complete Kubernetes architecture on AWS. We examined the control plane for cluster management, worker nodes for running workloads, and cluster networking for reliable connectivity among Pods, services, and external traffic. We also addressed security, access control, monitoring, logging, and observability, emphasizing that a production cluster requires both operational visibility and effective troubleshooting.

We also explored advanced features and deployment models, demonstrating that EKS supports more than basic clusters. This includes various approaches to node management, workload isolation, and designing for scalability, resilience, and operational simplicity. Ultimately, EKS combines Kubernetes flexibility with AWS reliability, enabling the creation of modern, portable, and scalable systems.

In the next chapter, we will shift from understanding Amazon EKS fundamentals to exploring how to make clusters more dynamic, efficient, and scalable. We will cover the Container Network Interface for Pod connectivity, the **Horizontal Pod Autoscaler** (**HPA**) for dynamic scaling, and service mesh solutions for improved traffic control, security, and visibility. We will also examine Karpenter for rapid, right-sized worker provisioning and discuss networking options that influence workload communication. By the end, you will understand how these features integrate to transform a basic EKS cluster into a responsive, production-ready platform.

References

1. **https://docs.aws.amazon.com/eks/latest/best-practices/control-plane.html**
2. **https://docs.aws.amazon.com/eks/latest/best-practices/scale-control-plane.html**
3. **https://docs.aws.amazon.com/eks/latest/userguide/kubernetes-concepts.html**
4. **https://docs.aws.amazon.com/whitepapers/latest/security-overview-amazon-eks-auto-mode/eks-control-plane-and-data-plane.html**
5. **https://docs.aws.amazon.com/eks/latest/userguide/eks-provisioned-control-plane.html**
6. **https://docs.aws.amazon.com/whitepapers/latest/security-overview-amazon-eks-auto-mode/amazon-eks-control-plane.html**
7. **https://docs.aws.amazon.com/eks/latest/userguide/Pod-id-how-it-works.html**
8. **https://docs.aws.amazon.com/eks/latest/userguide/Pod-identities.html**
9. **https://docs.aws.amazon.com/eks/latest/userguide/what-is-eks.html**
10. **https://docs.aws.amazon.com/eks/latest/userguide/automode.html**

Join our Discord space

CHAPTER 16
Service Mesh and Autoscaling for EKS

Introduction

This chapter introduces key concepts that keep an Amazon **Elastic Kubernetes Service** (**EKS**) cluster connected, responsive, and scalable as demand changes. We start with networking, as all Pods, services, and external requests rely on efficient traffic flow within the cluster and to **Amazon Web Services** (**AWS**) or users. Next, we cover the **Container Network Interface** (**CNI**), which enables reliable Pod-to-Pod communication. We also discuss service mesh in EKS, which provides enhanced control and visibility between services, particularly in microservice environments. We then examine the **Horizontal Pod Autoscaler** (**HPA**), which adjusts application capacity by scaling Pods based on demand, and Karpenter, which further enhances efficiency by rapidly adding required worker capacity.

Collectively, these topics demonstrate how EKS can evolve beyond a basic Kubernetes cluster to become a responsive, efficient platform that supports modern application patterns with minimal manual intervention. This chapter aims to help you understand how these components work together to design clusters that are functional, scalable, resilient, and easier to manage.

Structure

In this chapter, we will discuss the following topics:

- Networking in EKS
- Container Network Interface in EKS
- Service mesh in EKS
- Horizontal Pod Autoscaler
- Karpenter Kubernetes Cluster Autoscaler for EKS

Objectives

In Amazon EKS, networking enables secure and efficient communication between Pods, services, and external users. Effective network design ensures the cluster remains scalable, secure, and manageable as workloads increase. The **Container Network Interface** (**CNI**) connects Pods to the VPC network and assigns IP addresses that align with AWS networking, simplifying Pod communication and supporting seamless integration with other AWS services.

A service mesh provides an additional layer to manage service-to-service communication, traffic routing, retries, encryption, and observability. In larger EKS environments, it simplifies control over microservice interactions without embedding complex logic in application code.

Scalability is a key objective in EKS. The Horizontal Pod Autoscaler adjusts the number of Pods based on demand, enabling applications to respond to traffic changes automatically. At the cluster level, Karpenter provisions compute capacity efficiently by launching nodes that match workload requirements, improving utilization compared to fixed node groups.

Networking in EKS

Networking in EKS enables communication within the Kubernetes cluster and with external systems and ensures security. It connects the EKS control plane, worker nodes, Pods, services, and users across the AWS **Virtual Private Cloud** (**VPC**), enabling the system to function as an integrated platform rather than as isolated components.

From an AWS solutions architect's point of view, networking in EKS includes:

- How the control plane reaches the worker nodes.
- How worker nodes and Pods reach the internet, other AWS services, and external **application programming interfaces** (**APIs**).
- How users and systems reach the cluster (for example, through kubectl or via load balancers).
- How traffic flows between services inside the cluster.

All networking operates on one or more VPCs and subnets, integrating Kubernetes concepts such as Pod IPs, services, routes, and security with AWS networking features, including security groups, route tables, **Network Address Translation** (**NAT**) gateways, and load balancers.

EKS connectivity with control and data plane

An EKS cluster effectively lives in two networking spaces:

- The **AWS-managed control plane VPC**, where the Kubernetes API servers run in an Amazon-managed account. You cannot see or log into those instances, but they expose an API endpoint.

- Your **customer VPC**, where worker nodes **Elastic Compute Cloud** (**EC2**) or **Fargate** tasks run, along with databases, load balancers, and other AWS resources.

Worker nodes within your VPC connect to the control plane API endpoint to register, receive instructions, and report status. The connection method depends on your cluster endpoint configuration:

- Public endpoint only:
  - o Nodes may sit in public subnets or private subnets with a route to NAT.
  - o API traffic from nodes goes out onto the public internet but stays within AWS's network infrastructure.
- Private endpoint or both public and private:
  - o Nodes connect to the control plane through elastic network interfaces inside your VPC subnets.
  - o That keeps control-plane traffic within the AWS network instead of going over the public internet.

Note: **The public endpoint is the default for standard EKS cluster creation. EKS Auto Mode and some AWS console-guided configurations may default to different endpoint settings.**

This decision influences node deployment, subnet design, and access control for users and tools such as kubectl. You can further restrict the public endpoint using **Classless Inter-Domain Routing** (**CIDR**) rules to limit access to specific offices or **continuous integration** (**CI**)/**continuous deployment** (**CD**) IP ranges.

Pod's network identity

The most important networking layer in EKS is the VPC CNI, which is the default add-on:

- The VPC CNI assigns each Pod its own **Internet Protocol** (**IP**) address from your VPC subnet ranges.
- Instead of creating a separate overlay network, Pods get real VPC IPs, so they can behave like *normal* AWS resources.
- Because Pods use VPC IPs, you can apply security groups, route tables, and traffic-mirroring tools at the Pod level, not just at the node level.

As a result:

- A Pod can talk directly to **Relational Database Service** (**RDS**), **DynamoDB**, **Simple Storage Service** (**S3**) via VPC endpoints, or other AWS services as though it were an EC2 instance.

- You can secure traffic to and from Pods using the same security groups and network-ACL patterns you already use in AWS.
- The VPC CNI uses **Elastic Network Interfaces** (**ENIs**) attached to worker nodes to provide IP addresses to Pods, and newer modes like **Prefix Delegation** let you pack many more Pods per node by handing out IP address ranges instead of one IP per ENI.

To understand the EKS Traffic more clearly, you can refer to the following diagram, which illustrates three distinct traffic paths within an EKS architecture. Each path is styled to remain visually distinct, even when overlaid in the same VPC:

- **Path 1, User to Pod (solid line)**: The user's request enters through the internet gateway, passes through the ALB provisioned by the AWS load balancer Controller from a Kubernetes Ingress resource, is routed to a service, and ultimately reaches a Pod on a worker node in the private subnet.
- **Path 2, Pod to internet (dashed line)**: Outbound traffic from a Pod, such as external API calls, exits through the NAT gateway in the public subnet and then through the internet gateway, as Pods do not have public IPs.
- **Path 3, Node to control plane (dotted line)**: The kubelet on each worker node communicates with the EKS control plane, which resides in a separate AWS-managed VPC, using EKS-managed ENIs in the customer's subnets. This enables node registration, heartbeats, and Pod scheduling without direct access to the control plane from the customer's VPC.

The following figure illustrates EKS Traffic flow:

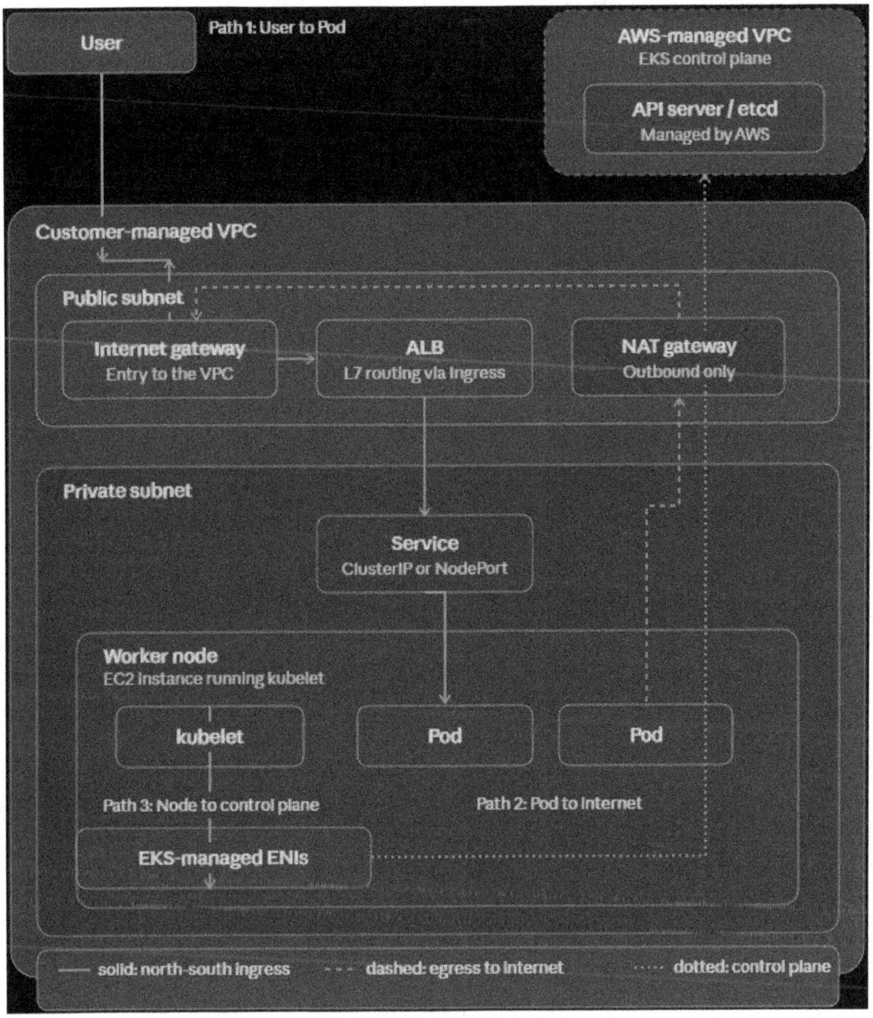

Figure 16.1: EKS Traffic flow

Inbound and outbound traffic in EKS

Incoming traffic usually follows this pattern:

- External users send requests to an **Application Load Balancer** (**ALB**) or **Network Load Balancer** (**NLB**).
- The load balancer lives in public subnets and routes traffic into the VPC.
- An **ingress controller** (for example, AWS load balancer Controller) or a Kubernetes Service routes traffic to the right Pods based on the request host or path.

- The Pods inside private subnets receive the traffic and send responses back through the same path.

For traffic going out of the cluster:

- Pods in private subnets route their outbound traffic to a **NAT gateway** or **NAT instance** in the public subnet so they can reach the internet for things like package updates, external APIs, or **software as a service** (**SaaS**) services.
- In some architectures, Pods can also be allowed to talk to the internet directly if they are in public subnets or if you use transparent proxies or service mesh sidecars for egress control.

Services and DNS fit in

Inside the cluster, Kubernetes uses:

- **Services** (ClusterIP, NodePort, LoadBalancer) to give Pods stable, abstract endpoints. A Service can represent multiple Pods and load-balance traffic across them, so applications talk to the Service, not individual Pod IPs.
- **CoreDNS** to provide **Domain Name Service** (**DNS**)-based service discovery. When one Pod talks to another using a Kubernetes service name (for example, database. default.svc.cluster.local where default is the namespace the service belongs to), CoreDNS resolves that name to the right IP addresses behind the scenes.

These features simplify networking for developers, as they do not need to track individual Pod locations. Developers use service names, and Kubernetes manages the routing.

Security and observability in EKS networking

Security in EKS networking is handled at multiple layers:

- **At the VPC level**: Route tables, NACLs, NAT gateways, and VPC endpoints shape how traffic flows between zones and services.
- **At the security group level**: Worker nodes, ALBs, and Pods (when using Podlevel security groups) can be locked down to only the ports and protocols they actually need.
- **At the Kubernetes level**: Network policies can restrict which Pods can talk to each other, for example, only allowing traffic from the frontend namespace to the backend namespace.

Observability is equally important:

- VPC Flow Logs, CloudWatch Metrics, ALB-access logs, and Kubernetes-level visibility (metrics, logs, and traces) let you see how traffic moves between services, where latency is high, and what might be causing errors.

- When you combine EKS networking with a service mesh like Istio or a managed solution like Amazon VPC Lattice, you get an even more granular view of service-to-service calls, including retries, latencies, and security attributes.

For an AWS Solutions Architect, networking in EKS is more than simply adding a VPC and subnets; it is fundamental to availability, security, and performance. A well-designed EKS network:

- Uses at least one private subnet per Availability Zone for worker nodes.
- Places internet-facing load balancers in public subnets with tight security-group rules.
- Uses NAT gateways or similar patterns to give private nodes safe outbound access.
- Limits controlplane access with private endpoints and CIDR restrictions where appropriate.
- Aligns VPC CNI configuration (prefix delegation, custom networking, custom security groups) with your scale and security requirements.

When properly implemented, EKS networking serves as a reliable backbone. Pods receive secure, VPC-native IPs, workloads scale automatically, and the system operates as a unified, well-connected platform rather than isolated components.

Container Network Interface in EKS

The CNI provides Kubernetes Pods with a unique network identity. In EKS, the CNI ensures each Pod is accessible within the VPC network, enabling secure communication between containers, AWS services, and users. Simply put, the CNI ensures that when a Pod is created, it receives the necessary networking to communicate effectively.

CNI concept

Kubernetes does not enforce a single networking implementation. Instead, it uses the CNI standard, allowing various networking plugins for different environments. In EKS, the primary plugin is the Amazon VPC CNI, which integrates Kubernetes networking with the AWS VPC. This allows Pods to receive IP addresses from VPC subnets, similar to other AWS resources.

This approach makes Pod networking consistent with standard AWS networking. Pods operate within VPC boundaries, utilize security groups and routing rules, and can access services such as RDS, S3, and DynamoDB seamlessly.

Significance of CNI

CNI is essential because networking underpins all Kubernetes operations. A Pod without network connectivity cannot serve traffic, call APIs, or interact with other system components.

The CNI plugin ensures each Pod receives the appropriate network configuration upon creation.

This integration is particularly valuable in AWS, as EKS is designed to work directly with the VPC. By leveraging the VPC rather than a separate overlay network, EKS achieves improved integration with security groups, routing, observability, and private connectivity.

Working in a simple flow

Once a Pod is created, the kubelet on the worker node requests the CNI plugin to configure networking for that Pod. The plugin assigns an IP address and connects the Pod to the node's networking stack, making it part of the VPC network and enabling traffic flow.

The simple flow is:

1. Kubernetes decides a Pod should be created.
2. The worker node receives the Pod assignment.
3. The kubelet calls the CNI plugin.
4. The CNI plugin attaches or uses an IP address from the VPC subnet.
5. The Pod gets network connectivity.
6. The Pod can now communicate with other Pods, Services, and AWS resources.

The CNI is a foundational component; without it, Pods cannot communicate, and workloads cannot function within the cluster.

Components of CNI

The following are the components of CNI:

- **Pod IPs**: Each Pod receives a unique IP address, making Pods first-class network entities within the VPC. This direct addressing simplifies communication between services and components.
- **ENIs**: In AWS, the CNI integrates with ENIs, which are virtual network cards attached to EC2 instances. The CNI plugin uses ENIs to allocate IP addresses to Pods from the subnet range.
- **Kubelet**: The kubelet is the node agent that instructs the CNI to configure networking when a Pod is scheduled, serving as the bridge between Kubernetes and the node runtime.
- **Security groups and routes**: Since Pods use VPC networking, you can manage traffic using standard AWS tools such as security groups and routing tables. This approach enhances cluster security and predictability.

- **Prefix delegation**: In larger clusters, IP address capacity is critical. Prefix delegation enables the CNI to allocate IP address blocks more efficiently to ENIs, supporting higher Pod density per node and improved scalability.

Example

Consider an EKS cluster running a microservices application: a frontend Pod receives a request and communicates with a backend Pod, which then accesses an RDS database in a private subnet. This workflow relies on the CNI assigning network identities to Pods and integrating them into the VPC. By using the VPC directly, the CNI ensures Pods function as integral parts of the AWS network, rather than as isolated containers behind a separate overlay.

As an AWS Solutions Architect, understanding the CNI is important because it impacts:

- Pod density per node
- IP address planning
- Network security design
- Communication between services
- Cluster scaling behavior

If you do not plan networking carefully, you may run out of IP addresses, create traffic bottlenecks, or make security harder to manage. However, when designed well, the CNI gives you a clean, scalable, and AWS-native way to connect your workloads.

The CNI provides Pods with essential network connectivity. In EKS, the Amazon VPC CNI integrates Pods into the AWS network, allowing them to communicate as standard VPC resources. Networking is a foundational component, as containers without connectivity cannot fully participate in the application.

Service mesh in EKS

A service mesh in EKS is a communication layer between microservices that manages their interactions. It enables smarter, safer, and more observable communication without embedding this logic in application code.

Concept

In a typical microservices setup, each service manages retries, timeouts, encryption, traffic routing, and request tracking independently, which can complicate code maintenance. A service mesh centralizes these networking responsibilities in a shared infrastructure layer.

In EKS, technologies such as *Istio* or *Cilium* are commonly used. The mesh manages service traffic, allowing applications to focus on business logic.

Working

A service mesh typically consists of a **control plane** and a **data plane**. The control plane manages rules, while the data plane enforces them. In Kubernetes, the data plane usually consists of sidecar proxies (Istio's classic mode use sidecar proxies) running alongside each application Pod, directing all traffic through these proxies. Some modern implementations like *Cilium* and *Istio Ambient* are sidecar-less. The process works as follows:

1. Service A sends a request.
2. The request first goes to Service A's sidecar proxy.
3. The proxy checks mesh rules for routing, retries, security, and load balancing.
4. The proxy forwards the request to Service B's proxy.
5. Service B's proxy sends it to Service B.
6. The response returns through the same path.

This approach removes traffic management concerns from application code, ensuring consistent behavior across the cluster.

Significance

A service mesh is particularly valuable in EKS as microservices scale and communication complexity increases. It centralizes dependency tracking, security enforcement, and traffic monitoring. It also provides greater control over deployment strategies, such as traffic splitting for canary releases and blue/green deployments.

Main benefits

The following are the main benefits of service mesh in EKS:

- **Security**: A service mesh can encrypt inter-service traffic using mutual TLS, enabling services to verify each other's identity and supporting Zero Trust networking within the cluster.
- **Observability**: Since all traffic passes through proxies, the mesh collects detailed telemetry, including request counts, latencies, errors, and service dependencies, which simplifies troubleshooting.
- **Traffic control**: A mesh enables advanced routing features such as retries, timeouts, traffic splitting, mirroring, and circuit breaking, providing greater control over request flow.
- **Reliability**: If a service becomes slow or unstable, the mesh helps isolate failures and maintain overall system health. Features like retries and timeouts enhance resilience without custom application code.

Example

Consider an order-processing system in EKS with checkout, payment, inventory, and shipping services:

- Checkout sends a request to the payment.
- The mesh ensures the request is encrypted.
- If payment is slow, the mesh can retry once or apply a timeout.
- If you are releasing a new version of the payment, the mesh can send only 10% of the traffic to it first.
- Observability tools can show exactly where the request slowed down.

Without a service mesh, each microservice would need to implement and maintain much of this behavior separately.

Use case

A service mesh is recommended when:

- You have many microservices.
- You need strong service-to-service security.
- You want deep observability and traffic control.
- You need safer release strategies like canary or blue/green deployments.

For small applications with few services, the overhead of proxies and mesh management may outweigh the benefits. In these cases, standard Kubernetes Services and ingress rules are often sufficient. Each sidecar proxy typically adds around 50 to 100 MB of memory per Pod and introduces a small amount of additional per-request latency. In clusters with hundreds of Pods, this overhead becomes a meaningful architectural consideration. This sidecar overhead applies only to proxy-based meshes such as Istio.

A service mesh in EKS acts as a traffic management and security layer for microservices, enhancing safety, visibility, and reliability. The key takeaway is to use a service mesh when centralized control of service-to-service communication is needed, rather than implementing it within each application.

Horizontal Pod Autoscaler

The HPA is a Kubernetes feature that adjusts the number of running Pods based on demand. It scales applications up as traffic increases and down as it decreases, eliminating manual intervention. In AWS EKS, HPA is essential for maintaining responsive and efficient containerized applications.

Concept

HPA operates at the Pod level, adding or removing Pods within a Deployment, ReplicaSet, or StatefulSet. It does not manage nodes. When application demand increases, HPA adds Pods; when demand decreases, it reduces them. This process is known as **horizontal scaling**, where additional application instances are added rather than increasing the resources of a single instance. Vertical scaling, by contrast, involves allocating more **central processing unit** (**CPU**) or memory to a Pod.

For workloads where increasing resources per Pod is more appropriate than adding more Pods, the VPA can automatically adjust CPU and memory requests and limits. HPA and VPA serve complementary roles, though they should generally not be applied to the same metric on the same workload simultaneously.

The following figure demonstrates that HPA automatically scales the number of Pods based on metrics from the Kubernetes metrics server to maintain optimal performance:

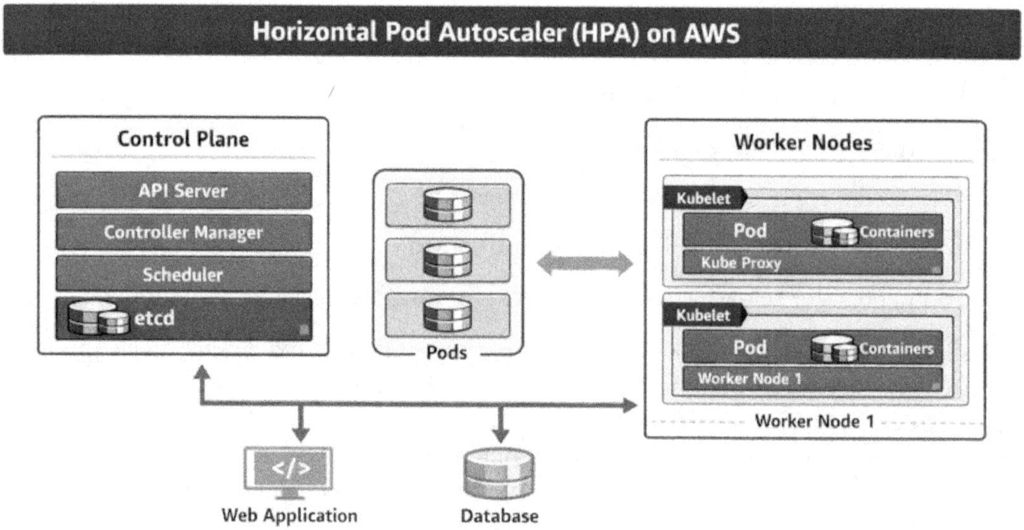

Figure 16.2: Horizontal Pod Autoscaler

Significance

HPA is valuable because application traffic often fluctuates. Some applications experience predictable daily patterns, while others face sudden spikes during events such as sales or batch processing. Without HPA, you would either:

- Run too many Pods all the time and waste resources, or
- Run too few Pods and let performance suffer during peak load.

HPA balances performance and cost by scaling resources only when necessary.

Metrics HPA watches

HPA usually watches metrics such as:

- CPU utilization
- Memory usage
- Custom application metrics
- External metrics

The most common configuration is CPU-based scaling. If average CPU usage across Pods exceeds a target value, HPA adds Pods; if it falls below the target, HPA removes them.

For event-driven scaling based on sources such as SQS queue depth or CloudWatch metrics, **Kubernetes Event-Driven Autoscaling** (**KEDA**) is a popular complement to HPA in EKS environments.

HPA in a simple flow

The process works as follows:

1. Your application runs as a deployment with a few Pods.
2. The Metrics Server or another metrics source collects resource usage.
3. The HPA controller checks those metrics at regular intervals.
4. It compares current usage with the target you configured.
5. If demand is high, it updates the number of replicas.
6. Kubernetes creates new Pods.
7. The scheduler places those Pods on available worker nodes.
8. If demand falls, HPA scales the replicas down again.

HPA operates as a continuous control loop, constantly adjusting the workload as needed.

Note: **The Kubernetes Metrics Server must be deployed separately in EKS clusters, as it is not installed by default. Without it, CPU and memory-based HPA will not function.**

Example

Consider an online shopping API running on EKS:

- During normal hours, 2 Pods are enough.
- During a flash sale, CPU usage climbs above the target.
- HPA notices the increase and scales the Deployment to 6 Pods.

- Traffic is spread across those 6 Pods.
- After the sale ends, usage drops.
- HPA reduces the Pods back down to 2.

This approach improves availability during traffic spikes and reduces costs during periods of low demand.

HPA limitations

HPA only adjusts the number of Pods and does not provision new worker nodes. If existing nodes lack capacity, new Pods remain pending until additional node resources are available.

These different layers work hand in hand: HPA adds Pods, which then go to a Pending state, triggering Karpenter or Cluster Autoscaler to provision the necessary nodes.

That is why HPA is often used together with:

- Cluster Autoscaler, or
- Karpenter

These tools manage worker nodes, while HPA manages Pods.

Best use cases

HPA works well for:

- microservices
- APIs
- web applications
- event-driven services
- workloads with changing traffic

HPA is especially useful when application load fluctuates frequently and automated scaling is required. For AWS Solutions Architects, HPA serves as the application-level scaling layer in EKS. It aligns Pod count with demand, enhances platform elasticity, improves user experience during spikes, and reduces unnecessary costs. In summary, HPA enables applications to scale out as traffic increases and scale in as demand decreases.

Karpenter and Cluster Autoscaler for EKS

In Amazon EKS, both Cluster Autoscaler and Karpenter manage worker node scaling as cluster capacity needs change. Cluster Autoscaler uses predefined node groups, while Karpenter dynamically provisions right-sized nodes based on pending Pod requirements.

Concept

Cluster Autoscaler is the established model for Kubernetes scaling. It monitors unscheduled Pods and adjusts the size of existing node groups accordingly. Typically, it operates with EKS-managed node groups or Auto Scaling groups defined in advance.

The following figure demonstrates that Cluster Autoscaler automatically adjusts the number of worker nodes in an AWS cluster to meet Pod demands:

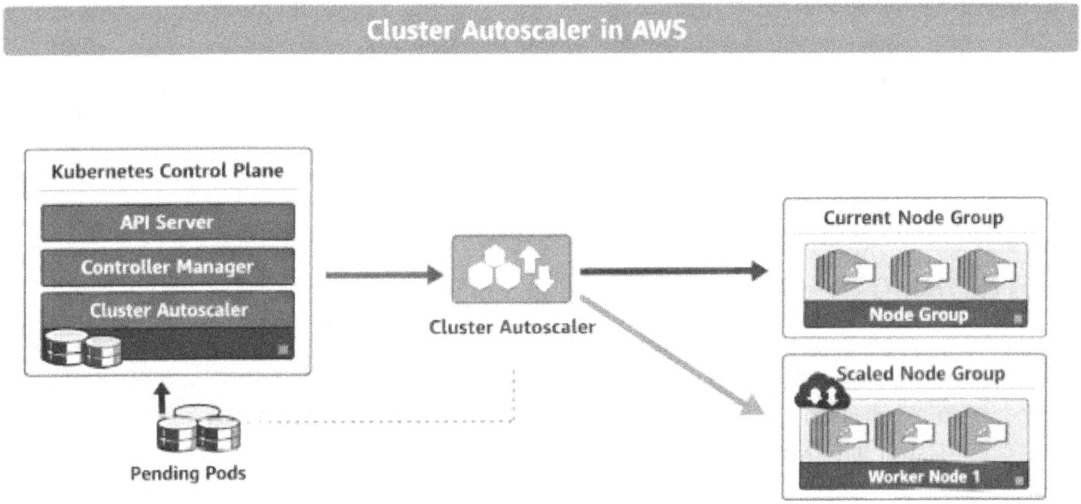

Figure 16.3: *Cluster Autoscaler*

Karpenter offers greater flexibility and performance in node provisioning. It evaluates pending Pod requirements and directly launches the most appropriate compute resources. AWS describes Karpenter as a flexible autoscaler that enhances application availability and cluster efficiency, and EKS documentation notes that EKS Auto Mode is built on Karpenter.

The following figure demonstrates Karpenter efficiently provisions and scales worker nodes in AWS based on cluster demands:

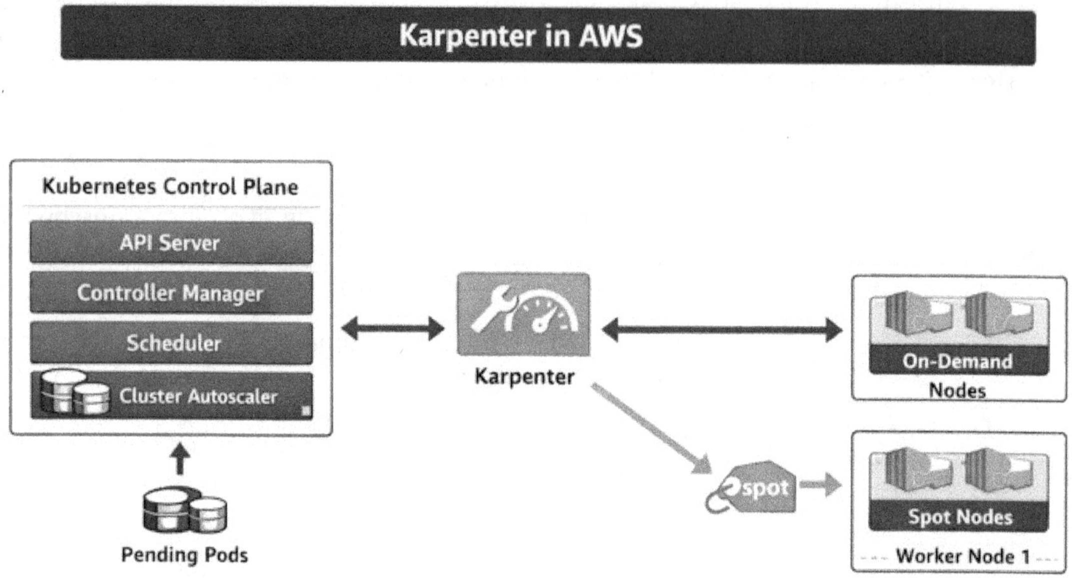

Figure 16.4*: Karpenter provisioning nodes*

Working of Autoscaler

Cluster Autoscaler operates by monitoring pending Pods. If no existing node can accommodate a Pod, it evaluates whether adding a node from a predefined group resolves the issue. It increases group size as needed and scales down underutilized nodes when safe. This approach requires you to define node types in advance, providing predictability but limiting flexibility, as scaling is restricted to existing node groups.

Working of Karpenter

Karpenter functions as an intelligent provisioning system. It monitors unscheduled Pods, assesses their CPU, memory, and placement needs, and provisions optimal nodes accordingly. Karpenter selects instance types dynamically, rather than relying solely on predefined node groups. According to AWS documentation, it provisions compute based on workload requirements such as compute, storage, acceleration, and scheduling needs.

Karpenter does not wait for node group expansion. It responds directly to workload demands by creating appropriately sized nodes, making it faster and more efficient for variable or mixed workloads. In the following table, we can find the main difference between Cluster Autoscaler and Karpenter:

Area	Cluster Autoscaler	Karpenter
Scaling model	Scales predefined node groups	Provisions nodes dynamically from workload needs
Flexibility	Limited to the node groups you create first	More flexible and adaptive
Speed	Usually slower because it waits for node group scaling	Usually faster because it provisions directly
Instance choice	Restricted to the instance types in your node groups	Can choose from many instance types dynamically
Best fit	Stable, predictable node patterns	Variable, bursty, or cost-sensitive workloads

***Table 16.1**: Differences between Cluster Autoscaler and Karpenter*

In practice, Cluster Autoscaler is linked to managed node groups and AWS Auto Scaling groups, while Karpenter provisions capacity by interacting directly with EC2.

Note: **EKS Auto Mode, introduced at AWS re-Invent 2024, fully automates compute, storage, and networking management for entire clusters with a single click. It automatically provisions right-sized nodes, manages OS patching, rotates nodes every 21 days for security, and includes pre-configured load balancing and storage. For teams seeking operational simplicity, AWS now recommends EKS Auto Mode as the starting point for new clusters.**

Use case

Choose Cluster Autoscaler if you prefer a traditional, predictable model and are comfortable defining node groups in advance. It is best suited for stable cluster layouts and straightforward operations. Select Karpenter for faster scaling, improved resource utilization, and greater flexibility in instance selection. It is ideal for dynamic workloads, cost optimization, and rapid response to changing demand.

Example

Consider a cluster that typically runs a few small services during the day but experiences a significant traffic surge at night. With **Cluster Autoscaler**, the cluster waits for a Pod to remain pending before expanding a predefined node group. If the selected group is too small or unsuitable, scaling may be slower or less efficient.

With **Karpenter**, the cluster identifies the pending Pod, selects an appropriate instance type based on its requirements, and launches a node that closely matches the workload. This typically results in faster placement and reduced resource waste.

Simple takeaway

Cluster Autoscaler focuses on scaling existing node groups, while Karpenter provisions the optimal node for each workload in real time. In modern EKS environments, Karpenter is generally more flexible and efficient, though Cluster Autoscaler remains valuable for those preferring a predefined scaling model.

Conclusion

This chapter examined how Amazon EKS clusters achieve greater dynamism and production readiness through advanced networking and autoscaling. EKS networking and the CNI provide reliable communication, while the HPA maintains application responsiveness by adjusting Pod counts based on demand. Service mesh introduces advanced traffic management, security, and observability, and Karpenter offers a faster, more efficient approach to node provisioning compared to traditional autoscalers. Collectively, these components enable EKS environments to adapt to changing workloads, maintain visibility under pressure, and reduce operational overhead, allowing Kubernetes to scale effectively within AWS.

In the next chapter, we will focus on securing and strengthening EKS clusters in production by applying AWS best practices that align security with your overall architecture. We will begin with the AWS Shared Responsibility Model to clarify the division of responsibilities, then address network security and segmentation to isolate workloads and manage traffic flow. The chapter will also cover data protection and encryption for safeguarding sensitive information. By the end, you will have a comprehensive playbook for building EKS environments that are robust, scalable, and secure against real-world threats.

References

1. **https://aws.amazon.com/blogs/containers/de-mystifying-cluster-networking-for-amazon-eks-worker-nodes/**
2. **https://docs.aws.amazon.com/eks/latest/userguide/eks-networking.html**
3. **https://aws.amazon.com/blogs/containers/deep-dive-into-cluster-networking-for-amazon-eks-hybrid-nodes/**
4. **https://docs.aws.amazon.com/eks/latest/userguide/autoscaling.html**
5. **https://docs.aws.amazon.com/prescriptive-guidance/latest/scaling-amazon-eks-infrastructure/workload-scaling.html**
6. **https://docs.aws.amazon.com/eks/latest/userguide/horizontal-Pod-autoscaler.html**
7. **https://aws.amazon.com/what-is/service-mesh/**

8. **https://aws.amazon.com/blogs/opensource/getting-started-with-cilium-service-mesh-on-amazon-eks/**
9. **https://docs.aws.amazon.com/eks/latest/best-practices/networking.html**
10. **https://docs.aws.amazon.com/eks/latest/best-practices/vpc-cni.html**
11. **https://www.redhat.com/en/blog/cni-kubernetes**
12. **https://docs.aws.amazon.com/eks/latest/userguide/eks-architecture.html**
13. **https://docs.aws.amazon.com/eks/latest/userguide/kubernetes-concepts.html**

CHAPTER 17

Security and Best Practices in EKS

Introduction

This chapter introduces the security mindset required for running **Amazon Elastic Kubernetes Service** (**EKS**) in **Amazon Web Services** (**AWS**). We begin with the AWS Shared Responsibility Model, which clarifies the division between AWS-managed and customer-managed security. Next, we address network security and segmentation to separate workloads, minimize unnecessary access, and control traffic between Pods, services, and external systems. We also discuss data protection and encryption of our sensitive data at rest and in transit. Finally, we cover incident response and recovery, emphasizing the importance of early detection, rapid response, and efficient service restoration.

These topics form the foundation for securely operating EKS in real-world environments. Kubernetes security extends beyond edge controls; it requires designing the platform to limit access, protect data, and manage incidents effectively. By the end of this chapter, you will understand how EKS security works in practice and why these best practices are essential for resilient, trustworthy, and production-ready applications.

Structure

In this chapter, we will discuss the following topics:

- AWS Shared Responsibility Model
- Network security and segmentation
- Data protection and encryption
- Incident response and recovery

Objectives

This chapter provides practical guidance for securing an Amazon EKS environment using cloud-native approaches. You will learn how the AWS Shared Responsibility Model defines security boundaries, how network security and segmentation reduce risk, and how data protection and encryption safeguard information at rest and in transit. The chapter also explains how incident response and recovery integrate into overall security, ensuring your team can detect, respond to, and resolve issues confidently. By the end, you should view EKS security as an integral part of designing and operating a reliable AWS architecture.

AWS Shared Responsibility Model

The AWS Shared Responsibility Model underpins security in EKS and all AWS services. AWS's responsibility is to secure the cloud infrastructure, including physical data centers, global infrastructure, and the managed EKS control plane. You are responsible for securing workloads, access, data, and configurations within your cluster.

Concept

A helpful analogy is to view AWS as the building owner and you as the tenant. AWS ensures the building is secure and maintained, while you control office access, storage, and information handling. In EKS, AWS manages the control plane, but you are responsible for securing nodes, Pods, container images, **Identity and Access Management** (**IAM**) roles, secrets, and network rules.

This model is important because many security issues arise from customer misconfigurations, such as public S3 buckets, overly permissive IAM roles, or open security groups. The shared responsibility model emphasizes that cloud security is a partnership, not solely AWS's responsibility.

AWS responsibilities

In EKS, AWS manages the supporting infrastructure, including the control plane, hardware, data centers, and systems that ensure platform availability and patching. AWS also maintains the reliability and security of the managed Kubernetes control plane, so you do not need to install, patch, or maintain master nodes.

While AWS patches the control plane, customers are still responsible for:

- Upgrading the Kubernetes version on their own schedule (AWS does not auto-upgrade clusters).
- Patching worker node **Amazon Machine Images** (**AMIs**) (managed node groups can be updated, but this is customer-initiated).

- Managing add-on versions (CoreDNS, kube-proxy, **Virtual Private Cloud** (**VPC**) **Container Network Interface** (**CNI**)).

This is a key benefit of EKS: you can use Kubernetes without managing the control plane. AWS handles the complex platform operations, allowing your team to focus on application design and cluster management.

Customer responsibilities

Your responsibilities begin when you create the cluster. You must secure worker nodes or Fargate tasks, manage cluster access, configure Kubernetes **Role-Based Access Control** (**RBAC**), protect secrets, and control traffic using security groups and network policies. You are also responsible for ensuring container images are trusted, patched, and scanned for vulnerabilities.

You must also consider application behavior within the cluster. While AWS secures the platform, poorly configured applications can still expose data or create vulnerabilities. For example, excessive Pod privileges or overly broad service account permissions introduce risks due to workload configuration, not the EKS service.

Security in practice

The shared responsibility model becomes practical when you consider questions such as:

- Who can create or change workloads in the cluster?
- Which IAM roles can a Pod assume?
- Are secrets encrypted and stored safely?
- Are Pods allowed to talk to only the services they need?
- Can users reach the cluster endpoint from anywhere, or only from trusted networks?

These questions highlight your responsibilities under the model. AWS provides the necessary tools, but you determine how strictly to apply them. A secure EKS cluster results from strong architecture and disciplined access control, not simply from using AWS.

Significance for EKS best practices

The shared responsibility model helps teams avoid the mistake of assuming that *managed* means *fully secure by default*. While EKS reduces infrastructure management, you still need governance, identity control, logging, scanning, and hardening. Effective architectures treat AWS as the secure platform provider and the customer as the security owner for workload design.

For example, AWS may manage the control plane, but you still need to:

- Rotate credentials and use IAM roles instead of long-lived keys.

- Restrict Kubernetes API access.
- Use least privilege for service accounts.
- Keep node images and container images updated.
- Monitor logs and alert on suspicious activity.

Note: **AWS recommends using IAM Roles for Service Accounts (IRSA) or the newer EKS Pod Identity to grant Pods scoped AWS permissions at runtime, instead of embedding long-lived IAM access keys in environment variables or container images. These methods bind IAM roles directly to Kubernetes service accounts, ensuring each workload receives only the permissions it needs and preventing credential sharing across Pods.**

Example

Consider a company running a customer portal on EKS. AWS ensures the control plane is available and secure. The company must ensure that only the DevOps team can deploy to the cluster, that only application Pods access the database, and that only approved container images are used in production. If an attacker gains access due to an overly permissive role, this reflects a customer-side security gap that requires improved design and governance.

The shared responsibility model implies AWS secures the platform, while you secure your use of it. In EKS, this distinction is critical: AWS manages the control plane, but all other aspects of your cluster require careful security design. Remember, managed does not mean you are not responsible.

Network security and segmentation

Network security and segmentation are critical in EKS as they govern traffic between users, applications, services, and external systems. In Kubernetes, workloads are distributed across many Pods and nodes, making a flat network design risky. A secure EKS architecture restricts communication to only what is necessary, ensuring that if one part is compromised, the rest remains protected.

Concept

Network security controls who can communicate, on which ports, and under what conditions. In EKS, traffic may flow from the internet to a load balancer, from the load balancer to Pods, between Pods, or from Pods to databases and AWS services. Each of these paths should be intentional.

Network security is similar to doors, locks, and hallways in a building. Not every room should connect to every other room, and not every visitor should have the same access. In EKS, only required traffic should be allowed, and all other traffic should be blocked by default.

Significance of segmentation

Segmentation divides the cluster and network into smaller, controlled areas. This reduces the impact of errors, attacks, or unexpected behavior. If one service is compromised, segmentation limits the spread to other services or sensitive systems. For example, a public-facing web application should not have the same network access as an internal payment service or database. Separating them into different network zones, namespaces, or security boundaries creates a safer design. Segmentation is a simple and effective way to reduce the impact of security incidents.

Control points in EKS

EKS provides several layers for controlling network access. At the AWS layer, security groups and subnet design define permitted traffic. At the Kubernetes layer, network policies restrict Pod-to-Pod communication. At the application layer, service design and ingress rules determine which endpoints are exposed or remain private.

An effective design combines these layers rather than relying on a single control. Security groups protect nodes and load balancers, while network policies secure traffic within the cluster. This layered approach increases reliability, as one control can compensate if another is misconfigured.

Public and private exposure

A key decision in EKS network design is determining what should be public and what should remain private. Typically, only the application entry point, such as a load balancer or ingress controller, should be accessible from the internet. Worker nodes, internal services, and databases should remain private whenever possible.

This is important because exposing more systems increases the attack surface. A private architecture limits potential entry points for attackers and simplifies operational control, as internal services are only accessible through approved paths.

Pod-to-Pod traffic

Inside the cluster, Pods often need to communicate, but this communication should be restricted. Workloads in the same cluster should not have unrestricted access to each other. For example, a frontend service may need to reach an **application programming interface** (**API**) service, but should not access a database or administrative service directly.

Careful network design defines allowed traffic paths, making the cluster function as a set of small trusted zones instead of a large open network. This model is safer, especially in environments with multiple teams, applications, or frequent deployments.

Note: **The following points should be noted with reference to the network for Pod-to-Pod traffic:**

- **EKS does not enforce NetworkPolicy by default.**
- **A compatible CNI plugin must be explicitly installed and enabled (e.g., Calico, Cilium, or AWS VPC CNI with network policy support turned on).**

Segmentation by environment

A robust EKS architecture separates environments such as development, testing, staging, and production. These environments should not share the same level of trust. Production data and services must be isolated from lower environments to prevent issues in one from affecting the other.

This separation can be achieved using different clusters, VPCs, namespaces, or a combination, depending on security requirements. Production should have stricter controls and minimal shared dependencies. Segmentation between environments reduces accidental access and the risk of change-related incidents.

Example

Imagine an online shopping platform running on EKS. The website is exposed to the internet through an ingress layer, but the order service is only reachable from the website and the internal payment service. The database is private and can only be reached by approved application Pods. Monitoring tools can read logs and metrics, but they cannot modify order data.

In this design, even if the public website is attacked, the attacker does not automatically get access to the payment system or the database. That is the value of network segmentation: it limits how far a problem can travel.

Significance for EKS best practices

Network security and segmentation are fundamental to a secure EKS strategy, as Kubernetes environments are highly interconnected. Without strong boundaries, one exposed service can compromise many others. Effective segmentation ensures each service has a smaller, safer trust area.

The key lesson for AWS architecture is clear: do not build EKS as a single open network. Instead, design it as a set of controlled zones with defined communication rules. This approach improves security, simplifies incident containment, and creates a more stable platform for application and operations teams.

Data protection and encryption

Data protection and encryption are essential for secure EKS design, as containers scale rapidly and often process sensitive data across multiple layers. In Kubernetes, data exists in transit, at rest, and in memory. Effective architecture protects data at every stage, ensuring that even if part of the system is compromised, the data remains secure and difficult to misuse.

Concept

Data protection ensures that only authorized users and systems can access specific data. In EKS, this involves safeguarding application secrets, customer records, configuration values, logs, and data in attached volumes or external databases. It also requires designing the cluster to prevent unnecessary data movement between Pods, nodes, and services.

This is critical because containers are temporary. Pods can be created, replaced, or deleted rapidly. Therefore, secrets and data must be managed to remain secure during scaling, updates, and node failures.

Encryption at rest

Encryption at rest secures data while it is stored. In EKS, this includes Kubernetes secrets, persistent volumes, EBS volumes, S3 buckets, database snapshots, and log storage. Even if an attacker accesses the storage, encrypted data remains unreadable without the encryption key.

A good EKS design usually encrypts:

- Persistent volumes attached to Pods.
- Secrets stored in Kubernetes or external secret systems.
- Database storage used by applications running in the cluster.
- Backups and snapshots kept for recovery.

This is important because storage often holds long-term sensitive data, even in dynamic container environments. Business data must remain protected for extended periods.

Encryption in transit

Encryption in transit secures data as it moves between locations. In EKS, this includes traffic between users and load balancers, ingress controllers and Pods, microservices, and external AWS services.

Proper encryption in transit makes network traffic difficult to intercept or alter. This is crucial in microservices architectures, where requests traverse multiple services. Without encryption, each step introduces potential vulnerabilities. Encryption in transit between Pods requires a service mesh (e.g., *Istio, Linkerd*) implementing **mutual TLS** (**mTLS**), or application-level **Transport Layer Security** (**TLS**).

For example, an application may receive traffic over HTTPS, forward requests internally over TLS, and connect to the database using encrypted channels. This approach provides consistent protection from the system edge to the backend.

Secrets management

Secrets, such as database passwords, API tokens, private keys, and service credentials, are among the most sensitive data. In Kubernetes, they require careful handling and should not be treated as ordinary configuration values, as they can grant access to critical system components.

Note: **Kubernetes Secrets are base64-encoded by default, not encrypted. EKS now enables envelope encryption for all Kubernetes API data (including Secrets) by default on clusters running Kubernetes 1.28+ using KMS v2 with an AWS-owned key. This protection is enabled automatically and requires no customer action.**

A robust EKS architecture avoids hard-coding secrets in container images or source code. Instead, secrets are stored securely and injected into Pods at runtime, ensuring applications access them only when needed and preventing secrets from being embedded in container images or repository history.

AWS services (Secrets Manager, Parameter Store) that store secrets plus open-source integrations that sync them into Pods (External Secrets Operator, Secrets Store CSI Driver) are as follows:

- **AWS Secrets Manager** (AWS Service recommended)
- **AWS Systems Manager Parameter Store** (AWS Service)
- **External Secrets Operator** (open-source integration)
- **Secrets Store CSI Driver** (open-source integration for mounting secrets from AWS Secrets Manager into Pods)

A key principle is that widely distributed secrets are difficult to protect. Centralized management and controlled exposure to the appropriate workloads significantly reduce risk.

Protecting data inside the cluster

Data protection also involves controlling Pod communication and visibility. If a service should not access another's private data, the cluster must enforce separation using roles, network policies, and namespace boundaries.

Kubernetes and AWS work together to enhance security. Kubernetes provides logical workload isolation, while AWS offers encryption, IAM, security groups, and network controls. Effective design combines both. For example, a frontend Pod may access a backend service but not the database directly, limiting potential impact if compromised.

Key management

Encryption is effective only if keys are managed properly. If unrestricted access to keys exists, encryption loses its value. In AWS, centralized key management enables controlled, logged, and auditable access. AWS **Key Management Service** (**KMS**) helps you create and manage encryption keys, protecting sensitive data in your EKS environment. KMS provides a secure platform for managing keys used to encrypt secrets, application data, and storage, while allowing you to control access and usage conditions. In EKS architectures, KMS is essential for securing data at rest, supporting compliance, and minimizing the risk of unauthorized exposure. For example, encrypting secrets or persistent data ensures that, even if storage is accessed without authorization, the information remains protected and unreadable without the appropriate key.

A well-designed EKS environment defines clear rules for key usage by workloads. Sensitive workloads may use separate keys for different data types. Administrative access to key management should be restricted to prevent unnecessary control.

A core principle of cloud security is that encryption must protect data from both external threats and over-privileged insiders or accidental misuse.

Example

Consider an EKS-based healthcare application storing patient records. The application runs in Pods, interacts with an encrypted database, and uses encrypted traffic between services. Database credentials are retrieved at runtime from a secrets manager, and Pods receive only the necessary permissions. Attached volumes, database backups, and logs are all encrypted, and access is restricted.

If a container image is stolen or a storage snapshot is accessed, the data remains protected because encryption was integrated into the architecture from the outset.

Significance for EKS best practices

In EKS, data protection and encryption are fundamental design requirements, not optional enhancements. While containers enable rapid workload movement, this flexibility must be balanced with strict control over sensitive data. As the platform becomes more dynamic, consistent data protection across all layers is increasingly important.

A secure EKS environment protects data at rest, in transit, and in use. Encryption and data protection provide a safety net, even in busy, distributed, and constantly changing environments.

Incident response and recovery

Incident response and recovery are critical security components when an issue has already occurred. In an EKS environment, these processes enable the team to detect problems quickly, contain them, restore services safely, and learn from incidents to prevent recurrence. Effective security design anticipates incidents and prepares the cluster, team, and processes accordingly.

Concept

Incident response is the structured approach a team uses to address security issues, service outages, or unexpected cluster behavior. Incidents may include leaked secrets, compromised container images, misconfigured network rules, failed deployments, or suspicious Kubernetes API access. The objectives are to understand the event, contain the impact, restore normal operations, and prevent recurrence.

This is especially important in EKS due to its dynamic nature. Pods and services frequently change, which increases the risk of rapid problem escalation without a defined response process. Effective teams prepare runbooks, alerts, permissions, and rollback procedures in advance.

Detection and visibility

Detection is the first step of any incident response. A cluster cannot be secured if warning signs go unnoticed. Logs, metrics, and alerts are essential for incident readiness. Security events may present as unusual API calls, failed authentications, unexpected Pod restarts, abnormal network traffic, or unplanned resource changes.

Good visibility allows the team to answer basic questions quickly:

- *What changed?*
- *When did it happen?*
- *Which cluster, namespace, or workload is affected?*
- *Is the issue still active or already contained?*

Without clear visibility, teams lose valuable time. With it, they can respond quickly and effectively.

Containment

Containment focuses on preventing further impact. In EKS, this may involve isolating a namespace, scaling down compromised workloads, blocking network access, revoking credentials, or removing risky deployments. The goal is always to minimize the blast radius.

For example, if a container is suspected of compromise, the team may stop traffic to the service, rotate credentials, and redeploy from a trusted image. If a secret is exposed, revoking or rotating it is the first priority. While speed is important, containment actions should be controlled and documented, not improvised.

Recovery

After containment, recovery begins. This involves restoring the cluster and applications to a trusted, operational state. In EKS, recovery typically relies on redeploying workloads using IaC and application pipelines, rather than manual intervention.

This is a key advantage of container-based systems. If a service is compromised, replacing it is often safer than attempting in-place repairs. Clean redeployment restores known-good versions of applications, configurations, and permissions, making recovery more predictable and reducing the risk of lingering issues.

Recovery also requires validating system health. It is not sufficient for Pods to be running; teams must confirm that traffic flows correctly, dependencies are accessible, logs are normal, and the issue has not recurred.

Rollback and redeployment

A robust EKS recovery plan includes rollback procedures. If a deployment or configuration change triggers an incident, reverting to the last known-good version is often the quickest way to restore stability. This underscores the importance of versioned container images, manifests, and controlled release pipelines.

With a well-planned rollback, teams can quickly and confidently restore stability. Without it, valuable time may be lost reconstructing previous states. In practice, redeploying a clean version is often more effective than manual repairs.

Post-incident review

Stabilizing the system is not the final step. Post-incident review is often the most valuable phase, where the team analyzes the incident and considers:

- *What caused it?*
- *Why was it not caught earlier?*
- *Did our alerts work?*
- *Did our permissions or boundaries allow the problem?*
- *What should we change so the same issue is less likely next time?*

This review should emphasize learning rather than assigning blame. A secure platform evolves when each incident results in improved guardrails, automation, and documentation. In EKS, this may involve tightening IAM roles, enhancing image scanning, adding network restrictions, or refining deployment checks.

Example

Consider a company operating an EKS-based customer portal. If a Pod exhibits unusual outbound activity, monitoring detects the behavior, and the on-call team declares an incident. The team isolates the namespace, rotates the Pod's credentials, blocks the suspicious network path, and redeploys the service from a trusted image. After restoring stable traffic, they review the incident and identify that the deployment pipeline image was not properly scanned. As a result, they implement stronger image validation and stricter deployment approvals.

This example illustrates incident response and recovery in practice: detect, contain, restore, and improve.

Significance in EKS security

Incident response and recovery are essential because no security design is flawless. Even robust EKS environments may encounter bad deployments, stolen credentials, misconfigurations, or runtime attacks. The difference between a resilient and a fragile platform lies in the ability to respond calmly and recover quickly.

The key message for AWS architecture is clear: secure clusters are designed not only to prevent issues but also to withstand and recover from them. EKS provides the tools for clean recovery, but the architecture must incorporate the processes, permissions, and automation necessary for effective recovery.

Security and best practices in a nutshell

The following summarizes the security and best practices discussed in this chapter:

- Understand the shared responsibility model clearly. AWS secures the cloud infrastructure, but you remain responsible for securing what you run inside EKS, including access, workloads, data, and network rules.
- Treat the EKS control plane as managed, but never assume the rest of the cluster is secure by default. Secure worker nodes, Pods, IAM roles, secrets, and application settings with the same care you would use in any production environment.
- Use least privilege everywhere. Give users, roles, service accounts, and applications only the permissions they truly need, and nothing more. This reduces the damage if credentials or workloads are ever compromised.

- Protect data at every stage. Encrypt data when it is stored, when it moves across the network, and when it is used by applications. Sensitive data should never be left exposed in plain text or weakly controlled storage.
- Manage secrets carefully. Keep passwords, tokens, and keys out of code, out of container images, and out of unsafe configuration files. Store them in secure services and inject them only when the application needs them.
- Encrypt storage and backups. Make sure persistent volumes, database snapshots, log archives, and other stored data are protected with encryption so that stolen storage does not mean stolen information.
- Secure traffic in transit. Use encryption for communication between users, services, Pods, and external systems so that network traffic cannot be easily read or altered.
- Control who can access the cluster. Restrict Kubernetes API access, review IAM access regularly, and separate administrative duties so that no single identity has unnecessary control.
- Build strong network segmentation. Do not allow every service to talk to every other service. Limit communication between Pods, namespaces, environments, and external endpoints to only what is required.
- Keep public exposure to a minimum. Only expose the services that truly need internet access, and keep internal workloads, nodes, and databases private wherever possible.
- Separate workloads by trust level. Production, staging, development, and testing should not share the same security boundaries unless there is a strong reason to do so. This helps prevent one environment from affecting another.
- Monitor logs, metrics, and alerts closely. Security issues are much easier to stop early when the team can see unusual behavior, failed logins, suspicious traffic, or unexpected changes quickly.
- Prepare for incidents before they happen. Create clear response steps, assign responsibilities, and make sure the team knows how to contain, investigate, and recover from a problem.
- Use rollback and redeployment as part of recovery. In EKS, it is often safer to replace a bad deployment with a trusted version than to try to repair a broken workload by hand.
- Keep workloads and images clean and current. Scan container images, remove outdated components, and update systems regularly so that known weaknesses do not remain in production for long.
- Review every incident and improvement opportunity. After each problem, study what happened, why it happened, and what should change so the same issue becomes less likely in the future.

- Design security as a continuous practice, not a one-time task. In EKS, the strongest environments are the ones where encryption, access control, segmentation, monitoring, and recovery are built into everyday operations.

These best practices are most effective when implemented together. A secure EKS architecture relies on multiple controls working in concert, rather than a single measure.

Conclusion

In this chapter, we examined EKS security as a shared discipline rather than a single feature. The AWS Shared Responsibility Model clarified the division between AWS's responsibilities and those of the user. We explored how network security and segmentation help control traffic, separate workloads, and limit the spread of vulnerabilities. Data protection and encryption further enhance security by ensuring the safeguarding of sensitive information at rest and in transit.

We also emphasized that strong security requires a clear incident response and recovery plan. Even well-designed systems may experience misconfigurations, attacks, or failures, making early detection, calm response, and rapid restoration essential. Collectively, these practices demonstrate that EKS security involves not only defense but also building a resilient and reliable operating model. Integrating these habits from the outset makes your EKS environment more trustworthy, manageable, and production-ready.

In the next chapter, we will shift from building secure EKS environments to articulating and defending design choices clearly and systematically. You will learn the essentials of system design interviews, focusing on problem breakdown, trade-off analysis, and selecting solutions that address real business needs. We will cover how to consider scalability, reliability, security, and cost, enabling you to discuss architectures confidently and connect technical decisions to business outcomes.

References

1. **https://docs.aws.amazon.com/eks/latest/userguide/security-best-practices.html**
2. **https://docs.aws.amazon.com/eks/latest/best-practices/security.html**
3. **https://docs.aws.amazon.com/eks/latest/best-practices/data-encryption-and-secrets-management.html**
4. **https://docs.aws.amazon.com/eks/latest/best-practices/identity-and-access-management.html**
5. **https://docs.aws.amazon.com/eks/latest/best-practices/Pod-security.html**
6. **https://docs.aws.amazon.com/eks/latest/best-practices/network-security.html**
7. **https://docs.aws.amazon.com/eks/latest/best-practices/cluster-access-management.html**
8. **https://docs.aws.amazon.com/eks/latest/best-practices/image-security.html**

CHAPTER 18
System Design Interview Essentials

Introduction

This chapter introduces essential habits for approaching system design interviews with clarity and confidence. We begin by explaining how to clarify problem requirements and constraints, as effective design starts with understanding system objectives, users, and key limitations. Next, we cover high-level architecture and component identification, teaching you to break down complex problems into manageable elements such as clients, **application programming interfaces** (**APIs**), databases, queues, caches, and storage layers. We also discuss trade-off analysis, enabling you to justify design choices based on factors like scale, speed, simplicity, and cost.

Throughout the chapter, we apply these concepts to key system design topics, including load balancing, Auto Scaling, distributed system design, data consistency, caching, **content delivery network** (**CDN**) use cases, API design, communication protocols, fault tolerance, redundancy, and disaster recovery. Security best practices are also addressed, emphasizing the importance of identity, access, and data protection. We conclude with strategies for effective communication and iteration during interviews, as articulating your reasoning is as important as the technical solution. This chapter aims to equip you with a structured, repeatable approach to system design interviews, enabling you to present your ideas confidently and professionally.

Structure

In this chapter, we will discuss the following topics:

- Clarifying problem requirements, and constraints
- High-level system architecture and component identification
- Trade-off analysis
- Load balancing and Auto Scaling principles

- Distributed system design and data consistency models
- Caching strategies and CDN use cases
- API design and communication protocols
- Fault tolerance, redundancy, and disaster recovery
- Security best practices in system design
- Communication and iteration strategies in interviews

Objectives

This chapter is designed to help you develop a clear and practical approach to system design interview questions. You will learn to clarify requirements and constraints before proposing solutions, identify key system components, and explain trade-offs effectively. The chapter also covers essential concepts such as load balancing, Auto Scaling, distributed system design, data consistency, caching, CDN use cases, API design, communication protocols, fault tolerance, redundancy, and disaster recovery. These foundational elements will enable you to transform ambiguous problems into well-structured architectures.

You will also learn to integrate security considerations into your designs from the outset and communicate your ideas clearly during interviews. Additionally, the chapter demonstrates how to iterate on your solutions as new information emerges, since effective system design often evolves through discussion. By the end, you will be prepared to approach interview problems with a calm, organized mindset and articulate your design choices with both technical accuracy and business awareness.

Clarifying problem requirements and constraints

Clarifying problem requirements and constraints is a critical first step in **Amazon Web Services** (**AWS**) solution architecture. Before selecting services or creating diagrams, an architect must understand the system's purpose, users, expected traffic, required security, and key limitations. When this step is handled thoroughly, subsequent design decisions are grounded in actual needs rather than assumptions.

Significance

In cloud architecture, it is common to select services like **Elastic Compute Cloud** (**EC2**), Lambda, **Elastic Kubernetes Service** (**EKS**), **Relational Database Service** (**RDS**), or S3 before fully understanding the problem. This often results in technically sound designs that do not address the actual business need. It is more effective to start with the problem rather than the tools.

Clarifying requirements enables the architect to distinguish between what the system must do and how it will do it. This process also uncovers hidden needs that may not be immediately apparent. For example, initial requests for a web application may reveal additional requirements such as rapid deployment, high availability, strict compliance, low latency, or budget constraints, all of which can significantly influence the architecture.

Understanding requirements

Requirements usually fall into two broad groups: functional requirements and **non-functional requirements** (**NFRs**). Functional requirements describe what the system must do. These are the visible business features, such as processing orders, uploading files, sending notifications, or storing customer records. The focus is on the system's functionality. Non-functional requirements describe how the system must behave. These include security, scalability, performance, reliability, availability, and maintainability.

A strong AWS architect listens carefully to both. If you only hear the functional need, you may build something that works but fails under real-world pressure. For example, an application may successfully place an order, but if it cannot handle peak traffic during a sale, the design is incomplete. Good architecture works for the business in normal conditions and in stressful ones.

Understanding constraints

Constraints define the boundaries for the solution. They may arise from budget, timeline, compliance, technology standards, existing systems, team expertise, or regional factors. Constraints are integral to the design process and should not be overlooked.

A common mistake is to view constraints as obstacles rather than essential design factors. For example, low-latency requirements may necessitate multi-**Availability Zone** (**AZ**) deployments or edge caching, while strict budgets may limit the use of managed services. Compliance needs may require encryption, audit logging, or data residency controls. Effective architecture is built around these real-world conditions, not idealized scenarios.

Questions to ask early

A good architect begins by asking clear, targeted questions. These questions help transform vague ideas into actionable design inputs.

- *What business problem are we solving?*
- *Who are the users of the system?*
- *What happens if the system is slow, unavailable, or incorrect?*
- *How much traffic do we expect now, and how much growth do we expect later?*

- *What data is sensitive, and what compliance rules apply?*
- *What is the budget for build and operations?*
- *Are there existing platforms, tools, or standards we must use?*
- *What is the timeline for delivery?*

While these questions may appear basic, they often reveal critical design boundaries. They shift the discussion from general needs to specific, actionable requirements.

Simple workflow

A practical workflow for clarifying requirements involves five key steps.

1. **Restate the problem in simple words**: This ensures all stakeholders share a common understanding and reduces confusion from broad or vague requests.
2. **Separate functional needs from non-functional needs**: This clarifies both the required functionality and the expected performance of the system.
3. **Identify constraints**: Identify constraints related to budget, security, compliance, timeline, operations, and technical limitations.
4. **Validate assumptions**: If any aspect is unclear, ask questions and confirm details before proceeding with the design.
5. **Translate requirements into architecture decisions**: After clarifying requirements, select services and patterns that address the actual needs instead of defaulting to familiar options.

Following this process creates a clear path from business problem to technical solution.

Example scenario

Consider a scenario where a company requests a customer portal on AWS. Initially, the request appears straightforward. However, clarification reveals the portal must support thousands of users, protect personal data, remain available during regional failures, and launch within three months on a limited budget. Additionally, the team is experienced with containers but has limited serverless expertise.

This information significantly influences the design. Rather than selecting services arbitrarily, you might choose a highly available web application with managed databases, robust IAM controls, encrypted storage, and automated deployment. If rapid scaling is needed and the team is comfortable with containers, **Elastic Container Service** (**ECS**) or EKS may be suitable. If quick delivery and minimal operational overhead are priorities, serverless could be a better option. The optimal solution depends on the clarified requirements and constraints.

Common mistakes to avoid

A common mistake is assuming the initial request is complete when it often lacks details such as backup, audit, scalability, or recovery requirements. Overengineering is another pitfall; simple problems should not be addressed with unnecessarily complex architectures simply because advanced services are available.

Another mistake is overlooking trade-offs. In AWS architecture, nearly every decision involves balancing cost, performance, complexity, and resilience. There is rarely a perfect solution for all requirements, so clarification helps prioritize the most important trade-offs.

Significance for an AWS architect

For an AWS solution architect, clarifying requirements and constraints is foundational to the design process. The best architecture is not defined by the number of services used, but by how well it addresses the actual problem with appropriate simplicity, reliability, security, and cost efficiency.

This approach also builds trust. When stakeholders see that the design is grounded in real needs, they are more likely to support it. Great architects invest time in asking questions before proposing solutions, recognizing that effective design starts with a clear problem statement and an honest understanding of constraints.

High-level system architecture and component identification

High-level system architecture and component identification mark the transition from concept to concrete design. In a system design interview, this is when you shift from defining the problem to outlining the major building blocks that will address it. Effective architects avoid detailing every aspect too soon. Instead, they first define the system's main components, assign clear responsibilities, and determine how these parts interact.

Concept

High-level architecture provides an overview of the system, highlighting major components, data flows, and key boundaries. At this stage, you do not select specific table columns or API fields. Instead, you identify the main services, entry points, storage layers, communication paths, and external systems.

In AWS architecture, this step is essential because cloud design begins with structure. Before selecting services such as EC2, Lambda, ECS, EKS, RDS, DynamoDB, or S3, you must first define the type of system you are building. For example, a file-sharing platform, a real-time chat system, and a batch processing system are all cloud applications, but each requires a distinct architecture.

Significance

Component identification involves dividing a system into meaningful parts, each with a clear responsibility. Well-chosen components make the system easier to understand, scale, and maintain. Poorly chosen components lead to confusion, tight coupling, and difficulty making changes.

For example, in an e-commerce system, you might identify components such as authentication, product catalog, cart, order processing, payment, notifications, and data storage. These represent core business functions, and treating each as a separate concern allows for cleaner design and easier scaling.

Thinking about responsibilities

To identify components, consider the primary responsibility of each part. Each component should focus on a single main function. For example, the frontend manages user interaction; the API layer handles requests and enforces rules; the application layer contains business logic; the database stores durable data; and background workers process tasks that do not require immediate responses.

This separation results in a clearer design and guides the selection of appropriate AWS services. Services requiring immediate user response should be part of the request/response path, while long-running tasks are better handled asynchronously. This approach is fundamental in system design interviews.

Mapping requirements to components

After understanding the problem, map requirements to components. For example, file uploads require a storage component; notifications require a messaging or event component; handling traffic spikes may require load balancing, caching, or autoscaling; and high availability requires redundancy and failure handling.

At this stage, architecture becomes practical as requirements are translated into design decisions. For example, a requirement to scale quickly may lead to caching, queues, stateless services, and elastic compute layers. A requirement for data durability may result in managed storage, backups, and a multi-AZ design. The component list should always reflect the system's actual needs.

Common component groups

Many systems can be organized into the following few common groups of components:

- **User-facing layer**: Web app, mobile app, API gateway, load balancer, or ingress.
- **Application layer**: Business logic, microservices, Lambda functions, or containerized services.

- **Data layer**: Relational databases, NoSQL databases, object storage, or caches.
- **Async processing layer**: Queues, events, workers, or workflow engines.
- **Security and identity layer**: Authentication, authorization, IAM roles, and secrets management.
- **Observability layer**: Logging, monitoring, tracing, and alerting.
- **External integration layer**: Third-party APIs, payment systems, email providers, or identity providers.

Not every system needs all of these, but most real-world designs involve several of them. The job of the architect is to decide which ones are necessary and how they should connect.

Simple workflow

A practical approach to component identification in interviews is to follow a straightforward workflow:

1. **Restate the problem in one sentence**: This confirms that you understand the goal.
2. **Identify the primary users and actions**: Determine the most common user actions and the essential system capabilities.
3. **Break the system into major responsibilities**: Group related behaviors into components with defined responsibilities.
4. **Place the main data stores and communication paths**: Define the flow of requests through the system and identify data storage locations.
5. **Check the design against the requirements**: Ensure the components address the problem and meet all constraints.
6. **Refine where needed**: Divide overloaded components, consolidate unnecessary ones, or add missing elements.

This workflow is straightforward and helps keep the design organized and easy to explain.

Example of a photo-sharing application

For example, when designing a photo-sharing application on AWS, the high-level system might include a web or mobile client, a login component, an upload service, object storage for photos, a metadata database, an image processing worker, and a notification service. To support fast photo browsing, you might add a cache or CDN. For large uploads, pre-signed URLs and asynchronous processing may be appropriate.

This example demonstrates effective component identification. Rather than simply stating *the app stores photos*, you break the process into authentication, upload, storage, processing, retrieval, and notifications. This approach clarifies the architecture and improves scalability.

This following figure aligns each functional stage mentioned earlier with a specific component, illustrating the proposed decomposition of *stores photos* into six distinct concerns.

- **Authentication**: The login component issues a token before permitting uploads.
- **Upload**: Instead of routing files through servers, the upload service provides a pre-signed URL, allowing clients to upload directly to storage. This approach avoids burdening the compute layer with large file transfers.
- **Storage**: The object store retains the original photo and asynchronously initiates the next stage, ensuring the upload request is not blocked.
- **Processing**: The image processing worker retrieves jobs from a queue, handling tasks such as resizing and thumbnailing. This process is decoupled from uploads, preventing delays for users.
- **Retrieval and notifications**: After processing, metadata is stored in the database, and a notification is sent. A separate CDN and cache layer supports fast photo browsing, independent of the write path.

The following figure illustrates the workflow of a photo-sharing application:

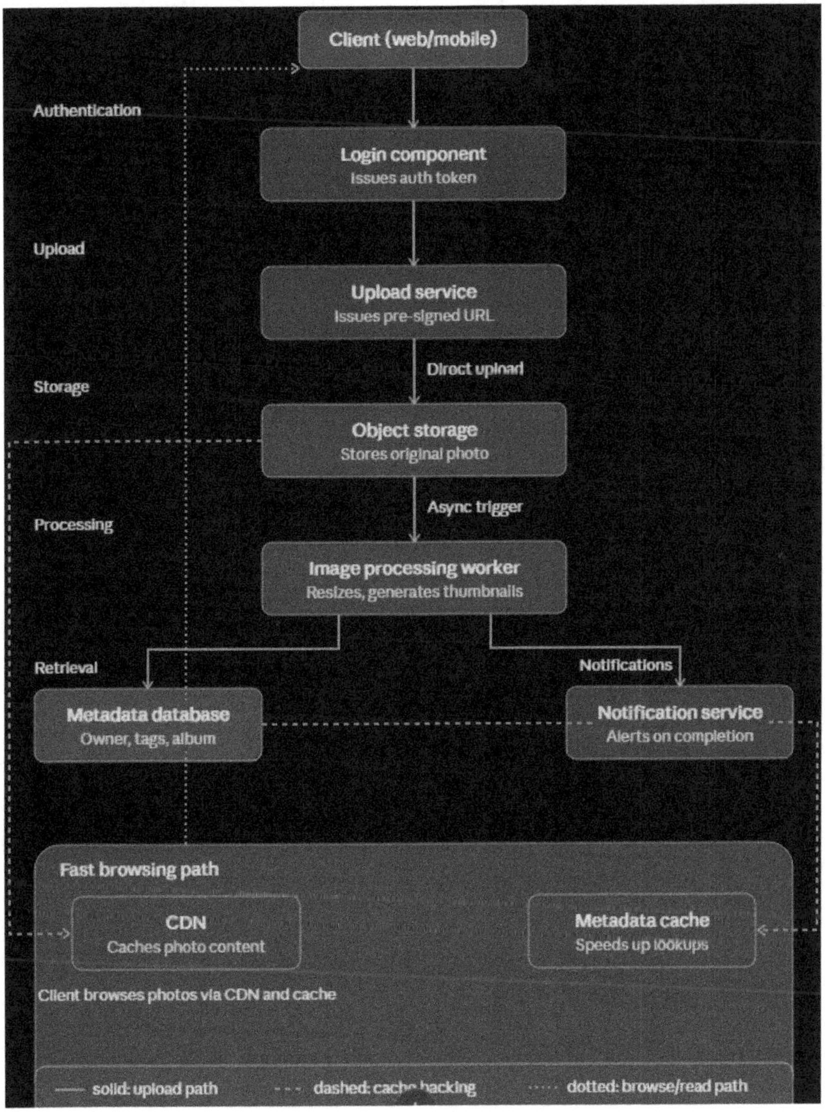

***Figure 18.1**: Photo sharing application workflow*

Example of order processing workflow

Consider an order system for an online store. The frontend sends an order request to an API, which validates the request and forwards it to the order service. The order service stores the order, sends an event to a queue, and a payment worker processes the payment asynchronously. Upon successful payment, another service updates the order status and sends a confirmation email.

This workflow illustrates the importance of component identification. Each part has a specific role and can be scaled, secured, or replaced independently. In AWS designs, this often results in a well-structured combination of managed services, queues, databases, and compute layers.

Things to keep in mind

A common mistake is creating components that are too large, making the system difficult to modify. Conversely, introducing too many small components too early can reduce clarity. The objective is not maximum separation, but appropriate separation.

It is also important to define clear boundaries. Components should have well-defined interfaces and avoid relying on each other's internal details. In AWS architecture, this typically involves using APIs, events, queues, and managed services rather than direct coupling.

Importance in interviews

In a system design interview, interviewers assess whether you can think like an architect. They are interested not just in AWS service names, but in your ability to break down a problem, identify key components, and explain how these parts work together in a scalable and reliable manner. A clear high-level architecture demonstrates your understanding of structure before detail.

This is why component identification is a critical skill. It shapes your design, supports discussion of trade-offs, and facilitates the transition from idea to implementation. At this stage, the system moves from concept to architecture.

Trade-off analysis

Trade-off analysis is essential in system design. Every choice offers benefits but also introduces drawbacks. For example, a solution may improve speed at the expense of cost, or enhance consistency at the expense of availability. In AWS architecture, this mindset is critical because cloud services provide many options, and the optimal choice depends on the system's priorities.

A strong architect seeks the best fit, not a perfect design. They compare options and select the most appropriate solution for the problem. For instance, a highly consistent database suits financial transactions, while a global social feed may prioritize speed and availability. In interviews, this reasoning demonstrates your understanding of both the services and the consequences of your choices.

Trade-off analysis enables clear explanations of your design. When justifying choices such as caching, queues, sharding, or managed services, also state what you sacrificed. This approach makes your answer thoughtful and realistic. In practice, this mindset leads to architectures that align with business priorities.

Interview points

A few points to keep in mind regarding Trade-off analysis are as follows:

- **Every design choice has a cost and a benefit**: This shows balance in decision-making.
- **Explain why you chose one option over another**: Interviewers want the reason, not just the answer.
- **Mention the impact on latency, cost, scalability, and reliability**: These are the most common trade-off areas.
- **Pick the design that best fits the requirement**: The *best* solution depends on the use case.
- **Be ready to discuss what you are sacrificing**: A good architect understands the downside of each choice.

Load balancing and Auto Scaling principles

Load balancing and Auto Scaling are fundamental in cloud system design because they help applications manage traffic efficiently. Load balancing distributes incoming requests across multiple healthy instances to prevent overload. Auto Scaling adjusts the number of running instances based on demand, allowing the system to expand during peak traffic and contract when demand decreases.

Combined, these principles create reliable and efficient systems. When traffic spikes, the load balancer distributes requests, and Auto Scaling adds capacity. When traffic declines, Auto Scaling removes excess resources, reducing costs. This elasticity is a key strength of AWS.

In interviews, describe load balancing as managing traffic and Auto Scaling as managing capacity. The load balancer directs requests to healthy targets, while Auto Scaling ensures sufficient resources. Effective designs combine both with health checks, multiple Availability Zones, and monitoring to maintain stability during failures or traffic spikes.

AWS provides three distinct load balancer types: **Application Load Balancer** (**ALB**) for **Hypertext Transfer Protocol** (**HTTP**)/**Hypertext Transfer Protocol Secure** (**HTTPS**) and content-based routing, **Network Load Balancer** (**NLB**) for low-latency **Transmission Control Protocol** (**TCP**)/ **User Datagram Protocol** (**UDP**) traffic, and **Gateway Load Balancer** (**GWLB**) for third-party virtual appliances. Selecting the appropriate type is critical, as the wrong choice can affect performance, cost, and routing capabilities. Understanding these differences is essential for AWS system design interviews.

AWS Auto Scaling covers more than EC2 instances. It also includes ECS task scaling, DynamoDB read and write capacity, Aurora replicas, and Lambda concurrency. Architects should recognize that Auto Scaling applies across the AWS service portfolio, not just to compute instances. Choosing the appropriate scaling target is as important as configuring the scaling policy.

More details about AWS load balancer and Auto Scaling can be found in *Chapter 3, Scaling with AWS Compute and Serverless*.

Interview points

Few points to keep in mind regarding load balancing and Auto Scaling are as follows:

- **Load balancing distributes traffic across multiple targets**: This improves availability and prevents overload.
- **Auto Scaling adjusts capacity based on demand**: This helps the system stay responsive and cost-efficient.
- **Use health checks to remove unhealthy instances**: This keeps traffic flowing only to working resources.
- **Design for multiple AZs when possible**: This improves resilience during failures.
- **Explain the difference between handling traffic and adding capacity**: Load balancing and Auto Scaling solve different problems.

Distributed system design and data consistency models

Distributed system design involves building systems from independent components that communicate over a network. This approach enhances scalability, fault tolerance, and flexibility, but also increases complexity. Distributed systems must address network delays, partial failures, data duplication, and synchronization challenges. The goal is not just to split services, but to ensure they operate reliably together.

Data consistency models define how and when data changes are visible across the system. Strong consistency ensures users see the latest data immediately. Eventual consistency allows updates to propagate over time, often increasing availability and scalability. The appropriate model depends on business needs; for example, banking requires strong consistency, while social feeds or analytics can often use eventual consistency.

A good architect recognizes that distributed systems require balance. Prioritizing perfect consistency can reduce performance or availability, while focusing solely on speed and scale may result in stale reads or temporary mismatches. In interviews, demonstrate your understanding of these trade-offs and your ability to select the appropriate approach for each situation.

As per the **consistency, availability, and partition** (**CAP**) theorem, a distributed system can guarantee only two of three properties: consistency, availability, and partition tolerance. Because network partitions are unavoidable, architects must choose between consistency and availability. This decision directly affects whether to use strong or eventual consistency models when selecting AWS services. Additionally, when there is no partition, the system must choose between **latency** (L) and **consistency** (C), known as **Partition, Availability, Consistency, Else, Latency, and Consistency** (PACELC), which is the extension of the CAP theorem. This theorem helps in understanding the trade-offs involved in designing distributed systems, particularly in scenarios where latency and consistency are critical factors.

More details on this topic can be found in *Chapter 5, Data Storage Strategies and Patterns on AWS*.

Interview points

Few points to keep in mind regarding distributed system design and data consistency models are as follows:

- Distributed systems improve scale and fault tolerance. They also add coordination complexity.
- Strong consistency gives the latest data immediately. It is useful when correctness is critical.
- Eventual consistency improves availability and performance. It works well when slight delays are acceptable.
- Mention replication, partitions, and network delays. These are central issues in distributed design.
- Choose consistency based on the business need. Not every system needs the same level of strictness.

Caching strategies and CDN use cases

Caching is a straightforward way to improve system performance. Frequently requested, infrequently changing data can be stored closer to the user or application, reducing the need for repeated computation or retrieval. This lowers latency, decreases database load, and enables faster responses during high traffic.

A good architect applies caching selectively. Not all data should be cached, as stale data can cause issues when freshness is critical. Product catalogs, user profile images, and static content are often suitable for caching, while payment status or inventory counts may require up-to-date information. The key is to distinguish between data that can be reused and data that must remain current.

On AWS, caching solutions include **Amazon ElastiCache** for in-memory application caching, **Amazon DynamoDB Accelerator** (**DAX**) for microsecond DynamoDB read performance, and **Amazon CloudFront** for CDN edge caching. Understanding when to use each service and how they work together is essential for AWS system design interviews.

A CDN is valuable when users are geographically distributed. Rather than serving content from a central location, a CDN stores data at edge locations near users, improving response times and reducing load on the origin system. In interviews, emphasize that caching supports not only speed but also scalability and cost efficiency.

Interview points

Few points to keep in mind regarding caching strategies and CDN use cases are as follows:

- Use caching for data that is read often and changes slowly. This improves response time and reduces backend load.
- Use a CDN for static and geographically distributed content. This brings content closer to the user.
- Be careful with stale data. Cached data must still meet business needs for freshness.
- Combine cache and origin intelligently. The cache should reduce load, not create correctness problems.
- Mention invalidation strategy. A cache is only useful if you know when to refresh or expire data.

API design and communication protocols

API design defines how system components communicate. In system design interviews, it demonstrates the practicality of your architecture. A well-designed API is simple, user-friendly, and stable, ensuring clients remain functional even as the backend evolves.

Interviews often focus on request and response patterns, particularly REST, but the best communication protocol depends on the use case. REST is popular for its simplicity and suitability for web applications. gRPC is preferable for fast, strongly typed service-to-service communication. Messaging systems and event-driven architectures are effective for decoupling components and handling asynchronous tasks. Also, **GraphQL** is an increasingly important API design option, especially for applications that require flexible data fetching where clients specify the data they need. AWS supports GraphQL natively through **AWS AppSync**, making it a strong choice for mobile applications, real-time dashboards, and multi-source data aggregation. These scenarios often require multiple REST calls or complex response shaping, which GraphQL can simplify.

The objective is to select a protocol that fits the problem, not just by name. Synchronous APIs suit scenarios requiring immediate responses, while asynchronous communication is better when tasks can be delayed. In interviews, also discuss versioning, error handling, idempotency, and authentication to demonstrate practical understanding.

Interview points

A few points to keep in mind regarding API design and communication protocols are as follows:

- Design APIs around clear business actions. The interface should be easy to understand.
- Choose the protocol that fits the use case. REST, gRPC, GraphQL, and events all solve different problems.
- Mention synchronous vs. asynchronous communication. This shows that you understand system behavior under load.
- Include versioning and backward compatibility. APIs should evolve without breaking clients.
- Talk about error handling and idempotency. These make APIs safer and more reliable.

Fault tolerance, redundancy, and disaster recovery

Fault tolerance helps a system to continue operating despite failures. Redundancy provides backup capacity or duplicate components to ensure continuity if a part fails. Disaster recovery is the process of restoring the system after major failures. These concepts are closely linked and are essential for reliable AWS architectures.

A well-designed system avoids reliance on a single server, database, or location. If one component fails, another should take over, or the system should recover quickly with minimal disruption. Architects often use multiple AZs or regions to achieve this. The aim is not to eliminate failure, but to minimize its impact.

Disaster recovery plans address required recovery speed and acceptable data loss. Some systems demand rapid recovery and minimal data loss, while others can tolerate longer recovery times. In interviews, mention backup strategies, replication, automated recovery, and clear recovery objectives to demonstrate a focus on real resilience.

Disaster recovery planning uses two key metrics: **recovery time objective** (**RTO**), which specifies the maximum acceptable time to restore service after a failure, and **recovery point objective** (**RPO**), which defines the maximum acceptable data loss measured in time. AWS provides four disaster recovery strategies aligned with these metrics: *Backup and Restore, Pilot Light, Warm Standby,* and *Multi-Site Active/Active*. Each strategy offers distinct RTO and RPO tradeoffs at varying cost levels.

Interview points

Few points to keep in mind regarding Fault tolerance, redundancy, and disaster recovery are as follows:

- Fault tolerance keeps the system running during failures. It reduces service interruption.
- Redundancy gives the system backup capacity. This avoids a single point of failure.
- Disaster recovery restores the system after major outages. It focuses on recovery time and data loss limits.
- Use multiple AZs when possible. This improves resilience within a region.
- Mention backup, replication, and failover. These are core reliability concepts.

Security best practices in system design

Security must be integrated into the architecture from the start, not added later. A secure design protects data, controls access, limits exposure, and isolates sensitive operations from risk. In AWS, this involves strong identity controls, encryption, network segmentation, logging, and least-privilege access.

Always assume every system contains sensitive components. Protect user data, credentials, tokens, keys, and internal APIs. Effective security design also reduces the blast radius of failures. For example, public-facing services should not have full access to internal databases or administrative functions. Limiting the power of compromised components increases overall system safety.

In interviews, present security as a layered approach. Access control manages entry, encryption protects data, network rules restrict traffic, and monitoring detects unusual activity. Clearly describing these layers demonstrates your understanding of security as a system-wide responsibility.

AWS offers a comprehensive set of native security services that architects should reference in interviews. These include **AWS Identity and Access Management** (**IAM**) for identity and access control, **AWS Key Management Service** (**KMS**) for encryption key management, **AWS WAF** for filtering malicious web traffic., **AWS Shield** for **distributed denial-of-service** (**DDoS**) protection, **Amazon GuardDuty** for threat detection, **AWS Security Hub** for centralized security posture management, and **AWS Secrets Manager** for secure credential storage. Presenting these services alongside security principles demonstrates practical AWS knowledge beyond theory.

Interview points

A few points to keep in mind regarding security best practices in system design are as follows:

- Use least privilege for users and services. Give only the access that is needed.
- Encrypt sensitive data at rest/transit. This protects data from exposure.
- Segment networks and limit exposure. Public access should be minimal and intentional.
- Log important actions and monitor for anomalies. Security needs visibility to be effective.
- Design for blast-radius reduction. A failure should not expose the whole system.

Communication and iteration strategies in interviews

Communication is as important as technical skills in system design interviews. Strong candidates explain their reasoning step by step, check assumptions, and adjust designs as new information emerges. This collaborative approach helps interviewers understand your problem-solving process under uncertainty.

Effective interviews progress in iterations. Begin by clarifying the problem and constraints, then outline a high-level design. Next, address key areas such as scale, storage, performance, failure handling, or security. If requirements change or more detail is needed, adapt your design. Flexibility is often more impressive than rigid certainty.

Clear communication requires a well-organized answer. Explain each component's purpose, function, and associated trade-offs. Revise decisions openly and logically when needed. Interviewers value thoughtful discussion over a polished but inflexible response.

Interview points

A few points to keep in mind regarding communication and iteration strategies in interviews are as follows:

- Think out loud in a structured way. This helps the interviewer follow your reasoning.
- Clarify requirements before designing. Good designs start with a good understanding.
- Iterate on the design as new details appear. Flexibility is a strong interview skill.
- Explain trade-offs openly. This makes your answer feel realistic and mature.
- Stay organized and calm. Clear communication often matters as much as the design itself.

Conclusion

This chapter summarizes the key concepts for approaching and explaining system design interviews. We began with clarifying requirements and constraints, as every effective design starts with understanding the problem and its limitations. We then covered high-level architecture, component identification, and trade-off analysis to help break down complex problems and justify design choices. These principles were connected to topics such as load balancing, Auto Scaling, distributed system design, data consistency, caching, CDN use cases, API design, and communication protocols, enabling you to consider system behavior under real-world conditions.

We also discussed fault tolerance, redundancy, disaster recovery, and security best practices, emphasizing that robust designs must withstand failures and protect data. Equally important, we reviewed communication and iteration strategies, as interview success relies on clear guidance and adaptability. The main takeaway is that strong system design is not about memorizing answers but about demonstrating structured thinking, sound judgment, and the ability to build practical AWS architectures step by step.

References

1. **https://aws.amazon.com/blogs/architecture/why-deployment-requirements-are-important-when-making-architectural-choices/**
2. **https://docs.aws.amazon.com/autoscaling/ec2/userguide/tutorial-ec2-Auto Scaling-load-balancer.html**
3. **https://docs.aws.amazon.com/autoscaling/ec2/userguide/autoscaling-load-balancer.html**

Join our Discord space

Join our Discord workspace for latest updates, offers, tech happenings around the world, new releases, and sessions with the authors:

https://discord.bpbonline.com

Index

T

V

W

www.ingramcontent.com/pod-product-compliance
Lightning Source LLC
LaVergne TN
LVHW060543061126
851857LV00017B/1881